Rebellions,
Perversities,
and
Main Events

Rebellions, Perversities, and Main Events

MURRAY KEMPTON

TIMES 𝕿 BOOKS

RANDOM HOUSE

*Grateful acknowledgment is made to the following publications for permission
to reprint previously published material, some of which appears in this book in
a slightly different form: Esquire, Grand Street, Harper's, The New Republic,
New York, New York Newsday, New York Post, The New York Review of
Books, The New York Times Book Review, New York World-Telegram, Playboy, Saturday Evening Post.*

Library of Congress Cataloging-in-Publication Data
Kempton, Murray
    Rebellions, perversities, and main events / Murray Kempton.—1st ed.
        p.   cm.
    Includes index.
    ISBN 0-8129-2294-8
    I. Title.
PN4874.K45A5   1994
814'.54—dc20   93-30569

Manufactured in the United States of America

9 8 7 6 5 4 3 2

First Edition

Book design by Chris Welch

For William F. Buckley, genius at friendships
of the kind that passes all understanding. And
for the whole army of those gone to be unforgotten
and those still here to be thankful for.

Contents

PERVERSITIES

MAIN EVENTS

Contents

Introduction

I WOKE UP one morning several years ago and found myself seventy years old. It is a matter of scant moment; my rounds will go pleasurably on as they always have, world without end, until my masters trade me in at the antiques show for some dubious bit of art deco. Still, the recollections press an unexpectedly insistent claim:

I have stood twice in St. Peter's Square and heard the oldest cardinal raise the glad cry, "Habemus Papam," once for Angelum Roncallus and once for Albinum Lucianus, and not Henry James, nor Stendhal, nor, for that matter, Michelangelo could ever have said the same.

I have had breakfast with Frank Costello, who commended me for the alacrities of my appetite and said that he owed his long life to three axioms. The first was: "Always eat a large breakfast." The second was: "Never try to cheat on your taxes." He forebore to mention the third, an abjuration perhaps to avoid sitting with one's back to a window.

I have sat a little after twilight in the Dexter Memorial Baptist Church in Montgomery, Alabama, with the congregation singing low and stirring to joy at the entrance of a young man who wore a hat so broad-brimmed that I took him for a sideman in the house band and who turned out, of course, to be Martin Luther King, Jr.

I have seen Robert Kennedy with his children and John Kennedy with the nuns whose fidelity to their eternal wedlock to Christ he strained as no other mortal man could. I have been lied to by Joe McCarthy and heard Roy Cohn lie to himself and watched a narcotics hit man weep when the jury pronounced Nicky Barnes guilty. Dwight D. Eisenhower once bawled me out by the numbers, and Richard Nixon once did the unmerited kindness of thanking me for being so old and valued an adviser.

But, if I have feasted with a panther or two, I can remember supping with only one god, and that one had been left without an undeflected worshiper except myself. It was Westbrook Pegler, and he observed at lunch that he had been misunderstood by those who imagined that he had been driven crazy by Mrs. Roosevelt. That, he said, was not the case at all. "It began," Peg explained, "when I quit sports and went cosmic. It finished when I began writing on Monday to be printed on Friday."

THAT GOSPEL HAS been so rooted in my heart ever since that I write every day for the next and walk wide of the cosmic and settle most happily for the local, a precinct less modest than I make it sound, since my local happens to be the only city under the eye of God where the librettist for *Don Giovanni* could find his closest friend in the author of "The Night Before Christmas."

I talked with Louis Armstrong one night in Basin Street and mentioned his record of "When You're Smilin,' " which I had early loved and too soon lost. "I was working in the house band at the Paramount when I was young," Armstrong said. "And the lead trumpet stood up and played that song, and I just copied what he did note for note. I never found out his name but there was kicks in him. There's kicks everywhere."

And then he went back to the stand and played "When You're Smilin,' " still thinking it remembered note for note even while he was quite transcending it, and he had made immortal a figure never vivid and faded long ago.

There are, in truth, kicks everywhere, and I have had all these and never one at my own expense. Most of life's epiphanies arise from its accidents, and it is never so much fun as when it conscripts us as prisoners to the luck of the day. Colette says in "The Vagabond," that bible for all us migratory laborers, that "If Chance ever got Herself called God, I should have been a very good Catholic indeed." And so, too, should I.

Rebellions

The Fate of Paul Robeson

"He must have been lying to me for five years, steadily. . . . Paul is not any different from any other Nigger man, except that he has a beautiful voice. His personality is built on lies. . . . No wonder white people don't want to let black men into their society."
—MRS. PAUL ROBESON, *to her diary*, October 1930

PAUL ROBESON'S WAS a career whose rise and fall were both tethered to his identity as a man of conspicuous color. His blackness conscripted him to a liftime of being held only on approval, first with a wide-spreading acceptance that thought itself particularly kind, and last with a near universal casting out that felt itself particularly wounded.

He was born into that tentativity as the child, as he would be the husband, of a mixed marriage. His father, the clergyman, had been a slave boy escaped from eastern North Carolina; and his mother had been one of the Bustills, a family whose blood mingled its black with Amerind and British Quaker strains, and whose history of modest prominence in Philadelphia ran back to the eighteenth century. Her choice of a partner so much darker than herself had been an abrasion to family pride; and the Bustills would be cool to their Robeson cousins until the fame of the youngest of them eclipsed every prejudice of color.

Eslanda Cardozo Goode, who would occasionally suffer and devotedly die as Mrs. Paul Robeson, had been born to a line grander than the Bustills could ever have hoped to be, since her hemi-demi-semi black grandfather had been treasurer of his state during its Reconstruction, and a Jewish cousin would in time be a justice of the U.S. Supreme Court. Eslanda Goode's mother had married darker and so had she; and yet, dedicated Africanist though she became, her wariness of the taints of a duskier brush was so ingrained as to press her to warn her mother not to take seven-year-old Paul, Jr., "to any nigger beach."

MARTIN BAUML DUBERMAN'S abundant virtues as a biographer in his new book, *Paul Robeson*, are of the variety seldom stimulated by promptings toward the ironic. But his explorations have brought forth a rich trove for those otherwise inclined; and the most telling lesson they might sift from these diggings is that Robeson's life was defined all along by blackness. It may well have been his consolation at the last but in between it was the blessing that exalted him as long as he gave satisfaction, and the curse that condemned him almost as soon as he did not.

The Carl Van Vechtens, who had been the most fashionable of the patrons of his youth, visited him in London in 1928 and he repaid their prior hospitalities with a reception at the St. Johns Wood house he had rented from the Countess des Boulletts. The guests included Fred and Adele Astaire; Mrs. Patrick Campbell; Ivor Novello; Hugh Walpole; Max, Lord Beaverbrook; and at least two ladies ennobled by titles much older than his.

The Van Vechtens had been gratified by their protégé's welcome and dazzled by the grandeurs of his station. But ten years later, when Robeson returned to the States and did not bother to call them, this neglect goaded Carl Van Vechten, whose *Nigger Heaven* Robeson had once admired, to complain to his wife Fania that "it's pretty obvious that Paul doesn't want to see *us* very much, or *most* of his old friends." Fania's response was an all but automatic tuning of the chords appointed for those who, having been favored beyond the deservings of birth, have swelled up with misapprehensions about their proper place. "Really," she wrote, "if it were not for his meagre talent and his great charm he would be just the traditional 'low-down, worthless nigger.' "

Justice would be happily served if we could with assurance refute any sibyl who, having found her divinations in the smoke of her spite, would scorn as meager the talents that had seemed to her vast when Robeson had been so agreeably employing them to sing to her guests for his supper. But to give Fania Van Vechten the lie direct is not as easy as we would want it to be. Robeson's presence was, of course, enormous, and his gift outsized; but ridiculous as it was to dismiss his talent, we have no sure way to measure its true proportions.

We get our gifts from nature, but we realize our talents with their cultivation. The substantial black artists of Robeson's generation were, in nearly every instance except his own, conditioned by an apprentice-ship, whose enforced obscurity gave them the chance to refine a style that ultimately won for too few of them the attention of a wider world.

If our eyes were keen enough, the image of Stepin Fetchit might show them not a little about the protracted term beneath the notice of the general public that the craftsman can use for scouring the murk where hide the subtleties that even coarse performers require if they are to stick in our memories. But the profits other black artists so painfully squeezed from the ill favor of the gods never came Robeson's way; his only misfortune was the luck that arrives too soon.

HE SEEMS TO have come to his career as Adam did to Eden; and throughout its subsequent progress there can somehow be sensed the operation of a universal conspiracy to preserve an illusion of his Ada-mism. Disguise though it did the Rutgers Phi Beta Kappa and the Columbia Law graduate, it suited the persona that the good intentions of his time were more than satisfied to keep swinging, like Tarzan on his vine, back and forth between what Duberman identifies as the "stereotype of servile childishness" and the "alternate caricature of simplistic nobility."

As early as 1920, when he had scarcely begun as the least-schooled practitioner in the Harlem Amateur Players, he gave forth resonances so commanding that there endures the tale that the set designer Cleon Throckmorton was moved to go backstage and urge upon him the title role in *The Emperor Jones*, which was then projected by the Province-town Playhouse.

It is said that Robeson asked for a synopsis of the part and was told, "A railroad porter from a lowly background becomes emperor of a

5

tropic island and then, under terror, slips back," and that he sent his visitors away with the "self-aware dignity" of a dismissive "You may know this kind of person, and Mr. [Eugene] O'Neill may know this kind of person; but I don't."

Duberman doubts this story; and his distrust is licensed by its presumption that Robeson would subject a stranger to treatment so uncharacteristically ungracious. But all the same it has some scent of artistic credibility. Brutus Jones was scarcely a symbol that any representative of the New Negro so refulgent as Robeson already was would care to put on display. He afterward told the writer Marie Seton that the role that was his first leap to fame had been repellent to him. Smoothly as they came, there would never be enough of his earthly glories without similar exactions of bits and pieces from his dignity.

Three years after he had turned down *The Emperor Jones* he had lost most of his hopes for a career in the law undeflected by the disabilities of his color. He had learned that no one who had found out how much lay beyond his reach could look down on Brutus Jones from heights as towering as, in his innocence, he had used to think them. He accepted the part when the Provincetown Players sweetened their dose by offering it to him in a package with *All God's Chillun Got Wings*, whose Jim Harris was so much more appetizing because so much more to be pitied. And, as too often happened, the more primitive the image, the more enduring its effect would be for him; and Jim Harris's aspirations for the stars were soon forgotten while Brutus Jones's satisfactions in the mud made Paul Robeson famous.

The world that had been so stingy with his chances at the bar now lavished him with opportunities in the theater, although their scope would in time turn out to be delusive, and some of us may suspect they inhibited the enlargement of his particular genius to dimensions appropriate to its potential.

IT GETS HARDER and harder to come by the materials that might remind us of how much Robeson managed to do inside the boundaries for whose narrowness social circumstance deserves most of the guilt, although he himself cannot be acquitted of some of the blame. The only record album of his still listed by Schwann is the survivor of his Carnegie Hall concert in 1958, when his powers had been eroded by sufferings that had extorted not a penny from his dignity but a king's ransom from his confidence. The exuberant clamors of the walls that tumbled down before Joshua have departed to distances beyond echo. There is a fragment of Othello's final speech with no trace in it of those reflective, resigned, and melancholy notes that sound in the head even when we are reading them in a public library.

All that is left is declamation; and we who never saw and can never see his original performance can only wonder whether it was ever more than this, and whether he might not have flourished and withered eternally noble and permanently unfulfilled, the tragic figure who never learned to be a tragic actor, and the extraordinary voice that settled for a single tune.

This constricted range was not at all a fault of indolence. Robeson seems to have been an assiduous student of music without ever being comfortably at home as a sight reader, a failure that suggests an intelligence richly nourished by education but underfed by tutoring. He was persuaded that all music flowed from a common folk root; but the folk he had in mind was seldom other than his own, and when he essayed departures from that source, the *Christus Lag* of Bach and the "Lullaby" of Schubert emerged from depths as profound as, and widths no broader than, "Deep River." He could only feed—and we were perhaps more content than he may have been to let him feed—on very little inspiration beyond what he had found in his father's church.

It seems sensible to accept Robeson, with no thought to diminish him, as less a musician than a messenger too possessed by the theme to be distracted by temptations to vary it. The late John Hammond once told me that, when he brought Robeson together with Bill Basie for the "Joe Louis Blues" he had to write out the chords and drum them in. The prescription did not work: Robeson and Basie simply traveled down the paths of each one's memory; and the result, however far from the true pattern of the blues, abides in the recollection as a superb statement. The younger Robeson had so little taste for blowing or even enjoying the changes that he thought Duke Ellington childish, having perhaps been put off by those "jungle" growlings that could have affronted him as parodies of the African rhythms he was himself beginning to venerate.[1]

Robeson began with the same chord and at once triumphed with it and had no encouragement to explore its varieties thereafter; and, lastingly impressive as the results remain, we cannot quite toss away the complaints of the *London Sketch* when it responded to the 1928 London reproduction of *Showboat* with a cartoon captioned "Despite ragtime and jazz, poor old Joe sings 'Ole Man Ribber' right through the years from 1880 to 1928."

Peggy ashcroft, the Desdemona to his first Othello, in London in 1930, remembers her shock when Nellie Van Volkenberg, their director, barked loud enough for the whole company to hear at one rehearsal: "Mr. Robeson, there are other people on the stage besides yourself." Dame Peggy told Duberman thirty-eight years afterward that, in her recoil "at this gratuitous humiliation of Robeson, [she] decided that Nellie was a 'racist.' "

That might have been an unfair surmise because Van Volkenberg's outburst does not quite permit the inference that her loss of patience with Robeson the person extended to revulsion from Robeson the man of color, a step that by the way seems to have been shamefully easy for people otherwise confident that, for them, this cast of mind was unthinkable. The New York *Othello* of 1942 was directed by Margaret Webster, who could be off-puttingly pompous in such public manifestations of her enlightenment as, "For the first time in the United States a Negro was playing one of the greatest parts ever written . . . and [the occasion] was trying to prove something other than itself."

---

[1]As time went on he grew to appreciate not just Ellington but Charlie Parker and Thelonius Monk too. That late-arriving taste ought not to have much surprised him; Julian Euell once observed that "Ornette Coleman plays field hollers," and the compliment fits as well for Parker and Monk.

Even so, when she took offense at a coalesced resistance to her will by José Ferrer, her Iago, Uta Hagen, her Desdemona, and Robeson himself, Webster could write to her mother with a clear conscience about the effronteries she was being forced to bear in order to "get a show out of that big, black jelly-fish and those two conceited little asses and make us all happy and bursting with harmony and enthusiasm."

In 1928, when Actors Equity suspended Robeson for failure to honor a $500 contract to appear in a "colored review," because he wanted to be in *Showboat* instead, the NAACP's Walter White wrote him that such evidences of light-mindedness "would react on all of us" and reported that, not long before, a "prominent white person" had explained his reluctance to accept a pledge of White's own with the observation, "Your people are not strong on keeping their promises, are they? Look at what your friend Paul Robeson is doing."

All the same, the force of Van Volkenberg's complaint asserts itself in films that too often register a presence too massive and too unpliant to blend comfortably into ensembles. When Brutus Jones sings his farewell to the congregants of the Georgia church of his childhood, there is almost nothing of the boy leaving for wider scenes and almost everything of the man returned from their conquest. Robeson never acquired the skills that enable actors more practiced than he to mingle, barely recognizable, in the crowd of the company and then emerge from it like thunder.

His range seldom rose beyond the limits of the solo and the duet. His singular charm could reach full expression only in circumstances of intimacy; and since he was untrained in the artifices of its contrivance, he seems to have achieved its effects by establishing a run-of-the-play liaison with nearly all his leading women, a pattern his wife blamed on "pursuing white meat . . . the curse of the race," with an anger that, however natural, may have debarred her from considering the alternative explanation. This chase and capture may have had much more to do with his sense of what the occasion required than with any lust to storm the walls of the dominant race. For he followed his impulses into transient conquests of and/or subjugation by Nina Mae McKinney and possibly Fredi Washington, both women of color however lighter than his own.

. . .

ROBESON ACHIEVED HIS summit in 1940 when the Republicans came close to inviting him to sing "Ballad for Americans" at their national convention. He was still on its plateau in 1946 when the widow of Harry Hopkins, President Roosevelt's closest coadjutor, asked him to sing at her husband's funeral.

But the downward slide had already begun, and it ended in 1950 in the dark valley where he could add the last citation on the list of his accomplishments as pioneer—the second Negro named All American in football, first Rutgers Negro elected Phi Beta Kappa as a junior—and now first in another vanguard as, in Duberman's words, "the first American to be officially banned from television" for the sin of empathy with the Soviet Union.

Robeson thereafter endured a species of internal exile throughout nearly a third of a life that ended in 1975. Duberman has committed roughly 250 of his 800 pages to this fall from the peak to the pit, and the sad years that followed; and, although his account is as devoted as it is extensive, it is the least satisfying portion of his narrative, because he is too determinedly resistant to each and every prompting to engage the mystery. For there is a mystery about Robeson's terminus; and its fascinations reside not in the afflictions of the victim but in the self-will of the hero. Ill-used though he was, we would cheat him of the respect he deserves if we failed to recognize that he proudly chose his fate.

Nothing in his prior existence had prepared him for the vehemence of that fate's blows; but when they fell, he appreciated the might of national purpose behind them so acutely that, when the young Sidney Poitier and Harry Belafonte sought his company, he warned them "to avoid being seen or connected with him" and risk careers that would in time delight him by spreading through the national consciousness even wider than his own career had done before its ruin.

The lesson he still thought he could most usefully teach an acolyte was to take special care not to be as contentious as he seemed to have become but to be as agreeable as he used to be—and remained, to a degree that would have surprised the spiteful. That agreeable quality belonged in the essence of Robeson's nature and, even as it confronts us with the most tantalizing of all the locks that bar his riddle's door, it may be offering us its key.

Robeson owed his first great chance to his agreeability, which he would never lose in the years when he had put all opportunities to forfeit. Brutus Jones had been played first by Charles Gilpin, who had not before had a part so grand and would never have another even as noticeable; and he had brought to it a rage stoked with the fires of a life experience that Robeson could not match. That disability was fortunate, because his frustrations had left Gilpin's temperament so fierce and stubborn that *The Emperor Jones*'s first run had been such an unremitting series of quarrels that Eugene O'Neill would have no more of him.

"I've stood for more from him than from all the white actors I've ever known—simply because he was colored," O'Neill wrote in a letter to Mike Gold, sour with Gilpin's dismissal and radiant with Robeson's welcome as "a young fellow . . . full of ambition and a damn fine man personally with real brains—not a 'ham.' "

His career had been launched from the wreckage of Gilpin's; and he could hardly be blamed if he was then inattentive to the cruel ironies of that circumstance, because he would have a long and happy journey before finding out that one man of color is not often enough given a copy book to write upon unless another has previously spoiled it for himself.

HE WOULD NEVER entirely give up taking every new face for as fair as it presented itself as being. Still, openhearted as he stayed, he could no longer be as unaware of the untrustworthy actualities of life as he had been before the term in England, which had been a succession of glittering rewards all turned to dust with a cheat at the end.

He had fallen in love there with Yolande Jackson, a sometime actress with a dubious leasehold in the aristocratic ambience whose pet he was. Their intimacy had lasted three years until he determined upon divorce and remarriage to her; and then she had suddenly and sickeningly rejected him, having, Eslanda Goode Robeson keenly surmised, "lost her nerve" in the face of "too risky an experiment."

Long afterward he would recall the time when he was driving with Yolande Jackson and her passion for his person inflamed her into displays wantonly indifferent to what the chauffeur might think. That, Robeson would say, was the moment when he recognized that hers was the class that cannot imagine that servants have sentience, let alone sensibilities, and he became finally aware of "the affinity of working people the world over . . . black and white."

He does not seem ever to have served up this parable without accompanying it with the demonstration of the native gentility that would invariably identify Yolande Jackson as "Lady so-and-so" and thus manage chivalrously to disguise her identity and gallantly improve her social station.

AND SO HE had departed England and returned to his again beloved country unshackled from an old fantasy and perhaps too ready to be enchained by another. The Van Vechtens no longer mattered to him; and, if they were correct in inferring the snub, they were profoundly mistaken when they ascribed it to frivolity, for England had taught Robeson, perhaps too lastingly, that there is no social defect more worthy of disdain than a failure to be serious; and who among us, once having lost patience with the Ladies Diana Duff Cooper and Edwina Mountbatten, would have looked to Fania Van Vechten for their replacement?

Robeson had been made at last aware that his color was both ineffaceable and a summons to duty; and he would henceforth prefer the comradeship of the Communists to the company of the Van Vechtens. Even if we set aside the unwarranted sufferings that would be its consequence, that choice cannot be considered a wise one. There is a good deal of room for adventuring in the directions of seriousness in the vast swath that lies between the errant paths traversed by an ill-tempered and self-struck Fania Van Vechten and a benignly moon-struck Elizabeth Gurley Flynn.

Even so, we should, I suspect, go wrong if we assessed Robeson's subsequent course as an abandonment of his residence with the sensible for lodging with the utterly foolish. The late Benjamin Davis was his closest friend in the American Communist party; and, in one of his conversations with Duberman, Angus Cameron remembers Davis observing once that "The Party was wrong when it held that blacks in America were a nation, and also when it held they were not a nation." The author of *Nigger Heaven* was hardly so placed as to condescend to any intelligence that could array the ambiguities of the case as neatly and subtly as Davis had.

THE PUZZLE THAT finally challenges us is not Robeson's arrival at this particular station but his resistance to getting back on the train and going away, which, so far as we have any license to believe, was sustained unto his last breath. His vision of the Soviet Union, however over-sanguine, was never impenetrable by evidence of its imperfections and even its taints.

Marie Seton has recalled references of his to "dreadful things" in the USSR as early as 1937; and no extreme of the adulation that greeted his return there in 1949 was sufficient to allay his unease at being unable to locate so many of his old Jewish friends—a disquiet that mounted to alarm when, having been released from police custody to visit his hotel, the poet Itzik Feffer began their colloquy with "mute gestures" signaling that the room was bugged, that their vocal exchanges should be limited to the social pleasantries, and that weightier matters could be less perilously discussed by passing notes back and forth.

Robeson's visits to the Soviet Union thereafter seem to have alternated the anticipated bouts of delight with intervals of gloom inexplicable to his hosts. His first attempt at suicide was the slashing of his wrists in Moscow's National Hotel in the spring of 1961; and he would later explain to an East German physician that "people whose parents or whose relatives were in jail had approached him—'Can't you help me'—this sort of thing had put him into conflict."

Three months later, after rest and presumed recuperation, he broke

down again, and the regimes of a London psychiatric clinic were prescribed. When the car that was transporting him there approached a
traffic light near the Soviet embassy, a companion on this unhappy
journey has since told Duberman, Robeson "thought we were driving
in there [and] he started muttering, 'You don't know what you're doing,
you don't know what you're doing . . . get down!!' . . . He was frightened,
cowering himself and trying to protect me." The memory that bore
witness to that scene belonged to a woman who was then and apparently still is a devotee of the Old Left and remains "astonished"—as we
ourselves may be as well—at a paranoid episode triggered by the
symbol of the very faith that had been cherished so long and at so
exacting a cost and that would survive until he died without a hint of
repudiation.

THIS TORMENTED MIXTURE of loving and fearing the USSR is the final
enigma of Robeson; and we are reduced to no better clue for its answer
than a remark he made, when, far from settled in his reason, he was
talking to Paul Robeson, Jr., who had meant little to him as a child and
everything as a man, and explained that he had tried to kill himself
because "someone close to me had done irreparable damage to the
USSR."

That is the voice that neither knows nor needs to know wherein it
has offended; and we hear sounding from its sorrows the echoes of Job's
"Though He slay me, yet will I trust in Him." Job speaks for all of those
who have been wounded not by the blows of God's enemies but in the
hand of God Himself and by a judgment so indifferent to mercy or
equity that "If I washt myself with snow water, and make my hands
never so clean/Yet shalt Thou plunge me in the ditch, and mine own
clothes shall abhor me."

Such was the Jehovah whose fierce covenant the boy Robeson had
heard his father preach; and such may have been the Joseph Stalin to
whose altars the man Robeson repaired with a faith that demanded few
of the nourishments of self-deception. If he never reached the dead
certainty, he seems to have entered upon the lively suspicion that Stalin

did not reserve his wrath for the guilty alone, but that "He destroyeth the perfect and the wicked. . . . He will laugh at the trial of the innocent."

Robeson may simply have found again and thenceforth clung, if with diminishing serenity, to his God in the image of the Old Testament that directs us so frequently to cherish God for what He is and in spite of what He may sometimes do. When we puzzle over the whys and wherefores of the case, we should, I think, do well to take note of how often men in their particular time choose a course not because they are guided there by reason, which is never so fresh and clear as when it is operating *post facto* like ours, but because they are simply tired and want to go home.

The black church was Christian in creed; but drew on the Old Hebrew for its soul's true cry. The spirituals pay an occasional tribute to the little Baby Jesus; but their home is Sinai and not the Mount of Olives, and their time is in Egypt's bonds and the desert's heat and not the day of Pentecost.

Even those of us devoted—but let us pray, not complacent—in our commitment to the truth of the Gospels, cannot in common sense overlook the extent to which they are false to the reality of the life around us. It would be curious indeed if they who created the spirituals, and the congregants who were their earliest auditors, enduring as they did the rule of masters cruel at worst and whimsical at best, had been altogether convinced that Peter had assessed the divine will more precisely than Job, or that the apostles, who bubbled over with the realization of their visions, were so much wiser observers than the Old Testament prophets, who dared to be peevish about the postponements of their own dreams.

Robeson had carried the spirituals about with him as the stock of his trade and art; and since they were the most intimate of his intellect's inspirations, they were bound to be the resource for its most prolonged reflections. If he had grown weary and aching for home and was by now too sophisticated to return to his childhood's church, we need not wonder that, for its substitute, he settled upon the Soviet Union, the ark of another covenant whose Jehovah also had his "fan . . . in his hand,

and he will thoroughly purge his floor, and gather his wheat into the garner; but he will burn up the chaff with an unquenchable fire," and, in both cases, with a distressingly coarse touch for distinguishing the chaff from the wheat.

The America that he had trusted so long in his innocence responded to the loss of that illusion with a meanness of spirit whose excesses reached their ultimate pitch when the 1950 *College Football Annual* "listed a ten-man All American team for 1918," having excised Robeson's name as conscientiously as Rutgers removed his picture from the gallery of alumni warrior heroes that ornaments its gymnasium.

His essential good nature insured him against cankering by bitterness toward white people; but even so, another tug toward his first youth suggests itself in the friends to whom he was drawn closest in age and isolation and who were not only Communists but, with few exceptions, black Communists, and most significantly, as he might have felt himself, beached remnants of the tide of the New Negro's Renaissance in the twenties. They had mostly been born to the more elevated castes of color: Benjamin Davis's father had been a Republican National Committeeman from Georgia; and Revels Cayton's grandfather had been the United States senator from Mississippi in the prereconstructed South.

THE ONE AMONG them Robeson had most cherished as guide and teacher was Max Yergan, executive secretary of the Council on African Affairs, the center of Robeson's first joint endeavors with the left. In the winter of 1948, Yergan commenced the strayings from the Party that would in time land him quite pathetically in the company of U.S. Senator James Eastland as a propagandist for the Katanga of Moise Tshombe.

The Communist majority on the council's board extirpated Yergan's heresy by accusing him of financial irregularities. Robeson's quick acceptance of these charges seems odd; of all those present at the table, he had the best reason to be familiar with imputations of boodling as a device for disposing of troublesome men of color, however innocent.

His own father had been the minister of a black Presbyterian church in Princeton; and, when he began to afflict the Presbytery's white overseers with his complaints against the poor lot of his congregation, he was visited with charges of " 'great carelessness' in keeping business records" that, for all their want of substance, were eventually effective enough to force his ouster. Mrs. Paul Robeson's grandfather was state treasurer of South Carolina until 1877, when its Democrats contrived to unseat him with a specious indictment and conviction for "embezzlement." This sort of thing is indeed so commonplace an instrument for purging black nuisances that even W.E.B. Du Bois employed it to push Marcus Garvey toward federal prison for marketing stocks about whose worth he was as guileless as anyone who bought them.

And yet there is no evidence that Robeson, for all his experience with prior injustices in the same key, paused to wonder if his comrades on the Council on African Affairs spoke fairly when they cried fraud against the apostate Yergan. There is a passage, dimly remembered, in Silone's *A Handful of Blackberries* when the hero tells an old peasant woman about his loss of faith in communism, and she replies that he has traveled a long way to find out that the world is round.

And so it is; but not many of us can accept that dreariest of revelations; and perhaps Paul Robeson was, at the end, one of those of us who turn back to our youth because it asserts itself in clouded memory as purer and freer of spite than pretty much everything we have met since. It wasn't, of course; but what else are we old men to do?

The New York Review of Books, April 27, 1989

The Champ and the Chump

J UST BEFORE THE bell for the seventh round, Cassius Clay got up to
go about his job. Suddenly, he thrust his arms straight up in the air in
the signal with which boxers are accustomed to treat victory and you
laughed at his arrogance. No man could have seen Clay that morning
at the weigh-in and believed that he could stay on his feet three
minutes that night. He had come in pounding the cane Malcolm X had
given him for spiritual support, chanting "I am the greatest, I am the
champ, he is a chump." Ray Robinson, that picture of grace who is
Clay's ideal as a fighter, pushed him against the wall and tried to calm
him, and this hysterical child turned and shouted at him, "I am a great
performer, I am a great *performer*."

Suddenly almost everyone in the room hated Cassius Clay. Sonny
Liston just looked at him. Liston used to be a hoodlum; now he was our
cop; he was the big Negro we pay to keep sassy Negroes in line and he
was just waiting until his boss told him it was time to throw this kid
out.

British journalists who were present remembered with comfort
how helpful beaters like Liston had been to Sanders of the River;
Northern Italian journalists were comforted to see on Liston's face the
look that *mafiosi* use to control peasants in Sicily; promoters and fight
managers saw in Clay one of their animals utterly out of control and
were glad to know that soon he would be not just back in line but out
of the business. There were two Catholic priests in attendance whose

vocation it is to teach Sonny Liston the values of organized Christianity, and one said to the other: "Do you see Sonny's face? You *know* what he's going to do to this fellow."

The great legends of boxing are of managers like Jack Hurley, who had taken incompetent fighters and just by shouting their merits, against all reason built them up for one big payday at which they disgraced themselves and were never heard from again. Clay had created himself the way Hurley created his paper tigers. His most conspicuous public appearance in the week before he was to fight had been a press conference with the Beatles. They were all very much alike—sweet and gay. He was an amateur Olympic champion who had fought twenty professional fights, some of them unimpressive; and he had clowned and blustered about how great he was until he earned his chance from a Liston who, if he could not respect him as an opponent, could recognize him as a propagandist skilled enough to fool the public. A reporter had asked Liston if he thought the seven to one odds against Clay were too long, and he answered: "I don't know. I'm not a bookmaker. I'm a fighter." But there was no hope Clay could win; there was barely the hope that he could go like a gentleman. Even Norman Mailer settled in this case for organized society. Suppose Clay won the heavyweight championship, he asked; it would mean that every loudmouth on a street corner could swagger and be believed. But if he lay down the first time Liston hit him, he would be a joke and a shame all his life. He carried, by every evidence unfit, the dignity of every adolescent with him. To an adult a million dollars may be worth the endurance of being clubbed by Sonny Liston; but nothing could pay an adolescent for just being picked up by the bouncer and thrown out.

On the night, Clay was late getting to the dressing room and he came to stand in back of the arena to watch his younger brother fight one of the preliminaries. He spoke no word and seemed to look, if those blank eyes could be said to look, not at the fighters but at the lights above them. There was a sudden horrid notion that just before the main event, when the distinguished visitors were announced, Cassius Clay in his dinner jacket might bounce into the ring, shout one more time that he was the greatest, and go down the steps and out of the arena and out of the sight of man forever. Bystanders yelled insults at him; his handlers pushed him toward his dressing room, stiff, his steps hesitant. One had thought him hysterical in the morning; now one thought him catatonic.

He came into the ring long before Liston and danced with the mechanical melancholy of a marathon dancer; it was hard to believe that he had slept in forty-eight hours. Liston came in; they met in the ring center with Clay looking over the head of that brooding presence; then Clay went back and put in his mouthpiece clumsily like an amateur and shadowboxed like a man before a mirror and turned around, still catatonic and the bell rang and Cassius Clay went forward to meet the toughest man alive.

He fought the first round as though without plan, running and slipping and sneaking punches, like someone killing time in a poolroom. But it was his rhythm and not Liston's; second by slow second, he was taking away the big bouncer's dignity. Once Liston had him close to the ropes—where fighters kill boxers—and Clay, very slowly, slipped sideways from a left hook and under the right and away, just grazing the ropes all in one motion, and cut Liston in the eye. For the first time there was the suspicion that he might know something about the trade.

Clay was a little ahead when they stopped it. Liston had seemed about to fall on him once; Clay was caught in a corner early in the fifth and worked over with the kind of sullen viciousness one cannot imagine a fighter sustaining more than four or five times in one night. He seemed to be hurt and walked back, being stalked, and offering only a left hand listlessly and unimpressively extended in Liston's face. We thought that he was done and asking for mercy, and then that he was tapping Liston to ask him to quiet down a moment and give the greatest a chance to speak, and then we saw that Clay's legs were as close together as they had been before the round started and that he was unhurt and Liston just wasn't coming to him. It ended there, of course, although we did not know it.

"I told ye'," Cassius Clay cried to all of us who had laughed at him. "I told ye'. I just played with him. I whipped him so bad and wasn't that good. And look at me: I'm still pretty."

An hour later he came out dressed; a friend stopped him and the heavyweight champion of the world smiled and said he would be available in the morning. His eyes were wise and canny, like Ray Robinson's.

The New Republic, March 7, 1964

The Clarity of A. Philip Randolph

I T IS NOT Asa Philip Randolph's style to embarrass presidents of the United States in large assemblies; and so, when he came as a vice president of the AFL-CIO to the White House along with three hundred other labor leaders, Mr. Randolph's brief comment on the President's televised speech on civil rights two nights before was at once a stately compliment and a measured reminder: "It was a magnificent speech, but it was, *unfortunately*, made rather late."

When the President had left the room and his audience was moving toward the outer air, a southern brother approached Philip Randolph and asked where he could find someone from the Labor Department. "I got a problem to tell him about," he said. "The colored people are doing all right in my state. It's the white people I'm worried about. They're being discriminated against."

Randolph gravely escorted this stray over to the nearest Labor Department official and went away. He returned to Harlem amused but unsurprised; he is the only figure in the American labor movement who has, for twenty years, been able continually to surprise his country, but nothing surprises him.

His Brotherhood of Sleeping Car Porters is aged and fading; it never had more than fifteen thousand members and no more than five thousand of these are working now. Porters with thirty years of service endlessly deal the brittle old playing cards in their recreation room on 125th Street in New York, awaiting their chance for an infrequent extra run. The porters may strike any day for the forty-hour work week which they alone among the operating railroad crafts have not achieved. They can expect the other unions to support their picket lines; this little group of old men could produce a national railroad strike. Nothing is new about their headquarters except the fresh picket signs.

The porter has always been poor and a menial; segregation created his job; the Pullman Company hired Negroes as porters because Negroes were inexpensive. And for most of the thirty-seven years of their union's history, the porters have taxed themselves for campaigns to destroy segregation on the railroads, but they seem to have been defeated by economic history. Their union has raised their pay scale to a basic $436 a month, which has made a porter's job one fit for white men, so fit in fact that occasionally a white youth comes to the Brotherhood in search of a union card; it cannot be given him, because there are not enough jobs for the old members, let alone new ones. There will be no white porters, and there will be no Negro engineers; the rule for employment on the railroads is not opportunity but seniority.

World War II was the best time they have known as workers. They used its rewards to finance Randolph's March on Washington movement, whose threat in 1943 won from Franklin D. Roosevelt the executive order which set up the wartime Fair Employment Practices Committee.

The first Freedom Rides into North and South Carolina and Tennessee were planned in Randolph's office in 1946. Bayard Rustin, a veteran of that first adventure into jail, remembers that everyone else had discouraged him until he came to Randolph. "It doesn't matter if you only get eighteen people," Randolph said then. "If you go down there, other people will rise and follow." He was looking seventeen years ahead as though they were the next day.

Ralph Bunche remembers traveling to Atlanta on the Seaboard line in 1947. South of Washington he went to the diner and was shown a table behind a partition. He looked at it, announced that he had not lived quite long enough yet to accept segregation, and went back to his room.

"About half an hour later, my door buzzer buzzed. I opened it and there were two sleeping-car porters and a waiter from the dining car with trays neatly covered and they told me that they had decided to bring me this food, because no Negro, in their view, who refused to eat at that Jim Crow table would ever grow hungry on a train where they served. They didn't mention it, but I took it that the food was with the compliments of the company."

The Brotherhood Building on 125th Street was headquarters for Thomas Patterson, Eastern Supervisor of the Sleeping Car Porters Union, who once traveled to Wilmington, North Carolina, to negotiate with the Atlantic Coast Line. He was ejected from its dining car for refusing to sit at the segregated table. The next morning, Patterson completed his union business with a Coast Line lawyer; that afternoon, he sued the Line for his humiliation on the diner. The railroad settled out of court and its Jim Crow partition was removed for all time; Patterson gave his award to the Brotherhood.

In 1955, Edward D. Nixon, a Pullman porter, summoned the Negro community of Montgomery, Alabama, to boycott its buses. Nixon knew that it would be politic to choose one of the Negro ministers as leader of the boycott. The youngest, and a stranger among them, was Martin Luther King, Jr., of the Dexter Street Baptist Church.

"He didn't say much, and I didn't know whether to trust him. But he had the richest church and he could hurt us," Nixon remembered. "So then and there, I nominated him to head our committee. I figured on pushing him out so far that he couldn't run away. And, with that bad guess, we got Moses."

Such is the history that suffuses this old command post set away in a Harlem that has changed hardly at all. Three floors down are the displays of studios that offer tap, ballet, and other lessons in how to escape to the great world, and the advertisements of employment offices that offer jobs for maids in New Jersey.

"WHAT WAS YOUR class at Harvard, Phil?" Franklin D. Roosevelt asked once, bemused by the massively cultivated tone of a man whose only degree was from Cookman College, a Negro high school in Florida. "Who is Randolph?" a World War II government lawyer asked as he brought in draft after draft of an FEPC order in 1943, only to be told that "Randolph" was not yet satisfied that any of them went far enough.

"I wish you hadn't said that, Mr. Randolph," Harry Truman answered when Randolph told him in 1948 that he would advise every young Negro to refuse to serve in the Army so long as it was segregated. Randolph answered that he was sorry to have to say it; and, when President Truman was restored to calm, he signed the order which integrated the armed forces.

In 1951, William Mills, a Pullman porter, escorted a detachment of American soldiers into his car at Spartanburg, South Carolina. The sergeant was a Negro; most of the men in his command were white. One of the white boys put his head out of the window and asked in the accent of the South, "Sergeant, what time we supposed to get off?" The sergeant answered, and turned to see William Mills looking at him. "Yes," the sergeant said. "It's true. It's true."

Randolph is seventy-four, thinner than he used to be. Men who have worked with him for thirty years call him "Chief" and treat him like a piece of old china; he tires more than he used to and lies down for a nap in the afternoon, like any country lawyer.

His only vanity is his manners. He has lived all his life in Harlem; he travels to the outside world as the ambassador of a Negro union. He carries a courtesy so old-fashioned that the white men with whom he negotiates are sometimes driven to outsized rage by the shock that anyone so polite could stick so stubbornly to what he believes; it was from such a shock presumably that George Meany breached the customary decorum of an AFL-CIO convention in 1959 by rasping, "Just who elected you, Phil, to represent all the American Negroes?" Randolph, almost alone on the convention floor, had been persisting in his insistence that the AFL-CIO had been derelict in its promises about civil rights.

"Every now and then," says Bayard Rustin, "I think he permits good manners to get in the way and that he even prefers them to sound tactics. Once I complained about that and he answered, 'Bayard, we must with good manners accept everyone. Now is the time for us to learn good manners. We will need them when this is over, because we must show good manners after we have won.' "

Yet the Black Muslims trust Randolph more than they do any other Negro leader. When he organized a neighborhood committee on Harlem's economic problems, he invited Malcolm X, the local Muslim prophet, to join. There were objections from the respectable. Randolph replied that when any group of citizens offered a representative, it "would be most improper not to recognize him, even though it will, of course, be most unfortunate if some of the ministers decide they can't go along."

Malcolm X came to his office. Randolph patiently explained how the Negro and the white will have to live together and how wrong he thought the Muslims were not to think so. Then he congratulated the Muslims on their campaign against whiskey and narcotics. "That," he said gravely, "may be the greatest contribution any of us have ever made," and arose to help Malcolm X on with his coat and see him to the door. Malcolm X has said since that all Negro leaders are confused, but that Randolph is less confused than any of them. Last spring the Muslims put a picture of this pacifist on the cover of their weekly journal.

"When Randolph began," says Bayard Rustin, "the Negro leader had the terrible problem of living by his wits. It was very important that there be one man who could not be corrupted. That man was Randolph. Even now, any time you have a plan and don't quite trust yourself, you go to Randolph and, if you are fooling yourself morally, you can trust him to point it out."

Randolph suddenly appears as the only figure who can reconcile the painful personal differences that have fallen upon the Negro protest movement at the height of its sweep and its fashion. We confront one of those occasions familiar in all revolutionary movements when doctrinal differences pass over into personal quarrels. Its moment of revelation came just after the murder of Medgar Evers, Mississippi secretary of the NAACP. Martin Luther King, Jr., called an NAACP official to suggest that together they proclaim a day of national mourning and self-examination and was told that he was always rushing into cases where he had no place or business.

THE ALLIANCE BETWEEN King and the NAACP has always been uneasy. They have moved by different roads in the same direction, King mainly in the streets, the NAACP in the courts. King's young can seem irresponsible to the NAACP's middle-aged; and the NAACP's middle-aged can seem stodgy to King's young.

Randolph is alone among these leaders because he neither feels nor incites hostility. He is a pacifist in a native American tradition; before most members of King's nonviolent army were born, he was reminding the Negro of Thoreau's prescription to cast the total vote with feet and voice along with the ballot. He has a natural sympathy for King. Still, there are ways in which he is more moderate than the NAACP. While the association has been in open war with the AFL-CIO, Randolph has kept his friends there, offending them only on matters of principle. The porters remain as they have always been, moderate in the particular that involves manners, and radical in the general that involves principle.

Not even a malignant imagination could assign Randolph one side or another in the quarrel between King and the NAACP. King he judges to be not just a modest man but a humble one, which, for him, disposes of the NAACP's complaint. On the other side, he reminds the radical young how important it is to respect the association, and Roy Wilkins, its executive secretary. "We must cultivate Roy," he tells them. "The association is the most important of all our organizations." He respects King because he has roused the poor Negro with results more consequential than any leader before him; and he respects the NAACP because it reaches the Negro middle class and can call upon its local chapters for hundreds of thousands of dollars in crisis; there is no other resource like this one.

Two months ago, Randolph had announced that he would call one hundred thousand Negroes to Washington to demonstrate against unemployment in October; it had seemed then just an echo of his 1943 march on Washington and scarcely relevant. Wilkins and King had different concerns and higher priorities, and without them, Randolph seemed reduced to the depleted resources of the porters. But then President Kennedy introduced his civil rights bill; Washington had again become the center and Randolph's march the critical item on the movement's agenda this summer. Randolph moved his march to August; he and King agreed to widen its scope to cover the civil rights bill. There was suddenly the surprising prospect that Congress would debate these bills with thousands of Negroes standing outside the Capitol.

Randolph and others were called again to the White House on June 22, just before the President was to leave for Europe. Mr. Kennedy said that he hoped that it wouldn't be necessary for Negroes to come to Washington in great groups while the debate was going on. Philip Randolph answered that he was afraid the choice was no longer whether Negroes came to Washington or not. "The choice, Mr. President, is between a controlled and nonviolent demonstration and an uncontrolled and violent one."

Mr. Kennedy answered that a president had many responsibilities and he wanted it made clear that he was not inviting them. Randolph's manners instructed Mr. Kennedy that he was talking for the record.

Randolph returned to plan a march that would be unlimited in aim, and that would remember above all the needs of all the poor and displaced, whatever their color.

"The Negro people are just one other depressed area," he said the other day. "As long as there is unemployment, it's going to hit us. The Negro is in the position of the white hod carrier and the white longshoreman. I should like all the unemployed to come with us. We complain because the building trades have no room for Negroes, but the real trouble now is that these unions are designed for profit through scarcity. If the crafts were open to us, that could not, in the present economy, create more than forty thousand jobs.

"When we have won, there will remain the Negro sharecropper. We shall end, great as this is, with a very sharp disillusionment when the great rallies are over. We had this experience with sit-downs in the thirties. We are basically a working-class group; we will not move unless we move with the rest of the working class."

More than anything else, Philip Randolph said, he would like to bring the displaced miners of Hazard, Kentucky, to Washington with him. He was silent just a moment, contemplating what all this sudden energy could mean, not just to the Negro, but to the whole United States. His secretary came in and reminded him that it was time for his afternoon nap. The Pullman porter, weary and depleted, has raised himself for just this one last effort to redeem his country.

The New Republic, July 6, 1963

Last Call

THE FOUR SQUARE Bar near Pennsylvania Station is a piece of Harlem set in midtown Manhattan. Most of its customers come to the Four Square between shifts at the main post office; and, since most postal workers are Negroes, they have made it a Negro bar.

It was into the Four Square that Bayard Rustin sank on the evening of the disaster of the March for Democratic Schools last week. It was sponsored by the National Association for the Advancement of Colored People and the Congress of Racial Equality, New York's most important instruments of Negro protest. They called upon the poor, whose hopes they represent and upon whose hopes they depend, to assemble at City Hall, salute the promise of the Supreme Court's school desegregation decision, and cry out against its nonfulfillment in a city 46 percent of whose Negro primary school students sit, ten years later, in substantially all-Negro classrooms.

Yet not five thousand persons answered the NAACP–CORE summons, and nearly half of these were white.

Bayard Rustin directed the pilgrimage of the two hundred thousand who marched on Washington last August; he managed the exodus of the five hundred thousand New York students who boycotted their schools for one day last February. Now he had exercised all the skills so important to these triumphs and all the authority they had given him, and only five thousand people had come to City Hall to affirm their faith in the power of mass witness. The March for Democratic Schools had been a failure in moral suasion and a defeat in tactics.

Near the end of March an estimated fifteen thousand white house-wives had walked across Brooklyn Bridge to ring City Hall and chant their objections to various proposals to improve the racial mix in substantially segregated areas by busing Negro pupils to white neigh-borhood schools. The opponents of any conscious effort at integration had gathered in such force in a snowstorm; Rustin had himself volun-teered the judgment that integration's supporters would have failed unless they could call up more than fifteen thousand in the spring sun. Now he had failed, and terribly. His marchers were trailing away, and a reporter gently asked him why so few Negroes had bothered to demonstrate this time. And Bayard Rustin had no answer except to remind his inquisitor that those who had marched against integration had been mere housewives, while those who marched for integration had listened, to choose an instance, to a rabbi, a priest, and a Protestant minister, who spoke not just for themselves but for the mighty host of believers in all New York's organized religions. What counts, he had suddenly been reduced to say, is not numbers but quality; the voices in the March for Democratic Schools had represented important power; the voices on the other side "come from nothing but the frying pan in the kitchen."

But now Bayard Rustin was in the Four Square Bar, among the people who had not come at his call, and now he had been on television in failure as well as in success; the Four Square Bar had been watching him. He sat down; a customer came over and put his hand on Bayard Rustin's shoulder.

"Man," he said, "I got to buy you a drink. You got to let me buy you a drink. Don't you know, you're a celebrity?"

Bayard Rustin had to give up and take a beer. "It's dreadful," he said, "to take a drink from another man. It's dreadful how they stop me and tell me I am a celebrity. I suppose it means something to people that we have done something they didn't bother to do."

You fail and you are just as celebrated.

The ordinary Negro has spent all his life sealed off from the rest of us. And could it be that we will come some day to know that we have even segregated him in our history? The period during which the ordinary Negro entered history as a general force began in May of 1954, and we may discover that it ended in May of 1964, an exact ten years, and a span of time as precisely framed and limited as the customs which have so long set the limits of the Negro's place in our national life.

The Supreme Court decided May 18 ten years ago that as a nation we owed it to the Negro child to be educated equal to and together in the classroom with the white child. That was the paper of a decision that the Negro was the ward of an enlightened society. But after the paper there came the flesh, isolated first in the faces of little children walking almost alone into Southern schools, then communal in the great throngs at Birmingham and in front of the Lincoln Memorial. The Negro had passed from being a ward to walking as a grown man. The Negro winter demonstrations in the New York schools had pushed the city's Board of Education into asking State Commissioner of Education James E. Allen to appoint a panel of consultants who could suggest ways to overcome the conditions of an increasingly segregated system. Commissioner Allen's advisers agreed that integration was "an overriding concern," and recommended that the state appropriate $250 million above the annual $800 million New York City education budget, to pay for the steps necessary to desegregate the schools and to repair and reinvigorate a straitened city education system. The Allen plan was both bold and expensive; the prospect of adding a quarter-of-a-million dollars to the budget chilled the state and city governments. The only real hope to realize any program so radical was in the rousement of radical public support.

The March for Democratic Schools had turned then, just before its disaster, from a mere concentration on the bad present to a projected affirmation of the better future the Allen program would offer. The NAACP and CORE had a chance at last to speak out for the right not just of the Negro for equality, but also of every child for a better school.

And then, at that moment of emancipation from the ghetto mind which was one great purpose of the history of the last ten years, there was the awful sense that the span of that history had run. The call went out and only five thousand people answered; the flesh had departed; this history, having begun with the paper of the Supreme Court decision, was ending with the paper of the Allen plan.

. The night before the March, Bayard Rustin sat with a dozen of his volunteer assistants, instructing them in the delicacies with which even the things that turn out badly have to be planned. There would be the demonstration boycott of one all-Negro East Harlem school; there would be the busloads of Negro children to four substantially all-white schools where they would sit in class as a reproach. There would be the Freedom School, where the children who had joined the boycott would have a day's instruction in the lives of Frederick Douglass and Mary McLeod Bethune and in the history of their own people in America.

All of the persons he drove through these details were young, and some of them seemed surprisingly new to the business. Near the end, a young woman asked Rustin why he had announced that the March would be a failure if fewer than fifteen thousand people came. She had been to Brooklyn that day seeking marchers and nobody seemed to care. The March might fail, and what would Rustin suggest she say then?

"I hope," he answered, "that I would do what Gandhi had done so many times; and that I can say that, if we had done what we should have done, the people of goodwill would have come out because the people of goodwill are there. Maybe the liberal community needs a failure. If that happens, let us say that we didn't do it this time, but we've got to do it. When you tell the absolute truth about what's wrong, then you help the truth."

The last detail was done; CBS had put together a documentary on the March, and Rustin went downstairs to the 125th Street bar to watch it. The television set was off; the customers were silent, lonely drinkers. The bartender turned the set on; suddenly, among the signs saying "Special, two for one, Carstairs, $1.15," there appeared on the screen the emblem "NAACP." It hung there and then there was the image of Rustin talking about how hopeless and empty life in Harlem is; in the back of the bar, the jukebox began with rhythm and blues and Rustin's voice on the soundtrack could be heard no more, and Rustin in the flesh was saying how old he looked.

Journalism talks about the long, hot summer of Negro militancy trembling toward violence that is ahead of us. But here in this room in Harlem, the customers looked each into his glass as though it were twenty feet deep. It will be a long, hot summer of sitting on stoops; it was hard not to believe that we looked at the abandonment of hope that private men can change the public order. The ordinary Negro, one suspects, was invited to apply for parole ten years ago, and now he knows that his parole has been denied him and that he must serve out his term with no real expectation of improvement by devices other than prison reform. The great demonstrations have shrunk down to public failures like the March for Democratic Schools, fragmented into isolated gestures like the World's Fair "stall-in." A chapter is over; all the energy, the imagination, the courage, and the hope which wrote that chapter could hardly not, before long, be revived again. But whatever chapter comes will be something new. We asked too much of the Negro when we expected him to carry almost by himself the burden of America as Eden, and endure and never get weary.

The day of the March was an exercise of the pride that instructs the best men that, if they are to fail, it will not be because they have been careless yesterday, or because they go slack today. More than six hundred pupils skipped classes in the overwhelmingly Negro East Harlem school which had been selected for the demonstration boycott, but few of them bothered to go to the Freedom School. Only ten little children could be found for the study-in at the overwhelmingly white elementary school on East 86th Street. They were kindly welcomed and escorted to class by little safety patrolmen. In the afternoon there were only one hundred pickets outside Governor Rockefeller's office; at night five thousand persons trailed across the Brooklyn Bridge, to watch Roy Wilkins of the NAACP and James Farmer of CORE tack— or more properly tape—their demands on the door of the Board of Education Building, and then to linger and sing the old songs.

"Ain't gonna let the power structure turn me round, turn me round," a young man sang; and then they went home, with no blessing except the preservation of their pride. Are there then to be no more parades?

At the Four Square, Bayard Rustin talked about going away for a week and trying to think through just what had happened.

"But," he said, "I must stay here. I must go up tomorrow and cut off the phone and clean the office and pay the bills. I cannot leave this behind me unfinished and in a state."

He is the sort of man who will be back, because he is the sort who makes formations, the first to arrive, the last to leave.

The New Republic, May 30, 1964

The Fruit of Islam

ND NOW THAT Malcolm X is dead, it is odd how sad some of us who knew him find ourselves and how pitiful, for all his dignity, he seems to have been all through our memory.

We knew him first and best as the preacher of the eternal separation of black and white; there is a theory that near the end he was struggling unevenly toward some idea of community. But I do not think he changed much with time; he lived with America for thirty-nine years and, whether from love or hate, I should doubt he really knew until the day he died.

Yet he was always a man of Harlem; he never entered white New York, except as ambassador from an independent, hostile nation. Never, that is, except the last night of his life, when he came to us as a refugee. He spent Saturday night at the New York Hilton because he did not feel safe in Harlem. That night he was a fugitive from black men; his dignity must have commanded him to go back among them Sunday and now he is dead.

Until the end, Malcolm X preached that Negroes must arm themselves against us, the enemy. And now he has been assassinated by armed Negroes at a meeting from which white people were barred.

It was his conviction that his father had been murdered by white men and thrown under a streetcar. Now his widow will have someday to explain to her youngest daughter Lomumbah that her father was shot down by Negroes.

The journalists always suspected that he was their creation, and in a way he was. He had both an exotic presence and considerable native wit; he came to New York at a time when he perfectedly suited the demands of electronic journalism. There have been very few public men whose message fit so snug and yet so lively into a two-minute segment of a news broadcast.

That gift would have made him notorious under any circumstances; but he had something else. I do not know a Negro so completely adjusted that some part of him did not respond to what Malcolm X was saying, just as I do not know a Negro so entirely alienated that some part of him does not respond to what Martin Luther King, Jr., is saying. Just by his insistence, Malcolm X created himself a nation to which every Negro owed a small allegiance. As Jimmy Hicks said yesterday, this *was* an assassination, for Mr. Malcolm was a head of state.

And yet he had a strange, trusting side. The longest I had ever talked to him was in Miami the night before the Cassius Clay–Sonny Liston fight where Mr. Malcolm had gone as Clay's spiritual prop. I remember his saying that, if you found a good white man, he was usually a Southerner, and how innocent that notion seemed to me as a hybrid Southerner. I tried to disabuse him and failed, and then the subject turned to Cassius and I said I hoped he wouldn't be immobilized by fear of Liston.

"To be a Muslim," Malcolm X replied, "is to know no fear."

And there he seemed to me correct, insofar as any white man can judge whether a Negro is correct about other Negroes; there was a quietness, a containment and a dignity about the young men around him that made you believe that Mr. Malcolm and they had been given a community and rescued from fear.

He lost that community when he was expelled from the Nation of Islam and it must have taken an immense amount of character to carry on as well as he did. Now what can we believe but that he was killed by young men very like the ones who used to surround him, and whom he had helped liberate from fear?

I do not think that, until now, I have ever really known what a terrible thing a ghetto is.

New York World-Telegram, February 23, 1965

Robert George Thompson:
American

"The cremated remains of Robert George Thompson will not be interred in Arlington Cemetery."
—THE DEPARTMENT OF DEFENSE, *January 27, 1966*

Buna was a long time ago. It had become a part of history three months after the battle for it was over; it was a rest area by the spring of 1943; and those who had been there before you were proud because they had seen the last time that the Aussies had charged with the bayonet in their shined shoes and because you never could.

Buna was the Aussies' last great battle in World War II and it was the Americans' first in New Guinea. The Aussies had begun it marching over the Kokoda Trail from Port Moresby and coming down in parade formation to the coast, singing "Waltzing Matilda," the legend insisted, until the Japanese began to fire. The 127th Infantry Regiment of our great 32nd Division came with them; Robert George Thompson was a staff sergeant in Company C of its 1st Battalion.

And there at the Monombi River, as his company commander later put it, Robert Thompson, "voluntarily led a patrol of five men in a successful attack and the establishment of a bridgehead . . . in broad daylight against a heavily fortified position, this patrol swam a heavily swollen and rapidly flowing river. . . . Clad only in shorts and with utter disregard for his own safety, Sgt. Thompson not only directed the crossing of his platoon but led them in a successful attack against two dominating pillboxes, thereby securing a small bridgehead."

These five soldiers held that patch of ground all day, and, when it was over, what they had done was thought to be one of the balances of the battle for Buna. Robert Thompson was awarded the Distinguished Service Cross and recommended for promotion to captain. A United Press correspondent asked who he was; and he smiled in the shy way he would never lose and answered, "Maybe you won't believe me, but I was a Young Communist League organizer in Ohio." He was sick by then and came home very soon with tuberculosis and malaria.

He stayed in the Communist party all his life. He paid more for that than for any sin there may be in that choice; all in all, he spent five years in prison; once, while he was waiting in the chow line in the West Street jail, an anticommunist hit him over the head with a hammer, and he lived on a very narrow edge ever after. When he died last spring, he was only fifty and was national secretary of the American Communist party.

This was a soldier. A soldier is not merely a man with a gun; he is a man who follows his commitments with that utter disregard for his personal safety which is the memory enshrined in Robert Thompson's citation. If he is in a war, he is in the infantry; if he is against a war, he is in the resistance. His choices are never for comfort; to live is for him to be a target.

It is not curious but natural that, dying, Robert Thompson should have wanted to be buried, not as the exile that civilians had tried to make him, but together with other soldiers in Arlington National Cemetery.

The Army could think of no way to deny his widow his wish; and his ashes were delivered the other day to Arlington for a military interment next Tuesday. The protests began to come in from the places from which protests always come, and the Army bucked the problem to the Justice Department, which came through yesterday with a finding that the Army did not have to bury Robert Thompson if it would be inconvenient.

And so an American who was brave has been judged and disposed of by Americans who are cowards of the least excusable sort, cowards who have very little to fear. Yesterday, the Army called Robert Thompson's widow and said that it would send his ashes wherever she wished.

Wherever those ashes go, the glory of America goes with them.

They belong to every soldier. They are all that remains of that afternoon at Buna, the guns in front and the vulnerable, half-naked body swimming to engage them. Those ashes had done everything for us but disgrace us; and now, by our treatment of them, we have disgraced ourselves.

New York World-Telegram, January 26, 1966

A Noble Itinerant

"Charles Keith, a real estate operator and campaign chairman for Paul O'Dwyer's successful bid for City Council President in 1973, died Wednesday . . . Mr. Keith, a native of Rutland, Vermont, was a merchant seaman during the early 1930s, very active in liberal causes . . ."
—THE NEW YORK TIMES, *February 17, 1978*

 "Very active in liberal causes" my foot. Lew Wasserman of the Music Corporation of America is very active in liberal causes. Charlie Keith was a dedicated Communist in the early thirties and into the forties and would probably have died one if the party, or any other party for that matter, had been adequate to his nobility of spirit.

It is both a sorrow and an advantage of the advance of the years that, more and more, the people in the obituary columns are people one knows. An obituary is, after all, the only story in a newspaper that comes at the end of the novel, and is thus uniquely the one that offers some chance for poetic truth.

And yet, in the absence of excessive fame, it is almost impossible to recognize the face you knew from the obituary portrait. What might remind us, now and then, how a life ought to be lived cannot even tell us how a life was lived. That is not even the fault of newspapers; they must depend for their facts on loving friends, who would think it a disservice to the departed if strangers thought him anything but respectable as the world judges respectability.

So then let me try awhile to talk about the Charlie Keith I knew who lived and died always better than respectable. I came up to the major leagues of the class struggle long enough to have a cup of coffee in the maritime unions in the middle thirties. Charlie Keith, young as he was then, had been in the old Marine Workers Industrial Union, a revolutionary Communist union pathetically unsuccessful until the upsurge of the New Deal gave its leaders a chance to be important in the formation of the National Maritime Union.

Keith was an open member of the Communist party in those days, but that wasn't the social disability it was later to be. Once the NMU became a piece of property with a treasury and an income, he might have made some claim to the rewards of the labor statesman.

Keith had, however, one of those natures Saint-Exupéry aspired to achieving when he said he preferred building a cathedral to serving as sexton in one. When the Spanish Civil War came, Keith showed himself lamentably unconscious of the duty of a political leader to send other people to be killed rather than go himself. He enlisted, was wounded, captured, and finally made his way home just before World War II began.

By then, the Communist faction in the NMU was in the hands of persons who had come later than Keith and who, although they weren't bad fellows, had already sunk into the time-serving habits of the union dodge. He had little in common with them, and went back to sea. By 1945, however, his old-fashioned romantic nature finally rebelled and he was thrown out of the Communist party with the *l'envoi* of a *Daily Worker* announcement that he was henceforth to be avoided as an enemy of the working class.

In 1946, Joseph Curran, president of the NMU, rose up and began a campaign to break the Communist party's power in the union. Curran was a particularly craftsmanlike product of the party's shop for the manufacture of myths, and he looked like the dream of the advancing proletariat in every agitprop drama. He was also possessed of the most formidably malignant cunning, and when he turned on his creators he broke them on his knees like matchsticks.

After Curran took full control, he appointed Keith to a staff job. It took about three months for the moral degradation of the piecard to become unbearable for Charlie. Not content with having purged the Communists from union office, Curran began an effort to drive them off the ships and very soon established a universal blacklist.

The notion that any man could be denied bread for no worse sin than calling him an enemy of the working class was so repugnant to

Charlie Keith that he protested, organized one more rebellion, lost, was denounced by Curran as a Communist and blacklisted. I was a labor reporter by then, and served the liberal cause by covering up for Curran much too long, until this sort of thing was just too noisome to go unrebuked, however faintly.

I shall die grateful to Charlie Keith for having provided the occasion when Joe Curran stopped speaking to me. Since he could not ship out any longer, he took to housepainting in Greenwich Village, and I never thought much about him thereafter, except to assume that he was mourning the romance of his youth in uncomplaining penury.

My daughter was living in the Village in the sixties and mentioned that her landlord, Charlie Keith, had said that he used to know me. Life has taught me that there are only 325 people in the world, and yet it seemed impossible that it could be *the* Charlie Keith.

And yet it was. I saw him next in 1973, back in politics as Paul O'Dwyer's campaign manager. Where else would any noble itinerant come at last to home? He was, by then, a substantial landlord. Communists are wonderful people: Not one of them has been able to produce a satisfactory example of socialism, and yet they waltz through capitalist acquisition.

Charlie died quite rich, setting aside enough money for Mrs. Keith to keep her in decent comfort and giving the bulk to a foundation to be spent by Paul O'Dwyer for the most useful social purposes his high soul can conceive. It is a lovely, romantic story that even has a happy ending, and it suggests what great opportunities we journalists disdain when we treat obituaries as routine drudgeries beneath our lofty talents.

New York Newsday, February 18, 1978

The Unpossessed

I T WAS BRAVE of Avon to retrieve Tess Slesinger's *The Unpossessed*
and put it to the risk of the paperback market after the thirty years it
has slumbered almost unremembered. To admire the spirit is easier
than to grant the hope; what appeal *The Unpossessed* retains is too
much more to our curiosity than to our affections; it seems, most of the
time, to insist too much on what we already know and learned long
since. To read Miss Slesinger is to remember how strident the thirties
were and how repetitively and how crudely they made their effects.
That was the very side of them Miss Slesinger protested; yet she could
only object to an age of manifestos in the tone of manifesto.

She gathers her barren women and their failed men in a living room
and then:

> My God, said Margaret Flinders to Margaret Banner-that-was
> (—*herself*—); we are sterile; we are too horribly girlish for our age,
> too mannish (with our cigarettes, our jobs, our drying lips) for our
> sex. Was this what you intended, Lady Mary Wortley Montagu?
> Rolling your fine eyes about the drawing room? Was this what my
> mother meant for me, sending me off to college, a book of Ibsen
> under my eager arm? O Economic-Independence Votes-for-
> Women Sex Equality! You've relieved us of our screens and our
> embroidery hoops, our babies and our vertigo; and given us—a
> cigarette, a pencil in our hair.

Norah, why don't we have children? she heard her own voice piercing like a fine horn through the din, battling its way through her pounding temples, cutting through time and space and clearing the air of confusion and wrong. And gazing straight at Norah as though the truth were out at last, she saw that the words had never been uttered, that her piercing voice had sounded nowhere but in her own astounded brain. 'God damn it,' Margaret Flinders suddenly said.

She could come no nearer to articulating her grievance against the voice of Man in his fortress on West End Avenue, affectionate, belittling, impossible to interrupt except by desperate expletive, never listening, always explaining, instructing, judging, anxious to be disappointed in her. She fled that voice, one thinks, because she was patronized; and now here it drones on, patronizing her still. In Tess Slesinger's New York, men, in the company of women, did not so much talk to them as to each other about them. And here we sit still unchanged after thirty years, still lecturing and scarcely noticing that she escaped us long ago.

Lionel Trilling in his Afterword tells us about Miss Slesinger with the reticent kindness we expect from the right sort of older brother when he talks about the little sister who ran away in the long ago. She was born in New York in 1905; a passing recollection of Damrosch concerts is all that is needed to fix our notion of a childhood in its established Jewish community. She was a graduate of the Ethical Culture Society School; Trilling first met her on the day of her marriage to Herbert Solow in the Society's meetinghouse on Central Park West. Her first husband was at the time an assistant editor of *The Menorah Journal*, remembered less for its own splendid merits than because Elliot Cohen, its managing editor, was to be the founder of *Commentary*.

"After her marriage to Solow, Tess Slesinger came into the circle of Cohen's tutelage," Trilling remembers. "No doubt she learned the more from him because he held her in great affection, as she did him." She was twenty-nine when she published *The Unpossessed*.

"Her natural charm," Trilling says, "was of a daughterly or a younger-sisterly kind, and in some considerable part consisted of her expectation of being loved, indulged, forgiven, or having permission to be spirited or even naughty."

The frame of reference is then of the family, and one for which Trilling retains the utmost affection; but the daughter of the house can be excused if she found it terribly confining. There was, first of all, its ghetto: The culture of her childhood had been high German and her new family did not take her far away from it. "Our tastes incline us to the left, our habits to the right; the left distrusts, the right despises us," her Bruno Leonard cries near the end of her book.

The isolation of Miss Slesinger's persona is just this total; even the Communist party is an abstraction of caricature outside their lives. All America seems light years away from them. That isolation is unexpectedly a factor of having been born Jewish and raised in an approximation of the ambience of Frankfurt. Nowadays the editor of *Commentary* has dinner with Mrs. John F. Kennedy and we have so forgotten the time when the Jewish intellectual was so little able to assert his authority in the general national culture that we need Trilling's painful reminder that his own appointment to the Columbia faculty in the twenties was an experiment.

For, to be *echt* bourgeois was to be cut off from the mass of the Jews of the thirties; and to be Jewish as well was to be separated from one's own class. The non-Jews one met must have been very seldom of one's own social position. Miss Slesinger rings least true when she introduces the Protestant rich upon her stage; there is the sense that these were persons she knew because she had confronted and inspected them at the money-raising events to which Jews of her class were invited only for their known munificence. Protestants with real property were simply outside her experience.

Part of her failure with them can be blamed on the temptation so many young novelists have to create characters upon whom they are unable to stand cross-examination. But another part of it must be honored for the courage of her attempt to engage the world outside the limits of the family. She is most appealing in the intensity of her curiosity about the "real" America; very seldom these days do we read a novel which so celebrates the rural, the fecund, the field as against the hothouse.

This nostalgia for a place she had never been must have been as necessary to her as repeated flights into a time unremembered are to her Margaret Flinders.

Trilling would hate to have it thought that *The Unpossessed* is "that so often graceless thing, a novel of feminine protest."

But it is difficult to read as anything else, from the beginning when Maggie Flinders remembers: "The real class struggle, Bruno said, is the struggle between the sexes, and rebellion begins at home," on through the reiterated moments when her husband feels her "alive and powerful, ten times more than he, as though she deliberately made the contrast."

In her family, the women are invariably the stronger and the men the weaker; the women natural, the men affected; the women the center to which the men repair either for refuge or rebellion. Miss Slesinger, you end up thinking, could hardly have been so insistent upon overrating her sex if it had been less persistently underrated in the family.

Trilling says she was born to be a novelist. He knew her, to be sure; but a stranger has to doubt it. The active motor behind the animus of *The Unpossessed* was her decision to divorce her husband; she seems to have waited barely long enough to see it published and fail to penetrate as an explanation, and then she escaped to Hollywood and a new husband and children. Norah then did not slam the door—who would have heard?—instead she wrote a novel. And, not thereafter having the need for another divorce, she was relieved of the necessity to explain herself; she became a happy wife, a mother, and a screenwriter.

The family's reaction, as remembered by Trilling, is a powerful testament for her grievance:

The burden of uneasy—of "guilty"—feeling must have been increased by the success the book achieved. . . . It was not success of an overwhelming kind, but it was real. . . . In the ethos of the time, the idea of "integrity" had great coercive power, and it was commonly supposed that success indicated an integrity compromised or even wholly lost; the gratification it brought was almost certain to be shot through with shame. That did not, of course, make success any the less interesting or attractive, and those who constituted the circle of Tess' friends wanted it for themselves, chiefly in the form of literary achievement. But it was Tess who first had it. That surely must have made a difficult situation for her. It would have been difficult for a man; it was even harder for a woman.

The illumination of this passage has a special sadness because Trilling can describe the environment that drove Miss Slesinger to revolt so much better than *The Unpossessed* can. To be a woman in that environment was to have the point of your complaint better made by man's response to your gesture than by the gesture itself.

Miss Slesinger failed as an artist because her true complaint could not be expressed with the means of discourse available to her. The language of feminism is just not subtle enough for what truly affronted her about her life; she never seemed to have been able to find in it the proper key for her own particular sense of loss; now she consciously parodies the feminist promise with the intent to deride, and now she unconsciously parodies it with the intent to exalt.

The difficulty seems to be that Miss Slesinger felt cheated of a promise of feminism so noble and so beautiful that it was seldom articulated by the normal feminist. The best of its daughters must have felt that the equality the woman's revolution promised was only useful as a way to a genuine intimacy between man and woman. Equality is a convenience; intimacy is a need. And intimacy was the promise of which Miss Slesinger properly felt cheated. That accounts for the mystery of how she could be so attractive and her work so without charm: *The Unpossessed* is, above all, charmless because its men and its women cannot talk to one another. It is unfair to blame a writer for a quality which so justly makes her point; but her circumstance made it a defect.

The claim of *The Unpossessed* on our attention, for example, is almost always pressed these days for what it can tell us about the state of mind of a special circle of New York intellectuals outside history at a moment of history. But there is very little life left in it as a social document; and, since that was not Miss Slesinger's concern, she cannot be blamed for that lack. She so well understood the element in the conversations of her men which was largely a device to avoid conversation with her women that, in being all too just to them in so many other things, she could not be just to that fraction of seriousness which had to exist in even this distorted an effort to engage political reality. What has spoiled *The Unpossessed* as a social portrait is not Miss Slesinger's hostility but her contempt for the importance of her subjects.

The life which endures in her grievance is instead in what is personal. As an instance, one reads most of the way through with less interest in than impatience with its old quarrels, and then one is suddenly caught up by that unspoken quarrel between Margaret and Miles Flinders, which ends the novel with her yielding to his demand that she abort their child.

This remains still an event so compelling that, shameful though it is to violate her privacy now, one cannot avoid the conviction that it happened to Miss Slesinger. Under stress of that conviction, it becomes possible to wonder whether those of our feminine novelists whose experience condemned them to the New York environment of the thirties might not more fortunately have died virgins. As it is, their words as teachers never quite talk to us as persuasively as do their wounds as victims; one remembers the woman forced into an abortion or the girl sitting all night in the park with her pessary long after one has forgotten the rest, all the figures in the landscape having been withered by that single stroke of autobiographical desolation.

"Norah, why don't we have children?" Maggie Flinders tries to call out. The thoughts that precede this strangled cry are, oddly enough, part Shaw, part Ibsen; she could think only in a language dictated to her by men, in the way that one African could communicate his hatred of French oppression to another African only by speaking French. Most of the time, at least in the early moments when being pregnant is only an abstract ideal to her, Margaret Flinders seems to confine its interior exposition pretty much to the terms of the Shavian notion of woman as life force. It may be that Miss Slesinger really believed that the Shavian formulas are enough by themselves to support a conviction this intense; but to think so is to read the Flinders marriage as no more than a power struggle. Miles Flinders thought it was, and Miss Slesinger gives his resentful and self-important ruminations more space than any author less just and kindly would have; but if either Miss Slesinger or her Margaret had thought the quarrel was about power she would have left us very little reason to care at all.

What makes one care is the scene that sets Margaret off to reflecting first with irony, then with rage, and at last with exultation, on the image of woman as life force. Her men are talking about men's work; and the customary disregard of their wives in such a conversation is made the more absurd because they are talking about a magazine they have projected but will never publish, and thus not about work at all but about a fantasy from which all save themselves are excluded. They are occasionally distracted enough to include the women; but when they do, it is to talk about man, woman, and sex in the vulgar clinical terms certain to turn the real into the fantasy.

At any such scene, the eventual overmastering cry is just for some-one you can talk to. I cannot remember that feeling better defined than it was by Ford Madox Ford when he had his Tietjens reflect that the best reason for having a mistress is to have someone to talk to. So perhaps, then, Margaret Flinders's demand to have a child is only a translation of the same lonely impulse.

Tess Slesinger seems by all accounts to have been very happy in Hollywood. She never wrote another novel, but one doubts that she felt this regret especially. This experience of peace and silence seems somehow a triumph over the New York man quite beyond the small competitive victory with the novel which made her place in the family so uneasy.

She even died a Stalinist, and Trilling reminds us that all the other members of the family had carried, in lonely rectitude, their resistance to that infection through a time remembered as one of great political loneliness. That reminder is the closest Trilling ever comes to that utterance so normal to the New York man: "I was right and you were wrong." But it is her victory that, even here, she manages so to enforce her personality that we are sure only that she was incorrect, and not that she was wrong. The insistence on being correct has had marvelous results for Trilling; I am not sure that its results have been all that appetizing in his inferiors. Stalinism, with all its vulgarity, had a sense of the family and an overvaluation of the common life, a tolerance, if you will, of romantic delusion that does not always suffer in comparison with superior judgment. A great part of its mindlessness was an over-acceptance of America. It was a movement in which a woman could, for a little while, delude herself that man was a comrade; and the point of *The Unpossessed* is that back here the family is full of cousins and brothers and uncles and empty of comrades.

The New Republic, November 5, 1966

Karl Marx: Reporter

D R. CHARLES BLITZER'S Introduction to *The American Journalism of Marx and Engels*, a selection of thirty-three of the more than five hundred dispatches which Marx and Engels composed for Greeley and Dana's New York *Daily Tribune*, is so exemplary a work of information without intrusion that it is embarrassing to begin by finding fault with its conclusion. If Marx seems "less striking and original today" than he must have seemed in the mid-nineteenth century, this is because, Dr. Blitzer says,

> the general approach to political history and analysis that he invented has been almost universally adopted in our time. If a preoccupation with the social and economic background of politics, and a determination to uncover the real motives that lie behind the words of politicians and governments are the hallmarks of modern political journalism, then Karl Marx may properly be said to be its father.

But these dispatches *are* striking and original, it seems to me, just because they have so little to do with most of the journalism I read or, for that matter, construct myself. The best of Marx's descendants are no closer to him than collateral. There is a puzzle here rather like that which arises when one confronts the early Carlyle: One sees at once that here is the way to get at the thing, and wonders why, with the sign painted this plain, the road has been so seldom followed.

That Greeley and Dana exploited Marx (and, without knowing it, Engels) is a piece of anecdote so familiar that President Kennedy sought to amuse the American Newspaper Publishers Association with the notion that the revolutionary specter might never have arisen had the *Tribune* not beggared its correspondents. Marx's contempt for Greeley had its side of self-disgust for having fallen so low in trade: "grinding bones and making soup of them like the paupers in a workhouse." "Mere pot boiling," Engels said long afterward. "It doesn't matter if they are never read again." Indeed Marx and Engels were not the unconscious future of daily journalism. They are only a sport in its past; and the conditions which have permitted their interlude were passing even while they grumbled at how trivial was the work which, as serious men, they never succeeded in trivializing. Greeley had his side; he was also cutting his own wage and Dana's, because early in the 1850s there had begun the process by which the *Times* slowly ground down the *Tribune*. "The *Times* was crowding us too hard . . ." Greeley wrote in 1852. "It is conducted with the most policy and the least principle of any paper ever started. It is ever watching for the popular side of any question that turns up, and has made lots of friends by ultra abuse of Abolitionists, Women's Rights, Spirit Rappers, etc., which I cannot do. Besides it has had the most room for reading matter the past winter . . ." That great instrument of collectivist progress, the journalism of accommodation had arrived.

"I HAVE WRITTEN nothing for Dana because I've not had the money to buy newspapers," Marx wrote Engels that same year. That remark is instructive, not for what it says about Marx's poverty but for what it tells us about his method. He was the journalist of the most despised credentials, the one who does not have access. Circumstance condemned him, of course, to be an outsider; but one comes to doubt that easier circumstance would have altered the method. Marx seems to have been incurious even about what was convenient to hand.

Did he ever visit the Crystal Palace? If he did, there is no evidence that this visual experience worked in any way upon his imagination. The most "unabashed hymn to industrial progress under capitalism"

George Lichtheim has found in Marx and Engels is their vivid conjuration of the immense shift that would come in the locus and proportion of commercial power with the discovery of gold at Sutter's Mill.

Marx had no use for the tactile and no infirmity of distraction by it. At the center of his imagination was the document from whose pages the historical moment jumped only for him. The successive lodgings in Soho, the British Museum, and Hampstead Heath are the only London places where Mehring sets him. It cannot be argued that direct observation would have been of no use to him whatever. If *The Eighteenth Brumaire* remains on a plane above even the best of this work, the difference, along with its higher passion, must be his direct experience with its events; he was acquainted with some of its personages and had at least seen many of the others. Even so, intimacy could never have been so important as the method itself. *The Eighteenth Brumaire* might be just as unique a piece of historical specification if Marx had got it up from nothing except the files of the *Moniteur*. The problem with any such surmise is that the *Moniteur*, superior though it might otherwise be to the run of the Parisian press, was inadequately stocked with the raw material of fact upon which the historical imagination depends for stimulus. A journalist whose needs and disposition confined him to the study of paper could hardly have worked, however uncommon his genius, anywhere except in the London of the 1850s. Periodicals embodying a special national idiocy can be found anywhere of course; but the British had those and something more. Their journalism was free and lively enough to provide a rich ration of revelatory anecdote. And what was more consequential, the British were the only social statisticians in Europe, which meant that they counted their sins along with everything else; Great Britain was the only European nation that bothered to compute its deaths during the 1848 epidemic. This material, primitive as it was, was all Marx needed; what is embarrassing, one hundred years and megatons of documentation later, is how much more he did with such treasures then than our journalism does now.

There were no limits of time and distance to the range of his mind. The House of Commons debates the British rule of India, "in the usual dull manner," and Marx is off on an examination of the question, impossible of course without a long consideration of the origins and the destruction of the Indian village system. The Duchess of Sutherland attacks slavery in America; and Marx notes the event as a definition of the "class of British philanthropy which chooses its subjects as far distant from home as possible and rather on that than on this side of the ocean." The definition would not, of course, be complete without a full account of the rapacities of the Staffords in Scotland since the end of the seventeenth century.

He notices points that appear to have escaped all public debaters, whatever their side; he even wonders—as no mere ideologue could have—whether India has not cost Britain more than it has been worth to her. Most of all, he is unchained from any notion of fixed place; he sits in his imagination wherever it would be most illuminating to sit. When he writes of the opium war, it is as though he were Chinese watching the barbarian ships come up the river; when he unearths the bluebook that describes revenue methods in India, he is the Brahman being tortured for his taxes. Sympathy does not take him there; sympathy was not one of Marx's weaknesses; he is simply impelled to find the seat that affords the clearest point of view.

There are none of the rewards of access in these dispatches. They are faintly suggested only by Engels in his sketch of Lord John Russell, where there is some of the small change of gossip we have got used to in journalism. But a man who rode the hunts might have picked that up, from the tone horsemen have always used about any Bedford, whether he was Tory, Whig, or philosopher. Engels does Palmerston from Hansard and the Foreign Office blue books, the documents in this case being quite enough even for lesser men. For Palmerston is one of those parliamentary dervi who leap up at us, dancing and dodging, from the official page:

> If not a good statesman of all work, he is a good actor of all work. He succeeds in the comic as in the heroic, in pathos as in familiarity, in tragedy as in farce, although the latter may be more congenial to his feelings. . . . Being an exceedingly happy joker, he ingratiates himself with everybody. Never losing his temper, he imposes on

passionate antagonists. If unable to master a subject, he knows how to play with it.

Of all the illusions we bring young to journalism, the one most useful to lose is the illusion of access to sources. To take two cases, I. F. Stone gets along splendidly by avoiding it, and Walter Lippmann gets on no less splendidly by having it and throwing it away before settling down to make up his mind. Persons privy to events either do not know what is important about them or, when they do, generally lie, as even Lincoln lied to Greeley for purposes of seduction. Marx had neither temptation nor opportunity of access; even so, his judgment again and again fits very closely the private observations of those persons safe inside the closed society that he speculated upon from across the moat.

By 1852, he had barely learned enough English to do the *Tribune* chores, which Engels had, until then, been composing under his name; yet he was already able to dismiss that summer's parliamentary elections:

The bribery and intimidation practiced by the Tories were, then, merely violent experiments for bringing back to life dying electoral bodies which have been incapable of production, and which can no longer achieve decisive electoral results and really national Parliaments. And the results? The old Parliament was dissolved, because at the end it had dissolved into sections which brought each other to a complete standstill. The new Parliament began where the old one ended; it is paralytic from the hour of its birth.

In that same month, James Graham was writing Gladstone: "It will be an impossible Parliament. Parties will be found too nicely balanced to render a new line of policy practicable without a fresh appeal to the electors." In 1855, even Disraeli, in a letter to a friend, embroidered for Palmerston a metaphor very like Engels's, seeing the Prime Minister–designate as "utterly exhausted. . . . and now an old pantaloon, very deaf, very blind and with false teeth, which would fall out of his mouth when speaking, if he did not hesitate so in his talk."

. . .

IN MARX'S JOURNALISM, then, we read dispatches which come as close as contemporary publication ever could to the journals the shrewder members of a ruling caste keep for themselves and the letters they write their friends. There the Outsider meets the Insider: Marx makes himself in his own work the embodiment of the Hegelian principle of the contact of extremes.[1] His intimacy with persons never seen extends as easily to ground never walked upon. When Marx deals with the Indian village system, there is the impression—he was not above cultivating it—that we look upon the distillation of long years of experience in the East set down by a man whose command of every possible detail of the picturesque is controlled by his determination not to let it distract our attention from his hypothesis. Yet all of it is the work of the historical imagination; it is difficult to think of anyone who approached its achievement except the Burke of Macaulay's grand compliment:

> His knowledge of India was such as few, even of those Europeans who have passed many years in that country, have attained, and such as certainly was never attained by any public man who had not quitted Europe. He had studied the history, the laws, the usages of the East with an industry such as is seldom found united to so much genius and so much sensibility. Others have perhaps been equally laborious, and have collected an equal mass of materials. But the manner in which Burke brought his higher powers of intellect to work on statements of facts, and on tables of figures, was peculiar to himself. In every part of those huge bales of Indian information which repelled almost all other readers, his mind, at once philo-

---

[1] "A most profound yet fantastic speculator on the principles which govern the movements of humanity" Marx begins his dispatch of June 14, 1853. "[Hegel] was wont to extol as one of the ruling secrets of nature what he called the law of contact of extremes. The homely proverb that 'extremes meet' was, in his view, a grand and potent truth in every sphere of life, an axiom with which the philosopher could as little dispense as the astronomer with the laws of Kepler or the great discovery of Newton."

sophical and poetical, found something to instruct or to delight. His reason analyzed and digested these vast and shapeless masses: his imagination animated and colored them . . . He had in the highest degree that noble faculty whereby man is able to live in the past and in the future, in the distant and in the unreal. . . .

But, aesthetic homage aside, these dispatches deserve that special praise reserved for works whose rediscovery makes us doubt every succeeding work that has neglected them. After Marx and Engels, even such an excellent model of the energetic and the curious as Asa Briggs seems disturbingly insular. I do not mean just that Briggs is philistine; Marx was pretty philistine himself. It was nearly impossible for a Victorian not to be, and it probably remains unavoidable when one has been long engaged with Victorian studies. But these occasional pieces by Marx and Engels leave you with the feeling that all general histories of the 1850s are incomplete, an impression which makes dubious Dr. Blitzer's assertion that the Marxist attack has been almost universally adopted in our time. For there is a sense that Marx's method is now never put to more than half its use: that Briggs understood the materialism without appreciating the dialectic; and that G. M. Young appreciated the dialectic without understanding the materialism; and that both travel Macauley's upward road past setbacks overcome and in progress ever ascending.

TO READ MARX is to commence to suspect that a great deal of what was to happen to Great Britain was determined by the forces which developed the nineteenth century's solutions, and thereby fixed their limitations. It has become, for example, almost automatic for even the soberest historians of the early Victorian period, when they come to the Ten Hours Act, to be carried away by the spectacle of an aroused national conscience. But Marx noticed even then how contained and confined that conscience has always been: The Established Church, having watched the Enclosures without protest, was suddenly aroused at the sufferings of the victims in the cities. The difference in response had an obvious root for Marx: The Church got its living from the landlords; the mills were owned by Dissenters.

We have grown used to dismissing the Marxist assessment of motive as simpleminded: Still, if this shot were wide of the mark, would there have been as much cant in the Victorian conscience as there was, could there indeed have been that indifference to all humans who were not Western Europeans? One reads all the way through *The Age of Improvement* without being reminded that Great Britain and France invaded China for no other reason than to force the opium trade upon her: It is an event described only in histories of China, and in the irony of Marx:

> While the semi-barbarian stood on the principle of morality, the civilized opposed to him the principle of self.

For the decay of Britain probably began, not so late as we usually set it, but in the years of Palmerston and Russell, who seemed farsighted when they were only indifferent; the one the most insular of foreign adventurers, the other the reformer who changed almost nothing. Great Britain, more lastingly even than France, established government as the theatrical art from which we suffer still. Its invention defeated Marx; one of his mistakes was his failure to recognize that no one is a fitter instrument for resisting history than the mime. England's lasting educational impress on the Indian subcontinent was not the railroad from which Marx expected so much, nor the English verse from which Macaulay hoped for so much. It was instead the mummery that has produced the Pakistan whose official lies are so like Sir Douglas Haig's and the India that lies in the cadences of the *New Statesman*. The post-Marxian world is an international of the insular.

Still one arises from this hack work of Marx's and thinks of him, defeated, in the heroic form Isaiah Berlin evokes during those years in Soho:

> The task of preparing the workers for the revolution was for him a scientific task, a routine occupation, something to be performed

as solidly and efficiently as possible, and not as a direct means of personal self-expression. The external circumstances of his life are therefore as monotonous as those of any other devoted expert, as those of Darwin or Pasteur, and offer the sharpest possible contrast to the restless, emotionally involved, lives of other revolutionaries of his time.

Journalism is certainly the less important of the two vocations that have forgotten his example of how a job of work should be done.

The New York Review of Books, June 15, 1967

The Man Who Hated Publishers

No HOPE OF private gain could have dictated *Westbrook Pegler: Angry Man of the Press*; Pegler is past all probability of rescue by fashion. Its author, Mr. Oliver Pilat, must have been drawn to his subject by one of those lonely impulses which are their own testaments of personal and professional honor. He is a newspaper reporter writing about the journey of another newspaper reporter with respect and a sense of duty to the history of an industry whose institutions seldom have a history that is not commissioned by their publishers. Westbrook Pegler's mature years have been a long cry that values like these have departed; and that "nowadays money is all that interests writers"; there is an unlooked-for justice in his having a biographer like this one.

One of Pilat's advantages is that he knows so much and that he takes for granted what he knows under the illusion that everyone else knows it. He will throw away as asides points about the practice of journalism that his lessers would inflate into whole themes; as an instance: "Particularly in later years, Pegler placed great stress upon his independence, but, *like any newspaperman*, he tended to absorb by osmosis the beliefs of his boss."

That is a lesson learned only by working for newspapers. The heart of the mystery with Pegler is that he worked so long for newspapers and thought hard about very little else, and still he never learned this simplest lesson from the experience.

The reason must be that to admit this knowledge would have been insupportable to him. Arthur Pegler, his father, was an itinerant worker on midwestern newspapers; stern at home, combative in saloons, but most of the time a tractable employee. During the First World War, Arthur Pegler wrote a magazine article on yellow journalism; a Hearst paper, he said then, sounded like "a screaming woman running down the street with her throat cut." He was fired at once by the Chicago Hearst paper for which he then worked. He recovered from this horrid fall into freedom to live thereafter in harness. Pilat traces Arthur Pegler to the city room of Hearst's *Daily Mirror* when he was in his seventies; occasionally he wrote editorials, in which sacred function he would "confer ill-naturedly with Frank Farley, the paper's political expert, over how things should be phrased to avoid annoying 'the high priest' "—meaning the managing editor. Ill-natured but accepting, Arthur Pegler worked into his eighties, after which his employers certified him as a legend and retired him with $780 in severance pay.

WESTBROOK PEGLER WAS fired for good last year, for the same cause that once got his father fired: He cursed the Hearsts in public for defiling the product. By then he was in his late sixties; it took him that long to discover what his father had known and had accepted as part of the game.

But there was one special difference between them. Westbrook Pegler had an Irish mother, and there would always be something in his life to call back Yeats's memoirs of the failed poets he knew in the nineties. They were Scots most of them; but there is the same Irish Jacobite madness of *great hatred, little room*, and there are the same passions larger than the narrow streets on which they were appointed to walk. With them we feel ourselves among Westbrook Pegler's true precursors: John Davidson, who told Yeats in the British Museum, "the fires are out; I must hammer the cold anvil" and, most particularly, Macgregor Mathers, whom Yeats met on the streets of Paris wearing his Highland clothes "with several knives in his stocking" and who explained, "when I am dressed like this, I feel like a walking flame." The effort to feel like a walking flame has been the business of

Westbrook Pegler's life. Journalism is not the proper place for that experiment. The American reporter has a better chance of acceptance as a gentleman and an equal than his colleagues anywhere in the world, but it is a chance spacious only by comparison.

Pilat finds just one instance of a private conversation between Franklin Delano Roosevelt and Westbrook Pegler: " 'Now look, West,' said F.D.R. at one point, gesturing with his cigarette holder. That tore it . . . 'What was that, Frank?,' [Pegler] replied, glowering." Pegler sat at that moment as the incarnate representative of the outraged dignity of his craft. And too few journalists of his time have been truer than Pegler to the pride that is the artisan's duty to his trade.

Yet none came to dignity and preserved it with less reason; Pegler's childhood and apprenticeship were one long argument against its claims. It is scarcely conceivable that the image of Arthur Pegler as untrammeled spirit could have survived the sight of Arthur Pegler in the office. Westbrook Pegler began life for himself with a Scripps-Howard paper in Des Moines and passed on to the United Press; Pilat makes it clear that these were animal existences. He must have been one of those men of special fiber who endure sweatshops and keep a fierce and unreasonable vanity about their craft, hating their employers no less for turning out a bad product than for exploiting them. The resentments of such men are peculiarly unappeasable by a social system which might be able to mollify their material resentment as workers but can only further abrade their pride as craftsmen because its reason for existence is to distribute more and more goods of worse and worse quality every year.

FROM HIS YOUTH at the United Press, Pegler has drawn this holy memory: "We had no assurance of pay during illness, no vacations and no severance. . . . I never knew such an outfit of workers. You could hardly sweep us out of the office." This ideal of labor, incessant, consuming, unrelated to gain or glory, lives on in Pegler; we almost forget that he is talking about the newsroom of a wire service. Heywood Broun thought it unreasonable for Westbrook Pegler to sit for eight hours with the blood running into his shoes for nothing more consequential than the fabrication of a newspaper column; Westbrook Pegler found it sacrilegious that Heywood Broun would cast off in forty minutes something so extraordinary as a newspaper column.

All sense of proportion argues that Broun was right; nothing argues for Pegler except what is left of us from the way we felt when we were young. To have been young and a reporter and to have met Westbrook Pegler was to have been surprised at how gentle he was, and how glad to see you. Tristan, I suppose, would have been like that when he met young men in the fit of first love and swearing that they would live no other way; and then they would go off and get fat and bulge at conventions of the Association of Former Knights Errant or give lectures on their adventures in the Middle East or endorse candidates for King; and Tristan would sit there, still held by that old potion, and he would hate them and quite properly too.

Pilat tells us that in the thirties Westbrook Pegler was traveling to Poughkeepsie and met the mother of a friend. " 'Will you see the President?' she asked. 'I hope not,' he answered. 'Why not?' 'Because he bemuses me.' " Anyone outside the newsroom was the enemy tempter.

HERE IS ONE of the few American workingmen who has heroically and stubbornly struggled to remain class-conscious. I know he is not thought of that way; even Pegler thinks of himself as a Tory, but he is correct only if he means that word in its precise original sense, which was to designate a Popish outlaw who, from pride and necessity, offered his resistance to Oliver Cromwell from an Irish bog.

A cold, proud bias for the athlete as against the promoter—for the craftsman as against the merchandiser—informed Pegler's work as a sportswriter in the twenties. He was not a Marxist sportswriter, but something better, an anarcho-syndicalist one. It is forty-four years since the Chicago White Sox threw a World Series, but the Westbrook Pegler who would rail at a Postmaster General if he stole a five-cent stamp still thinks of Joe Jackson and Hal Chase as toilers so badly paid that taking bribes was only a way to get back a bit of their own. It was hard for him to believe that an athlete who took had violated the meaning of his life and the honor of his sport, since that meaning and honor seemed to Pegler to have been already violated by his employer.

Scripps-Howard raised—or more precisely dissipated—him into the station of general columnist in December of 1933. An argument might be made that Pegler owed this elevation to Franklin D. Roosevelt; in any atmosphere except the one which Roosevelt was creating, a newspaper syndicate would hardly offer as public educator a columnist of Pegler's peculiar credentials. His first general column began, "As a member of the rabble. . . ." He had not completed high school; the most distinguished scholar of his close acquaintance was either Al Munro Elias, the baseball statistician, or Nat Fleisher, the boxing historian. Now, Will Rogers was also a common man and he had been a popular columnist in the twenties; but he had specialized in the message a proprietor wants most to hear from his chattel, *i.e.*, "I never met a man I didn't like." But Pegler was the common man with a grievance; in him, the resigned wisdom of simple folk came out as the snarl which is so often their real private speech.

The national new beginning of 1933 infected him with the misapprehension that was the most disabling distraction of his career. President Roosevelt is still blamed by the unreconciled for developing class hatred in Americans; but his true consequence was to weaken and confuse the class sense of the ordinary citizen beyond any hope of recovery. The strongest illusion the common man drew from the New Deal had little to do with socialism; it was instead a mistaken faith that he was emerging to own property and be independent. Under Herbert Hoover, Westbrook Pegler knew that he worked for a living at his boss's mercy; under Franklin Roosevelt, he thought himself a free man and his own proprietor.

His quarrel with the American Newspaper Guild, really a quarrel with Broun, is admirably reviewed by Mr. Pilat and might be summarized as a case study in this misconception. In the spring of 1937, Broun was ready to go on strike against *The New York World-Telegram*, which seemed illogical to Pegler, because he and Broun were not ordinary employees but independent contractors. Their difference was that

Pegler trusted Roy Howard, their publisher, as an old friend and an equal. Pegler broke with the Guild on that issue, first among others, in 1937. Seven years later, his distaste for unions had made him a commercial liability in New York.

"In 1944," Pilat instructs us, "Roy Howard visited David Dubinsky to suggest that he was publishing a liberal paper which deserved a better circulation in the labor field. How could he get it? 'That's easy,' said Dubinsky. 'Fire Pegler.' "

We do not ordinarily think it the function of a representative of workingmen to suggest to an employer that he solve a commercial problem by firing another workingman. That is because the New Deal confused us. Labor leaders happened to be among the few common men who had acquired property under the New Deal; Dubinsky and Howard shared the bond of men who really have power to hire and fire. In the end, Howard let Pegler go to Hearst; he had been an independent contractor to just the extent that a General Motors dealer is a free entrepreneur and a friend of Harlow Curtice. Pegler may have begun to understand by then how it was; that unreal quality in his public rages may have resulted from their being fired at targets so different from the true objects of his anger. He really hated publishers. As he grew older much of his work began to seem distracted—and in some areas even deplorable. Suddenly the rhetoric was just so much terrible evidence of an interior grievance to which the wooden ducks he was shooting were quite irrelevant. Pilat is too honest not to give us our fill of samples of Pegler when, as *The New Yorker* once said, he was writing about Mrs. Roosevelt as though she were a crooked wrestling promoter. There are values in Pegler, but they are not in his determination to offend. Brutal, remorseless rage does not liberate but only imprisons.

I should judge that the best things from the later Pegler, both as art and social criticism, are his judgments on journalism in the fifties; how stale it was, how inoffensive it wanted to be, how mechanical it had become, how clumsy publishers were in all functions except the crook of the knee to power. Only Pegler could find the precise word for those syndicated columns which make every newspaper seem like nearly every other. He called them "packaged goods"; it was the judgment of the handcraftsman about the product that had displaced his, a thing only stamped out and distributed without touch of human hand.

His valedictory was that speech last year to the Christian Anti-Communist Crusade. Pegler knew the real enemy at last—he could only talk about William Randolph Hearst, Jr., his boss—and he was left only an audience held together by an inflamed ignorance of who their enemy really is. He might better have delivered his testament to a convention of editors, publishers, or union journalists; but the best platform was any one Pegler could get that afternoon; the point was not the scene but the words.

What could this audience have made of this judgment of the Hearst syndicate, which is not that much worse than the others?

[King Features] is a sub-division of the Hearst empire dealing in comic books, comic strip books, sweet powders to make soda pop, toys and a very ingenious variety of dingbats for the immature.

The minimum compliment that sentence deserves is that it renders unnecessary, by the act of poetic concentration, every previous essay on mass culture.

Mr. Pilat tells a sad story and one often errant, confused, and lonely; but the dignity of its subject endures because there was in this life not one act of real betrayal. Pegler damaged himself, he wasted himself on what did not matter, but he never told a lie that he had not told himself first.

I used to be depressed when radicals talked about Pegler and said how they wished they had him on their side. If the radical impulse is some dubious but lovely notion from one's youth and the radical faith a struggle to preserve it, chipped but whole, against every erosion by maturity, then Westbrook Pegler *was* on their side.

The New Republic, June 8, 1963

[Postscriptum]

THE FINAL SADNESS, the only sadness really, is that there is no child of Peg's to whom to write. The sorrow about him is a private one, hard to explain to strangers. Curiously, the lines that come to mind are Robert Lowell's about quite somebody else.

> . . . *I miss you, out of Plutarch, made by hand*—.

Peg *was* made by hand, and then warped, never yielding, by process. His last respectable employer was the Hearst Corporation; it fired him for a speech.

He was disposed of by Hearst at the moment of revelation, like a Bolshevik at the execution wall. He passed a while at *American Opinion*, the journal of the Birch Society, but he could not endure that either. He died blacklisted.

THE CRAFT WHICH he honored so long and so alone can be found, by a fortunate accident, if you sit in the audience of *The Front Page* this season. The characters in that police headquarters are, if not quite Peg's contemporaries, the reporters who read him in the sports pages of the *Chicago Tribune*. They are casual about suffering; they are harsh about losers; but they know something that has escaped those of us their juniors who have lunch with the White House assistants. They know that the sheriff is a thief and that when the Mayor says that he stands against the Red Peril he means only that he confronts the approach of the first Tuesday after the first Monday in November.

They know, in other words, what Lord Acton studied for years to find out: "Great men are almost always bad men . . . There is no worse heresy than that the office sanctifies the holder of it." Just to have learned that much and to have been given a fanatic heart are all you need to get through life. Yet, Peg, more than anyone I ever knew, had that knowledge and that heart; and those of us who cherished him, not just as a writer but as a person, are thought to be whimsical when we say so, and the young are warned against going his road.

I AM SORRY. The only argument against Peg's road is its risks, and you affront the young—or ought to—when you advise them against risks.

New York Post, June 26, 1969

Saving a Whale

A CHOICE OF DAYS and *On Mencken* make up Knopf's testament to Henry L. Mencken on the hundredth year since his birth. We should, of course, be grateful to have any memorial less degrading than those essays of R. Emmett Tyrrell through which Mencken's ghost now and then flickers like some damned soul in hell. All the same, these garlands, though altogether worthier and more scrupulously worked, seem somehow not quite up to their subject.

But then there are subjects that fairly prohibit adequacy. Whales are the only mammals that the museums have never managed to stuff and mount in their original skins. The great whale in New York's Museum of Natural History is a styrofoam reproduction; and the museum's orca, despite its more modest proportions, is only a compound of burlap and plaster. These counterfeits are the best the taxidermists can do, because, they have found, something in the very nature of the whale's original skin makes its preservation impractical.

Mencken is a very great whale and can stove all boats that sail too close too soon. The careful sailor begins at a respectful distance and looks for what the creature is not before grappling with what it might be.

THE FIRST SIGHT is the spouting, and who cannot be forgiven for coming upon such a spectacle and henceforth and forever deciding that this sportive play in the warm waters is most of what whales are about? Alistair Cooke, who knew him well and read him keenly, settles for defining Mencken as "a humorist in the classic American tradition, about halfway between Mark Twain and Woody Allen."[1]

Even those of us least satisfied with the notion that his spout is all there is to the whale have to concede that any geyser is a joyous sight indeed. Here, as an instance, is the thirty-six-year-old Mencken on Tchaikovsky's Sixth Symphony:

> In this grand complex of tunes, indeed, Tschaikowsky tells all his troubles—how he was forced into marriage against his will; how he lost three thousand roubles on Russian government bonds; how his pet dog Wolfgang was run over by the Moscow–Petersburg *D-Zug* and lost an ear; how the concert-master was in liquor at Dresden and spoiled his *Romeo and Juliet*; how ill he was after eating that *gekochter Schellfisch* at Prague; how the wine merchant, Oroshatovich, swindled him with synthetic Burgundy; how he lost his baggage between Leipzig and Berlin, and had to conduct in borrowed cuffs; how the summer boarders at Maidanovo played "Monastery Bells" on their tin-pan pianos; how that *Schuft* of a critic at Köln accused him of borrowing his Capriccio in G sharp minor from Offenbach; how his friend Kashkin won a hundred roubles from him at *yeralash*; how he cut his hand opening a can of asparagus; how melancholy it was to come to fifty-year.

This is, of course, pure sport with no destination except the disposable tissue that is any day's newspaper, and we would not even know this flight existed if it were not for Carl Bode's exemplary efforts at retrieval in *The Young Mencken*. Such stuff goes about as far as Woody Allen has ever contrived to go. But, after the mockeries of all self-seriousness, there comes the note of appreciation of the serious that lifts the man of true sensibility above the one who merely jests for the ostentation of the cap and the bells:

[1]Dorsey, John, ed., "Mencken and the English Language," in *On Mencken* (New York: Knopf, 1980), p. 112.

And yet, for all that maudlin confidence, a great work of art. A work to torture and delight the sentimentalist, but at the same time a work to interest and edify the musician. In the midst of all its mawkishness it is written superbly.[2]

The point of Mencken is not just the ear for those elements of the ridiculous that are pretension's close companions but the eye for those elements of genuine feeling that can redeem the worst pretension. He knew that what deserves to be esteemed lives very often with what deserves to be laughed at. It is this ability to render justice and what he would have scoffed to hear called his capacity to love that separate him from so many of those who mistake him for their model.

COOKE'S JUDGMENT THAT Mencken's claim upon posterity resides mainly in his place among classic American humorists is, I am afraid, one more example of the trouble we have accepting ungainly, outsized, and troublesome articles of our cultural furniture unless we trim and trivialize them into domestic comforts.

The special service of Bode's anthology is the help it gives us in understanding that Mencken's mind took its mold very early on. Just because he so recognized the difference between himself and the run of his countrymen, the brands preserved in *The Young Mencken* glow especially with anticipations of the mistaken identity his shade now threatens to carry through the eternal snows.

That fate had, after all, been Mark Twain's:

While he lived he was several times labeled and relabeled, and always inaccurately and vainly. At the start the national guardians of letters sought to dismiss him loftily as a hollow buffoon, a brother to Josh Billings and Petroleum V. Nasby. This enterprise failing, they made him a comic moralist, a sort of chatauquan in motley, a William Jennings Bryan armed with a slapstick. Foiled

---

[2]Bode, Carl, ed., *The Young Mencken: The Best of His Work* (New York: Dial, 1973), p. 541.

again, they promoted him to the rank of Thomas Bailey Aldrich and William Dean Howells, and issued an impertinent amnesty for the sins of his youth. Thus he passed from these scenes—ratified at last but somewhat heavily patronized.[3]

And then, after Mark Twain was buried and his habitual alarms about being a cause of scandal were no longer relevant, those black posthumous works *What Is Man?* and *The Mysterious Stranger* were at last published, and in Mencken's words:

> The parlor entertainer . . . completely disappears; in his place there arises a satirist, with something of Rabelais's vast resourcefulness and dexterity in him, and all of Dean Swift's devastating ferocity. . . . No wonder the pious critic of the New York *Times*, horrified by [*What Is Man's*] doctrine, was forced to take refuge behind the theory that Mark intended it as a joke.[4]

Mencken had barely passed his apprenticeship before he resigned himself to the same destiny of misunderstanding. While still young, he demonstrated a knack for clarifying and compacting the ideas of alien and distant prophets. His first appearances between boards were *vade mecums* to Nietzsche and Shaw; and his formidable learning owed itself in considerable part to the force-feeding such drudgeries extort. He was only twenty-seven when he was at work on *George Bernard Shaw: His Plays*, and gave voice to his doubts that:

> Shaw will ever become a popular dramatist, in the sense that Sardou and Pinero are popular. . . .
> One cannot expect a man, however keen his sense of humor, to laugh at the things he considers eminently proper and honorable. Shaw's demand that he do so has greatly restricted the size of the Shaw audience.[5]

[3]Bode, p. 566.
[4]Bode, p. 564.
[5]Bode, pp. 73 and 75.

This early insight may best explain why the Mencken manner, to the extent that it survives at all, has its awkward existence in the language of disciples who reserve their scorn for whatever the respectable conceive as improper and dishonorable, and who confine their nonconformity to mock heroic gestures of refusing to crook the knee to anyone who declines to conform. Thus we have R. Emmett Tyrrell, who walks so lamely among us as Mencken's bitterest enemy, the enforcer of loyalty oaths, born again in the disguise of Mencken *revivivus*.

Would he be ashamed to have progeny no seemlier than this one? We can by no means be sure that he would. There sits, by no means uncherished, some Aunt Polly at the back of all our minds, and as the years go by, her voice grows ever more compelling. What we rejected we now embrace; suddenly we are ashamed to be a trial and long to be accepted as a comfort.

Mencken was forty when he caught the pathos and arraigned the betrayal of Mark Twain's later years:

> returning to the native mob as its premier clown—monkey-shining at banquets, cavorting in the newspapers, shrinking poltroonishly from his own ideas, obscenely eager to give no offense.[6]

And yet, if they are free of pathos and innocent of betrayal, what are those yarns that Knopf now abridges and reissues as *A Choice of Days* except the effort simply to please that overcomes all of us in an old age anxious to be amnestied for the sins of our youth?

Both *A Choice of Days* and *On Mencken* are almost all *allegro*, youth as sunrise in Baltimore as Eden. They are delightful, but they are far from the whole symphony. *On Mencken* beguiles us with a full chapter of tributes to the city of Baltimore collated by Huntington Cairns. We are in Cairns's debt for *The American Scene*, the most acute and discriminating of all selections of Mencken's work. But in this case the

---

[6]Mencken, H. L., *The American Scene: A Reader*, Huntington Cairns, ed. (New York: Knopf, 1965), p. 108.

employment assigned him is the mining and exhalation of roseate memories of Mencken's native place. His Baltimore was certainly charming and easy enough, but there were cruel limits to the tolerance Mencken celebrates.

It was, after all, Baltimore whose citizens grew so abraded by his enthusiasm for the German cause in the First World War that by the autumn of 1916 their *Sun* papers were driven to put him on forced leave. The city he loved was also the city that exiled him from its journalism for three years and the city whose public librarian declined to stock the novels of Theodore Dreiser while they sat untrammeled on the shelves of Philadelphia, Kansas City, and Indianapolis. There was darkness as well as sunshine in this life; and the swimmer swam against the current, gaily to be sure, but all the same strenuously.

HIS COMMUNITY WITH Dreiser was the expression of Mencken's nature that comes nearest to an accurate perception of him:

> All the latter-day American novelists of consideration are vastly more facile than Dreiser in their philosophy, as they are in their style. In the fact, perhaps, lies the measure of their difference. What they lack, great and small, is the gesture of pity, the note of awe, the profound sense of wonder—in a phrase, that "soberness of mind" which William Lyon Phelps sees as the hallmark of Conrad and Hardy, and which even the most stupid cannot escape in Dreiser.... In the arts, as in the concerns of everyday, the American seeks escape from the insoluble by pretending that it is solved. A comfortable phrase is what he craves beyond all things—and comfortable phrases are surely not to be found in Dreiser's stock.[7]

> One swiftly forgets his intolerable writing, his mirthless, sedulous, repellent manner, in the face of the Athenian tragedy he instills into his seduced and soul-sick servant girls, his barbaric pirates of finances, his conquered and hamstrung supermen, his wives who sit

[7] *The American Scene*, p. 112.

and wait. . . . Such a novel as *Sister Carrie* stands quite outside the brief traffic of the customary stage. . . . It is not a mere story, not a novel in the customary American meaning of the word; it is at once a psalm of life and a criticism of life—and that criticism loses nothing by the fact that its burden is despair. . . . The thing he seeks to do is to stir, to awaken, to move. One does not arise from such a book as *Sister Carrie* with a smirk of satisfaction; one leaves it infinitely touched.[8]

Cooke notices a strain of cruelty in Mencken; and it is inescapably there, although you rather wish that he had found a specimen more inarguably gross than the obituary of William Jennings Bryan that was printed the day after his death and polluted the attendant clouds of incense with the stink bomb of the insistence that the deceased was "a charlatan, a mountebank, a zany without sense of dignity . . . full of an almost pathological hatred of all learning, all beauty, all fine and noble things."[9]

This style of having at the carcass pays the price of getting itself thought cruel but that cost seems meager when set against its rewards. For the Mencken who was unafraid to violate the proprieties is the Mencken who speaks most eloquently to us still; he dared in that high fashion Whitman marked in Thoreau: "his lawlessness—his dissent— his going down his own absolute road, let hell blaze as it pleases."

But then Mencken's grand advantage over the journalists of his or any later time was not merely that he did not worry about Hell or Heaven. Indifference to and even disbelief in an afterlife of blessings and punishments are more common than unique to man. But, if it is a rare journalist who quakes at the prospect of the Lake of Fire, it is a rarer one still who does not worry about the hot water that can scald anyone who gives cause for scandal.

The conventional obituary escorts the defunct to the bar of heaven

---

[8] *The American Scene*, p. 128.

[9] A revised version of this grand remonstrance, more carefully groomed but in no way tamed, can be found in Mencken, H. L., *A Mencken Chrestomathy* (New York: Knopf, 1956), pp. 243–248.

with a deference made particularly ceremonious by the fear of being caught jogging the elbow of the Recording Angel. Mencken did not believe that there is such a being as the Recording Angel; and yet the precipitate death of William Jennings Bryan, whom he had watched raving and fuming at the Scopes trial only days before, pressed upon him the awful transience of everyone's life. We could hardly otherwise explain the image he summoned up at the opening of his dispatch to the Baltimore *Evening Sun*:

> Has it been duly marked by historians that William Jennings Bryan's last secular act on this globe of sin was to catch flies? A curious detail, and not without its sardonic overtones. He was the most sedulous fly catcher in American history, and in many ways the most successful. His quarry, of course, was not *Musca domestica* but *Homo neandertalensis*. For forty years he traced it with coo and bellow, up and down the backwaters of the Republic. Wherever the flambeaux of Chatauqua smoked and guttered, and the bilge of idealism ran in the veins, and Baptist pastors damned the brooks with the sanctified . . .—there the indefatigable Jennings set up his traps and spread his bait.[10]

This is an image of the sort that is started by the most vivid intimations of your own mortality and the sharpened perception that all of it could end for you tonight as it had so suddenly for so many men, run over, say, by some rackety Ford on the way back to bed after filing at the Western Union office.

These then might be the last lines you would write on earth, and that thought serves to expel every inhibition about how they might look to the proper-minded. Mencken once remembered or perhaps imagined that he had composed his *envoi* to Bryan on a July night in a Chattanooga hotel room sitting in his undershorts with all the windows open and nothing between him and suffocation except a languorous overhead fan. We can conceive of him standing up when he had finished and putting his shirt back on and saying to himself, "What I

---

[10]*A Mencken Chrestomathy*, p. 243.

have done this night no man alive could have done and I am the king of the cats."

The kingdom runs to fairly tame cats with ribboned necks and clipped claws; and in the times when their king runs raucous on the rooftops, he has very little company; but no matter: Moments of self-coronation like those excuse staying too late at the journalist's trade.

I DON'T THINK it can be sensibly argued that Mencken did not stay too late at his trade. Victimage has its uses. Blacklisting deprived Zero Mostel of every chance except that of being a very great artist at the $75 a week Equity minimum; and absolution only liberated him for increasing excesses of clownish vulgarity, irresistible in their way but travesties of his higher self. Mencken was expelled from daily journalism for his heresies in wartime; and when his term of banishment was over, he had made himself the first American editor to publish Joyce and the first living American critic to earn the admiration of Joseph Conrad.

In exile, he had brought himself to the place from which great leaps are made. And then the *Sun* papers opened themselves up to him again and he went zestfully back to inspecting statesmen, reporting on prize-fights, and exulting in the stable smells of conventions and campaigns. He did this kind of thing better than any other first-rate journalist has done since the death of John Reed; but it is easy work really, and third-rate novelists try it now and then and almost automatically do it better than first-rate journalists, and novelists like Gore Vidal, Norman Mailer, and Truman Capote, being well above the third-rate, do it better than anyone else on earth.

Still Mencken's turn back to the journalism he had outgrown was not so much a surrender as an engagement with a felt duty to a cause. He always boasted that he had no more social conscience than a cat; and yet now he took up the sword and threw away the scabbard, and there ensued a great war with the American consensus of the twenties that could not have been pressed so vehemently unless fructified by the anger of a victim of intolerance who felt himself one with every other victim.

A month before the Armistice, he had written Ellery Sedgwick at the *Atlantic Monthly:*

> Once it is over, I'll be glad to write you, if you dare me, a frank statement of the feelings and sensations of an American of German blood, facing for a year or more the ecstatic Germanophobia of the rest of the population. It has been a curious time and I think it has changed me a lot.[11]

It had changed him into a radical in unremitting conflict with the spirit of his age. I confess to thinking of him with idolatry; and it is idolatry's worst defect that the idolator molds his idol from the clay of his personal prejudices. The minimal respect we owe any man is to begin by taking him at his word; and Mencken never presented himself as other than a Tory, contemptuous of democracy and scornful of the masses. But, faithful as he tried to be to that vision of himself in the abstract, he was almost invariably false to it in confrontations with the here and now. He had the luck of the disability that afflicts William F. Buckley: His nature was not cold enough to make a good Tory or a good Bolshevik; he was deficient in the high-mindedness the disciplined coldhearted need. He worked as best he could to corral his sentiments and pen them away; and yet some fugitive feeling constantly drew him into places where the complacent do not choose to travel.

[11]Forgue, Guy J., ed., *The Letters of H. L. Mencken* (New York: Knopf, 1961), p. 130. This is a collection full of flaws and of fascinations, a deplorable example of the dangers of loving not wisely but too well. Knopf's adoration for Mencken was of that doting variety that blinds the lover to every danger that the beloved might go about the streets untidily arrayed. I doubt if any artist of Mencken's proportions has ever been edited with a hand as slovenly as this one. One even comes upon a letter identified as addressed to F. Scott Fitzgerald which the most casual reader would at once recognize as written to the child Frances Scott Fitzgerald. And yet, for all the indifference of publisher and editor to minimal dictates of grooming, what they so carelessly served forth to us remains sufficiently wonderful.

He was only too successful at making us think him the bourgeois undiluted. But for all his origins in the overheated, overbundled, overfed cocoon of a German-American–middle-class household, he was thrown into a workingman's world while barely out of adolescence. He was established on the old Baltimore *Herald* when he was eighteen and had already learned to look with a detached and eventually ribald eye while sheriffs lurched through hangings they could not execute until they were drunk enough not to notice. He saw men die of rabies in the country's earliest Pasteur clinic and suicides with their mouths distorted by carbolic acid and the cops badgering their distracted mothers. These experiences were a permanent coarsening; but they also bred a lasting tenderness toward the victims of life.

"It seems plain to me," he once wrote Dreiser, "that the most valuable baggage that you carry is your capacity for seeing the world from a proletarian standpoint. It is responsible for all your talent for evoking feeling. Imagine *Sister Carrie* written by a man without that capacity, say Nietzsche. It would have been a mess."[12]

There is no explaining their affinity unless we understand that Mencken, incompletely and therefore rebelliously, and Dreiser, entirely and therefore resignedly, each saw the world from a proletarian viewpoint.

Even in the thirties, when he was bleakly and even grouchily conservative, Mencken never forgot that society is divided between those who own property and those who work for a living, and he could continue to describe the American Newspaper Guild as a necessary instrument to protect "working newspapermen . . . against the forays of the predatory Babbitts who control only too many of the American newspapers."[13]

. . .

[12]Forgue, p. 221.

[13]Mencken, H. L., *A Gang of Pecksniffs and Other Comments on Newspaper Publishers*, selected by Theo Lippman, Jr. (New Rochelle, N.Y.: Arlington House, 1975), p. 187. Persons innocent of the reality of class can instruct themselves by noticing that these sentiments, prepared for the readers of the Baltimore *Evening Sun*, went unpublished therein.

THERE WAS A black strain of pessimism beneath the motley he so often affected. As it early convinced him that all gods were illusions, it almost as swiftly persuaded him that all rulers were frauds and most social action a futility. When the New Deal is finished, he wrote Ezra Pound in 1937, "the poor fish who now sweat with hope will still be slaves, doomed to dull and ignominious toil for scoundrels, world without end."

Pound had solicited his interest in Major Douglas's Social Credit Movement a few weeks before, and Mencken had replied:

> You made your great mistake when you abandoned the poetry business, and set up shop as a wizard in general practise. . . . All your native common sense oozed out of you, and you set up a caterwauling for all sorts of brummagem Utopias, at first in the aesthetic region only but later in the regions of aesthetic and political baloney. Thus a competent poet was spoiled to make a tin-horn politician.

It does not seem unfair to suspect certain suggestions of the confessional in the harshness of these words. Mencken had made a choice not unlike Pound's when he congratulated Louis Untermeyer for the promise that

> You will escape from literary criticism, too, as I am trying to do. The wider field of ideas in general is too alluring. . . . We live, not in a literary age, but in a fiercely political age.[14]

He had traded detachment for alienation and, throughout the twenties, he would treat politics as a grinding of victims by their oppressors. The continued imprisonment of Eugene Victor Debs galled him almost as much as the prohibition amendment, which especially galled him as an assault upon private liberties.

The political commentaries that Malcolm Moos collected under the rubric *A Carnival of Buncombe* deserve to be read not so much for their

[14]The letters to Pound can be found in Forgue, pp. 411 and 413. The letter to Untermeyer is on p. 210.

gibes at charlatanry as for their social outrage. Consider his 1924 endorsement of the Progressive party presidential candidacy of Robert M. LaFollette,

> ... the Wisconsin Red, with his pockets stuffed with Soviet gold. I shall vote for him unhesitatingly, and for a plain reason: he is the best man in the running, *as a man*. ...
>
> Suppose all Americans were like LaFollette? What a country it would be! No more depressing goose-stepping. No more gorillas in hysterical herds. No more trimming and trembling. Does it matter what his ideas are? Personally I am against four-fifths of them, but what are the odds? They are, at worst, better than the ignominious platitudes of Coolidge. ...
>
> The older I grow the less I esteem mere ideas. In politics, particularly, they are transient and unimportant. ... There are only men who have character and men who lack it. LaFollette has it. ... He is devoid of caution, policy, timidity, baseness—all the immemorial qualities of the politician. He is tremendous when he is right, and he is even more tremendous when he is wrong.

And this on the mind of Calvin Coolidge:

> Every idea that is honorable and of good report in Pullman smoke-rooms, on the verandas of golf clubs, among university presidents, at luncheons of the Kiwanis Club and where sweaters and usurers meet—all this rubbish he has welded into a system of politics, nay of statecraft, of jurisprudence, of epistemology, almost of theology, and made himself the prophet of it. He has shoved himself an inch ahead of his lieges. He is one degree hotter for the existing order than they are themselves.[15]

But the commitment to politics leads down two roads, each with a pit at its end. One is the path of embracing, the other is the path of

---

[15]The comments on LaFollette are in Moos, Malcolm, ed., *H. L. Mencken on Politics: A Carnival of Buncombe* (New York: Vintage, 1960), pp. 119–120. The judgment on Coolidge is on pp. 102–103.

rejecting; and you finish either embracing or rejecting everything. When the time came to recoil from Franklin Roosevelt as from every other incumbent, Mencken could only recoil on the terms and in the posture of the plutocracy he had always reviled; and sixteen years afterward, when he chose his own favorites among his writings, he included a philippic against the New Deal that reached the apogee of its disgust in the revelation that Harry Hopkins had a staff of nonentities so dim that they were not even listed in *Who's Who in America*.[16]

The matter had shrunk down to no more than the manner. We may suppose that he was surprised to meet that empty hour, for he had long before shown the acuity with which the true critic anticipates his own twilight in the fallings-off of his elders. He had seen that shadow in 1920 in the remarkable *tour d'horizon* he called "The National Letters" when his eye fell upon "the literature that fills the magazines and burdens the book counters of the department stores":

> One constantly observes the collapse and surrender of writers who started out with aims far above those of the magazine nabob. ... It is, indeed, a characteristic American phenomenon for a young writer to score a success with novel and meritorious work, and then to yield himself to the best-seller fever, and so disappear down the sewers. ... The pull is genuinely powerful. Above lies not only isolation, but also a dogged and malignant sort of opposition. Below, as [Gouverneur] Morris has frankly admitted, there is the place at Aiken, the motor-car, money in the bank, and the dignity of an important man.[17]

"We all end up as packaged goods," Westbrook Pegler remarked a little while before he died. The dreary road to the wrapping and bundling counter is probably inescapable: there is the hunt for the

[16] *A Mencken Chrestomathy*, p. 427. We might not imprecisely define the whole of Mencken's thought as rising from the assumption that we live in a country where anyone curious about a truly interesting fellow citizen can look him up in *Who's Who* and seldom find his name there.

[17] *The American Scene*, p. 70.

discovery of what works, then the erosion of curiosity about what else might work, then the disappearance of all curiosity about anything unfamiliar, and at last the prison of the safety of one's own accepted manner. Yeats was a little way off the mark; the peril for the artisan no less than for the artist is not that his circus animals may desert him but that he will let slip past the time when he ought to turn them back to the forest.

I do not suppose it makes too much difference that Mencken lodged too long with his circus animals. The worst result of this capitulation to the habitual was that it distorted his reputation and limited him to followers drawn to the frozen model of his manner instead of the warm example of his intelligence. And yet the manner had been only a device to make a savage indignation less lacerating by transmitting uncomfortable thoughts in the language of an hyperbole so exuberant as almost to turn them into jokes.

But then, if it is one of life's major blessings that, in time, savage indignation ceases to lacerate, it is one of life's minor curses that the cured sufferer so often loses interest thereafter. The loss of interest was the likely reason why, in his last twenty-five years, Mencken produced so much that remained engaging and so little that is still exciting.

His FLAGGING ATTENTION to literature may have been the most discernible cost to us. Mencken the critic was the very best Mencken, for, as it was his pose to look at the affairs of the Republic with monarchical disdain, it was his nature to confront the institutions of the kingdom of letters with the passion of a Leveller.

His most fervid responses were reserved for young and otherwise half-buried writers whose motive force was, as he said of Dreiser's, "to depict the life of struggling peoples." He forgave their infelicities mostly for the sake of the poetry that infused their mission but partly because he took such delight in the banalities of common speech.

His editorial functions at the *American Mercury* continued after his decampment from aesthetics to politics in the twenties, and they conscripted him to keep an eye on the literary marketplace. That eye retained its keenness whenever it lighted upon whatever came from below or outside the conventional culture. He displayed a quick appreciation for Ring Lardner, Willa Cather, and Ruth Suckow; and Sinclair Lewis dedicated *Elmer Gantry* to him. That last piece of homage was a symbol of what was happening to him; he had begun to harden into a monument. He appears to have disliked Hemingway's work no less than his person; and what scraps of their correspondence we have suggest a larger affection for Fitzgerald's person than for his work. There is no evidence that he even read Faulkner.

Dreiser seems to have spent his life with a peasant's timidity about being detected in semiliteracy, and, in 1937, he wrote to ask Mencken for a list of the more notable works of fiction produced in the last decade.

"I suggest," Mencken replied, "that we have dinner alone and go through the matters you discuss. It seems to me that there is a great deal of quackery in literature, as there is in politics. Most of the geniuses discovered by the Communists are simply imbeciles. But I have considerable confidence in young [James T.] Farrell, despite his political hallucinations."[18]

Dreiser had never much kept up with the course of letters, and by then we may surmise that Mencken had stopped keeping up with it too. He was coming to rest in that lovable anecdotage whose fragments Knopf now serves forth as its ceremonial wreath. Here is a deservedly admired publishing house; and here was quite the most original American mind ever to be sent forth under its imprint. And the samples of that mind the owners of its copyright have now judged the most relevant memorials have little more fresh and original to tell us— however marvelously they tell it—than that the kitchen was more fragrant and the carnival livelier when the teller was young.

And about that kind of circumstance Mencken would, I suppose, have only said what he did in the final sentence of his obituary of Theodore Roosevelt, which was, "Oh well, one does what one can."

The New York Review of Books, June 11, 1981

[18]Forgue, p. 413.

A Narodnik from Lynbrook

O*DYSSEY OF A Friend: Letters to William F. Buckley, Jr., 1954–1961*
are the letters Whittaker Chambers wrote to his last and his *best*, that
is, his most *respectful* employer. The compliment is less than Mr.
Buckley's kindness of nature deserves, since his most conspicuous fellows in the company of Chambers's former employers happen to be
Colonel Bykov of the Soviet Secret Police, the late Henry Luce, and
John F. X. McGohey, "then United States Attorney" for the Southern
District of New York. These documents will come as a surprise to
those persons who think of Chambers as simple and evil, since they
begin in 1954 with a warning to Buckley against Senator Joe McCarthy
and approach their end in 1959, with Chambers complaining, like any
other sensitive American traveling abroad, about the embarrassments
inflicted upon the home country by the Chairman of the Senate Committee on Internal Security and by the Strategic Air Command.

They also provide as much as we can know of Chambers's last
endeavor at factional agitation: He seems to have been Vice President
Nixon's man on the Board of Editors of *National Review*. This operation was anything but covert: Chambers indeed held back from joining
National Review at its outset largely because its other editors so distrusted Mr. Nixon for being a centrist. "I am an *org* man," he once wrote
Buckley. Mr. Nixon was General Secretary of the last *org* he had; his
faith in the Vice President remained a major point of difference with
those of his colleagues, whose conservative principles were so much

superior to those of Mr. Nixon that they had vaulted to the higher level
of those of Senator Joe McCarthy.

"Something . . . in your letter," he writes to Willi Schlamm in
December 1954, "leaves the impression that there is an affinity between
the *National Review* and a third party movement . . . a third party will
be Senator McCarthy and his rally. I shall not be blaming him or them
exclusively, if I say that such a move seems to me to be completing by
suicide the wreck of the Republican party . . ."

Four years later, when he is abroad, he explains to Buckley:

> The masses must be won by the Republican Left while keeping the
> Republican Right within the family. Once I hoped that Mr. Nixon
> could perform this healing bond, holding the Right in line, while a
> Republican Left formed about him a core. . . . The Republican Party
> will win the masses, or history will find for it a quiet, uncrowded
> spot in the potter's field . . ."

That Mr. Nixon occasionally took counsel with Chambers was no
secret; if it had been, Chambers would certainly have broken it, because, if the connection amused Buckley, it also impressed him. Perhaps
it was Chambers's loneliness, the experience of having to begin life
again so often as a stranger in new surroundings, which explains his
need always to carry the aura of an ambassador from some Other Shore:
The Hisses, he says, were drawn to him because they thought him a
Russian, which, to the extent that the will could conquer an origin in
Lynbrook, Long Island, he certainly was and remained. His colleagues
at *Time* knew that he had been an agent of the G.P.U. so long before
the fact became notorious that we have to conclude that he told them
early and often. Mr. Nixon was then only the last of those princes and
powers of the outer air the suggestion of whose portfolio he bore.

His enjoyment of the mystery which was his alone to understand
comes up now and again in these letters as the hint of knowing more
than he can say. Some gossip had said that the Vice President did not
always speak kindly of President Eisenhower. "But in this area," Chambers wrote, "I must have Mr. Nixon's permission to write (and espe-

cially to quote); and if he should feel it better to let the matter die, I am afraid I should have to agree with him" (October 8, 1957).

"There is some very big news in the making, which I am bound not to hint at . . . I think I can and must say this: the first stages of what I refer to have already taken place, and been widely discussed. Only no one sees what is implied. So look, if you are interested, at seemingly minor news of the past fortnight or so. . . . I guess I may say this too: the President's news conference disclosure of an arrangement with No. 2 [Nixon] was not an accident, though the succession was not the big news." (Buckley's explanatory notes make no reference to whatever great event was there portended and subsequently revealed: the chances are that there was none, since the Eisenhower administration was as scrupulous in the avoidance of great events as it was in working up truly interesting secrets.)

CHAMBERS SEEMS TO have been troubled early on by worry that Buckley might think he was using his *National Review* essays to reflect Mr. Nixon's mind. "I should expect our (his and my) position to be loosely similar on most issues. Yet I shall never be speaking for him: while I, like him, reach my conclusions independently. Conclusions I reach that may be of any use or of any interest to him, I freely submit. His rejection or concurrence is not my affair" (October 1957).

Mr. Nixon, he went on to suggest, had consulted with him in 1952 over whether the cause might be better served by supporting General Eisenhower rather than Senator Taft for the Republican nomination. "We disagreed 'sharply' . . . He was judging in political terms and, in those terms, was absolutely right." Mr. Nixon's disregard for Chambers's advice made possible, of course, that happy betrayal of the Republican Right which earned him the vice presidential nomination and constitutes, along with his part in the Hiss-Chambers affair, the only substantial achievements of his career prior to his ascension to the presidency.

Still, the consultations endured at least into 1960, although the bond between the two seems, like so many of Chambers's other commitments, to have been a domestic affection dressed up as the summons of history: He was always curiously sentimental about persons who from kindness had ruined his career—far from having any need to forgive he seems positively grateful to the old friend who liked him so much that he drafted him into the Communist underground—and Mr. Nixon, more than most other men of affairs, is sentimental about persons who have advanced his. They drifted apart not because Mr. Nixon was distracted by larger matters—he remained indeed most properly solicitous—but because Chambers in the end found that there was very little about Mr. Nixon which could sustain the historical imagination:

"My rule," he finally tells Mr. Buckley, "is never to mention to anyone my contacts with him. I'm going to break it this once, for a reason, but I wish you not to mention what I shall say. Not long ago I had lunch with him. He asked us down one Sunday, and we had a long talk. What was said? Except for two minor points I could not say . . . I suppose the sum of it was: we have really nothing to say to each other. While we talked, I felt crushed by the sense of the awful burden he was inviting in the office he wants . . . If he were a great, vital man, bursting with energy, ideas (however malapropos), sweeping grasp of the crisis, and (even) intolerant convictions, I think I should have felt: Yes, he must have it; he must enact his fate, and ours. I did not have this feeling . . . So I came away with unhappiness for him, for all" (March 10, 1960).

And yet, against all Chambers's habits, how peaceful this last apostasy seems. In the first case, horror, terror, and guilt; in this one, only the moment of inconsequence, when the side of Nothing is left for no side whatsoever. Still, it could be one of Mr. Nixon's better qualities that he makes so small a wrench for those who give up on him and that, in his case, there have always been so few illusions whose destruction might embitter the memory at the moment of parting. The emptiness of the terms of enlistment has at least the use of making peaceful its abandonment.

We have gone on about Chambers's engagement with Mr. Nixon longer than it is worth. But then it has been Chambers's general fate to have struggled to be an historical *presence* and to end up being treated merely as an historical *object*, to be offered for notice only when it can be presented as current. By now this object's one remaining topical tag is no more than the accident of its place in the career of a sitting president and its last Witness just one among so many testaments to that president's inadequacy.

AND YET I think Chambers is worth more of our attention—indeed our sympathy—than that. There are, of course, barriers to that attention, let alone that sympathy. Richard Rovere said very early that he did not expect much market for books supporting the official verdict on the Hiss-Chambers case simply because people would rather be told about innocence than about guilt.

Then too there are the distasteful associations of the act for which he is best remembered, not the espionage but the naming of his partner in espionage. The second is a kind of betrayal far worse thought of by private men than the first. Afterward Chambers's society would seldom extend beyond persons like Mr. Nixon and Buckley, who revered him for his service to his country; yet they brought him no comfort. The harshest words of his enemies could hardly have exceeded the bleakness and the self-contempt of his own picture of himself during the performance of the deed which made him so notorious:

> The informer is different, especially the ex-Communist informer. He risks little. He sits in security and uses his special knowledge to destroy others. He has that special information to give because he knows those others' faces, voices and lives, because he once lived within their confidence, in a shared faith, trusted by them as one of themselves, accepting their friendship, feeling their pleasures and griefs, sitting in their houses, eating at their tables, accepting their kindness, knowing their wives and children. If he had none of these things, he would have no use as an informer.
>
> Because he has that use, the police protect him. He is their creature. When they whistle, he fetches a soiled bone of informa-

tion . . . He has surrendered his choice. To that extent, though he be free in every other way, the informer is a slave. He is no longer a free man. . . .[1]

These are among the few sorts of feelings it is difficult to imagine any man attesting to insincerely. The gap between Chambers and the persons most outraged by him is that great: They condemn him to the degradation of having lied, while he writhes in the degradation of having told the truth. We can understand his persistence in regretting Buckley's invitations to the occasional evangelical tent shows of the Right. He was a long way from being able to present himself as a Justified Sinner.

HE IS CUT off from us last of all because, while few of his contemporaries were written about so extensively, almost none has been written about less persuasively. For the last ten years of his life, he engaged no subject without coming back very quickly to himself, and I think he tried to present himself as candidly as he could. But he could not overcome the habit of anointing himself as legate from some Other Shore; he had carried the Mystery too long to put it aside; one's impression of him on stage is of someone perpetually explaining, and still as much a stranger as he was when he appeared. The flood of explanations by others, friendly or hostile, carry no more sense of our being brought closer. Indeed one of the various curiosities of Whittaker Chambers is that the only persuasive picture of him was published in 1947, a year before many Americans had ever heard of him.

Gifford Maxim, the focal figure of Lionel Trilling's *The Middle of the Journey*,[2] is modeled on the Whittaker Chambers whom Trilling knew best, when Chambers was between the Communist party and *Time*, on the transitory ground of the *Menorah Journal*, and more distinct than

[1]Chambers, Whittaker, *Witness* (New York: Random House, 1952), p. 454.
[2]Trilling, Lionel, *The Middle of the Journey* (New York: Viking, 1947; reprinted by Anchor Books, 1956).

he could be under the historical disguises assumed or imposed upon him before or since.

Trilling had known Chambers as a Communist: The memory is both more compelling and purer than it would ever be again, and accords with the moral authority which Chambers tells us he exercised in those days:

> For to Laskell [Trilling's liberal hero], Maxim was never quite alone. Laskell saw him flanked by two great watching figures. . . . On one side of Maxim stood the figure of the huge, sad, stern morality of all the suffering and exploited men in the world, all of them without distinction of color or creed. On the other side of Maxim stood the figure of power, noble, fierce, indomitable. Behind Maxim and his two great flanking figures were infinite dim vistas of History, which was not the past but the future.

Laskell's first reaction, when Maxim tells him of his break, is "surprise . . . contempt . . . revulsion . . . It was one thing for a man to abandon his loyalty to the cause he had lived for; it was quite another thing, and far sadder, for him to spread foul and melodramatic stories about it, such terrible stories as were contained in Maxim's silent stare, in his talk of ocean bottoms and pistols behind the ear.

"But, although Maxim might have lost authority, he had not lost his skill." Very soon, although he could not be trusted quite as he had been and the moments of revulsion recurred—"Perhaps only because Maxim spoke them and spoke them often, Laskell felt that never again could anyone say the words tragedy and love"—he retained some of his power to compel belief. For one thing, although those two invisible presences had departed from his side, he seemed otherwise so much what he had been; there was the same "ironic revolutionary eyebrow and the ready, almost maternal, look of solicitude with which he habitually gazed upon human suffering."

It is a while before Laskell can define the difference:

"When you yourself were a member of the Party," he says the last time he is really angry, "you tried to involve us all in your virtue. Now you try to implicate the whole world in your guilt. . . . You have a very fancy kind of mind, Maxim."

That was the single great change; otherwise Maxim, the counterrevolutionary, was surprisingly like Maxim the revolutionary, even to that air of special access to the occult which had been useful to heighten his bearing as a representative of History and which he needed still for his protection as its victim: "He still pretended to his knowledge of hidden motives, but the hidden things he pretended now to see were different from the hidden things he had pretended to see before."

> Maxim had the trick of really good fortune-tellers and palmists of putting things so generally and so dramatically that what was said had to have some sort of relevant meaning, and then if you asked them what they meant, they looked at you with mockery and annoyance, as if you were being willfully stupid, you with your intelligence and sensitivity.

Trilling could, then, recognize the charlatan and still say in 1949, "Whittaker Chambers is a man of honor." It is unlikely that we can ever get a fix on Chambers, but it is certain that we never can if we think there is a contradiction in those two assessments by the same observer. Chambers was not one or the other but both, man of honor and fraud together.

THE HABIT OF the general, dramatic statement which seems somehow relevant persists in these letters. For example, in 1954, Chambers tells Buckley what drew him to Communism, an image which, if its relevance is still not as vivid to him as ever, would hardly seem to have meaning at all:

> In 1907, the Russian government instituted a policy of systematically beating its political prisoners. One night, a fashionably-dressed young woman called at the Central Prison in Petersburg and asked to speak with the commandant, Maximovsky. This was Rago-

zinikova, who had come to protest the government's policy. . . .
When Maximovsky appeared, she shot him with her revolver and
killed him. . . . She was sentenced to be hanged. Awaiting execution, she wrote her family "Death itself is nothing. . . . How good
it is to love people. How much strength one gains from such love."
When she was hanged, Ragozinikova was twenty years old.

Now this is an anecdote which might appear more calculated to
unhinge than to strengthen Buckley in his commitment to the defense
of established order. Still he seems to have drawn from it the inspiration to go on as he has, it being the nature of anecdotes to have one
revelation for me and quite the opposite for thee. Their nature indeed
is such that Chambers could take the historical tableaux which had
explained to him why he was a Communist and trot them forth intact
to explain why he was no longer a Communist. He did add a few more
personages, of course, most notably Yurovsky, who shot the Romanovs,
and Nechayev, "the nineteenth-century Russian who carried the logic
of revolution to its limit, teaching (Lenin among others) . . . that all
crimes are justified if they serve the socialist cause." (Curiously enough,
after twelve years in the party, considerable immersion in the legends
of nineteenth-century revolutionaries, and a term under commanders
who had learned far more from Nechayev than from Ragozinikova, he
had never heard of Nechayev until Colonel Bykov mentioned him in
1937, which is rather like serving the Papacy of Alexander VI while
focusing all one's attention on *The Pastoral Care of Gregory the Great*.)
But, in essence, the tableaux remain what they were—the attitudes of
the Narodniki.

The anecdote as revelation ought then to seem to us a pretty
suspicious bit of goods. Still the trick is infectious; trying to understand
Chambers, you clutch gratefully at Victor Serge's quarrel with Miguel
Almereyda, an old comrade he had begun to suspect of taking German
money to arouse the French against the First World War:

I told him, "You're just an opportunist." . . . He answered, "As far
as Paris is concerned you are an ignoramus, my friend. You can

purify yourself with Russian novels, but here the revolution needs cash."

Those, of course, are the two points from which one set of revolutionaries has always quarreled with the other. And, if these letters seem to tell us more about Chambers than he was ever able otherwise to tell us, it is because they reveal him accommodating both points within himself: He was able to know himself at once purer and more worldly-wise than the others.

WHETHER THE SUBJECT was the higher morality or practical affairs, he was a serious, although never malicious, snob. Buckley had established *National Review* to shore up the present with various fragments of the ruins of the future; and, ahead of Chambers, he had assembled into his cadre William S. Schlamm, who had been wandering since he left the Austrian Communist party in 1929; Frank Meyer, who had been educational director of the Chicago Communist party in the forties; and James Burnham. Chambers's tone about them all seldom descends below affectionate condescension. "Willi [Schlamm] was heaved out of the Communist Party. I broke out. . . . But I have known a dozen minds of the same size and shape as Willi's. He has no surprises whatever for me. . . ." "If the Republican Party cannot get some grip on the real world . . . [it] will become like one of those dark little shops which apparently never sell anything. If, for any reason, you go in, you find at the back an old man, fingering for his own pleasure some oddments of cloth (weave and design of 1850). . . . You are only slightly surprised to see that the old man is Frank Meyer." "Burnham is a man of honor. . . . He was a Trotskyist, precisely at the moment when Trotskyism was worn to a shadow by reality."

Chambers explains what sets him apart from all such drabs: "Unlike most Western Communists . . . I remained under the spiritual influence of the Narodniki long after I became a Marxist. In fact I never threw it off. I never have." It is the assurance of purification by reading Russian novels which survives all changes; there is no spite in that assurance but just a degree of hauteur whose equivalent can be remembered only from the evening Malraux went to a working-class quarter to defend de Gaulle against his Socialist opponents and asked: "What do they know of the Left? Were they in Spain?"

YET CHAMBERS IS no less snobbish about his superior sense of the practical, being in Buckley's service first the former senior editor of *Time* and only after hours the counterrevolutionary. "I am for a magazine . . . if its first and steadfast purpose is to succeed. . . . Another crusade does not interest me at all." In that key, whatever briskness he brought to his last assignment was devoted to the preachment that the first task of a magazine is to reach a market: One's models for style ought not to be mixed up with one's notions of sound public policy. Buckley passes on to him a complaint from Rebecca West about the *New Statesman* and Chambers gives back the cold reply: "If the *New Statesman* is a 'muck heap' I wish General Grant would tell me what whiskey he drinks so I could send the same brand to the other generals." It ought to be odd to find that, having come to rest with a cadre of persons who shared his despair for the West, he should have written pieces for *National Review* rather more casual and less portentous than those he used to compose for *Time* at the dawn of the American Century. But the tone in both cases must have been commanded more by his impulse as a craftsman than by his inspiration as a prophet, his voices having told him that *Time* needed darkening with trombones to be rounded for the market and that *National Review* needed lightening with strings.

Yet he has not changed but simply come to rest; he is still so much the fortune-teller; he remains too mischievous to leave off the intimations of the occult. Even when he is the tipster, he pretends to be the seer:

I think I am obliged to tell you, if you are interested in a quick turnover, to have a thought to Phila. and Reading Coal Company. It stands at 27 and a fraction. . . . I have reason to believe that, within the next 12 days, it will make interesting gains. . . . I know, I know we old revolutionists are peculiar birds. (January 23, 1957)

He departed after a while, having lost hope of being able to teach Buckley but grateful for the affection. He had a history of serving his employers faithfully and being parted from them indifferently.

"Some time after the Hiss Case had formally closed, certain of my effects, including Kafka's *Parables*," he says, "were sent back to me from *Time*—somewhat as the effects found in the pockets of a man who has met a fatal accident—his wallet, driver's license, social security stub—are mailed to his relicts."[3]

Thinking of that cold parcel, we have to be glad that Chambers could this once part from an employer who cherished for him an affection and respect which amounted to reverence. Still what Buckley made of him otherwise is hard to say.

IN MAY 1959, Chambers made his last effort as Teacher before giving up. Could not the Right, he asked Buckley, begin to "examine and define with a special scrupulousness the civil liberties field." Take the internal Communist peril: ". . . as of now, there seems to me a certain unreality about the Right's general treatment of this subject as if no drastic change had occurred. . . . Why for example should we leave it to liberals to give tongue against the frightening developments in wire-tapping? . . . The Right I feel more and more must find its conscience and make it explicit, first of all to the Right."

Ten years later, *National Review* remains as alarmed by the Communists within, as if no change at all had occurred. Buckley has even joined Mr. Nixon as an adviser to his information service. Poor Chambers could not even teach him from genuine experience that Mr. Nixon is someone with whom everyone finds himself left eventually without anything to say. In this small case, as with the large one of Alger Hiss, Chambers's ghost could say: "Scratch across my effort:

[3]Chambers, Whittaker, *Cold Friday* (New York: Random House, 1964), p. 209.

Canceled." Buckley worshiped and did not listen; the real affection aside, the Chambers of his vision is a saint whose icon hangs in a Church where his message is never read.

The icon is not recognizable. Neither, to be sure is that mask of the goblin which survives in more general circulation. But perhaps the tricks of Maxim were the most important part of his nature; and so—the thought is not meant cruelly—may have been the masks of Whittaker Chambers. He always, except here, when so plainly what he really wants most is to rest, must have *seemed* to be so much larger than he really *was*. There was always an invisible other presence: He says Hiss thought him a Russian, which added the presence of *Chapayev* and the sailors of Kronstadt; at *Time* there were those sentences about his long nights at the window, adding the presence of the sword over the head. Chambers suggests that Alger Hiss did not understand him. That Buckley did not understand him either is strongly suggested by Buckley's apparent deafness to any intrusion of common sense into the syllabus. Yet Chambers's most intense recollection of his time with the Hisses was of rest and domestic tranquility; and it must have been very like that with Buckley also. We are glad to find him happy here at the last even though it was the curious happiness of the man to find peace of soul and comfort of spirit in The Friend Who Does Not Understand.

The New York Review of Books, January 29, 1970

Alger Hiss, Again

GOOD LORD, DELIVER us: Everyone seems to be talking about Alger Hiss again. I wish they would stop and I am ashamed of myself for starting again.

Alger Hiss has done his time. He has paid his dues. I know that those are hackneyed expressions; but a statement doesn't get to be a cliché unless it reminds us of an important truth that no one has found any fresh way of putting as well.

I have never met Alger Hiss, although I have now and then run across his son Tony, who is there to evoke for us all the luminosity with which his father seems to have dazzled his contemporaries and his elders alike in the long, long ago. I didn't read Tony's book about his father. I felt it noble of him to invade his own privacy and I would have felt it ignoble to listen.

But Tony did once tell me a story about his father that I think absolutely beautiful and I hope it is in the book. Just before he went to prison nearly thirty years ago, Alger Hiss was held at the old Federal House of Correction on West Street. It was his first day in jail; and along with the natural trepidation of any new boy in school, he may well have suffered from the then-prevailing illusion of the respectable that convicts are intensely patriotic and would shun, if they did not do worse to, anyone convicted of having been a Communist.

Hiss was then taken to the West Street jail's roof for his morning exercise with no great expectations of fraternity. He was joined upon his arrival by another detainee in a pearl gray hat and a coat of sharp cut and indubitably expensive provenance. This mysterious but some-how familiar companion walked once around the roof with him with-out saying a word. When they had completed the circuit, he paused and shook Alger Hiss's hand. Everyone seemed to be watching; and Hiss had the sudden sense of having been made part less of a gesture of courtesy than of some high demonstrative exercise.

"Mr. Hiss," the stranger said—it was all he ever said—"my name is Frank Costello. I have always been a great admirer of Mrs. Roosevelt."

Alger Hiss always made his debut escorted by the gods: He came to Washington with a reference from Felix Frankfurter and he went to Lewisburg with a reference from Frank Costello.

But at Lewisburg, he became a very great con on his own, in fact the greatest con who was in his cell for having been convicted of radical subversion since Alexander Berkman. I have since run across one or two ex-convicts who were there with him, and their reverence was authentic beyond question. He was kind; he was helpful; he was indeed a comrade you could ask to hide your contraband and know he'd never either use it himself or hand it over to a guard. In short, the man Whittaker Chambers, even after he testified against him, went on affirming Alger Hiss was the man "of an unvarying mildness, deep considerateness and gracious patience."

Think though I always have that his jury was correct, I shall never dismiss Alger Hiss as no better than a traitor so long as I know that he never finked at Lewisburg. The fact that he was a truly great con may in fact explain the mystery of why, if he really did what he was convicted of doing, he hasn't just confessed it after all this time. Which of us has ever known anyone who has attained the curious moral purity it takes to be a great con and who has then stooped to confess that he came there guilty as charged?

The heart of the argument for Hiss's innocence has always been that he was too respectable to ever have been a Communist and that Whittaker Chambers was too disreputable to have ever been worthy of credence.

To take up the minor point first, it is ridiculous as well as malignant to speak of Whittaker Chambers as though he were merely or even really disreputable. He talked a deal of nonsense about God and history; but it is a common sin for people to take themselves too seriously. I doubt if his detractors would snatch *Bambi* from the hands of their children; they know that *Bambi* is work of great moral and spiritual beauty although they avoid noticing that these qualities were preserved and may even have been enhanced when they were translated from the German by, yes, Whittaker Chambers.

The rug Chambers gave Hiss had been selected for him by Meyer Schapiro, the greatest of our art historians; it is no small point that, try their patience as he often must have, Chambers died with both Schapiro and Lionel Trilling remembering him as essentially a man of conscience. A reference from Trilling and Schapiro when you die is at least as impressive as a reference from Felix Frankfurter when you have barely begun to live. After all, Frankfurter paid almost as high a testament to Thomas Corcoran, who may have subsequently done his country rather more damage hustling than Hiss ever did betraying it, while remaining nonetheless an honored guest at all reunions of the old New Dealers.

The imputation that Hiss was too respectable to be a Communist is one of those taints from which it isn't as easy to acquit him as it is to absolve Chambers of disreputability. I. F. Stone, who could not be our most transcendent realist if he were not our most enduring romantic, has argued that he knew Hiss in Washington in the thirties and that he was too obvious a careerist to have the guts to be a Communist.

I have, as I have said already, never met Alger Hiss; and my claim for intuitive belief that he could have been a Communist is a meager one. But we happen to have been born in the same city in the same circumstances, which were, believe me, of no massive social distinction. They were circumstances of shabby gentility; and I know of only two, and perhaps a third of their children, who grew up in precisely that place and that environment and joined the Communist party. One had the honor to say so publicly while he was. The other was myself. Let us, *arguendo* as Bill Buckley so nicely puts it, assume that Alger Hiss *was* a Communist. It occurs to me then that all three of us shared the condition of having had our fathers die when we were almost infants. The theory that deprivation produces Communists makes little sense unless you remember that deprivation is not always or even that often only economic deprivation.

Alger Hiss is being talked about again because of the massive arraignment mounted against him by Allen Weinstein's *Perjury*. I have nothing but affection for those who are now attempting to refute Weinstein; it is wise to prefer persons who persist in believing a man is innocent to persons who hasten to assume his guilt.

Still I do not envy Weinstein's critics their task any more than I would want to be a defense counsel who had listened for three days while a prosecutor read Weinstein's book aloud to the jury and who now had to arise for rebuttal.

Alexander Bickel once wrote of a legal argument that some lawyers have an instinct for the jugular but that this one had a genius for the capillaries. The best that can be said for the critiques of Weinstein is that they have done some slight damage to his capillaries.

Sidney Zion has accused Weinstein of failing to establish the date of Chambers's break with the Communist movement which Weinstein himself had begun thinking the central mystery of the case. Except to the extent that it bore on the evidence, that happens to be one mystery Weinstein was wise to give up trying to solve. Understanding the way of a man with a maid is nursery school work next to locating the moment when he becomes entirely aware that he has lost the faith he had until then lived by.

There *is* one central mystery in the Hiss case which is almost never mentioned by either side and which, since it obsesses only me, may not be as important as I think. Weinstein does refer to it; but then Weinstein refers to everything. His summary, however brief, seems to me exemplary.

This particular mystery has to do with Alger Hiss's interior, and involves the otherwise forgotten international incident of the Robinson-Rubens case. Robinson was a Soviet agent in the United States who was recalled to headquarters in Moscow during the 1938 purges. He took along his wife, who was an American citizen. Two weeks after their arrival, Stalin's government recognized his services to the revolution by arresting him. His wife went to the American embassy and asked its help. She wasn't the sort of citizen the State Department was ready to do much for; but she was a citizen, and the Moscow embassy began asking Washington how far it ought to go to protect her.

A copy of one of its resultant cables was among the documents that Chambers produced as evidence against Hiss ten years later. It was in Hiss's handwriting. Hiss did not remember writing it or manage to think of any reason why he should have; it had no connection with any of his duties in the State Department. What he wrote then came into the hands of Whittaker Chambers who by his account duly transmitted a copy of it to Moscow. I'm sorry; but I cannot conceive of a jury imagining any plausible way for Chambers to have gotten it except that Hiss gave it to him.

What the message had suggested was that the American embassy in Moscow was disinclined to get much excited about any disposition, however drastic, the Soviet government might choose for one of its employes. It certainly didn't; a few weeks later, Robinson's wife was arrested too, and like her husband has never since been heard of. Her only resource had been her American citizenship; and, since nothing except an American protest could remotely inconvenience the GPU in any plan to do away with her, it could only be a source of comfort to the Soviet police to know that America didn't much care.

Again I'm sorry; but Alger Hiss ought to have thought a long while before deciding that he couldn't say how he happened to copy that telegram. No more than anyone else in official Washington had he given much evidence of deep sympathy for Stalin's victims. And absent such concern, and the slightest indication that the Robinson-Rubens case had anything to do with his job, of what interest could the case be to him?

I have to say, until there is some real effort to persuade me otherwise, that I cannot but believe that he helped, and probably knew he helped, assure the Russian police that they need not worry that a comparatively innocent woman in their custody might have friends to help her. In that case, Alger Hiss would have been doing a job for the cops, and pretty lousy cops. And that would be something for a truly great con to be ashamed of.

New York Post, April 23, 1978

The Memory of Lillian Hellman

*S*COUNDREL TIME IS the third of the meditations of Lillian Hellman's memory. Its single theme is her summons by the House Committee on Un-American Activities in 1952, her decision to refuse to yield up the names of Communists she had known, the worse trouble with the Hollywood blacklist that followed that trouble, and the dignity and the shrewdness that carried her through both.

Miss Hellman has developed a style for these discourses very close to the ideal for letters, say, from an aunt who is envied for her experience of the world and enjoyed for her candor and her comic sense whenever they are directed at persons other than yourself—always a comfortable majority of the cases—amusing, affecting, persuasive, entirely charming, if you don't too much mind being hectored now and then.

Her nieces seem somehow luckier than her nephews. Nieces, I suspect, read her letters for that feminine wisdom condemned to be misunderstood as womanly folly: the sensibility that armors itself with a Balmain dress for the ordeal by the Committee on Un-American Activities, the taste that notices the habit awkward social occasions have of being accompanied by bad food, the gaiety that conquers dread with shopping sprees. It is hard for nephews to find that much unforced pleasure in Miss Hellman; they have to be wary of possible disapproval.

· · ·

I HAVE NEVER quite understood upon what altar Miss Hellman's moral authority was consecrated; but that authority is there, was there even before the apotheosis of her risky yet grand appearance before the Committee on Un-American Activities. To measure how far and for how long a time her writ has run we need only to consider the case of Elia Kazan, who had decided that it was necessary for him, as they used to say in those days, to "come clean" with the Committee on Un-American Activities. Kazan is one of those persons who would have especially profited from the injunction, "Never Apologize, Never Explain." As it was, in his ignorance, he spread apologies for his small sins and explanations of his vast redemption all over the advertising pages of *The New York Times*, and lifted them like prayers to heaven to Spyros Skouras, president of Twentieth Century Fox.

That was an acceptance of humiliation for the sake of survival in a confiscatory tax bracket, an impulse for which, if we cannot often find enough excuse, we can at least locate an identifiable source. But then, in the midst of his flagellations, Kazan sought out Miss Hellman, who had not yet appeared before the committee, to explain himself to *her*. It was an overture to humiliation for humiliation's own sake that does not now lend itself to reasonable understanding. The scene can only be guessed at among the clouds that surround Miss Hellman's reincarnation in the memoir, but we can glimpse in it the Confederate lady who uplifted the soldier in the heat of his youth and waited in the twilight to receive, but in no measure to entertain, the veteran's apology for having joined the board of directors of the carpetbagger's railroad.

MISS HELLMAN'S STRENGTH of character is great, but of a kind that is hard to comprehend apart from its candid snobbishness. When she searches for the core of the self that enabled her to resist and left Clifford Odets naked to surrender to the House Committee on Un-American Activities, she can return with no discovery more useful than:

It is impossible to think that a grown man, intelligent, doesn't have some sense of how he will act under pressure. It's all been decided so long ago, when you are very young, all mixed up with your childhood's definition of pride or dignity.

Many [American intellectuals] found in the sins of Stalin Communism—and there were plenty of sins and plenty that for a long time I mistakenly denied—the excuse to join those who should have been their hereditary enemies. Perhaps that, in part, was the penalty of nineteenth-century immigration. The children of timid immigrants are often remarkable people: energetic, intelligent, hardworking, and often they make it so good that they are determined to keep it at any cost.

Observations of that tenor somehow suggest that for strong spirits like Miss Hellman's, the Sunday family dinner is material for rebellion in childhood, comedy in middle age, and attitudes in final maturity. What is here intimated is some doctrine of predestation by growing up with servants in the kitchen, but it is not easy to think such a notion prepossessing and impossible to find it serviceable as a measurement for moral development. We are left to wonder why Senator Harry Flood Byrd, whose mother was in every way a Virginia lady, should have arrived at his fullest spiritual bloom ringing changes on the word "nigger" on public platforms, or why John Foster Dulles, grandson of an American secretary of state, should have managed a career whose most striking achievement was the avoidance of any suspicion that the impulse of a gentleman might ever intrude upon his conduct. Let us settle for saying that *Commentary*'s tone was lamentable in the early fifties, when its editor was Eliot Cohen; for what worse epithet must we thereupon reach to describe *Time*, the weekly newsmagazine, in the days when its managing editor was Thomas S. Matthews, son of the Episcopal Bishop of the Diocese of New Jersey?

WE MOVE, I think, closer to the truth about those years when Miss Hellman swam against the current and Odets sank beneath it if we think of the fifties as a time not much different from this one and a majority of others when most people acted badly, and public faces passed by as a succession of gray embarrassments infrequently illuminated by displays of dignity like Miss Hellman's. Banality is the only sort of chic that always has its fashion; and we need not be surprised that Miss Hellman, thanks to her superb hour of resistance to banal chic, should now be punished with the comfortable indignity of being enshrined by it.

". . . An intense, moving moral," *Time* says of her story now. "She was brave because her private code would not allow her to be anything else. She dabbled in radical politics and befriended Communists because she thought it was her right as an American to associate with whomever she damn well pleased. . . . *Scoundrel Time* is a memorable portrait of . . . a polished stylist and an invaluable American."

The tone of *Time*'s original report on Miss Hellman's encounter with the House Committee on Un-American Activities had, of course, been faithfully cast into the cadences of what Edmund Wilson once called its "peculiar kind of jeering rancor."

> Her sympathies [had] led her to attend countless Red-inspired rallies and lend her name to various Communist-front crusades . . . as the record shows, a skilled playwright and a great meeting goer.

Caption on Miss Hellman's photograph, *Time*, May 10, 1976:

> AUTHOR HELLMAN: "I cannot cut my conscience to fit this year's fashions."

Caption on Miss Hellman's photograph, *Time*, June 2, 1952:

> PLAYWRIGHT HELLMAN: "An expert at smooth dialogue."

But after all, as Burke said, "We are very uncorrupt and tolerably enlightened judges of the transactions of past ages. . . . Few are the partisans of departed tyrannies." So, when Mr. Nixon was in his terminal throes, we were treated to the spectacle of White House Counsel Dean Burch, who had come first to our notice as manager of Senator

Goldwater's presidential campaign, complaining to the journalists about the "McCarthyite tactics" of the House Judiciary Committee. A year or so ago, *New York* magazine published an interview with Ted Ashley, the talent agent. Its most inspiring passages recited Ashley's brave, lonely, and, so far as his own memory seemed to suggest, successful struggle to defend Philip Loeb, the actor, against the blacklist. It seems to have been of no consequence to the glory of this Iliad that, if not by Ashley's will, certainly with his ultimate compliance, Loeb had been so effectively blacklisted that throughout the year before his suicide he had been able to find no employment above the $87.50 a week Off-Broadway scale. Those who can forget their own history are rewarded by having it forgotten by pretty much everyone else.

WHEN WE CONSIDER the general practice of using memory so earnestly as an instrument for mendacity, it is a sufficient miracle for Miss Hellman to be so honest a witness; and our admiration for her integrity cannot grow smaller for a final impression that *Scoundrel Time* is not quite true. Honesty and truth are not just the same thing, since the first has to do with character and the second with self-understanding of a cruder kind than hers.

Miss Hellman cannot be blamed for *Time*'s having spoken of her political history as a business of having "dabbled in radical politics." But, even so, the very light brush she brings to her treatment of what must have been a commitment of high self-discipline could well contribute to such a misapprehension. She was, by every evidence, what she most puzzlingly denies she was—one of "those serious, dedicated people"—and she would not have needed to rely so entirely upon herself in her troubles if she hadn't been. It is therefore rather unsettling to come upon musings like:

> the mishmash of those years, beginning before my congressional debut and for years after, took a heavy penalty. My belief in liberalism was mostly gone. . . . There was nothing strange about my problem, it is native to our time; but it is painful for a nature

that can no longer accept liberalism not to be able to accept radicalism.

Now except for the lonely period when she could have used their goodwill most, the run of liberals have shown great respect and no little affection for Miss Hellman, and for more substantial reasons than the reverence liberals render to success and the odd pleasure so many of them draw from being scolded. But all the same it would be surprising if Miss Hellman could have been left with many illusions about liberals by the time, long before McCarthyism, when she had completed her apprenticeship with Horace Liveright. By the late forties, the most prominent liberals were busy antagonists of her two most heartfelt causes, Henry Wallace's campaign for president as a Progressive in 1948, and the Cultural and Scientific Conference for World Peace at the Waldorf-Astoria in 1949.

The Waldorf conference was beset with more obloquy than it deserved; but I cannot think that Garry Wills has come quite up to the lofty mark for historical objectivity that he has maintained almost everywhere else when he speaks, in his introduction, of Miss Hellman's having, in her wartime trips to the Soviet Union, "formed friendships there not subject to any government line, so she helped arrange for artists and scholars to meet and discuss what would later (when a new line came in) be called 'detente.' " What had been arranged might less enthusiastically be described as a discussion between Americans who spoke critically of their government and Russians who could hardly have offered theirs any such treatment and safely gone home. It is doubtful that the Waldorf conference provided any historical lesson more significant than that Lillian Hellman got in trouble because she attended it and Dmitri Shostakovich risked worse trouble if he hadn't. But, all the same, there is, I suppose, a case to be made for encounters of this sort, and it seems a loss that Miss Hellman takes note of the affair in terms so cursory as to afford us no reflections upon it at all.[1]

[1]Cedric Belfrage's *American Inquisition, 1945–1960* (Bobbs-Merrill, 1973), the best per-haps because it is the most radical account that I know of those days, contains a tidy

MISS HELLMAN DOES tarry longer with the Wallace campaign, but her pause there is not productive of one of her better effects. Very little about Wallace himself seems to have endured in her memory except for "certain embarrassing scenes" in restaurants arising from his inadequacies as a tipper and "the stingy, discourteous supper" (poached eggs on shredded wheat) that he served her when last they parted. Granted that Miss Hellman's generosity of spirit is not one of her more remarkable qualities, she is in no way a trivial woman; and it is some trial to the patience to see her reducing what, for someone like her, must have been convictions intensely and even fiercely felt to stuff so trivial as this.

She remembers that she quarreled with the Communists over the conduct of the Progressive Party's campaign because she would not abate her "constant pleas that we turn attention and money away from the presidential campaign and put them into building small chapters around the country in hope of a solid, modest future." Again there is that uneasy sense of diversion to the marginal. Are we really to imagine that Miss Hellman found the influence of the Communist caucus on the Progressive Party more objectionable when it was merely blundering about tactics than when it was upholding its stern principles by persuading the 1948 convention to reject a motion that the party platform include the statement that "it is not our intention to give blanket endorsement to the foreign policy of any nation"? For the Old Left had principles, good ones and bad ones, or for that matter bad good and good bad ones, and they must have held a substantial place in Miss Hellman's consciousness a long while before the day she embodied the

---

summary of the Waldorf conference, and makes it sound much more interesting than most of us permitted ourselves to imagine. The remarks of Harlow Shapley, Norman Mailer, and I. F. Stone sound especially notable for critical independence; for the flavor of the Russians we can be satisfied with this: "Shostakovich described Russia's mushroom growth of music activity, *especially in Soviet Asia*, which had neither an orchestra, a chorus nor an opera house thirty years ago."

simple and pure principle that she served so well in her troubles. It is an annoyance to have her leave so many mists around them.

We do not diminish the final admiration we feel owed to Dashiell Hammett when we wonder what he might have said to Miss Hellman on the night he came home from the meeting of the board of the Civil Rights Congress which voted to refuse its support to the cause of James Kutcher, a paraplegic veteran who had been discharged as a government clerical worker because he belonged to the Trotskyite Socialist Workers party. But then Hammett was a Communist and it was an article of the party faith that Leon Trotsky, having worked for the Emperor of Japan since 1904, had then improved his social standing by taking employment with the Nazis in 1934. Thus any member of the Socialist Workers party could be considered by extension to be no more than an agent of Hitler's ghost. Given that interpretation of history, Paul Robeson spoke from principle when a proposal to assist the Trotskyite Kutcher was raised at a public meeting of the Civil Rights Congress. Robeson drove it from the floor with a declaration to the effect that you don't ask Jews to help a Nazi or Negroes to help the KKK.

SUCH RECOLLECTIONS, OF course, by no means tell all or even much about either Robeson or Hammett. But they do suggest that the matter is not entirely simple; and to appreciate its complexity is to recognize that what was imperishable in the hour of Miss Hellman's witness was that she managed to extract and make incarnate its one important and authentic element of simplicity. Hammett had served a prison term the year before for refusing to surrender to the police the names of contributors to the Civil Rights Congress bail fund. Political considerations had hardly entered into his choice at all: He endured his punishment not for the advancement of Marxism-Leninism but because he felt that to keep inviolate the privacy of those who had contributed to a bail fund for Communists had "something to do with keeping my word."

It would be unjust to Miss Hellman's independence of will to suggest that she was brought to her position by the force of Hammett's example. But all the same, if you presumptuously imagine her offering her objections to his course, if only from tenderness, her words hanging there as though unheard, and being left to argue the dilemma through by herself, then you have to suspect that this was one of those experiences that, however otherwise painful, serve to bring its victim to the confrontation of an essential point, which like most good points was a domestic and not a political one.

The enduring eloquence of her statement to the Committee on Un-American Activities belongs not to rhetoric but to conversation:

> I am not willing, now or in the future, to bring bad trouble to people who, in my past association with them, were completely innocent of any talk or any action that was disloyal or subversive. . . . But to hurt innocent people whom I knew many years ago in order to save myself is, to me, inhuman and indecent and dishonorable.

That is not just a fine way of putting the question but the only way, and it seems sufficient to itself. It was enough for Miss Hellman to have done the single great thing of having once and for all defined the issue.

SHE WAS BY no means the only one who acted well. Arthur Miller acted as well as she—if he could not be said to have performed as superbly—and he took a larger risk of going to prison. If what we call the serious theater otherwise ran short of representatives anxious to enlist as embodiments of its will to resist, comedians like Lionel Stander and Zero Mostel took their places handsomely.

The open Communists absorbed the beatings inflicted upon them by an indifferent official malignity with barely a whimper, not just Robeson and Hammett but scores of others more ordinary. It is ridiculous to give grades in matters like this; but if I had to select just one man who ennobled that age, I think it might be Steve Nelson, Communist party chairman of western Pennsylvania, to the press then only a piece of boilerplate ("Atom Spy Clams Up"), to prosecuting attorneys only a basic natural resource for the process of conspiracy trials.

Standing on his crutches, he acted as his own defense counsel, questioning with some good humor the newest of the prosecution's witnesses ("Tell me, Mr. Stoolpigeon . . ."). It is unlikely that Steve Nelson had ever known many conscious moments when he had not been a Communist, and by then he may no longer have been entirely certain of the wisdom and kindness of Stalin, but he was dead sure that the one inexcusable act was to be a fink. Miss Hellman did not act better than people like those; but what she alone did had its special grandeur: Without mentioning any of them, she drew them about herself and, as none of them had ever been quite able to do, spoke their real reasons for acting as they had.

"I am not willing to bring bad trouble to people. . . ." Rather that I endure my own. That is all that seems finally important about the way she did what she did, and it is a great deal. It would be too much to credit it with any more tangible historical result. The Committee went on just as it had; the blacklist grew if anything more savage and its depredations wider. Miss Hellman's words are memorable not for what they did but for what they said.

IT IS HARD to believe that she ran her course with much risk of going to jail. These doubts have nothing to do with her courage; she would have done her time and been no doubt an excellent con. She might have run serious danger all the same (dignity is always risky) if she had not, quite by accident, come as close as it was ever possible to get to an iron-clad promise of immunity when she retained Joseph L. Rauh as her counsel. She had no way of knowing how seldom an unfriendly witness represented by Joseph L. Rauh ended up convicted of contempt. Rauh's professional skills and high personal honor were the major factors in this record; but it could also be suspected that a less measurable element in his success may have been the general knowledge that Rauh was not inclined to take a client he thought to be a Communist party member, not because of any want of fervor for the rights of such people but rather because he felt that their difference of temperament might make mutual confidence difficult.

Justice Felix Frankfurter's was the crucial vote on a Supreme Court whose rulings on Un-American Activities Committee prosecutions were by then gyrating so wildly that there seemed to be no way of explaining them except by Justice Frankfurter's solicitude for the liberties of any American so long as it was reasonably certain that he was not a Communist. If Miss Hellman had been indicted, Rauh's name would have been on the brief for her appeal to the Supreme Court, and Rauh's name by then may well have carried for Justice Frankfurter enough assurance that the appellant was not a Communist to permit him to consider the issues in those abstract realms where freedom debates order. There Justice Frankfurter could often be a libertarian.

But if Miss Hellman had been to any degree calculating in her choice of Rauh, she would hardly have treated his advice as starchily as she did. *Watch on the Rhine*, her anti-Nazi drama, had opened in New York, most tactlessly in the Communist party's view, a few months before Hitler's tanks announced the demise of his friendship treaty with the Soviets. The *Daily Worker* had criticized Miss Hellman for warmongering and Rauh suggested that this evidence of her independence of the Communist line be submitted to the Un-American Activities Committee as a defense exhibit. (These were days, as Stefan Kanfer has observed, when "the artist was pitiably grateful for bad reviews.") Miss Hellman refused to avail herself of any such umbrella because:

> my use of their attacks on me would amount to my attacking them at a time when they were being persecuted and I would, therefore, be playing the enemy's game. . . . In my thin morality book it is plain not cricket to clear yourself by jumping on people who are themselves in trouble.

We would pay Miss Hellman much less than the due such a sense of honor deserves if we credited it solely to a primal innocence. You feel here the operations of a genuine nobility and no small part of a shrewd instinct about the future, an awareness and such senses have much to do with honor—of how the thing would look in due course. I hardly know Miss Hellman; our only real conversation happened a few days after her testimony. I had read *The New York Times* summary of her statement, and had been moved to express my admiration for it in print, haltingly but with very little competition. Miss Hellman was grateful; but then I was no less grateful to her as I was becoming more and more grateful when members of the Old Left entered my consciousness, reminding me not just of their general humanity but of their personal dignity, and throwing sand into what had for a long time been the mechanical workings of my anti-Communism.

She told me then about her discussion with Elia Kazan, which had preceded his acceptance, and her rejection, of HUAC's demands. She had observed to Kazan at that time, as I remember her account, that they did not, after all, *have* to make as much money as they had over the years and that, if Hollywood was closed to them, there would still remain the theater and the smaller but by no means uncomfortable living it could afford.

It was her recollection at that time that Kazan had replied that it was all very well for her to say that, because she had spent everything she had ever earned, but that *he* had savings. And then she told me that her first thought was of how her aunt used to say that you don't go into capital. In her book she remembers a quite different interior response to Kazan's observations—something her grandmother said. Although her memory is clearly the authoritative one, the years have given me too much affection for my own version to give it up; because it seems to me that one of her most important lessons is that there come times when you have to go into capital, and be ready to face up to the loss of a lot, because you are wise enough to sense that the alternative is to lose everything. You will get through, and there will be a time to come when all that will be remembered about you is whether or not you gave the names.

I HAVE TO confess, although it is never gracious to say such things, that Miss Hellman's voice in these discourses does not fall upon my ear as coming from someone I should want overmuch as a comrade. She is too vain about judgmental qualities that seem to me by no means her best ones; she is a bit of a bully; and she is inclined to be a hanging judge of the motives of persons whose opinions differ from her own.[2]

But such feelings, even if they were just, would not finally matter when set against that one great moment of hers. It is her summit. We can ask from her nothing more; I do not suppose that, in the only critical sense, we really need to. The most important thing is never to forget that here is someone who knew how to act when there was nothing harder on earth than knowing how to act.

The New York Review of Books, June 10, 1976

[2]It is a matter of limited moment except to me perhaps, but I cannot contain a desire to express the liveliest resentment of Miss Hellman's statement that James Wechsler "not only was a friendly witness" before the House Un-American Activities Committee "but had high-class pious reasons for what he did." The least offensive thing about this assertion is that it is factually in error. What is far less forgivable is a rancor that Miss Hellman's very eminence and authority ought to instruct her most carefully to ration. Wechsler was never called by the House Un-American Activities Committee: he was subpoenaed by Joe McCarthy after he was made editor of the *New York Post*, and, far from being a friendly witness, he was a manifestly hostile one. ("I may say," he told McCarthy's committee, ". . . that we have repeatedly taken the position that the *New York Post* is as bitterly opposed to Joe Stalin as it is to Joe McCarthy and we believe that a free society can combat both.")

He did decide that the fight against McCarthy would be damaged if he as a conspicuous opponent did not demonstrate his good faith as an anti-Communist by submitting to the committee a list of persons he had known when he was a member of the Young Communist League. I considered his reasons idiotic and told him so; I thought this action lacking, among other things, in proper concern for his personal welfare, because it is seldom possible to explain the giving of names, no matter how high your motive. But if there have been many occasions when I have wondered about Wechsler's good sense, I have never known a time when I felt the smallest doubt about his honor. Perhaps I have a right to say this because, as it happens, I was one of the former Communists that Wechsler named in public while he was wrestling with McCarthy. I also think it a duty of fairness to Miss Hellman to say that my strictures on her disposition are inspired in part by personal feelings in this matter.

The Ambivalence of J. Robert Oppenheimer

I N THE SUMMER of 1945, Robert Oppenheimer looked across the New Mexico sands, took the fireball's measure, and knew that he was the usher who had escorted all the creatures of the earth to the tenebrous dawn of the atomic age. Afterward he would remember—or prefer to believe—that his first conscious thought had been Krishna's: "I am become death, the shatterer of worlds."

It is unlikely that he himself could say with any assurance whether here was the cry of the stricken sinner or the exultation of the conqueror. His essence was, as always, in the ambiguities of the divided soul and equivocal presence of someone who had come in triumph to a world that would have been safer if he and everyone else who tried had failed.

BUT THEN HE would himself have been safer if, at the hour that so precipitately discovered him, he had known enough more about the world than it had about him. He had been wrapped at birth in the soft bunting of a well-to-do German Jewish household on Manhattan's Riverside Drive. He came to consciousness in an ambience secure—indeed, smug—about the refinement of the air it breathed but timid about the rough winds beyond. He began his education at the Ethical Culture School, a place of refuge for families that had cast aside the few rags of superstition still adhering to Reform Judaism and swaddled themselves in the credulities of secular humanism. He passed on to Harvard, where Jewish applicants from New York had no large chance of arriving unless they brought with them the promise of departing summa cum laude. He was graduated with honors more than justifying Harvard's confidence and embarked at once for England and Christ's College, Cambridge, and then to Germany and the University of Göttingen. At Cambridge he met Niels Bohr and Paul Dirac, and at Göttingen he studied with Max Born; the great men of theoretical physics had become familiars to him while they were still strangers to the most cultivated of his countrymen.

He carried his German doctorate back to Harvard; he had already begun to robe himself in folds of mystery; Philip Morse, a Princeton graduate student who met him at a Harvard conference on molecular vibrations, had no more vivid recollection of their first encounter than "I didn't know what he was talking about."

His four months at Harvard and five at the California Institute of Technology made the year 1927 the least purposeful he had ever experienced; and it was a relief for him to accept a Rockefeller Foundation grant and escape for twelve months in the European centers of the new physics that were altogether more congenial to him for being so much more aware.

He returned in the summer of 1929 to an assistant professorship at the University of California in Berkeley, where, as he afterward remembered, "I was the only one who knew what this was all about." But even though, or perhaps because, Berkeley had so long been a desert for theoretical physics, he found it most suitable for cultivating a comfortable, if modest, bloom. Its experimentalists never quite found out what he was talking about; but they learned quickly to trust and more and more to depend on the sound and clear assessments of the practicalities of their projects he drew up from his reservoir of the indecipherable.

But for all their affectionate admiration, they never got over the sense that they were in the company of an abstract being, and they were correct in that judgment. His father's textile properties were essentially undamaged by the Depression; and Robert Oppenheimer often recalled that in those days he so seldom glanced at the newspapers that he did not know the stock market had crashed until a long time after it had. The world's coarse rubbings had never chafed his flesh until Hitler shocked him into a political activism that was the more febrile because belated and that so faithfully followed the customary courses of his divorcement from reality as to make him a fellow traveler of the Communists. Those delusions had already grown wispy when the outbreak of the war drew him into research of the potentials of nuclear fission for weaponry.

It was an area of exploration that gave the new physics an authority it had never known before; and Oppenheimer swiftly displayed such unique attributes as a bridge between the abstract and the concrete that he was recognized as essential. His earlier leftward excursion was a source of doubts and trepidations, but they yielded to the overpowering necessity for his special qualities, and he was appointed director of the Los Alamos laboratory.

There he showed gifts of command quite beyond any suggested by either his prior history or the highest expectations of his sponsors. He persuaded a hundred scientists to leave the cozy precincts where they were already satisfyingly engaged in military research and to come with him to a closed military outpost in the desert. In the end he was managing a work force of over three thousand.

He was their inspiration, their supervisor, and even their housekeeper, and, collective triumph though theirs was, they all knew that he had done more to build the bomb than anyone else at Los Alamos. Here had been the utmost prodigy of practical achievement; and yet it had been brought about in an isolation sealed off from the run of humanity; there, as always, he had been protected from the routine troubles, discontents, and worries that instruct even while they are cankering ordinary persons, and he was transported to his glittering summit innocent of all the traps that every other man of affairs has grown used to well before he is forty-two years old.

AFTER THE WAR the United States government established an Atomic Energy Commission, and one of its earliest decisions was to approve

Robert Oppenheimer as chairman of its General Advisory Committee. One of the commissioners, Lewis Strauss, was also a leading trustee of the Institute for Advanced Study at Princeton. He saw his chance to add to its collection a jewel hardly less precious than Albert Einstein and went down on his knees to persuade Oppenheimer to be director of the institute.

The slow work of Robert Oppenheimer's undoing began in the awe that Strauss brought to their earliest encounters. For it was the awe evoked by a presence whose singular curse was that he was easier to adore than comfortably like. The aura of otherworldly properties is the riskiest of capitals, because the gullible, once disappointed in imagining them divine, are apt to fall into imagining them diabolical. Strauss was one of nature's gullibles, and, having come to worship, he would remain to destroy. There would be others.

As director of Los Alamos's laboratory, he had been all else but the solitary creator of the nuclear weapon; but he had been master of its macabre ceremonies and he could not escape becoming its personification, not just for the public but for a government too quick to assume that since he produced the riddle, he must have brought along its answer. But it did not take long for his country's governors to recognize that Oppenheimer was more a riddle than an answer.

To their ultimate common despair, he was conscripted as physics tutor to paladins like Undersecretary of State Dean Acheson and Wise-About-Everything John J. McCloy; and he was an automatic choice as scientific member of his country's delegation to the United Nations Conference on International Control of Atomic Energy, the first flight in a search of ever-diminishing expectations.

He complained early in his tenure as chief adviser on international atomic policy that whatever he proposed was uncritically accepted. His wait for relief from that distress was a short one; within a few months his advice was being just as uncritically disregarded.

He first began to sense the limitations of his writ when President Truman asked him, in 1946, to guess when the Russians would develop their own atomic bomb. Oppenheimer replied that he did not know; and Mr. Truman said that he knew the answer and that it was "Never." The misapprehension of Robert Oppenheimer's supernatural qualities had done its worst damage; Mr. Truman could not conceive that the Russians could find the secret because he could not imagine a Soviet Oppenheimer and did not understand that no such ultimately delicate instrument was needed for work rather coarser than he knew.

But even if he had consumed a bit too much of his credit as sage, Oppenheimer's repute as mechanic resided so far beyond doubt that, for the first six years of the AEC's history, it was a matter of course for him to have been the only chairman of its General Advisory Committee.

ON NOVEMBER 25, 1947, the young, standing or sitting in the auditorium of the Massachusetts Institute of Technology, listened as if at their devotionals while he recited science's general confession: ". . . in some sort of crude sense, which no vulgarity, no humor, no overstatement can extinguish, the physicists have known sin; and that is a knowledge they cannot lose."

Half a week before, the eight other members of the General Advisory Committee had watched with no less admiration for their chairman's dedication as he led them through the preliminaries of what they had agreed upon—"without debate [but] I suppose not without melancholy"—as their prime task: "to provide atomic weapons and many atomic weapons."

His ambiguities were already traveling into the ambivalence that is the first leg of every journey toward exhaustion.

Long afterward, in his troubles he replied to the charge that he had been less than wholehearted in serving his government's desires, if not its truest interests, by saying: "I did my job, the job I was supposed to do." There was in those words a cold tone stripped of every ideal except the rules of function. It was just that pinnacle of spiritual dispossession that Robert Oppenheimer tried his best to reach, and he would fall short only because he traveled encumbered with too many pieces of baggage he could not quite bear to throw away.

He had crashingly entered the great world without bringing along enough familiarity with the ordinary one. Every famous American

physicist before him had been a species of grand tinkerer more conspicuous for the size of his machines than the breadth of his concepts.
Oppenheimer represented instead that first generation of theoretical
physicists who had voyaged to Europe and brought it home with them.
He thought of science almost as a religious vocation, and the higher
physics as the sublimest poem in its liturgy.

This susceptibility to abstraction seems the most plausible explanation for his attraction to communism in the years before he fell into
practical affairs. Marx's message could never have been as compelling
as it was if he had not presumed to call his system "scientific socialism."
Oppenheimer would always say that his fear of the Nazis had first
brought him close to the Communists; and yet in 1939, when Stalin
consummated a treaty of friendship and even a spot of collaboration
with Hitler, Oppenheimer's reaction, while by no means uncritical, was
somewhat this side of repulsion: Stalin was, after all, a scientific socialist
and might know something he didn't.

In July 1945 Edward Teller had solicited Robert Oppenheimer's
support for a muster of Los Alamos physicists petitioning Mr. Truman
not to drop the bomb on Japan itself.

"He told me in a polite and convincing way," Teller said later, "that
he thought it improper for a scientist to use his prestige as a platform
for political pronouncements. . . . Our fate was in the hands of the best,
the most conscientious men in the nation. And they had information
which we did not possess."

Now he had taken upon himself the felt duty of speaking for
physics to government and for government to physics. He would be
guardian angel over an alliance with too much of the imbalance that
obtains when one side is the caterer and the other is the customer and
disputes about taste are settled by the palate of the payer.

Oppenheimer maintained this singular legation for five years. He
was all but final judge of what could be done and what could not and,
consequently, keeper of the gate between the ambitions of others and
the official funds that could give them life and force.

The earliest recruits to the army of enemies that eventually overbore Oppenheimer were assembled, not unnaturally, from his oldest

friends in the physics department of the University of California, the home where he had grown up and where he had met all of those he had ever consciously harmed and too many of those who would harm him.

He had risen beyond Berkeley and even beyond physics to that grandeur that is at once an affront and a promise, because its object arouses envy and inspires emulation. He had shown the way to an eminence there was no reaching except by a conquest more resounding even than his. He had become a huge shadow between other men and whatever bright particular moon they happened to be baying at.

At Berkeley Oppenheimer had never been more than an honored guest in a house whose master was Ernest Lawrence. Lawrence had earned his Nobel Prize with the great machines he had forced to the outer limits of those laws of physics he insecurely understood and expected someday successfully to defy.

In 1946 Lawrence designed his Materials Testing Accelerator, a piece of hardware too expensively enormous even for the magnificoes who were his private patrons. He laid the MTA's conception before the AEC's General Advisory Committee, where he sustained the shock of having it dismissed by Oppenheimer as a vision that, "imaginative" as it was, "cannot do what is expected of it." Lawrence was too powerful for any such summary disposal; he turned, in his wrath, to the Department of Defense and the Joint Congressional Committee on Atomic Energy and so intoxicated them with his promises that the AEC could only give way and buy Lawrence his Materials Testing Accelerator, which swiftly burned itself out.

This demonstration of Oppenheimer's sound judgment increased rather than abated Lawrence's rage at his presumption. For at Berkeley he had taken on the ineffaceable taint of the deserter. He himself had all but ceased to search, whether because he had realized his ambition or because he had shrunk from its consequences. He could be seen as someone who existed only to frustrate the ambitions of others, having lost and perhaps, indeed, deserted the high American confidence that overrides all doubts and compunctions.

Major General Roscoe Wilson was sitting, in January 1951, as the Air

Force's representative on an AEC panel on long-range weapon objectives. As always, Oppenheimer was its chairman; and General Wilson went back to headquarters deeply shaken as "a dedicated airman" at having found his country's most authoritative scientific adviser dubious about current prospects for a thermonuclear weapon, pessimistic about any early improvement in devices for detecting atomic explosions, and chilling to notions that anyone present would live long enough to see a nuclear-powered aircraft.

After this cold bath for his dreams, General Wilson felt that he had to "go to the director of [Air Force] intelligence to express my concern over what I felt was a pattern of action not helpful to the national defense."

By the time General Wilson cast his stone at its consecrated object, the odor of incense had already grown faint around it. After September 1949, and the fact of the first successful Soviet nuclear test, Oppenheimer could never again be the symbol, or even personally the sharer, of a national complacency secure in the possession of a weapon beyond any alien enemy's attainment.

Ordinary laymen and officials had taken for granted their country's monopoly of a secret uniquely Robert Oppenheimer's, and they could see no way it could have been lost if it had not been stolen. They kept faith with that misconception well after it had been blown to vapor by executing Julius and Ethel Rosenberg, whose crimes could never have run beyond pilferage too petty to explain the triumph of Soviet research.

Edward Teller knew better than that; he was a theoretical physicist whose attainments and even intuitions were barely less commanding than Oppenheimer's. Teller's contributions at Los Alamos had been smaller than the promise of his talents, because he had spent the war hunting after a thermonuclear weapon quantitatively more dreadful than the bomb delivered upon Hiroshima. His first reaction to the Soviet accomplishment was to recognize in it a public necessity and personal opportunity to renew that pursuit.

He telephoned Oppenheimer to ask what should now be done. "Keep your shirt on," Oppenheimer advised; and that reply left Teller lastingly certain that the chairman of the General Advisory Committee of the Atomic Energy Commission had dropped out of a race it was his duty to run.

There were doses of moral qualm in the mixture of Oppenheimer's objections to what Teller zestfully called the Super, but they were rather smaller than his practical doubts. His remedy for the advantage lost to the Soviets was not to aim for the prodigious but to give more attention to the comparatively modest and to concentrate upon smaller nuclear weapons designed for "getting the atom to work on the battle-field as well as the heartland" and to develop a defense system that might diminish Soviet confidence that the United States could be destroyed.

All five of his colleagues on the General Advisory Committee joined him in recommending a low priority for Teller's quest for the absolute. Oppenheimer later professed himself astonished by a unanimity that his enemies could never afterward explain except as the workings of his malicious animal magnetism.

All but one of the AEC's commissioners seem momentarily to have been given pause by the unity in opinion of their scientific advisers; but that one happened to be Lewis Strauss, a minority of undiscourageable militance, who trundled his alarms to the secretary of defense and there raised the battalions that would prevail upon Mr. Truman to decree a crash program for the Super.

Oppenheimer's immediate response to this defeat was the sugges-tion that he yield his General Advisory Committee chairmanship to someone who would bring the necessary enthusiasm to the Super. Secretary of State Acheson responded to this overture by sending back word, "for heck's sake, not to resign or make any public statements to upset the applecart but accept this decision." Oppenheimer stayed on, puzzled, as he afterward said, that anyone could have even transiently mistaken him for the sort of crank who would seek, let alone "find a way to make a public conflict."

He was able to husband a somber hope drawn from his despairs about the Super's feasibility until June 1951, when Teller arrived at a weapons conference in Princeton with the formula that made the hydrogen bomb workable.

Oppenheimer's certainties had eroded and his will was ebbing; but the old intuitive faculty was swift as ever; and he seems to have divined Teller's breakthrough sooner than anyone else there. "Sweet and lovely and beautiful," he is reported to have observed. There was a sudden reglowing of what embers remained from the fires of his earlier conviction that what could be discovered ought to be discovered, wherever it tended. Once more, elegance was for him its own absolution.

He set himself thenceforth to do whatever he could to help Teller. But he had lingered too long in the sin of dubiety to earn gratitude or forgiveness from those he had transiently obstructed. A few months after he had speeded Teller on his road, Oppenheimer's term as GAC chairman expired; and neither he nor his masters had any itch to have it renewed. He was sent off with Mr. Truman's warmest thanks ("You have served your country well").

And then President Truman gave way to President Eisenhower, Lewis Strauss became the Atomic Energy Commission's chairman, and Malice put on the robes of Judgment.

Even though Strauss had never quite been tutored up to his pretensions as an amateur of science, he still deserved to be thought of as a professional of sorts, because he had so often profited as a banker alert to the market potential of the by-products of scientific curiosity. In the years when research funds still depended upon private generosity, he had been Enrico Fermi's patron; and now the federal budget had made him a dispenser of benefices so much more opulent that when he retired as AEC chairman, defense agencies were spending five times as much on scientific research as they had in the Second World War.

Strauss did not carry his empire in his eye. His face, with its rosy hue and the blandness of its spectacles, gave no hint of his resentments; and his manner infrequently deviated from an all but universal disbursement of deferences. The Strauss who had been obdurate when alone in the Commission's minority would be tyrannical as commander of its new majority.

Extremes in the worship of anything, even reason, inevitably arrive at superstition. Strauss had made out of science his cult; and, all the time he was sure of himself as a child of the Enlightenment, his devotions bore him farther and farther back toward those smoking altars where men adored or shuddered before idols they thought either kind or malign but never indifferent.

For Strauss, science had become confused with magic; and since he saw Oppenheimer as the apotheosis of the scientist, he saw him as a species of wizard who would not withhold his powers for good unless he proposed to employ them for evil.

Oppenheimer had abandoned his resistance to the Super as soon as Mr. Truman had approved it; he had been scrupulous, if not quickly enough enthusiastic, about assisting its achievement; and then, having already laid down his arms, he had with no visible complaint yielded his office and withdrawn from the center of affairs.

The very propriety of such conduct was particularly disturbing to Lewis Strauss, whose own disposition so scorned the concept of majority rule that he never thought a question closed until it had been finally settled in his favor.

Insulating the Atomic Energy Commission from Oppenheimer was no problem at all: He was still on call as a consultant, but Strauss had only to abstain from taking the opportunity to consult him.

But in 1953 Strauss and Air Force Secretary Thomas Finletter learned that Oppenheimer had rebounded to a seat on the Office of Defense Mobilization's Scientific Advisory Committee, which had been moldering unnoticed until President Eisenhower suddenly adopted and lodged it in the National Security Council, the privatest chamber in his household. The image of their presumed grand antagonist, his radiance rekindled, bearing his potions and reciting his incantations before the President himself, threw the Strategic Air Command and the AEC into the determination that there was no remedy for Robert Oppenheimer's mischief except to get him stripped of the security clearance that was his license.

He had obeyed the state too conscientiously to afford it an easy excuse to find points where he had strayed. He had, of course, been close to the Communists in the lost time when such sympathies were the private citizen's options; but he had candidly confessed his excursions, and even Lewis Strauss had assessed them as nullities when the AEC reviewed them before approving Oppenheimer's security clearance six years before.

In the interim, to be sure, his security file had grown to a width of four feet and six inches from its birth late in the thirties, when the FBI recorded him as a new subscriber to the *People's World*, a Communist daily. He himself had contributed little to its engorgement since his enlistment to Los Alamos; and the small scraps of his own giving had all been the consequences of the infrequent times when his official discipline had fleetingly been overcome by private feelings:

1. Late in the thirties he had been informally betrothed to Jean Tatlock, an on-again, off-again member of the Berkeley unit of the Communist party. After their courses diverged, Jean Tatlock had wandered into those forests of depression that would lead her to suicide in 1944. At one point in the months before the end, she sent word to Oppenheimer that she was anxious to see him. He was too occupied to respond to her appeal until June 1943; but he must have been touched in places he had thought forgotten, because he missed the Los Alamos train to sit with her, talking through the night in her father's house.

Oppenheimer did not yet know that he had embarked upon an existence that did not hold many hours of unobserved privacy. His government's agents had watched them enter the Tatlock home and had remained outside it until the next morning when she drove him to the airport.

2. During his affair with the Left, Oppenheimer's nearest and most mutually ill-fortuned masculine friendship had been with Haakon Chevalier, who taught French at Berkeley. Chevalier's romantic and innocent ardor for the Marxist-Leninist simplicities endured after Oppenheimer's disenchantment with them; but their personal affections survived. One evening, while Oppenheimer was mixing their martinis, Chevalier told him that he had been approached by an industrial chemist on the lookout for physicists who might be willing to use the Soviet consulate as conduit for transmitting information to Russian scientists.

Oppenheimer's only recollected comment was, "That would be a terrible thing to do." But later he had thought it no less than his duty to warn the authorities against the intrusive chemist without identifying Chevalier as his go-between.

This effort to serve both his friend and his nation failed so utterly that the government's agents did not relax their pressure until he surrendered Chevalier's name. He had revealed the weakness that those who thought they knew him best would be the last to impute to him: He was a man who could be bullied.

With this revelation, Chevalier's career commenced a steady decline; and now and then, from stirrings livelier in his conscience than his affections, we may suppose, Oppenheimer would make a feeble stab at clearing his name.

3. Communism had attracted—or as the fifties would prefer to say, infected—several of his Berkeley graduate students. In 1949 the House Un-American Activities Committee called him to an inquiry on two or three of them. By now Oppenheimer was thoroughly infused with the developing spirit of his age and in that key he poured out his direct suspicions of Bernard Peters, who had come to California as an exile from Nazi Germany and had gone on to teach physics at the University of Rochester.

Oppenheimer told the Committee that Peters had brought with him to California an abounding fraternal affection for the German Communists, beside whom he had fought Nazi gangs in the Berlin streets before being imprisoned in Dachau, from which he had escaped by guile. To Oppenheimer any such history betrayed a character "not pointing to temperance," an assessment most curiously founded upon little more evidence than the indications of light-mindedness that Peters had shown when he had been so wanting in respect for Hitler's system of justice as to commit the insolence of levanting from one of its concentration camps.

The Committee had listened to Oppenheimer in an executive session and he had been sent away with a warm testimonial from Congressman Richard Nixon for this among so many even larger services to his country. He had felt secure against anyone outside the hearing room ever knowing what he had said about Peters; but he was about to learn how much more careless the government was with his secrets than he would ever be with its.

The Committee's staff provided a Rochester journalist with snippets of Oppenheimer's strictures on Peters; and their publication left the accused jobless and the accuser beset with protests from other physicists. The harm done Peters only too probably distressed him less than the damage he had inflicted upon himself with portions of his old fraternity. He sought to repair both with a letter to a Rochester newspaper, taking note of Peters's denial of affiliation with any Communist party anywhere and hoping that no word of his own would be taken as impugning "the honor and integrity [of] a brilliant student [and] a man of strong moral principles. . . ." That disclaimer seems to have been little meant and was even less effective; after a futile canvass for some haven in an American academy, Peters went off to teach in India.

An unhopeful attempt to comfort a woman the world thought a Communist and he once thought he loved, a failed essay at shielding a friend who may or may not have made a pass at espionage, and a halfhearted try at calling the dogs off someone against whom he himself had raised the scent—those three uneasy passages were the only departures from prescribed discretion that could be found against him by prosecutors whose obsessive curiosity would have been more than up to discovering any others.

But no more than this was more than enough. His judges needed those dry straws because they dared not engage the whole, awful bale. Oppenheimer's damning offense was the sin of moral qualm; he had contemplated the shadows of the thermonuclear age and shrunk back, however briefly, at a tidal point in what might or might not be man's march toward his own extinction.

This could inarguably be taken for a high crime, but it was one for which the spirit of his time forbade any man's condemnation. The Enlightenment is to be distinguished from the Age of Superstition not because it is invariably so much nicer in its treatment of heretics but because it would never burn one without being careful to condemn him for any and all sins except heresy.

Jean Tatlock, Haakon Chevalier, and Bernard Peters were broken fragments from long ago; but their excavation was essential to proceedings whose verdict could not be satisfactory unless it could contrive to define Robert Oppenheimer's departed past as his present. These minor trespasses adumbrated the major crime; his dealings in each case were signs of a piece of Robert Oppenheimer that some might think the redeeming piece: Not even his uttermost self-rigors could uniformly subsume the private into the public self. The same unruly heart had given itself away in the gesture to Jean Tatlock and the recoil from the specter of the Super.

Oppenheimer was tried before a three-member Personnel Security Board chosen by Lewis Strauss, a prosecutor uniquely blessed with the right to select his jury. The hearings lasted over three weeks and consumed some 990 pages of transcript. Large portions of them were engaged with inconclusive burrowings into the history of the hydrogen decision. Six of the eight prosecution witnesses gave evidence whose main import fell upon the bad advice they felt the accused had given to his masters.

Two of his three trial judges found Oppenheimer guilty. Their names are dust now but they were paladins in their day; and both were obedient to commands of a time never more zealous, with genuflections before the temple of liberty of thought in general, than when it was punishing somebody or other it suspected of liberty of thought in the particular.

Thus, they so wanted it understood that Oppenheimer's hesitations when faced with the Super were no crucial element in their judgment that they felt themselves impelled "to record [the board's] profound and positive view that no man should be tried for his opinions." What they could not forgive was Jean Tatlock, Haakon Chevalier, and Bernard Peters: a man could be tried for his ghosts.

Their findings were sent upward to the Atomic Energy Commission, where honest venom resided. Lewis Strauss himself undertook the composition of the AEC majority opinion that ruled Robert Oppenheimer unfit for future service.

"The work of Military Intelligence, the Federal Bureau of Investigation and the Atomic Energy Commission—all at one time or another have felt the effect of his falsehoods and misrepresentations."

After these savage rites there followed the customary national drill of accommodation. Oppenheimer was allowed to wither with every material comfort. He was still director of the Institute for Advanced Study, and Strauss was still a trustee, and each kept his place.

The motion to retain Oppenheimer was, in fact, tendered to the institute's board by the same man who had, only three months before, officially found him to have "lived far below acceptable standards of reliability and trustworthiness." If Strauss's principles had been the equal of his rancors, he might better have given the board the option of finding either a new director or a new trustee; but he had sounded the temper of his fellow trustees, and he preferred to keep one of his honors at whatever expense to his honor and did not press his vengeance beyond the limits of his convenience.

Whatever outrage any of the physicists felt never extended to troubling anyone above and beyond their own specialized community, and soon stopped troubling even them. Edward Teller was snubbed at the first physics conference he attended after the revelation that he had been a witness for the prosecution at Oppenheimer's trial. But there was no change in the deference of the physicists when they encountered the formidable Strauss; an unassailable immunity is reserved for the man who pays.

Enrico Fermi and I. I. Rabi had joined Oppenheimer in the General Advisory Committee's early remonstrance against the Super; and yet Strauss went on showering them with his blessings and they went on rejoicing in them. Perhaps the distinction between democratic and totalitarian societies is in economy of victimization: Totalitarians suppress wholesale, and democrats, when a like fit is upon them, manage a decent retail measure of the same effect by pillorying a representative specimen of a class and depending upon his example to cow the rest of its members. It could now be understood that Robert Oppenheimer was the archetype of the physicist not least because he was someone who could be bullied.

In the summer of 1945 he had done what he could to convince a doubting Teller that this country's governors were "the best and most conscientious men . . . who had information that the rest of us did not possess."

He had believed those words, against increasingly intimate access to contrary evidence, all the while his glory blazed; and even now, when it had been extinguished, he seemed somehow to believe them still. Government, not Krishna, and not even science, had turned out to be God for him; as there could be no disrupting a government's decision to immolate Hiroshima, there could be no real disputing its decision to immolate him.

When the curious approached with questions about himself and his life, he would often recommend the closest attention to the transcript of the Hearings of the Atomic Energy Commission in the Matter of J. Robert Oppenheimer. This record of his degradation seemed almost to have become for him the authorized biography; but then, it bore the authority always most requisite for him: It was a government document.

One day, shortly after his disgrace, he sat with a visitor painfully better acquainted with his history than his person.

"What bothers me," Robert Oppenheimer said, "is the complicity."

But where, his visitor wondered, did the complicity lie?

Was it in making the atomic or resisting the hydrogen bomb, in denouncing Bernard Peters or defending Bernard Peters, in leaving Jean Tatlock or returning to her for a few skimpy hours in the night, in hurting Haakon Chevalier or trying to help him, in serving his government too unquestioningly or not questioningly enough—in all the mess we make of life and life makes of us, just where do we locate and house the complicity?

"In all of it," Robert Oppenheimer answered.

THE POINT OF him? Who can feel safe in saying? A clutch at a guess might be the sense that it is probably an illusion that any one man much alters history even in the short run, and it is certainly a fact that history crushes every man in the long, and that Robert Oppenheimer can touch us still because he was one of the few of those who have lived with both the illusion of being history's conqueror and the fact of being its victim.

But that is a surmise too grand for the almost domestic thoughts that start when we look at his eyes in the old photographs and confront the inexplicable nobility of stuff so adamant that it can be passed through every variety of the ignoble, do the worst and have the worst done to itself, and somehow shine through all its trash and its trashing.

His death of throat cancer on February 18, 1967, was discreet and his memorial service impeccable. The Juilliard played the Beethoven C-sharp Minor Quartet at the funeral, up through but not beyond the third adagio movement. We ought to assume that his was the choice of the C-sharp Minor and that his was the decision to cut it short. Personages of consequence would come to his funeral and bring with them a few troubles of the conscience; and it had never been his way to make uncomfortable the bottoms of his betters.

But all the same, dying as he had lived, he had tried to find some means of expressing at once his sense of his own culture and the perfection of his manners.

The C-sharp Minor had been the emblem that Oppenheimer and the aspiring theoretical physicists at his feet in Berkeley had held up to proclaim the difference between their own refinement and the crudities of those stranger cousins, the experimentalists.

Now his votaries were scattered, a few by the main force of public contumely, one chased to India, another to Brazil, and he himself dead, each in his exile.

Young and obscure though they were then, they would have been much too pure to distract themselves from their reveries over the C-sharp Minor to read the program notes and discover that Beethoven had instructed his publisher that "it must be dedicated to Lieutenant General Field Marshal Von Stutterheim." All the while, the portrait of the warrior had hung upon the walls of the little rooms where they dreamed, incarnating the future that would be the unpitying judge of each and all.

Esquire, December 1983

The Husband from Dow

THE DEBATE OVER those Harvard students who surrounded and held prisoner a Dow Chemical Company recruiter has so far been conducted in those terms of abstraction which are our way of missing the point about most experiences in this country. Only the *Harvard Crimson* took the trouble to try to engage the scene.

When Fred Leavitt arrived to begin his stint as Dow's missionary to the graduating seniors, he was met by four hundred students, some of whom bore posters showing children burned in Vietnam by the napalm that is among the wonders of scientific progress available from Dow. "Aren't you embarrassed?" one of the protestants asked Leavitt. "Don't you feel guilty?"

"I'm against the war," Fred Leavitt answered. *"I have the same objection as you.* I just don't know enough about what goes on in the military. No, I don't feel guilty. The whole situation is so complex, I don't know enough to accomplish anything."

Leavitt was held thereafter for seven hours, and released on the promise not to come back again. Very early, the *Crimson* suggests, his custodians began to feel a little embarrassed. One protester, who had brought his lunch bag, sacrificed it in pity to the prisoner. It is, after all, unsettling to one's sense of fitness to have seized a war criminal and have him turn out to be a mild and troubled man who, to the extent he believes himself capable of an opinion, rather thinks he agrees with you.

. . .

BUT THEN WE may be the first nation so refined that we have to adjust to the condition that complicity and the conviction of innocence are inextricable. America getting near the end of its moral tether does not, it seems, even get the pleasure of feeling wicked; it only feels helpless.

It was generally agreed that, if a Dow representative wanted to deliver a speech in favor of napalm, he should be welcomed.

The only difficulty with this expression of faith in the free market of ideas is that the napalm side has no takers. "None of us here really likes napalm," the president of Dow Chemical told *Newsweek*.

The private citizens who make it won't defend it, and the government which uses it won't discuss it.

One thinks of the melancholy futility which surrounded the scene of Fred Leavitt's martyrdom when one reads Miss Mary McCarthy's *Viet Nam*. This is an extraordinary document not just for its intelligence but for its *wifely* point of vantage. Mary McCarthy is the perfect witness to our condition, not because she is so bright, but because so many awful things have been done to her by so many helpless American men.

SHE WAS, BEFORE she became anything else, a girl who went to Vassar. The common experience of girls who went to Vassar seems to have been that they married men who fell helplessly into one of the several disgusting ways of making a living available in this country and that the wife then spent breakfast asking the husband why he did such things.

Miss McCarthy has by now so absorbed that experience that she had only to meet an American male in Vietnam and he became, without touch of flesh, her husband, long past the youth when he promised her so much, and sunk into the middle age where he chews over the surrenders he keeps explaining he could not help. She moves us even when she scorns us, because we know she wants the illusion that we are fit to be loved again.

Her final judgment on America is, of course, wifely. We have become a country, she says, pervaded by the feeling of having no choice: "just as in American hotel rooms you can decide whether or not to turn on the air conditioner, but you cannot open the window." Damn those children at Harvard; damn that wife from Vassar; why do they keep blaming that husband and father from Dow because he is resigned to being unable to open the window?

New York Post, November 7, 1967

Bombs Away

THE REVOLUTIONARY COMMITMENT may or may not be a waste of time, but how much profit can we expect to draw from an account of the experience that does not often come close to the reflective except when it is asking a question like: "Did all of us feel interested in bombing buildings only when the men we slept with were urging us on?"

To answer "yes" would cause the reader to lose all interest in the questioner; sexual bondage is not a motive but a sickness. But then, to suspend judgment and search for something beyond this self-abusive question is, I am afraid, to end up losing a deal of patience with a narrator so disinclined to bother herself with, let alone help the rest of us understand, what that something beyond might be.

It is a puzzle how an undeniably appealing young woman could have composed an autobiography called *Growing Up Underground* that leaves us with so little to respect except her troubles. Jane Alpert, to be sure, inflicted as many troubles as she endured. In November of 1969, she was arrested for having helped to plant dynamite in the Manhattan headquarters of the Marine Midland and Chase Manhattan banks, the Standard Oil offices, the Federal Building in Foley Square, and the Whitehall Selective Service Induction Center. No one was hurt in any of the bombings she planned. She disappeared two days before she was due for trial, costing her parents a $20,000 cash bail bond, sustained an aimless fugitive's life for four years before surrendering to serve a total of two years in prison. When these ordeals were over, Sam Melville, the lover who had been the moving force in her deeds, was dead and only a bitter thought to her; the woman to whom she had been closest was unjustly reviling her for treason to the revolutionary code; and she could hardly think of a comrade who was still a friend.

ALL THESE ELEMENTS add up to a most impressive cargo of experience and yet Miss Alpert's reflections upon them seem so trivial that they can hardly be called reflections at all; and what most persuades us of the shallowness of the illusions that made her a revolutionary terrorist is the patent shallowness of the disillusion that followed their crash.

She is almost the first *ancienne combattante* of the youth vanguard of the sixties to seek the explanation of the examined self. Her failure at the attempt may, of course, be to some degree generic; the overindulgence of the collective voice in solitary circumstances leaves the user with rhetorical habits that work badly for translation into the personal.

Politics are all too often a coupling of the manipulator and the manipulated; and Jane Alpert is, perhaps irretrievably, one of the manipulated. The manipulator's strength is altogether less attractive than his quarry's weakness; and the difference accounts for a certain gentleness about Jane Alpert that surprised many of those who met her after her arrest for actions that, however without malice, could hardly be called unaggressive.

She is a brave woman and has no small gifts of intelligence; but those qualities of deference and passivity that drew her to us as a kind of victim turn out to be the ones that estrange her from us as a writer. There is too much the sense of someone who cannot find an idea unless someone else locates it for her first. She seems unready for, because unconfident about, the risks of irony, subtlety, or for that matter the cultivation of the mind. She is one of those who dwell among the too-trodden ways that are the ruts of formula rather than the paths of thought.

Her memories abound with occasions that might have been moments of revelation, and yet her account of them reads like transcriptions from a parrot. Her narrative is not without its uses as a portrait of the student rebellion of the sixties; but it would, I think, be a mistake to think it typical because to take it as such would be to dismiss the dramas of that time as played out on a landscape all too like the island of legend that was exclusively inhabited by mares impregnated by the wind.

Jane Alpert seems instead to have been tangential to the radical movement until her dreadful susceptibility to suggestion made her a terrorist and set her to dreaming so giddily of herself and Sam Melville as revolutionary celebrities that she half hoped they would be caught so that the world could know what they had done.

HER ACTUAL INTRODUCTION to the catharsis of dynamite came when she was fifteen and read Ayn Rand and was implanted with "the idea that bombing a building could be a morally legitimate form of protest." Rand's "brilliant, powerful, yet sexually passive heroines who submit to the men they love remained my role models long after I had forgotten where I first heard their names."

It would be delightful to send Senator Jeremiah Denton off on the hunt after Ayn Rand as inspiration for the crimes and follies here set forth; but it seems more plausible that what we are hearing is the mechanical click of Dr. Susanne Schad-Somers, the feminist psychiatrist, who seems to have been the last of the avatars who led Jane Alpert down such a variety of roads; and we are left with the impression of hour after therapeutic hour scouring after the sources of her distraction with intervals when the patient cries out, "There, now I see; that's it," and the "it" turns out to be nothing more profound than Ayn Rand.

After her graduation from Swarthmore, Jane Alpert spent six weeks at the American School of Classical Studies in Athens:

> When it was too hot to sleep at night, we took refuge in the lounge that opened onto the porch, where there was a record player and

a small collection of American records, of which two by the Lovin' Spoonful were favorites of those of us under thirty. I played "Daydreamin'" so many times I could hum it all the way up the steps to the Acropolis.

Hers was a journey with trash as too constant a companion.

The barrenness of culture that she carried from inchoate thought to all too coherent deed seems to have been a characteristic she shared with all her lost comrades. But the triviality of motive just has to be unique. Her earlier involvements had been as tentative as they were fleeting. She traveled to the 1967 Vietnam protest at the Pentagon and fled back to New York from rumors of tear gas. She was a Columbia graduate student during the 1968 strike and was so far from being an activist that she almost crossed one of the picket lines when she was enjoined not to "let those people intimidate" her by a teacher she revered—as she was conditioned to revere all teachers, including Sam Melville, whose only credential was the air of command. A year afterward, she was living with Melville and had become an urban guerrilla. She did not so much rise to the challenge of her time as yield to infection by its vagrant air; and it would be too much to call any such history typical.

STILL SHE DOES not seem utterly singular; and after a while one commences to hear notes that belong to the orchestra more than the soloist and to sense that Jane Alpert's might be, while not *the* voice of her generation, at least a not uninstructive voice from it. The children who came to adolescence when the fifties ended seemed at the time more to be envied than any great number of the young who had lived in America before them. They breathed the air of a nation whose children were recognized as judges rather than the judged, as the young had generally been before that deliverance.

The year 1960 was an *annus mirabilis* for the unchallenged possession of the national imagination by the illusion of happy families and golden childhoods. Miss Alpert's account of her own growing up is packed full enough with the normal miseries and insecurities to suggest that she ought to have known the reality better. But then the atmosphere of those times may have been so overmastering as to make each unhappy child think his family an exception in the great herd of idyllic ones. In any case, her parents, for all the multitude of their misfortunes, do not seem to have recognized, or anyway admitted, that theirs was an unhappy family. A large part of their insulation from that uncomfortable knowledge was owed to their assurance that their children would lead lives easier and more fulfilling than their own; and it is a very short step from thinking that someone is luckier than yourself to imagining that he is better.

Along with an almost reckless love, there is an element of tribute to presumed superiority in the sacrifices Jane Alpert's parents made and the trust they continued to extend to a daughter who, by every evidence, had fallen, if only transiently, into a state of possession where she could neither appreciate the sacrifices nor deserve the trust. The impression of being at bottom a good woman that Jane Alpert conveyed even when she was a fanatic and that can still somehow survive the otherwise alienating tone of her autobiography can in some measure be credited to the fine character of her mother and father; but, their virtue aside, there was common sense in their stubborn adherence to a delusion, because to reject a child is to abandon most of the hopes of life.

And then, if the young had been as mistaken as their parents in thinking of their childhood as a blissful dawn, could there have been the proliferation of those communes whose most plausible attraction must have been the promise of re-creating the fifties babyhood, that myth enduringly mistaken for a fact?

Not to have known a happy childhood home may even have spurred in Miss Alpert a special intensity for contriving its counterfeit when she might have been more usefully engaged with the demands of maturity. It seems then only natural that we enter the realm of the domestic memoir when she recalls the ragtag and bobtail of the purposelessly violent with whom she traveled to her supreme crisis:

> For my part, I came to think of the four [of] us as a family. At times we seemed a single consciousness, divided randomly into four bodies, four biographies, but sharing a vision to which we had implic-

itly sworn loyalty. . . . Our revolution would create a universe in which all consciousness was cosmic, *in which everyone would share the bliss we knew from acid* [my italics].

The note here struck is one new to the recollections of a radical experience that, if it ended all too often in withdrawal into self-absorption, had seldom begun there. But then Jane Alpert arrived at revelation in an hour when the only real revolution was the one that chemistry had achieved with the Pill and the hallucinogen.

There were no limits to the permissible and no barriers to sensation; and there seems to have followed the "painfully familiar phenomenon in mental history" that Henry James defined as "the demoralizing influence of lavish opportunity." The gift of Miss Alpert's spiteful fairy had been this shower of temptations multiplied and rendered apparently safe.

The not-to-be-trusted bliss of acid, the numb peace of the reefer, the ecstatic moans of the arrived-at orgasm, and the promise of the revolution are all mixed in her chronicle as aspirations of equal value. Vices turn into virtues and virtue into a species of vice; fidelity comes to be seen as selfish and promiscuity as a sacrifice to the communal ideal. These, of course, belong to the order of lies that men have been telling women since shortly after the sun rose in the sky; but it would be sad to think that all our advances toward freedom have only meant a proliferation of the lies women tell themselves.

THESE UNGRACIOUS OBSERVATIONS are not meant to suggest that the young radicals of the sixties were all that much worse than their predecessors. Sam Melville was the baddest of news; and yet Miss Alpert's portrait of him has lines strikingly like those Emma Goldman drew for Johann Most, author of "a manual of instruction in the use and preparation of Nitroglycerine, Dynamite, etc." Emma Goldman lived with Most and ended up horsewhipping him; and although her description of the relationship is altogether more inhibited, it seems likely that their conjunction would have been more satisfactory if she had discovered, as Jane Alpert did with Melville, that Most was someone most easily to be stirred to erection by his mate's murmur of "Yes, Master."

Still, Most was in most other ways a far less distractable revolutionary. We have not before been confronted with a generation of radicals with so high a proportion of those who became tragic figures without ever managing to seem serious ones. And yet, even though the contagion of Miss Alpert's self-contempt works very powerfully indeed, might not her candor be one more piece of self-deception, some new operation of an incurable habit of refusing to give due notice to the complexities of nature?

The "revolution" had already passed from the assurance of universal community to fragmentation into tiny, almost accidentally coalescing colonies by the time she joined it. Chance brought her to one such group, and illusion made siblings of persons different from her, because she was a fugitive from a publishing career while the others had swum ashore from shipwreck in various streams of the rebellion.

Their comradeship sounds fortuitous and casual in everything except sexual passion or, anyway, sexual coupling. Pat Swinton went to Tanzania on her own, married an academic, left him, returned to New York where she taught in the Queens College SEEK program, judged it an instrument for infecting the black poor with middle-class fantasies, and quit to go on welfare. They met when a Swarthmore friend of Jane Alpert's picked up Pat Swinton at the post office; and in due course Jane and Pat and Sam Melville were pursuing self-awareness in bed together. Nathan Yarrow was Pat Swinton's lover and soon enough the four of them were on the sheets expanding one another's consciousness.

MELVILLE WAS THE child of an activist Communist whose withdrawal from the party had disgusted him. His choice of Herman Melville's surname suggests a nostalgia for the grandeurs of the party's Popular Front period. His only possession was his expensive guitar. He had seceded from the world of work and occupied himself with a series of scourings for nothing, the latest as a part-time circulation hand for the *Guardian*.

These were all partisans without a party and consequently bereft of those limitations of purpose that pass the affiliated radical's time in purposeless seasons. They had entered that condition of a rebel's affairs when there is too little that lies between inanition and the deed.

On their first night together, Jane Alpert was surprised to find that Sam Melville wore no underwear.

"I realized just a month or so ago that I didn't need socks either," he told her. "But I've still got a bourgeois hang-up that my feet might smell."

"How serious he was!" she reflected. "His revolution encompassed everything from the universities to the wearing of socks."

She had, of course, disablingly mistaken the caricature for the true likeness. By the time she met him, Melville had been left with so few responses to anything except whatever impulse his senses pressed upon him that, by her account at least, he was drawn to terrorism less by its social utility, if such there be, than by what Jacobo Timerman has called its sensuality.

After various fumblings, their program was set on course only after the day she told Sam Melville that she intended to assert her independence by accepting a blind date, and he thereupon placed a bomb at the Marine Midland Bank, which caused several people to be injured.

"Because I had threatened to abandon him," she says now, "even for one night, by sleeping with another man, he had taken revenge on a skyscraperful of people."

This note of vanity brings a certain relief from the monotony of her self-abasement; but here, as there, she remains a prisoner of her habit of imputing every effect to a single cause. Melville arrived at his madness after no end of frustrations until the universe subject to his control had shrunk down to Jane Alpert and his guitar; and rage at innumerable generalities may have been more his motor than any transient threat to one of the only two possessions he had left. Still she was certain that nothing moved him except his anger at her; and the more sure she grew that he was crazy, the more pressed she was to take up her wifely responsibility and put her unstable husband's business on a sound footing:

Most of the tasks associated with the bombings were extremely simple and required less coordination than preparing a dinner party. Rather than leave the stolen dynamite in Sam's less-than-competent care, from then on I placed myself at the head of the conspiracy and prodded everyone else into action under my direction.

She was the only member of their band who had lately functioned in a responsible job, and whatever efficiency it achieved seems to have been owing to the habits of discipline she had preserved from that employment. Her intervention was a distinct service to the deprived classes; Melville was too careless a fellow to leave a time bomb and then alert the occupants of the premises to its presence; and Jane Alpert's administration was admirably scrupulous in its concern to protect the charwomen who might otherwise be the only victims of late-night *attentats* against corporate headquarters from which the common oppressors of mankind had long since departed for Greenwich, Connecticut.

BUT WITHOUT HER talent for organization, Melville might have been largely ineffective and gone unnoticed and therefore unpunished. Only careerists can manage careers, even ones as bizarre and foredoomed as this one. She was unlucky to know Melville; but he was not all that lucky to know her. The firmness of her purpose could well have been more fatal to him than any instability of his; she made it possible for him to find himself for the first time in his life in command of an organization that was, in its way, a success; and he used that new eminence to ruin them all by inviting a government informant into the firm.

When caught he sank into catatonia and went numbly off to prison, where he was quickened back to life by the Attica riots and ran about the yard seeking the means to make another bomb until the state troopers killed him. Jane Alpert had already begun tending toward her radical feminist phase; and, after grieving for his death awhile, she repudiated him in a manifesto that ended:

You fast and organize and demonstrate for Attica. Don't send me
news clippings, don't tell me how much those deaths moved you.
I will mourn the deaths of 42 male supremacists no longer.

The feminist ideologue Robin Morgan had by then made her appearance as the newest of Alpert's succession of proctors and had led
her to the conviction that Sam Melville was not a communist at all but
a fascist. Persons less confident of labels may wonder whether he had
ever been either one or the other or anything at all except the hippie
of the fifties marooned in the sixties that a Columbia strike veteran
remembers from the days when Melville was hanging about the Students for a Democratic Society.

He had in any case conquered her from the grave as he had domi-
nated her in life. He emerges in his craziness somehow the hero of her
narrative, because he has again profited from her weakness for being led
too far. He had debased her when she loved him; and now she debased
herself through hating him. Simply by being there as a ghost, he had
become the object of an injustice from her; and he had beaten her once
again.

Miss Alpert has one of those minds that can first bless and then
curse forty-two dead convicts without at any point in the swing of its
pendulum exhibiting the smallest inclination to consider the possibility
of differences among them as individuals. To live awhile in the company of such a mind is to grow not just bone weary but alarmingly close
to thoughts as cold as hers.

A CERTAIN SENSE of proportion is confessedly wanting in someone
who felt drawn to Miss Alpert when he met her as an indicted terrorist
and who likes her less now that he has dealt with her as a writer. No
one can reasonably quarrel with her renunciation of her old courses or
fairly censure this new undertaking as a betrayal of her former friends.
They were bad courses and bad friends who have, in most cases, been
more false to her than she ever was to them. It is not simply her
conduct then or now that alienates us but rather the cast of mind that

she seems to have carried unaltered through multiple changes of attitude.

She remains someone so overloaded with grievances that she cannot distinguish between those that are proper and those that are beside the point. It is that confusion, I think, that accounts for the extraordinary absence of generosity that seems to compel her to name nearly every man who ever seduced and abandoned her and then shroud the identity of pretty much everyone who helped to hide her when she was a fugitive. Resentment remains a more powerful force in her nature than gratitude. That imbalance was, you finally decide, a plague that all too few of her comrades had the luck or character to escape; they were in too many cases persons who brought more passion to quarreling than to coupling. Because, for all their professions of love, they could not trust one another, they could not restrain one another:

> No one wanted to admit that with explosives already in our possession, we were having second thoughts about using them. No one wanted to be the first in the group to look like a coward. . . . Not one of us was capable of handling this new power; not one of us was brave enough to back away from it.

The dream of power had displaced and overcome the fantasy of comradeship; and each of them was alone with the self. It is from such states of perceived isolation that men and women proceed to the worst of political follies, which is to follow one's ideas to their logical conclusion and visit one's aggression upon targets as inappropriate as Brink's guards, airport peacekeepers, and cleaning women. Those who had begun assured of their warmth and their concern had ended cold and careless.

There is, I think, something curiously American in this incapacity to concede that you have wasted a sizable part of your life. Not to be able to make that concession keeps us somehow stunted, cuts us off from the redeeming sense of irony that rose up to rescue Swann after his long agony with Odette: "To think that . . . I've longed to die, that I've experienced my greatest love, for a woman who didn't appeal to me, who wasn't even my type." Life runs like that in all too many of its varieties; and disablement by the self-importance that assumes that one is so special as to have deserved a better reward is a considerable handicap to reconciliation with reality. Miss Alpert would be altogether a more helpful witness if she understood that the least useful way to look back at your mistakes is to be pompous about them.

The New York Review of Books, January 21, 1982

Dead End Kids

I

A DISTINGUISHED BRITISH journalist, whose name has faded in the memory, was dispatched to cover the revolutionary tumults of the Paris Commune of 1870.

The Rue de Rivoli, he wrote, was full of ruffians.

"And they are," he went on, "ruffians of the worst sort. They are ruffians with principles."

The suddenly blazing funeral pyre of the revolution of the sixties has made ruffians of once-principled people and principled people of formerly simple ruffians. A very few of the affluent have joined a very few of the indigent in a coalition of common destructive passions.

Malefactors have come upon the stage whose motives baffle and whose vehemence frightens law officers used to commonsensical criminals.

This strange chain of events may have begun last month when a group of demonstrators came to Kennedy Airport armed with mason jars filled with battery acid to register their protest against the departing South African Springboks rugby team. In the absence of the Springboks, this cadre threw the acid at the Port Authority security personnel instead, leaving Patrolman Evan Goodstein legally blind.

The all-white, predominantly female band now proclaiming itself the Springboks Five was sent to Rikers Island at $10,000 bail per arrestee. On Friday, Eve Rosahn, their leader, was bailed with her mother's cash. In the interim, the license-plate numbers on an automobile seen near last week's Brinks payroll robbery had been traced to Eve Rosahn.

This discovery led District Attorney John Santucci to get a court order forbidding the release of any of the Springboks Five without examining the bail money for the chance of its having come from the fruits of crime. Those suspicions were dissolved when Eve Rosahn's mother took the stand and turned out to be a woman with a substantial property in the wool trade and an income of no less than $100,000.

Eve Rosahn's companions came to Queens Criminal Court yesterday to argue their right to bail and she was with them at the bar. She wore an Afghan scarf of rare and beautiful weave, small imitation pearls in her ears, a black velvet blouse and coarse blue denim pants; those puzzled by the ambivalence of this last half-choked cry of the revolutionary impulse could not have found it more nicely exemplified than by a costume that was half the cocktail hour and half the street.

On Friday Samuel Smith and Nathaniel Burns, two alumni of the Black Panthers, went for a ride in a car that had also been connected to the Brinks robbery. They roamed about to no visible purpose in a vehicle with license plates whose numbers were indelibly engraved in the memory of every law officer in Queens. They were stopped; there was a shoot-out and Samuel Smith was killed and Nathaniel Burns captured.

If they had bothered to find another pair of license plates, they would be free men still. The terminal writhings of the revolution had produced a cast of characters who had shown themselves vicious at Kennedy and the Nanuet Mall, had turned up unexpectedly wealthy in a Queens courtroom, and were now revealed as suicidal.

They have become, however appallingly, evocators of classic American literature. In *The Great Gatsby*, Nick Carraway sums up Tom and Daisy Buchanan and a lot of other Americans, when he says that they were careless people. These are careless people; but the Buchanans were careless only of other people; the last lost warriors of the revolution are careless of themselves and everyone else.

By now you begin to think most of Katherine Boudin, if only because, however brighter, she is like so many children who have lived in ours and others homes. She was brought, one thinks, to her terrible pass because she was unable to accept what reality had done to the future she had embraced ten years before. She had been underground since 1970 and the war whose triumphant end she expected had become increasingly irrelevant.

She had, in different ways, arrived at the place Jean Harris reached when she was unable to admit to herself that she had wasted fourteen years of her life upon the wrong man. Jean Harris shot him; and Kathy Boudin may have ridden with armed and homicidal robbers because she, too, could not admit that she had wasted her life for an idea that had fallen out of everyone else's consciousness. You do wish these two women had read Colette and that Nathaniel Burns had read Frederick Douglass.

II

THE ARREST OF Katherine Boudin sounds more like a collapse than a capture. Michael Koch, the off-duty prison guard who made her his prisoner, reports that the last words she is ever likely to pronounce as a free woman were, "Don't shoot me. I didn't shoot them. *He* did!"

With that cry of desperate solitude, a twenty-year search for comrades and communities had reached its destination. She had ended as the companion and apparent accomplice of strangers, who were mad, bad, and dangerous to know. So, too, one feels forced to say, had she become or anyway thought she had until the awful Tuesday afternoon near Nyack when all that remains of the upper-middle-class urban guerrilla corps moved at last to the suburbs.

Something stubborn in Katherine Boudin had kept her a fugitive through the eleven years since she fled the exploded ruins of the townhouse on East 11th Street on the afternoon when Cathy Wilkerson's father was away and her friends were assembling a bomb in the cellar. Kathy Boudin left the body of Diana Oughton, her Bryn Mawr roommate, behind in the wreck; and now her travels have brought her to one of those places where the living envy the dead. Friends like Mark Rudd, Bernardine Dohrn, and Cathy Wilkerson have left the Weather Underground, given themselves up and accepted the punishment appointed by law enforcement agencies that, having almost forgotten them, were, in most cases, disposed to be lenient.

The mocking sadness of Kathy Boudin's reentry is that, if she too had surrendered, the law would likely have been easy upon her. She was in the bathtub when Cathy Wilkerson's father's house blew up; and, if that circumstance did not entirely remove every suspicion of guilty knowledge, it did make plausible a claim that she had only stopped by to tidy up.

But she would not give in. The Weather Underground dreamed at first of reaching and rousing the working class; but, as time went on and it faded from the public consciousness, its members withdrew to themselves and became one of those communes that have very little in common with any substantial element in the society around them. First comes isolation and then despair and at last the determination never to concede failure.

Kathy Boudin had become the last of the children of the fifties, the survivor and terrible tragic queen of a generation appointed to be golden. The fifties children were thought of as the reason for the struggles and the promise of the triumph of the dreams of their parents. The difference between lower- and upper-middle-class atrocities is that, in the first case, we feel sorry only for the families of the victims and in the second we feel sorry for the families of the victims and the criminals alike.

Kathy Boudin is the daughter of Leonard Boudin, a radical lawyer who lived and fought through the loneliness of the radicalism of the fifties and endured to become an eminence in the sixties. Mrs. I. F. Stone is Kathy's mother's sister; Kathy's brother and cousins moved into shining legal careers, and she seems to have been accounted the brightest of them all. And yet somewhere there was the anger that brought her to the shock and the horror of the moment when, abandoned, she yielded herself to her shocked and horrified captor. It is an anger that cannot be explained and its result would in any case cancel any excuse; but perhaps the fact of a loving family sustained her brother and cousins through the years when, to be a radical's child was to be a kind of pariah, and perhaps, for Kathy Boudin alone, the shelter of that love was not enough. All that was left from her childhood was the shame of admitting the failure of one's promise.

There is very little purpose in preaching over persons who will, in all probability, die in prison. Terrorism had been this lovely word and now it was this horrid deed whose roots lay in some dream of striking at the oppressor and whose reeking flower is the death of two police-men, either of whom, if he had seen Kathy Boudin at a loss on the street, would have come up to her and, with great respect, inquired, "Is there anything I can do for you, Miss?"

III

TWELVE YEARS AGO Sekou Odinga climbed a hill on Manhattan's Harlem River Drive and prepared to fire upon a police precinct across the river in the Bronx. He was interrupted by a squad car and made his escape to a place where the police could have arrested him whenever they chose.

There is reason to suspect that the police preferred to let him go his way, confident that he would do worse in due course and be eligible for long-term imprisonment. By the spring of 1969, they thought they had him; he became one of twenty-one Black Panthers indicted for conspiracy to bomb New York department stores in Easter week. But he eluded this raiding party, too, and found refuge in Algeria.

There had been far less to the Panther bombing conspiracy than met the headlines; it seems in fact to have been a compound of the imaginations of the Police Department's Bureau of Special Services and of young black fumblers after revolution, and the evidence of true intent was so slender that a jury that had listened to it for eight months acquitted the defendants in two hours.

Nothing was heard of Sekou Odinga thereafter until Friday when he finally had the shoot-out with the police he had always sworn he would. When it was over, he was found hiding under a truck in a warehouse near Shea Stadium and his traveling companion was dead. And so once more the old yearbook photographs come up again from dust; it is reunion time on the parched and deserted campus of Revolutionary U., that arena whose crowds and tumults defined the end of the sixties. What we watch is not the dawn of the revolution, but the dark and lurid night of its end. Only the despairing toughness is left. The protagonists are no longer young and they have raised no children to take their place. There is no one except themselves to play their parts; they have been broken to the knowledge that they cannot trust anyone under thirty.

Here is the last ditch; the rear guard has gathered the remnants of all the lost battalions and turns desperately at bay. In Nyack, Rockland District Attorney Kenneth Gribetz brought before Village Judge Robert P. Lewis the only four parties he is so far in a position to charge with the death of a Brink's guard and two policemen in Tuesday's assault on a payroll truck at the Nanuet Shopping Mall.

Kathy Boudin looked as though she had spent the years since her disappearance in the woods. The eyes of wild children are wounded and frantic like these. She seemed in some way different from the others; but then never had any group no larger than four persons appeared so disparate—Judith Clark, solemn and adamant; the black mystery of Samuel Brown, alternating somnolence and groans of pain; and David Gilbert, putative father of Kathy Boudin's baby, smiling, a shade silly, no little embarrassed. It had been their last defeat that, by the evidence, Kathy Boudin and David Gilbert had failed in the implacability true terrorists require. Detective Arthur Keenan, a survivor of the police party that had stopped their U-Haul truck at the entrance to the New York State Thruway, remembered that Kathy Boudin had gotten out of the front seat, put her hands to her cheeks in a gesture that was half surrender and half despair, and gone and stood quietly in the grass. Keenan had barely noticed David Gilbert, who seems to have debarked from behind the wheel and to have left in the aftermath of the ensuing horror and made his escape without her. Then the rear of the truck was opened, and out, by Keenan's account, came real terror in the person of Samuel Brown.

Brown was sitting in court with his head resting on Judith Clark's shoulder. When Keenan was asked to identify the man who had shot Sergeant Edward O'Grady, Brown lifted his head with obliging dignity and allowed Keenan's finger to point unmistakably at him.

Brown, Judith Clark, and Gilbert were caught when the Honda they were driving crashed into a wall a few miles down the road. Only Brown was hurt in that accident, and it could be duly noted that Brown was the only one of the three with a weapon, and it could be duly remembered that, in that long lost time, the black militants used to complain that the white radicals were out to get them killed.

Samuel Brown is the only one of them with no prior claim on historical memory; until now he had knocked about obscurely on the street as a burglar, a small robber, a suspect car thief, and a jumper over subway turnstiles. The lawyer Leonard Boudin, her father, met Kathy with a tender smile and she calmed and warmed noticeably; and, as they quietly talked during the recess, it could be understood that she had been again enfolded into a family and, deserve this great comfort or not, she at least was not alone. The others were. She and Samuel Brown were strangers again; and it would have been better for both, let alone the victims, if they had always been.

IV

THE FEDERAL GOVERNMENT has begun the trial of six persons suspected of having planned and helped execute the Nanuet Shopping Mall payroll robbery in an atmosphere curiously amiable for the unfolding of a history that encompasses four homicides.

Much of the credit for the pleasant, if not altogether appropriate,

allegro of the opening passages was owed to the conductor, Judge
Kevin Duffy, who regularly addressed the defendants as "you guys" and
"you fellows," and as regularly evoked responses no less sociable in their
informality.

Three of the four male defendants wear Muslim shawls that announce their self-definition as revolutionaries who have seceded from
the United States and proclaimed themselves citizens of their own
Republic of New Afrika. Their colloquies with Duffy have the air of
exchanges between ambassadors.

Ruins run to population by the abandoned and the savage, victims
who know no recourse except to be victimizers. The Brink's gang is an
odd mix from the wreckage of the white Weathermen and the Black
Panthers, and if all those in the dock are guilty, they can only belong
to the category of ruffian hardest of all to understand, which is, of
course, the ruffian with principles.

As Assistant U.S. Attorney Robert Litt told the government's version of their tale yesterday, it was not easy to distinguish their downward progress from that of the ordinary ruffian.

Litt's history began with 1976, when Sekou Odinga and fugitive
Mutulu Shakur, two survivors of the Panthers, robbed a bank in Pittsburgh. There began an obscure succession of similar adventures until
their little group began to aspire to broader public recognition of its
endeavors and achieved it in 1979 when Odinga breached the casual
security of the Clinton, New Jersey, reformatory, smuggled two guns
into the cell where Joanne Chesimard was lodged for robbery and
murdering a policeman, broke her out, and hid her safe in Pittsburgh.

By now Odinga and Shakur had refined their structure and, by
Litt's account, vehemently coarsened their methods. They had a five-
member central command that they called "the Family" and
the white auxiliaries they later recruited called "the Collective." The
Family, said Litt, "did the planning and led the attacks."

Because they thought of themselves as bandits with a cause, they
kept careful account of the robbery proceeds and invested them in an
acupuncture clinic and a store in the Bronx; and because they were
careful enterprisers, they rented a network of safe houses, equipped

themselves with bulletproof vests and weapons extending to a machine gun, and never completed an operation without compiling a report on its technical lessons.

In due course they began to understand the uses of middle-class whites as allies to survey their target areas, drive the panel trucks concealing the action squad, and otherwise serve as protective coloration. There were no murders early on; the Family had but to show its weapons to cow the payroll guards. But, at Danbury, Connecticut, in 1981, a Brink's guard locked his door and drove away, leaving the Family in the dust. Thereafter, by Litt's account, the Family came out shooting. Whatever principles the ruffian brings to the road, he generally meets murder somewhere on the way.

When Litt had finished, Sekou Odinga made the opening statement in his defense. He began with almost winning good cheer. ("I do not agree with the government's interpretation of what this is all about.") He went on to describe himself as an armed fighter for the revolution. "If that means killing, taking up arms, and fighting for our liberation, we are ready to do so." It was a display rich in the dignity of an accused too proud to pretend to be a victim of mistaken identity, but it might have had an appeal more resonant if the blood of four workingmen could be wiped away.

V

TYRONE RISON GIVES the inescapable impression of someone whose life has left his soul a bleak and barren place. And yet, if any remembered name could still warm that arctic space, you have to guess that it would be Sekou Odinga's.

They met as fellow citizens in the Republic of New Afrika in 1976. Rison affirms and Odinga conscientiously scorns to deny that together they robbed banks and armored cars by force of arms. They shared the view of themselves as not mere hoodlums but freedom fighters; but,

Rison says, their war turned sour for them in the spring of 1981 when a payroll guard was killed on one of their forays. After that, according to Tyrone Rison, they agreed that the time might be at hand for hanging up the gun.

By then, their five-member family had widened to untrustworthy proportions and they were jointly alarmed about the risk of future adventures with untried and undisciplined forces. That judgment was sound; in October 1981, a horridly botched armored-car holdup in Nanuet, New York, left a Brink's guard and two policemen dead.

Tyrone Rison had not gone for that ride, and it is far from certain that Sekou Odinga had either, although he is charged with direct participation in the Brink's disaster. These two comrades would not meet again except as enemies in a federal courtroom. Rison had robbed a bank in Georgia, been caught, made his deal, and satisfied the bargain by accepting service as a government informant.

Now, Sekou Odinga is on trial in U.S. District Court, Manhattan, as one of six parties accused of various parts in a conspiracy whose history crashed at Nanuet. Tyrone Rison is the government's witness-in-chief. Odinga is his own defense counsel, which is to say that in essence, he disdains to offer a disclaimer of imputations that seem to him cause for pride.

Yesterday morning, it came Sekou Odinga's turn to cross-examine Tyrone Rison. "Free the land," he said as pleasantly as though they had arrived for breakfast at one of the safe houses of their former dispensation.

"Free the land," Tyrone Rison replied.

"What should I call you?" Odinga asked, and Tyrone Rison answered, "Whatever you feel like calling me." And then all suspicion that the accused was about to call down some imprecation upon the accuser's head dissolved when, in a voice of almost fraternal regret, Odinga reminded Rison that he used to call Rison "La-Lupe," his African name.

Rison conceded they had formed their highwaymen's cadre to help the black poor because "we couldn't do the things we wanted to do, in our opinion, any other way." They had joined not to be robbers but to free the people, Rison agreed. "Do you feel you're fighting for black people now?" Odinga inquired.

"Yes, in my way," Rison replied.

He had not changed his mind, he went on; he still thought of his old friends not as criminals but freedom fighters. The difference now, he explained, is in "the way the United States government views our actions."

Odinga passed to Rison's testimony about the sortie that broke Joanne Chesimard out of the jail where she was a long-term prisoner. He did not bother to dispute the details; he seemed rather to have brought them up to savor them. That hour remains his highest glory.

The oddly gentle tone did not alter even at the end when Odinga asked if Rison thought of himself now as working for the government. "No," Rison answered. "I'm working for myself."

And Sekou Odinga turned from this ice floe and sat down with no sign of recrimination. He could do his time and would not descend to harshness with someone else who couldn't. The passage had done no noticeable service toward lightening the proof against him; but that had hardly been its point, for Sekou Odinga does not care overmuch about staying out of prison. What counts far more is to be remembered as, in his rough way, a man of honor. Forgiveness is an aspect of honor.

VI

TO THINK OF the Brink's armored car holdup in Nyack is to remember the deaths of two policemen and a security guard; and to watch the resultant murder and conspiracy trial is to sit in the graveyard of a dozen dead revolutions.

One of those revolutions had its transient hour in the sixties when a medical commune took control of Lincoln Hospital in the Bronx.

Jeral Wayne Williams and Sondra Margo Mitchell met as comrades in that uprising; he was the new administration's acupuncture specialist, and she was a public health officer.

All too soon, they lost the ground they had seized; he went off to an acupuncture clinic in Harlem and she to precincts as alien to her prior dedication as the sales counter at Saks. By then, Jeral Williams called himself Mutulu Shakur and in December 1980, he asked her to lend him her apartment in Mount Vernon for his workings in mysterious ways.

For Margo Mitchell, the revolution's business had become her own; and she agreed to do its bidding for $200 on the first occasion and $500 on the next. The first time Mutulu Shakur and friends gathered, she says, she tarried long enough to see the white women put on wigs and the black men strap on holsters. Her recollections, if accurate, are vague: The only paying guest she claims vividly to recall was Eddie Joseph and his bare chest was better fixed in her memory than his face.

Eddie Joseph had, she swore, observed that she was a pretty lady. Eddie Joseph has always had an appreciative eye for some women, and even more women have had an appreciative eye for him. Then Margo Mitchell left the premises to her tenants and had nothing else to report except that a few days later, she was disturbed to find a stock of handguns under her bed.

She called Mutulu and told him he had "to take the stuff out of here," and apologetically he complied. It was many months before the FBI agents found a bulletproof vest under her mattress; the lost and found desk of Chateau Margo had become a trove of exotic treasures.

Still, she remained greedy enough for the cash if not the company of the customers; and she says that she last leased her apartment to Mutulu and friends on October 20, 1981, and that she went to work before they arrived and returned after they had left. The next night, Cheri Dalton knocked on her door to report that "things went bad" and to hand her a bundle of clothes to be disposed of. Margo Mitchell carried this consignment of what may or may not have been damaging evidence to the Salvation Army for the sake, no doubt, of the tax deduction. Mutulu later stopped by to suggest that if the FBI intruded, she should tell its agents that theirs was no more than a doctor-patient relationship. By then, the Lincoln Hospital revolution was a long way back; the FBI seems to have had minimal trouble working Margo Mitchell around. Now, she is a federal witness testifying in the conspiracy trial of six of the alleged armed robbers whom Mutulu Shakur left behind when he escaped arrest.

Yesterday, Margo Mitchell appeared for cross-examination; a summer cold had borne her down over the weekend and her voice was a croak and her sniffles confined her answers to monosyllables. There was nothing to do but send her home; the gnawing of the revolution's trapped children by its escaped ones would have to wait another day.

But it will grind remorselessly on; and for all the awful sins imputed, it is nonetheless a pitiable sight. Eddie Joseph and Mutulu Shakur were stranded together in a Greenwich Village apartment a year ago last March and being bugged by the FBI. As evidence of robbery and murder, the transcripts of their talks are scrappy; but their sense of abandonment is all-pervasive.

By now, these shipwrecks agree, they can trust only each other. They talk of selling cocaine to stake a new beginning for the struggle. The revolution had come to a place where junk was all that was left of it.

New York Newsday, Fall 1981 and Spring 1983

The Promise of Huey P. Newton

W E KNOW THE year almost to the day when Huey P. Newton set out to redeem the streets of Oakland. But who among us can identify the hour when he ceased to try?

The chief disciplines left to his existence seem to have been governed in the end by the schedules of criminal courts. Had he not died by gunshot, he could hardly have been noticed until September 15 next, the deadline for repayment of the $15,000 he had conceded lifting from the funds of a community school.

For Huey Newton's was one of those lives whose tragedy abides not in the death but in a dying that began a while back on the road to yesterday.

We cannot even fix the time he died: It might have been yesterday when he was killed on just the sort of Oakland street whose dreams of better things he once embodied, or it might have been nine years ago when he took a portion of an allotment for the children of those streets and spent it on himself.

The image of Huey P. Newton was first widely established as a poster, and the ambivalence of the feelings it evoked would sit unresolved until the end. It was the vision of a young stranger, a spear in his left hand and a rifle in his right. He was seated in a wicker chair. The first thought was of the revolutionary despoiler of a club for white hunters and the second, and more lasting, was the vulnerability of his face.

He was founder and minister of defense of the Black Panther Party, which had entered the history of publicity when a small band of its members left Oakland to appear suddenly on the steps of the California State Capitol carrying their rifles and asserting the right of the people to bear arms.

By the time his poster had spread his fame, Huey Newton was in prison, charged with the death of one Oakland policeman and the wounding of another in a shoot-out after a motor vehicle dispute in the fall of 1967. That event established what would be the permanent incompatibility of his two images of the baddest and at the same time the best, so *bad* that he had killed a cop, and yet so *good* that he could never kill anyone with malice.

Newton himself appears never to have known what had happened that night, and he was by no means alone in that confusion. His first jury could find him guilty of no worse than manslaughter and, when its verdict was reversed and remanded, two other juries dissolved in disagreement as to whether he was guilty of anything. Juries that tried Huey Newton had a way of always ending hung, simply because, like pretty much everyone else and perhaps himself not least of all, they did not know who he was.

So long as he was invisible in prison, he was concrete as a conception but, once he came out to the open air, he became an abstraction as a presence. There were never more than three thousand Panthers in all, and they differed from one another as widely as is the usual case with those whom cops and journalists are inclined to group under one all-encompassing label. They fell into quarrels, some of them cunningly stimulated by the FBI, until Huey Newton's high quotient of mother wit convinced him to lay down the gun and put himself to community work.

But he could not find a community. Perhaps he never could have. I remember having a drink with him in the early seventies in the Palm Room of the Plaza Hotel, to which he had shrewdly repaired because none of the factions then breathing mayhem would think to look for him there. The trio played a little Brahms and Huey Newton looked about him and said that this was not a premise where he'd be hanging out much. Shortly thereafter, the crimes imputed to him settled into the pattern all too familiar to the street.

He had given up and apparently yielded to the street he had sought once to save. Now it has given him the death that is the street's too familiar wage for those who obey its rules. He will, I suppose, have his place in history. His good qualities, not unmixed though they were, might have entitled him to the far higher place that belongs to those who have been permitted to help change it.

New York Newsday, August 23, 1989

G. Gordon Liddy:
Knight Errant

G. GORDON LIDDY came to New York Friday to cut the ribbon on the New York branch office of Gordon Liddy Associates, worldwide security consultants. His film biography is ready for the fall television season, he summers on the four hundred feet of Potomac River beach he recently bought from Allen Drury, and now he is becoming a conglomerate.

He is proof incarnate that no one succeeds like the man who establishes a monopoly. Gordon Liddy has a corner on honor, a commodity in the shortest supply; and, thanks to the prodigal expenditure of that resource, the most masterly strokes of shrewder men cannot match the coup he has brought off with his blunders.

He reached this summit, of course, through a prodigy of incompetence followed by an extreme of suffering. First, he botched the Watergate burglary. After his arrest, he scorned to proclaim his repentance and to turn in his fellow conspirators. He paid for violating the code of dishonor that official convention has taught the trapped felon with fifty-two months in nine different prisons, through which he was successively shunted because his stubbornly resistant disposition made him the most obdurate and inconvenient of cons.

Why, a skeptic wondered Friday, would he expect a corporation to hire him of all possible guardians of its security? There are questions with smaller foundations in common sense after all; the last client who trusted his security to Gordon Liddy was rewarded with a one-way

ticket to San Clemente on Air Force One. "My reputation," Gordon
Liddy replied. "Anyone who hires me knows that he won't read what
he told me this afternoon in the next day's newspaper."

He is, he pointed out, barred from active service in his new enterprise's fieldwork because his criminal record still makes him ineligible
for a private investigator's license. This disqualification could at once be
recognized as a particular commercial asset, because nothing could so
solidly guarantee the success of any plan devised by G. Gordon Liddy
as the assurance that he was forbidden to have any part in carrying it
out.

At his worst, there was something comforting about Liddy; there
will always be plots against human liberty, and how can we be safer
than with someone this certain to mess up their execution? Not the
least of his manifold talents is for getting caught.

He was consultant-in-residence on the set of *Will*, his autobiographical film. One of the scenes showed him campaigning for Congress in
Poughkeepsie. One of the props was a dish of prize cookies. After the
shooting had passed through various stages of repetition, a production
assistant noticed that some party unknown was pilfering the cookies
between takes. A surveillance was set up and the perpetrator detected.
He was, of course, G. Gordon Liddy. Some guardian angel of his
essential purity protects him from getting away with even the tiniest
trespass.

His larger trespasses are all behind him. His juices have cooled. The
old rigid guardsman's posture has softened; he permits a few vagrant
hairs in a mustache that used to look as barbered as an East Hampton
hedge; and he even allows himself a trace of a slouch, the way old ball
players feel free to go to fat after their plaques go up in the Hall of
Fame. He has proved what he was made of, and he does not have to
display it any longer.

He had anticipated very little derring-do when he conceived of his
security service. His first intention was to concentrate on computer
fraud, an advance in criminal technology he discovered through exposure to a number of its practitioners who were his prison companions.
He was surprised to find that most of the corporate executives he

approached were rather more alarmed about the prospect that terrorism, in time, might grow into a fashionable enough article of import to
confront them with the risk of being kidnapped.

And so, he will put his mind to methods of counterterrorism, and
all of us ought to pray that he can come up with some means half as
effective as the only sovereign remedy, which would be to produce a
strain of terrorists as inept as G. Gordon Liddy. No matter; there are
higher qualities than competence. The rarest and highest is honor;
G. Gordon Liddy put his to the test and endured; and no one has a
better right to franchise it. He can be to the market in honor what
McDonald's is to the market in hamburgers, and he has less reason to
worry about competition, since knights errant are an otherwise extinct
species.

New York Newsday, July 12, 1981

The Imaginary Country

ACAUTIONARY NOTE: These articles are impressions without credentials as findings. I can only hope that they are at least true to my own feelings, because I have not learned the truth about Nicaragua and would be surprised if I ever could. I have been left wondering indeed whether, beyond her immemorial sorrows and her pitiful and by no means unheroic struggles for some new and better beginning, there exist such things as definable, inarguable truths about Nicaragua.

There are at best only clues, and one of the more suggestive comes from an open letter dispatched in April 1986 to then President Daniel Ortega by a woman active in the Social Christian Party. "When you speak for and in the name of the people," she wrote, "I think you are referring to a people of your imagination."

If such be the case, the president of Nicaragua is not alone in his confusion. Nicaraguas of fantasy are universal realities in our discourse: The assistant secretary of state for Latin America describes an imaginary Leninist Nicaragua; our President urges us to the colors of an imaginary army of imaginary freedom fighters; and every Nicaragua that is introduced into our congressional debates is, in its way, an imaginary Nicaragua.

And try though I may, I too must depend on too little that is better than my own imagination; and anyone with the patience to read what follows would do well always to keep it in mind that what he will get is not what is known but what at best is only what can be surmised.

I

"The National Commission for the Promotion and Protection of Human Rights was created in June 1980 as an autonomous government agency charged to promote respect for human rights in Nicaragua.

The Permanent Commission on Human Rights in Nicaragua is a non-governmental organization created to promote human rights . . . relations between [it] and the government are tense."

—*AMERICAS WATCH REPORT ON NICARAGUA, April 1983*

To DIAGRAM THE institutions of Nicaragua is to chart a kind of symbiosis of the polarized. Every action in its public life has an unequal and opposite reaction.

There is the Catholic Church of tradition and the Church of the People. There is the government labor federation and there is an exiguous bloc of independent unions, and each has nothing in common with the other except a shared deprivation of the right to strike.

In every aspect of institutional life, the voice of the revolution resounds and back comes the reply, enforcedly feebler, in the name of one or another beleaguered constituency. There seem to be two of everything, and, naturally, there are two human rights commissions.

Lino Hernandez is national coordinator of the Permanent Commission on Human Rights, which is, as Americas Watch puts it, "an organization highly critical of the Sandinista government."

On June 16, nine women of the sort sometimes referred to as "of the people" were sitting in the antechamber below his office. Theirs were the faces that wait in the reception rooms of clinics for the poor.

Lino Hernandez greeted his visitor with a handshake and the delivery of the month-by-month reports of his commission since January last. Until last April they were, like the stock in Managua's dollar store, products reserved not for the native but for the traveler from another shore, because, for a while before, the government had refused to allow their distribution to its own public so long as Hernandez refused to submit them to the censor.

The opening pleasantries are essayed and Lino Hernandez does not laugh. Until now on this journey, every Nicaraguan has managed to muster a smile, however weak the joke, but here at last is one too tired and too saddened to laugh even for the sake of the courtesies he is otherwise scrupulous to observe.

But then the visitor has already been warned by a person highly trustworthy that Lino Hernandez has been at his vigil so long that his views can sometimes be "a bit hysterical" and that it is wise to be cautious about accepting them whole.

In any case, the truth about Nicaragua is approachable, if at all, not through documents but by reliance on random chance. Would it be possible for Hernandez and the visitor to go down to the waiting room, unselectively pick one of its occupants, and ask her to come and tell us what had brought her there?

She sat down in a chair in the middle of Hernandez's office in a dress the color of a paper bag with two aching holes that wear and tear had designed in her skirt. The visitor would fix his gaze and she would turn her head to profile almost as though she were too embarrassed to display her misery in its full frontal force. Once in a while, she would pause in her narrative and slowly, mutely, wipe her eyes and nose on her sleeve.

She said as best she could through these intervals that four evenings earlier, her husband had disappeared and her neighbors had told her that four members of the Security Police had come to the house with their rifles and in their red jeep and taken him away.

He and she and their two children lived in Granada, thirty miles to the southeast, and he was an ice cream vendor. She did not know what he could have done to offend; his relations with the local Committee of Sandinista Defense had been amiable; he had stood guard when told to, and he had never before been in jail. She had inquired of the police and they told her that they would declare her husband missing.

"Every day he would come back with the money to find food," she said, "and that night he was unable to do it."

A neighbor, whose son had once been missing in circumstances similarly opaque, had told her about the Commission on Human Rights, and she had come to Managua by bus and taken a taxi because she would not otherwise know how to find it.

By then the eye had settled itself on the hand that was almost fiercely grasping the whole of her fortune, a wad of brown paper currency thick enough to choke a camel and, since it was in cordobas— tens, twenties, and with luck an odd hundred or so—perhaps worth enough to buy five tortillas. She went off at last to recite her sorrows for formal transmission to Lenin Czerna, commander of the General Office of State Security, who has not yet quite flatly told Hernandez that complaints in writing will pass entirely unconsidered.

She identified herself in her declaration as Mercedes Moreira Amador, twenty-two. It seemed impossible that she could be this young and so swiftly linked to the chain of helpless subjugation that has run immutably through generations of the Nicaraguan poor. Her grandmother might have sat, equally ashamed of tears, in the same state of baffled bereavement and talked about her affliction by some whim of one of the Somozas.

No more than the tyrants it came to sweep forever into history does this revolution think it a debt of mere decency to tell a woman whose husband has been taken by the security police where he is or why he is there. But, if this habit of indifference to the victim has not altered, its application to the suspect appears improvedly less cruel.

If Mercedes Amador's husband's case is average, the chances are that in two weeks or so, his experience with this variety of the revolution's attentions to the poor will end with his release, physically unharmed and with his detention officially unexplained. Of course, Hernandez speculated, he may owe his misfortune not to his possible heresies but to his trade. Nicaraguan Security Police have traditionally set a high value on the assistance of ice cream vendors: They are uniquely privy to the gossip of the squares and they are all but unnoticeable seated by the front doors of suspect political deviants.

But it is unlikely that Mercedes Amador's husband was physically mistreated; even those who oppose it generally concede that the government does not practice torture unless we mean to define as such the state to which Mercedes Amador had been brought down.

The visitor's pot luck turned up just one Nicaraguan who had remained in detention long enough to be familiar with the means employed. Roger Guevara is a lawyer who has defended priests in trouble before the Popular Anti-Somocista Tribunals.

He was arrested in January 1985, and conveyed to El Chipote, the Somoza family's old prison on a hill above Managua. He sat in a dark closet for four hours and then was brought to formal interrogation at eight in the evening. He remained there for seven hours of questioning by Commander of the Revolution Bayardo Arce's brother and another policeman.

"They told me that my wife, who was eight and a half months pregnant, was outside the prison frantic and weeping. They knew who my friends were and where I went. I was most impressed by how much they knew about me. And, after they had given me their own analysis of my own personal and political life, they told me I could not leave until I told them my secret truth."

He could provide no secret truth, and thereafter they left him severely alone in the solitary darkness of days in a small cell with a straw cot, water for one hour, and a toilet that was a hole in the floor. His only contact with the human species was the hand that thrust in the rice and eggs that was his unchanging meal.

What Roger Guevara remembers most acutely of all was his terrible tormenting need to "talk to someone, almost anyone." But he did not give way and, on the tenth day of his imprisonment, "they took me out and shaved me and put me on the roof to give me some color and put some lotion on my face and left me at home saying that they hoped the experience would do me some good.

"One of them asked, 'What do you think of the process?' I answered, 'What process?' Arce's brother then said that I had been staying first-class."

And, perhaps Guevara had. It would take an ice cream vendor of special distinction to be eligible for interrogation by a *comandante*'s brother.

Every morning, when he comes to work, Lino Hernandez says he finds at least six women like Mercedes Amador waiting for him. He may have been too long at this sort of thing to sustain the detachment requisite for precise and irrefutable proffers of evidence, and he may indeed have grown "a bit hysterical." If he has, it is a disability earned on a field of honor.

II

ESTELI—BACK IN Managua, Carlos Humbes's visitor had scoured for whatever light might help him divine what an indefinite subsistence in independent inanition must be like for the general secretary of CTN, the wind-tossed umbrella of the Catholic trade unions.

At length the visitor could find no better question than:

"From where you sit are things better or worse or just the same as they were before the revolution?"

"Better" would be the inconceivable from this quarter. "Worse" would be only the expected from a labor leader unevenly competing with rivals whose nurse and keeper is the Sandinista government. No possible answer could surprise except "the same."

"El mismo," Carlos Humbes replied.

"El mismo." The same. The same cruel futility of things.

The visitor is contemplating the shoe factory the revolution has brought to Esteli. Its air is pervaded with the tune of hammer plinking upon nail that fell silent long ago wherever there exist methods of production that can reasonably be called processes of manufacture.

Here hunch twenty figures from centuries gone, cobblers with no machines but their fingers. Each would have worked alone in his cottage before the Industrial Revolution; the only perceptible difference is that now he has been collected in a shed with nineteen other handicraftsmen, each cutting, shaping, and fitting his own materials.

The establishment's best artisan is introduced. He is stitching the side trim on a boot. A young boy sits beside him threading a needle. It is an image from seventeenth-century genre painting, the apprentice learning his trade by observing his master, and the inference is inescapable that, now as then, the apprentice's mother is paying a small fee for the lesson.

The master displays his latest completed work with eminently justifiable pride. It will retail for roughly fifteen dollars and half of that will be his pay for ten ten-hour days of loving care. We have come upon one of Nicaraguan labor's aristocrats, and he fairly glows with the satisfaction of bringing home four dollars every day. Are we to suppose upon such scenes that we have penetrated a core sector of the fearful machine that pours forth the jackboots for what our own President seems seriously to conceive as the imminent trampling of Latin America?

At the cigar factory, a crew of workers, mostly women, puts the tobacco leaves through their preparatory stage by breaking off their stems and stacking them on tables. Things are done here just as they must have been when Samuel Gompers wrapped cigars in Tampa in 1865 before breaking his chains to bemuse the toilers and himself as the first president of the American Federation of Labor.

The revolution's "Outstanding Child Worker," a transient television celebrity, is a member of this work force. She is twelve years old, an intact artifact from the beginnings of capitalism. Nicaragua's methods of production are still so primitive that its Ministry of Labor can find no way to increase output except to encourage all hands to work harder with pay incentives.

She who sorts and stacks 70 pounds of tobacco has achieved the day's norm where her incentive pay begins. At the end of any month where she has averaged 30 percent above the norm, she will have earned 28,000 cordobas while an equally motivated sister will take home 38,000 cordobas thanks to the higher level of skill required to wrap the cigars and bundle them.

For the great majority of Nicaraguans who have no access to the black market, a thousand cordobas is worth but a shade more than one American dollar.

The visitor travels on to the garment factory named after Luisa Ajuda Espinoza, a revolutionary martyr, and there he beholds a sight he has all but lost hope of seeing in a Nicaraguan industrial premise—a working spread of mechanized devices.

They are sewing machines, gifts of the unions affiliated with the Belgian Socialist Party.

Nicaragua's sympathizers blame most of her difficulties on the Reagan administration's economic boycott, but, in point of fact, she is the beneficiary of an extraordinary volume of foreign aid not merely from the Communist bloc, but from those Western democratic nations whose kindliness is stimulated by their pleasure in the discreet thumbing of noses at the White House. But it is not often enough aid of the sort that is useful.

For all the pride and even the vainglory of her *comandantes*, Nicaragua is a beggar nation and cannot be a chooser. She must take what she can get, whether from charity or from barter. Most of the paltry stock in the supermarket at Esteli is of foreign import and so all else but appropriate that customers from a town that could hardly have many more than 100 flush toilets can find a whole shelf stuffed high with toilet plungers delivered by Bulgaria in exchange possibly for Nicaraguan cigars.

When the Belgians donated these sewing machines, they conferred a treasure upon the Luisa Ajuda Espinoza Cooperative; and its rewards manifest themselves in the schedule on the wall that establishes a forty dollar a month raise for a worker who doubles the norm that expects her to attach fifty-six collars a day. There aren't many trades of moderate skill where the employer can pay even that comparatively decent a wage unless he has functioning machinery.

Still, a few young girls activate the needle even here; and the visitor observes, as delicately as he can, that child labor is no entirely appetizing example of revolutionary social advance. The forelady replies that it is only a temporary recourse in the exigencies of the war that has conscripted the men who would otherwise be working for the national defense. Hers is an answer that serves better to excuse than explain.

Men do not operate sewing machines; it is women's work the world 'round. There are indeed necessities that force a female child into a garment shop, but they are her family's and not her nation's necessities, and they are not temporary: Luisa Ajuda Espinoza's nineteen dollar monthly minimum wage will for a long time mean for these children the difference between an exigent existence and a one nearly unbearable.

Nicaragua's revolutionary leaders demonstrate an inarguable quotient of incompetence, but it increases their difficulties only because their situation allows them not one inch of the wide margin for mistakes available to developed industrial societies. If they were masters of planning, they would have too little with which to plan; the only material that is not in short supply in Nicaragua is the stuff of dreams.

The citizens of Cordoga have been assembled to celebrate the anniversary of one of the earliest Sandinista victories there. Cordoga is perhaps four hundred yards and not less than a hundred years from that lonely symbol of capitalist development, the Pan American Highway.

Nothing seems new there except the Wall of Revolutionary Martyrs and the cellophane banners of the Sandinista National Liberation Front. A troupe from the Nicaraguan National Ballet offers a program of dances from progressive portions of the earth, including a snatch of *The Red Detachment of Women*, the ballet to which his People's Chinese hosts subjected President Richard Nixon, and it appears to baffle this audience as much as it had him. The occasion is nonetheless unexpectedly pleasant, and not least because of the brevity, the quiet tones, and the notes even of apology for past inadequacies in the keynote address of Jose Francisco Mendietta, secretary of the Sandinista Party for the Zone of Esteli.

It is fifty years since the murder of Augusto Sandino, and yet if he had ridden into Cordoga this day, he would have found not one change to surprise him except the martyr's wall and the pictures of himself plastered on so many of the others. A whole forty-three of those years belonged to the Somozas and only seven belong to the revolution, and none of them have brought a detectable difference in the life of Cordoga.

III

ESTELI—THE VISITOR'S northward journey had been enlivened, if scarcely enlightened, by the company of a sociologist tenured at a university in the American Southwest.

"Isn't Managua wonderful?" she asked in the familiar American voice that proclaims the answer in the form of the question. "There are no poor sections and no beggars and no homeless."

How much time, her companion wondered, had her researches needed to bring her to a judgment likely to stupefy a *comandante* of the revolution as profoundly as it had himself?

"I have been here two weeks," she replied. So, then, she had sailed blithely through an ocean of penury and never seen or felt a wave. Her compass had been set on the chart of her imaginary Nicaragua; and it had steered her safely past all the snags and rocks of reality.

Her companion reflected that, as is too much his habit, he had spoken too soon when he said that Nicaragua is short of every material except the stuff of dreams. Nicaragua is possessed, in addition, of a surplus of holy fools, the most conspicious among them the Americans who tour.

But then there are the Americans who have come here, found out the worst, and stayed on the course of struggle to make it better. There will be those who condemn them for having chosen the wrong side, for these are times when too many of us have forgotten that the side of the poor can never be entirely the wrong one. Only those who remember that can understand something of what Paul Rice has tried to do in the service of his notion of his country's honor.

Paul Rice: economic planner for Zone One of the Nicaraguan Ministry of Agriculture, a curiously orotund job description to be attached to an economy that is scarcely more than subsistent and seems impervious to any remotely plausible plan.

It is, all the same, a professional's title. Paul Rice is no longer a tourist.

Perhaps he was never equipped to be, for, had he been, he probably would have wandered away long ago.

"I went through the normal three stages," he explains. "You come here expecting Nicaragua to be paradise. Then you see a beggar and the feeling of disillusion starts and, after a little of that, most people go home. But if you wait long enough, you settle into understanding how hard the job is and you stay and try to do it."

Those who stay are different from the run of us; and, if the sense of having always felt that difference does not weigh as heavy on Paul Rice as it did before, it still has some of its weight.

He is three years out of Yale and has been here almost since he was graduated.

"I don't think I was brought here by an ideology so much as by an identification with the poor."

His kinship with the deprived could not have been the hardy plant it has turned out to be if it had not been grown in the stony ground of deprivations of his own. Paul Rice's mother was an Oklahoma textile worker whose husband had drifted away early on. She worked her way through college and emerged with a master's degree in psychology. She had bettered herself and she was as determined to better her son, and, as even souls as large as hers so surprisingly often do, she adhered to the standards convention appoints.

"We lived in one room," her son says, "but she always sent me to good schools. Most of the time I was the only poor kid there and I felt the difference all the way until I wound up as one of Yale's token poor."

And here, at last, in Esteli's dust, he was comfortable with the difference. He had found his peace in a place that seemed least calculated to provide it, an arena where hope wrestles endlessly with the impossible. He commenced to talk with a candor unique in official Nicaragua, because it is the candor that cannot exist until the speaker has been candid with himself.

A year ago last spring, he remembered, the Nicaraguan army began converting portions of the border below Honduras into a free-fire zone and evacuating the civilian population. One purpose of these measures was to drain the area of the pool where, as Mao Tse-tung used to put it, the guerrilla swims. The peasants isolated there were all else but converts to the revolution.

"They have no radios, and the literacy campaign had missed them. All they knew about the revolution was that, when they rode down to a town to buy a machete, it cost twice what it had the year before. They believed the contras when they said that anyone we caught would be made into soup."

The ideal of a People's Army is a splendid abstraction, but an army is an army, and the Ministry of Agriculture was acutely aware that this one was not invariably well-behaved. After some argument, the army agreed to go about the business with a delicacy reflecting an appreciation that its problem was not merely military but political.

Things must be done correctly, and the ministry commissioned Paul Rice to go along to make sure that they were. It was, however, easier to be correct than ceremonious, and the peasants were carried away before they had time to pack. As soon as they landed, they demanded their rights to return and collect their possessions.

"The army argued that this was dangerous stuff," Paul Rice recalls. "But we said that it just had to let Juan Gomez get his cow. It was a long debate, but we won, and our trucks made forty-five trips carrying these people to the end of the road and leaving them to hike the rest of the way on their own. And every one of them came back. We settled them and put them to planting with the fastest seed we could find and, by August, when they could see the crop growing, they cheered up."

Difficult as it remained to believe that happy endings round themselves out quite this simply, there was a distinct refreshment in being able at last to listen to a voice pregnant with its consciousness of the complications of the search for even tolerable solutions.

Paul Rice's puzzlements turned to the new peasant cooperatives that lie so naked to the spite of the contras.

"There are times," he confessed, "when I have my doubts about our ideological bias toward cooperatives. How can we protect them? And, until we can, so many of those who die are our best leaders, the sort of people who will take the chance of going there, the activists who know and can tell the others what we are trying to do. We just lost one of our best technicians at Miraflores."

Sergio Chavarra was but a few years older than Paul Rice and his closest Nicaraguan friend. He had taken two days leave to work on his house, and, as he was driving a nail, a comrade ran in to say that there was danger at Miraflores. Chavarra had driven twenty-six miles to be killed on a field where lines of defense could hardly have been adequate in any case, and had not even been made ready in this one.

Paul Rice began asking what war was like. His visitor gave his own puny witness, which brings a glaze to the eyes of most auditors. But this one kept pressing for the last scrap of detail in a small stock of reminiscence until the visitor was drawn to the suspicion that there could only be one source for any fascination this intense.

"Are you asking all these questions," he inquired, "because you think you might be in a war?"

"In a year or two," Paul Rice answered, "the American army will land and I may have to defend myself, and it won't be from the Nicaraguans."

"I wish," he said suddenly, "I had been with Sergio."

They would only have shared a death without purpose, but then there do come times in the life of any man who has engaged its impossibilities day after wearying day when he almost longs for a climax that would settle matters once and for all.

Of all the images of Nicaragua, the one that will sit longest in the mind is of Paul Rice, waiting for his countrymen to arrive in arms and wondering if he would meet them with his gun. It was not a thought as offensive as it ought to be to what patriotism the visitor had left, because it was intruded upon by the recollection of the Edmund Burke who belonged to the British House of Commons and was yet aggrieved whenever the American rebels sustained a reversal. That Burke might very well have understood the temptation of Paul Rice, and what is good enough for Edmund Burke's understanding is good enough for the likes of my own.

IV

MANAGUA—DR. EMILIO Alvarez Montalban may or may not be the last Nicaraguan still addressed by acquaintances and identified by admirers as "Don Emilio." That ancient Spanish term of respect is dying with the revolution or departing with its exiles, and Don Emilio is an artifact.

When he was active in the Nicaraguan Conservative Democratic party's leadership, he spent a year in a Somoza family jail. The revolution is unlikely to mark him for a similarly unpleasant distinction, if only because no *comandante* is alienated enough from tradition to trust his eyes to any other ophthalmologist.

Don Emilio is still the Conservative party's Nestor, even though his last direct labor on its behalf was to compose and publish an unexpectedly respectful critique of the philosophy of Karl Marx four years ago. Since then he has limited himself to his studies of the history of the eye and to his conversations.

It is at once a sorrow and a solace that the voice of Emilio Alvarez Montalban promises to resonate longer in the visitor's head than any other he brought home from Nicaragua.

Don Emilio's conversation sets forth down only too familiar channels—the decline in living standards, the increase in infant mortality, the ineptitude whose consequence is the death of two hundred baby chickens because the planning authorities forgot to provide their feed and the unassailable self-satisfaction that inspires the minister of agriculture's assurance that there are still a million left alive. It is an exhausting catalog of the failures that have left the litany of triumph as loud as ever.

But then the voice ceases its quiet complaint about present troubles and passes to the tone of historical memory.

"The Americans came to us, and they organized money and the National Bank and the National Guard. They were the preachers of the modern. And yet they never developed a taste for our culture.

"And they are not alone in that confusion. One of my patients is a Bulgarian engineer brought here for an aid project. He told me that communism is impossible with people like ours.

" 'In Bulgaria,' he said, 'the whistle blows and we rush in and it's work, work, work all day, and I go home exhausted. But these people come in and then just wander off for coffee and talk, and I have to round them up.' " We are to take it then that Nicaraguans are unfit for the Marxist-Leninist ideal because they decline to be worked to death?

"The Bulgarian had, of course, overlooked the poor Nicaraguan's want of nutrition, the fact that he is always tired," Alvarez Montalban pursued. "But the Americans make the same mistake. We are unable to understand one other. We say of Anglo-Saxons, 'They are easy to fool and they are materialists.' And they say of us, 'They are liars and lazies and they don't like to work.'

"You must understand that our lives are a mixture of the reality and the dream, because the reality is otherwise too hard to bear. The Sandinistas dream of waking to find that they have made us into Los Angeles.

"Look at the photographs of our *comandantes*," he said suddenly. "They are *indios*. Before them we were ruled by Spanish faces; this is our first *mestizo* government."

His visitor had commenced to sense disdain, and, as is his weakness, he had sensed too soon.

For Don Emilio went on to talk, with no sign of dissatisfaction, about some of the changes since 1979.

"Women have a new role. The *caballero*'s old double standard is gone. And the common people believe at last that they are important. There are differences in their treatment. Now they call you '*companero.*' The language is more informal. It is a sadness of our history that it has trained the bulk of us to think that equality means more than freedom.

"But," he ended, "the Sandinistas will have a long agony, because they will never create their world. One of our problems is that we are not radicals. The Catholics have been trying to convert us for four hundred years. Our culture swallows all missionaries."

Nonetheless, the revolution presses its endeavors toward what Carlos Tunnermann Bernheim, its minister of education, has called the "formation of the New Man," and third-grade pupils steel their characters and refine their penmanship by copying sentences like: "Culture is the artistic rifle of the revolution" and "The children of Sandino never surrender . . . we will protect the workers and the peasants." And yet there are a dozen pictures of Mickey Mouse and Donald Duck and none of Marx or Lenin in the schoolroom where they transcribe their vows and exercise their devotions.

In Esteli one Sunday morning, the sound of a drum is heard and a column of children approaches. Here in full force can only be the armed New Man grown from dragon's teeth planted by the revolution. And then there arises from this formation a martial chant at once and unmistakably translatable as "Gimme an E, gimme an M, gimme an A . . ." The uniforms are pin-striped; what confronts the visitor's shuddering eye is the terrible presence of the Little League baseball team of the Barrio of Emaor.

Children very much like these were killed in a contra raid not twenty miles from Esteli three weeks before, and now, in its ineffable poltroonery, the Congress of the United States has tripled the subsidy that bought this milestone on the march to Nicaragua's redemption and will now speed the business along three times as fast and three times as far. Let the glad cry ring forth from bastion to bastion in the United States, fortress of cowards and draft evaders: "Yesterday three kids in a peasant's compound in the hills; tomorrow the Little League team from Emaor."

V

"On May 20, 1986, at 7 P.M., at least 800 contras attacked two cooperatives in Miraflores, 18 miles northeast of the city of Esteli. Eight people were killed and sixteen wounded and property was destroyed."
—*A report from Witnesses for Peace, issued June 10*

MIRAFLORES—"MIRAFLORES" CAN be loosely translated as "see the flowers."

The Ministry of Agricultural Development and Agrarian Reform speaks of it as the seat of sixteen world cooperative communities; but, as with so much of the revolution, the declaration has preceded the fulfillment it proclaims.

The frames and the fresh nicalit fiberboard of two of the Miraflores sixteen stand very close to where the Teodoso Pravia cooperative used to be. They are unfinished and uninhabited, because they are still waiting for their share of MINDRA's pinched supply of bricks.

The Sandino and Pravia cooperatives had been their near neighbors before falling under assault by anti-Sandinista guerrillas three weeks before one visitor arrived. Sandino's brick is half ruined and Pravia's wood has vaporized in a fire that had to have been carefully set and supervised down to the last ashes.

A few women gazed from the doorways of Sandino's one-room houses with the not unfamiliar Nicaraguan face that seems to endure all things and wait in expectation of none. There are children about; but the bedding in these interiors runs too much to the sleeping bags of soldiers to suggest family quarters. When dark approaches the women and the children depart in the main down the hill. Sandino lives 'round the clock only as a military outpost and an unassailable one, especially because the contras have left nothing they would think worth the risk of assailing.

There is the promise that the families will resettle in Sandino in due course; but it would be understandable if they felt the need for encouragement by tangible measures of security; and the interval of suspension seems so far to be passing without intrusion by the bustle and noise that signify works of reconstruction.

A troop of soldiers occupies the dirt in front of the porch of Sandino's largest structure, perhaps a school or a store or an assembly hall for peaceful times lodged indefinitely in its future. This formation is identified as a signal company assigned to restore communications; but, as it is, these corpsmen merely stand in drowsy attention to quiet tones of their commander. The impression is of some lesson taught in the open air and the suspicion is that they have been unable to bring along the equipment that would have made their presence more purposeful. It is a suspicion devoid of mockery; surplus wire is hard to find in Nicaraguan emergencies.

Ramon Gomez, who is wearing a white shirt, appears to be in charge and is asked to describe the battle of May 20 last. He obliges with evocations of the eight hundred contras and the firefight that lasted on and on for five hours until a Nicaraguan military detachment arrived to drive them away. The visitor casts about a searching eye dimly illuminated by his own memories of combats altogether pleasanter, looks for cartridge shells and finds almost none, tries to locate points that might have been a skirmisher's line and sees only some furrows suggestive of entrenchments but too shallow to have been in any way serviceable.

Just three judgments seemed fairly safe: (1) If a pitched battle had been fought in this vicinity, it could not have been fought on the ground within an immediate view; (2) and yet the deaths of six civilians—three of them children—are a fact abiding beyond reach of doubt or question; (3) Ramon Gomez, narrator, is not talking about anything he had seen for himself. If he had been in Sandino that evening, he would be dead, because his white shirt, however modest, was plainly not a *campesino's* and because, unselective as the contras appear to be when they are shooting peasants they seem to be very careful when it comes to marking out for special attention anyone within their range who is recognizably a servant of the revolution.

There could be no disputing Sandino's six civilian dead; but most of the rest of this story would have to lie on a bed of surmises. The visitor commenced to frame his assessment on experiences half forgotten and ended at last peopling this scene not with wires in battle but with hunters and their quarry in a turkey shoot.

The contras had come down as wolves to the fold; not eight hundred but forty would have sufficed for their will. Nothing apparent could be called a fortification; this had to have been a place that was in its essence undefended. Those who had lived here had not been frightened enough in advance to be prepared to resist being terrified into panic by the horror when it burst. The visitor settled with that guess with entire respect, having not seldom panicked himself on fields where he had been barely in danger if in any at all.

There are a few ceremonies more familiar than panic among wars' rites of passage; and it is particularly to be hoped that this government will talk less about heroes and take more account of ordinary people and that, whatever the outcome of its other dreams, it will try with genuine self-discipline to make whoever comes back to the Sandino cooperative ready for the next time round.

The visitor is pointed to the house where the three Talevara children were killed by a grenade. Or was it a mortar? The conflicting versions are not worth sorting out; the murder would be the murder in either case. A side of the interior wall has been whitewashed; but there are black splotches on the ceiling that the guides identify as blood and that may very well be, although the visitor comes from a country too profligate about shedding blood and too tidy about wiping it up for any citizen to know what its stains look like after three weeks.

The thought of these two dead boys and this dead girl is not a light one; but it is no more than a thought. Nicaragua is a country of martyrs who have given no offense; and these children are already slipping into abstraction for anyone who never saw them alive or dead.

Nothing about Nicaragua can be known in your bones except what you see with your eyes. And then the visitor goes off to what was once the Teodoso Pravia cooperative and discovers that just what you see can be quite enough.

The only observable ruins are a sack of potatoes, lightly baked, and the twisted roofs preserved from entire cremation by the asbestos mixed in their fiberboard. Otherwise there are only a few ashes and earth not merely scorched but charred; the wood frames that once defined floors have been evaporated in a fire that has not left so much as a scent.

A job so complete had needed time, patience, and a certainty of freedom from interruption. All that survived on the scene was the mark of cold and disciplined malice. And just a few yards away, the frames of two other projected cooperatives stood intact and untouched; and the sight of them fixed the conviction that they owed their immunity to their unfinished and empty state.

Teodoso Pravia had been obliterated because it was complete and occupied and, after its fashion, an accomplishment in a country that has only too few.

The tidal fact about the contras had come down in all its thunder. What they truly hate is not the dreams that are still fantasies but any small bit of a dream that demonstrates some sign of realization. They had waited until these buildings were finished and a living presence and then they had burned them down, because what they hate is the slightest feeling of having accomplished something in the bosoms of peasants so seldom permitted that somber joy.

Why are we to suppose these families came to this patch from which they have been cast forth without being permitted to leave so much as a trace? Is it too much to imagine that they came for a life moderately improved? Is it treasonable for an American to wonder what difference it would have made in the balance of power between great nations if these struggling souls were still settled in a shelter whose topmost amenity is for keeping out the rain and not choking you with the smoke of the cook fire, if they were still painfully raising potatoes for sale at twenty-five cents a bushel, and if the years were going on while the best that could be said for them was that the child was a little better off than his parents had been at his age?

Who, when all is said and done, you masters of the earth, goes to glory when you burn a farmer's potato crop?

The remains of Teodoso Pravia are the brand of a beaten army. Soldiers begin pretty much as a rabble; they are molded together and they fight and, when they are defeated, they become, in all but the best of cases, a rabble once more. The contras cannot have been reduced to futile malignities like this one unless they were already a rabble incapable of employments less dingy than the rape of an innocent hope. Until now the visitor had not been much more impressed with the troops around him than they would have been if they would have seen him younger in his fatigues and with his grease gun and his gas mask emptied to make room for his tobacco. Still they looked more than fit to engage an enemy sunk into the condition where the most it can do is the thing it had done here.

New York Newsday, Summer 1986

El Salvador: Our Bracing Desert

I

Come to our bracing desert
Where eternity is eventful
For the weather-glass
Is set at Alas,
The thermometer at Resentful
—W. H. AUDEN, "For the Time Being"

SAN SALVADOR—IN the desert of advanced civilizations the son of the poor travels across seas to death in war, and the mother's anguish arrives by cable. Here the son of the poor dies in front of his own house, and day by day the mother scrubs away at the encrustation of blood on her flagstone.

The guerrilla war fell upon Cuscatancingo on Saturday, November 11. Very little of it touched the powdery dust and rocky outcroppings of Colonia San Luis. "Colonia" is official theory's designation for a suburb. Fact identifies San Luis as an isolated passageway of modest but permanent dwellings whose residents have grown up with one another through a generation or more. Its soccer team is San Luis's symbol of pride and stability.

The noise that announced the imminence of rocket and shell drove the women and children from San Luis early; but a few of the men stayed behind to keep watch on their meager household effects. By Saturday, November 18, battle was done and the air somnolent; and six San Luisianes, three of them footballers, were playing cards in front of José Esteban Crespin's house.

Their coach had seen them on his way up the hill toward the larger town shortly after 4:00 P.M. He had also seen a patrol of perhaps seven soldiers sweating in their jungle gear a hundred yards or so farther along, and they had warned him in tones not unkindly to stay away because an air strike was impending.

A half hour later, it would appear, this patrol came down upon these players at their table, seized their identification papers and lined them up against José Crespin's door. The wall was just wide enough for five, and the assault force set two others at the right- and left-hand corners. One was Oscar Lopez, who had but recently finished his two-year tour with the army and who, with better luck might have been looking at the humble citizens down the barrel of his own official M-16. The other was Manuel de Jesus Medrano, fourteen, who had bread to sell and was stationed nearby. To bystand was to be guilty; Manuel Medrano's liquidation left no eyewitness; and no soul remained to tell the tale except another youth who had hidden in his house and heard the guns discharge so rapidly that he could not be sure whether they came from rifles or a machine gun.

The seven bodies lay in their blood until the next day, when their fellow San Luisianes came to dig and lodge them in a common grave.

The justice of what passes for peace in El Salvador came last week to supervise the ceremonies of formal interment, and six of the seven were carried to rest in the ever-populating cemeteries of Cuscatancingo. Only Manuel Medrano, bread seller barely in his teens, was left behind in the ditch he had lately shared with his elders. His parents were too poor to pay for a cemetery plot.

The only conspicuous flower in San Luis is a great splashy purple bougainvillea. In Salvador, every noticeable expression seems somehow extreme and with no company but silence all around it. Three or four men of the place did what they could to reconstruct this event from the chronicles of Salvadoran military glory, and, it can reasonably be assumed, in the body count of guerrillas killed in combat. One of them was San Luis's soccer coach, who declined to proffer his name. In the cases of scenes of the sort with which this country is all too prodigal only the dead are identified; the surviving preference inclines toward anonymity.

The wall where José Crespin lived and died at twenty-one is pocked with the holes that heavy caliber leaves. The pavement is white as if from incessant scouring, except for the clots of blood residue perhaps a foot by a yard or so at its edge. José Crespin's mother is plainly a housekeeper of high conscience, but sorrow had slowed her arm.

All the same, the sorrow on her face did not look fresh but im-memorial; tragedy here is a school for stoics, for who among these dusts and rocks with the green hills away in the distance does not know that in the midst of life death may be waiting up the hill or in the sky above?

There was a soldier or two or three about the passageway that is San Luis's only street. They did not speak to the residents, nor the residents to them.

These are troopers officially conscripted for the protection of children who neither care, nor dare, to play with them.

> *Come to our old world desert*
> *Where everyone goes to pieces.*
> *You can pick up tears*
> *For souvenirs*
> *And genuine diseases.*

And where the poor are made the enemies of the rest of the poor and divided from them by combat gear and an M-16.

II

THE FIRST PHASE of the battle for San Salvador has softened into a desultory dying fall that is at best an affliction for its poor and at worst a nuisance for its rich.

The tourist of a mind to follow the itinerary of these small skirmishes at a properly respectful distance will find available a variety of quarters ranging from the first class of the high- down to the fourth or fifth class of the low- or no-rent districts. His options in lodging are, however, like all elements in the order of battle, dictated by the guerrillas who are his cicerones but do not post schedules of the events of the day.

On Tuesday, the squads of the FMLN rebels chose to fight in Delgado and the other eastern fringes of San Salvador where the impoverished live under tin and the marginally more propertied have built with brick in the semi-sylvan reaches farther out.

On Wednesday, the guerrilla squads improved their social environment while disturbing the peace of the comfortable by carrying the taunt of their defiance and the economy of their fire to Escalon and close proximity to the residence of the president of the Republic of El Salvador.

One tourist arrived at Delgado Tuesday afternoon four hours after hostilities had ceased and its residents had begun returning to inspect the damage done their houses by the rockets, the cannon, and the .50-caliber machine guns of the Salvadoran Air Force's helicopters.

One ought plainly to have gotten up earlier to adjust to the timing patterns of guerrilla warfare. The tourist had been joined in this exploration by two other journalists, one Australian and the other Mexican, and they would soon enough give him cause to reflect that one would also do well to be circumspect in one's choice of comrades in such adventures.

One goes to war here by taxicab at an eight-dollar hourly rate. One arrives to find the army rousing from its somnolence to inspect one's credentials and point the direction of the enemy without allowing the slightest inference of any temptation of its own to join the hunt.

One proceeds down the hill to the inspection of an occasional house unroofed and a mattress still smoldering from an army rocket through its walls.

A resident who had stayed the night explained that guerrillas had been there into the morning and been distinctly less bothersome than the air gunners bent on defending him from aggression. The FMLN cadres were by now, he assumed, quietly established in the woods and ravine down the way.

The Aussie signaled the advance and the Mexican fell into a line of march that compelled the tourist's allegiance because it would otherwise separate him from the only accessible strip of the white cloth that announces a coming in peace and an abstention from the savage quarrels of brothers not your own.

The thought had commenced to intrude that more than forty years had quite obscured a once vivid awareness of the properties of patrol, along with the memory of Aussies so scornful of their cautionary prescriptions that they would shine their shoes in the morning and then go forth into New Guinea's high grass, draw fire, and head into it.

The march went on through a silence that even the Aussie confessed to finding a bit ominous and ended at a small cliff looking down upon a creek and a pebbly bank where, had forty years not gone by, it might have been delightful to picnic with a chaste and lovely girl.

Then every dream of what is nevermore was expulsed by a solitary gunshot at a distance of perhaps two hundred yards. The cartridge's whine past the ear suggests that intimate hostility had been refreshingly absent and one could linger a while.

After five minutes or so of a silence broken by a rooster's crow or two, there was another gunshot and then a third; and even the Aussie took this possible hint of a welcome overstayed; and one took one's place in the line of withdrawal sheltered behind the walls of the trail, hoarsely crying *"prensa"* and never so much appreciating the esthetic grandeurs of brick and fieldstone until we three came at last to the rear echelon, which identifies itself here with the appearance of the first soldier one has lately seen.

The government troopers ask the Aussie for a report on his visit to the frontline. An army that needs to get its briefings from journalists does not stimulate overconfidence in its combat initiative.

The charms of Delgado's outskirts have been rural, while Escalon's are uniformly upper-suburban. One lay in the grass beside soldiers clustered together in common sloth and clustered together so close that it seemed a blessing to them and to one's self that the guerrillas hadn't brought a mortar.

The grass across from Escalon's grandest plaza made so pleasant an ambience that one stretched as though to pose for Manet's "Dejeuner sur l'herbe" and rather resenting the nearby street vendor's neglect of her duty to stock wine and cheese. It seemed quite ridiculous to go on creeping and crawling while all other civilians about you serenely strolled or drove. Still, it is never easy to escape the sense of one's own absurdity in a war where one can so often meet murder on the way and find its sovereignty proclaimed by a roadblock the army has set up with a flowering pineapple at its flank.

There was a lonely gunshot now and then no nearer than four blocks. The guerrillas were believed to have installed themselves in or behind the Discoteque Luzenne, where the rules of engagement in San Salvador render them invulnerable so long as they wish to stay.

Here the lives of the humble may count cheap, but real estate is vested with sanctity as soon as it reaches the requisite level of expense. The helicopters could not rocket Escalon; and, since the government's ground troopers have but the dimmest aquaintance with foot-soldiery, they were thereby immobilized.

Reconnaissance had, however, located a few fringe shacks whose corrugated tin roofs marked them as licensed targets, and their inhabitants had been ordered to relocate and were departing down the avenue. None carried a white flag since all knew that here they were still immune to whatever terrors might greet them down the stonier road toward which they traveled.

Even so, one felt embarrassingly naked without his own flag of cowardice and knocked at a door with thoughts of borrowing one. It was an introduction to the Imberton household, whose head replied with dignified courtesy as a government loyalist that he did not have a white flag, because "it means that you are neutral, and I am not neutral." He indicated, however, that it would be want of courtesy not to offer the stranger a drink. One soothed one's self with ice water among furnishings in Señora Imberton's taste for the English style and talked of New York and exchanged addresses until thoughts of the war returned from their transient oblivion and Señor Imberton observed that "They had been beaten in the countryside, and so they have come here." Suddenly the mind was intruded upon by that story of Kafka's whose opening sentence's vague recollection approximates as "Something may have gone wrong with the war at the frontier, because this morning the enemy set up his camp in the square of our capital."

There was settling upon the heart a heavy sadness for the future of a people as incorrigibly pleasant as Salvadorans tend to seem.

Yesterday, the FMLN squads offered a morning cease-fire. What they offer is what now prevails as always in an order of battle whose options for beginning, sustaining, and leaving off free of encirclement are their monopoly. The tourist's opportunity to approach inspection of their works again is theirs to dispose of as it may please them.

III

THE FORTUNES OF war run to infinite varieties of the unexpected, not to say the treacherous; but no happy accident could have seemed less probable than a chance to observe the domestic manners of the FMLN guerrillas taking their temporary ease in the suburbs of Soyapango.

The unlikelihood of an encounter this odd may excuse this tourist's protracted failure to recognize it when it came. One had made one's entry into the Colonia Santa Barbara Friday alongside a strand of rubbered wire that looked too much like stuff of the sort employed for detonating land mines.

The puzzlements of this object were compounded when the eye traveled its length to end at a half-open iron gate where a soldier sat in a uniform that had about it an air of the random entirely at variance with the neat if scarcely spruce appearance of government troopers whose clothing always looks as if it had been washed last night and is still unsoiled by the ungainly sprawls toward the sanctuary of the dirt that are the inevitable exigencies of combat. But here were garments not issued but picked up and assembled along the road.

"Of course," one too quickly decided, "this is the militia enlisted by the Republic from the loyalists among its citizens."

They were moving about the pathways in rags and tags of martial costume and in numbers enough to uplift the hearts of any U.S. military adviser as misapprehending as oneself.

Mark Uhlig of *The New York Times* had most attentively served as guide and oiler away of the rust from one's too-long unattended body of experience with the clatters and clutters of war. His companion had frequently admired and seldom deplored the qualities of the men and women of the *Times*, but not even from one of them could there have been imagined a display as exemplary as Uhlig's of the virtues summed up by the catcher in *Bull Durham* when he observed that you play this game with fear and arrogance.

We took a bend in the road behind Uhlig's white flag and then he began a conversation with a young man in a baseball fan's cap with the device "El Salvador, C.A." and another, bulkier man with a bit of red ribbon around his wrist. The younger introduced himself as Vladimir and the slightly elder as Daniel, and if Vladimir's Spanish tongue was incomprehensible to the tourist's ear, his tone was unmistakably that of political discourse and of Radio Venceremos. We had met the enemy in a guise so compellingly Garibaldian that, if just for a moment, one yielded him one's heart. There aren't all that many human creatures more attractive than some revolutionaries can be, at least until they win.

Grenades were crumpling and scattered gunshots crackling from distances by no means comfortably far. One flinched automatically after each; and yet Vladimir and Daniel continued their expositions without trace of tremor, and with a bearing that seemed to assume itself safer in loudly ominous clamors of the fields of war than many Salvadorans feel in church these Sundays.

We had come at last into the company of combat soldiers. Courtesy compelled one to bear with homilies of the political tenor; but it was a relief to arrive at the intimacies of reminiscence of three weeks' fighting.

"There has been a mess of combat around LoCinco," said Vladimir, "but the rest has been routine. We are not always fighting. We have our moments of peace. This is one."

This moment of peace has grown even more disturbingly noisy and the temptation larger to do as Ted Koppel does and say, "Gentlemen, I'm afraid our time is up." Even so, the fascinations of this particular absurdity still held its pull; and Uhlig asked Daniel why the FMLN forces had profaned the quarters of the rich in Escalon.

"We want the rich to understand as the poor do what it is to really feel the war," he replied. "Peace for the rich has ended and the war for the poor has begun."

He was asked which elements at the government's disposal were the opponents' most troublesome. He replied that the Elite—"so-called"—Brigades were the best trained but they all have a low combat morale.

"Morale is the essential all troops must have, and that is what they have shattered. We are willing to offer our lives. Of course some bullets will hit us. That is what war is about."

The intermittent rumbles were turning toward thunder; still one tarried to visit with three women warriors, two of them only girls ready with their smiles and one with the look of an NYPD female sergeant, circa 1958. Inside the otherwise barren room of their fleeting sojourn, there was a sofa and a game board with a small screen dividing and concealing one player's pegs from the others. It was that game where the child arrays his pegs one by one in hopes of matching the space where his opponent has concealed his battleship so exactly as to win the battle by sinking the enemy's navy. The warrior girls had passed part of the rest period playing the game called "Tactics."

At last the moment for parting too insistently pressed; and back down the exit trail our party went between intervals of pause when mortality's intimations broke forth too intrusively and one waited them out in the comfort of walls of brick and corners of concrete. Two hundred yards farther on, a detail of thirty or so Treasury Police slumped at the ready, each formidable as to weaponry and morose as to countenance.

It is a singularity of official El Salvador's military formations that nobody visible seems charged with command responsibilities. Perhaps nobody is, and the radioman just calls the rear for helicopter and rockets; and the rear eventually calls back with orders to move. The prospect of waiting a long while for instructions directly to engage may well be the only source of contentment available to troops like these. It hardly lay in the lips of one who had so recently been gimping about on decreasingly serviceable ankles waving his white flag with passionate timidity to impute cowardice to anyone else; but all the same the sight of this pre-battle assemblage scarcely suggested the demeanor of soldiers set for fighting or enough used to it to have learned the trade from the combatant's best instructor, the enemy combatant. It would be two hours after one had quit the oddly delightful company of the guerrillas that the battle to disturb their peace began.

After such spectacles, the tourist could only seek advice and counsel from a NATO diplomat sympathetic with our own embassy's cause but detached from its imbecile optimism.

"What worries me," he observed, "is that the FMLN has the discipline and controls the battle order and knows now that they can sustain contact with this army and may be starting to understand that they have a chance to break it." One had seen nothing all day that inclined him to dispute that assessment.

IV

EVERY MEMORY OF this misfortuned capital will be lastingly engraved and protractedly haunted by the images of three citadels, the rubbled warrens in the suburb of Soyapango where an FMLN detachment barracked awhile Friday, the national palace where President Alfredo

Cristiani takes his unease, and the great wall of the embassy of the United States.

The fortresses of the FMLN cadres are itinerant and formidable for their combat élan and their contempt for the government foot soldiers whose first rule of engagement seems only too frequently to be "Don't." The embassy's mass is made formidable by design. The traveler skirts masonry thicker and higher than the Maginot Line, makes his entry through gates like the ones that serve as exits in unattended subway stations, runs the gauntlet of platoon formations of Wackenhut guards, and arrives at an entrance with a canopy that would seem grandiose for the Beverly Hills Hotel.

This architect had met the challenge to his powers of excess by bringing off the ultimate symbol of the outsized complacency and equally outsized alarm that abide in a bizarre companionship of opposites in the castle keep within.

Little President Cristiani cannot exhibit quarters that mount the show of strength embodied in the high spirits of his enemies and the high walls of the embassy of the United States.

His palace can, however, claim a substantial edge over the other two in the matter of amenities. It is in the style and survives the illusions that used to beguile the hopes of the fledgling Central American republics for a future when peace, order, and progress unendingly unfolded. It is two virginally white stories tall and built as a rectangle with its interior loggia looking down on a grassy patio. One had come to Cristiani's Friday press conference from a visit with the rebels in Soyapango; and it was not unnatural, although it was patently unreasonable, to climb the carpeted stairs to the Sala Diplomatica with a head resounding with their shudderings from the dusty boots of ragged mountain warriors come in triumph on some day not far enough off.

Cristiani met the journalists beneath a panorama of notables assembled in 1821 to sign the act of San Salvador's independence, and the new president sat there under a red canopy with a crucifix at his back and with the reverend clergy waiting their turn to add their signatures. El Salvador's first president was slumped in a posture intimating a dejection inappropriate for an occasion this glorious but nonetheless too soon to become familiar in the bearing of his civilian successors at intervals in the hundred-odd years to come.

Cristiani is the latest of that so often ill-starred line. His parents came here from Italy in 1946, and he has some of the softness without the pomposity that distinguishes Italian public men and, like them, he inclines to responding to inquiries that intimate a condition of crisis by asking the questioner which of the various definitions of crisis he had intended to employ.

He has a mustache and beseeching eyes, is balding slightly, and was wearing a blue blazer, gray trousers, and loafers that would be the more magisterial for a shine. He is only forty-two and could take on a rather distinguished appearance if he grows older in office, a prospect not too likely.

He is the United States's present reliance for arrival at the ever-glimmering and ever-receding El Dorado, a center between the granitic right and the inextinguishable left in Salvadoran politics. Cristiani's views are about as far from the center as a statesman can get without reinvoking the Fugitive Slave Act; but he does have an appearance quite lamblike in the tigerish company of his ruling Arena party; and there are reports that he has embittered many old stagers in Arena by allotting to persons of some technical competence the cabinet posts to which they thought themselves entitled by long and not unsanguinary service against the weaponless.

Colonel Wayne Wheeler, the embassy's chief military adviser, is especially heartened by Cristiani's attentiveness to these cultivations of the goodwill of the Salvadoran army that former President José Napoleon Duarte had too carelessly overlooked. Cristiani is reported to all but live in the Army High Command headquarters. The army's friendship may be Cristiani's best shield against the spites of his own Arena party comrades; but it is not a treasure he can expect to survive the smallest lapse toward offense.

He feels forbidden to take notice of the two most conspicuous features of the army's performance in the last three weeks, which have been the boldness of its assaults upon peaceful and disarmed church workers and the timidity of its approach to armed and dangerous rebels.

On Friday, he confronted the rising mountain of evidence of the persecution of churches Catholic and Protestant with a flat denial of its existence and explained that the army could hardly be asked to dislodge an enemy that "doesn't present a target," an observation that fell most curiously upon the ears of a visitor who had but lately been chatting with FMLN troopers who did not just present but fairly flaunted a target whose only inconvenience was the degree of hazard it offered the shooter.

Since there is no statesman in Salvador to satisfy its test for a moderate, the embassy has the excuse of necessity for having had to invent this one. And Cristiani isn't all that ungainly a fit for these clothes, for like every moderate, actual or imaginary, the embassy has anointed before him, he is helpless and the plaything of an army invincible everywhere but on the fields of battle.

New York Newsday, Winter 1989

The Wisdom of Goya

I HAVE BEEN three times to the Metropolitan's great Goya exhibit; and I find myself less and less able to understand. When we speak of the Goyaesque, we mean, I have come to suppose, the presentation of the mysterious with a clarity of direct statement that somehow renders it more elusive than mists and shadows ever could.

Consider the hanged civilian in just one of the etchings from "The Disasters of War." It could not be plainer as story-telling. The dead man had been a Spanish peasant taken, fairly or not, for a guerrilla in the resistance to the Grand Army of the French Empire. His trousers have fallen to his calves, because his executioners have, with strict economy, used the sash that held them up for the rope.

There are no leaves on the tree that is his gallows, and he has no company except a soldier who peacefully contemplates his afternoon's accomplishments; his uniform, the hussar's hat and crest, identify him as one of Napoleon's Polish auxiliaries.

The image that finally holds us is not the hanged man but this witness. His elbow is on a stone slab, and his head rests on his hand as support for raising itself up for a clearer view of his work. The true and lasting shock is that Goya has drawn this murderer in the very attitude of the connoisseur in the artist's studio studying the new piece offered for sale and growing ever more content the longer he looks.

The French Revolution has come to Spain, incarnate in this figure that, having begun with the acceptance of the Terror as a necessity, has arrived at its enjoyment as a pleasure. The French Revolution mixed benign concepts and malignant notions, and in these bicentennial days when charity most urges us to celebrate the benign, the malign rises up somewhere else in the world with a new reminder of its enduring force.

The French Revolution cannot enter a fair claim to inventing the Rights of Man, which had been affirmed in terms no less artistically declamatory in our own. Its only authentically new aspect was the Terror, and small excess though the successor outrages in this century now make it seem, it has been immense as an example for them.

Its most seductive and soul-destroying appeal has been to revolutionaries of the left to whom it offered the means that pretended to justify an ever-receding end. Lenin would not have shot the children of the czar if the French Revolution had not beheaded Louis XVI and Marie Antoinette.

Begin to rule by killing a fallen and helpless woman and you will inevitably wind up as a regime that kills peasants. And you will be of no use; what has happened to the Soviet Union and is happening in China is a demonstration in proof that the Terror cannot create a viable system of government. To wallow in the blood of others means eventually to coagulate your own.

The Metropolitan has called its Goya show "Goya and the Age of Enlightenment," a title that would work as well with a question mark at its end. None of us can come any closer to the state of Enlightenment than pretending to it. Our old dark devils never leave, and they start forth in Goya's images of witches half-mocked and half-believed in, or bandits on peaceful landscapes detachedly exterminating the last survivor, or the fantastic and baleful shapes that swirl about the sleeper's head in the etching upon which he put the title, "The Sleep of Reason Produces Monsters," which would be no less satisfactory if it were shortened to "Reason Produces Monsters."

Perhaps what confuses me so much in Goya is simply the clarity of these distillings of the confusions that contend within each and all of us and that must be accounted for in all serviceable reflections on the French Revolution. When Napoleon had been driven out, Spain's *ancien régime* was restored and matters were as they had been before the

Enlightenment. Goya decamped to Bordeaux. France had returned to its senses, and Spain was back with its old nonsense. Whatever else can be said for or against the French Revolution, Goya's final choice was no small compliment.

New York Newsday, June 30, 1989

Thurgood Marshall

MEMORIES COME BACK to uplift the hearts of old men with powers to exhilarate that reside far less often in the recollection of grandeurs than of struggles.

And so Thurgood Marshall could hardly forget that the best time life gave him was not when he was a U.S. Supreme Court justice but when he was general counsel of the National Association for the Advancement of Colored People, traveling a South where there was no room at most inns for such as he.

All of what made Mr. Justice Marshall is distilled in a single anecdote in *Simple Justice*, Richard Kluger's distressingly neglected classic history of the NAACP's legal wars through the forty years before *Brown v. Board of Education*.

Thurgood Marshall's father was chief steward of the Gibson Island Club in southern Maryland and could dispose a summer job as a waiter for his son. One night, when the younger Marshall was at his station, a visiting congressman from Iowa, high flown with insolence, wine, and ignorance of the customs of the region, called out, "Come here, nigger."

And then Ellison DuRant Smith, the senator from South Carolina, rose up to demand in thunder, "What did he call you, Thurgood? I will not hear that word spoken in this club."

The offender was driven into the night, exiled for a private racial slur by the wrath of Cotton Ed Smith, the most tireless public race-baiter on the Senate floor. The "n" word was Smith's common currency for the campaigns he debased; but he would not hear it in the company of gentlemen.

Thurgood Marshall had to grow up in a white South so unsettled in its interior quarrel that no piece of its behavior could be taken for granted: It could often be cruel and sometimes be kind and would always be a mystery. But if southern white people were never easy to understand, northern ones would remain forever inexplicable.

He who would deal with either could never afford the mistake of trusting or distrusting absolutely. No one is redeemed and no one is irredeemable; the hostiles are no more without better sides of their natures than the friendlies are without worse of theirs. At no point in his last press conference Friday did Thurgood Marshall appear to come closer to bristling than when some questioner tried to press him toward pious denunciations of their presumed mutual inferiors in sensitivity to injustice.

We are saying farewell to one of those best of men and women, the sort who hate the *unco' guid*, which may be why President George Bush seems so much bitterer a thought to Thurgood Marshall than Senator Smith ever could be. The senator knew his bad side only too well; but the President's sits complacently unexamined.

Marshall's face broods now as with the dissatisfied contemplation of a great work of history begun, left incomplete, and not to be taken up again any time soon. He was making his triumphal exit with the look that says it belongs to a failure. He had beaten the spiteful again and again, but the indifferent had worn him out at the end.

The year had left him no further resource than the grand remonstrance of the outsider. He was obsolete. He had learned about life from prisoners in cells, farmers without land, sheriffs without pity, and children without enough food, and now he had ended where the actualities of suffering human flesh were dissolving into abstractions.

There was nothing more for him to do but register objections in what has to be the terminal loneliness of anyone whose father and mother had trained him in good manners as carefully as Thurgood Marshall's did. No gentleman likes to make himself a nuisance when being one is no longer useful to the public good.

Thurgood Marshall may or may not have gone away weighed down by the suspicion that the history he created is over. He should know it isn't, and his proudest thought must be that the unknown young who begin it again will take up a journey that seems far closer to hope than his did when he started it.

New York Newsday, June 30, 1991

Felled Oaks

"**W**E ARE CERTAINLY witnessing the death of Europe.... We are the last Europeans in Europe, which was Christianity," Charles de Gaulle says to André Malraux in this last talk of theirs in December 1969, now published as *Conversation with de Gaulle*. Such was the good-bye of fallen President to the Minister-of-Culture-become-odd-job-man: Our Passing is the Death of Europe.

Two adventurers twice raised by their own despair and self-esteem to the station at the very least of great pretenders, and now no more to rise. The only mistake that might seem worse than to swallow all Malraux's terms for taking them seriously would be not to take them very seriously indeed. Something terminal *can* be felt in these conversations; but it is not the death of Europe; it is the dying of Europe's last great mythic figure in the arms of her last grand mythomaniac.

Many of us outsiders came to think of de Gaulle as France; and, if these conversations reinforce that incarnation, it may be because no one can be said to embody a nation unless his person carries within itself both the good sense and the nonsense that have timelessly abided together throughout its traditions.

We approach de Gaulle, as we ought to approach France, with diffidence, that is, with both respect and distrust. There is something in so many Frenchmen that afflicts them with the dream of being Napoleon as there is something in so many Italians that redeems them with the dream of being St. Francis. Yet all this pretension has never lived free from the intimate proximity of those who found it ridiculous. France seems a family of those who puff up and those who deflate. There can be no Versailles without its Saint-Simon, and the Proust who felt himself trembling as the spirit of the Guermantes passed over him at a great height was inextricable from the Proust who was the parodist.

So de Gaulle's claim to *be* France is most powerful when his speech mixes the self-serious with the self-mocking. The incarnation of the myth quite often, of course, retains a common sense lost to those possessed by it. The General was the balloon to be sure, but he was also the pin.

"Your predecessor," Malraux tells him "is not a politician—not even Clemenceau. It is Victor Hugo."

"Actually you know," the General replies, "my only international rival is Tintin." "We are the little fellows who refuse to get taken in by the big ones. No one sees this, because of my height." One had come rather to conceive him as the husband in the Feydeau farce, taller and stiffer and more nearsighted than anyone else on stage; and he is most authentically the hero in the gravity of farce with which he evokes his final situation: "I shall not be able, for the third time, to grab France by the hair at the last moment."

He reflects on his time in office: "*I entertained them with banners. I persuaded them to be patient while waiting for*—for what if not France?"

He remembers, as a magician might, the fall of his props and his crash in May of 1968: "In May everything was slipping from me. I had lost my grip on my own government. That changed of course when I appealed to the country at large when I said, 'I am dissolving Parliament.' . . . I felt [I had] a way of awakening the country, of making it aware of its own existence, of shaking it up. But it had already made its choice. . . . I said what I had to say. But the game was over."

And now he looks upon the snow on the abandoned countryside around his window and mockingly imagines his monument: "They will set up a great Cross of Lorraine on the highest hill there. It will be visible to everyone, but, as there is no one, no one will see it. It will rouse the rabbits to resistance."

For here is a *hauteur* so lofty as to condescend even to its own person. For all his "old boys," his smile withers slightly even when it is most affectionate. The General invites the minister of culture to discourse on the Soviet Union; and Malraux is off on one of those bouts of rhetoric of his that seem so often to reduce nature into the most implausible imitation of art:

"Long ago Bukharin and I were pacing the Place de L'Odéon—it was surrounded with sewer pipes taken out of their trenches—and, in a distracted tone, he confided, 'And now he is going to kill me.' And he did." . . . " 'Russia is still full of Karamazovs,' Ehrenberg used to say. I was with him when . . ." "I met Stalin at Gorki's house; cunning and strange." One feels an absolute confidence about Malraux when he remembers his experiences and an absolute distrust when he retails his anecdotes; he is honest in the weave but suspect in the embroidery. We can believe he met Stalin, but *at Gorki's house?* We can accept the memory that his resistance band took cover in a cave, but *Lascaux?* We end trusting Malraux in pretty much everything except this insistence that history casts its tableaux as though Irving Thalberg were its producer and Norma Shearer its star; and that is no small area in which to distrust a man.

And, after the anecdotes, he passes to the imagery, equally suspicious:

"The past is always there in Russia! In Lenin's office beside maps of the civil war fronts, a small bronze Darwinian ape-man stood on a pile of Marx's works. . . . I visited the Marx-Engels museum. It was empty enough for me to find several pairs of lovers clasped together in the last room, more secluded than the benches in the square."

"And," the General intervenes, *"beyond the picturesque?"*

Malraux remembers their conversation after the General returned from President Kennedy's funeral.

"You added: 'She is a brave woman and very well brought up. As to her fate, you are mistaken. She is a star and will end up on the yacht of some oil baron.' "

"Did I say that?" de Gaulle replies. "Well, well. . . . Actually I would have thought she would marry Sartre. Or you!"

The merciful teasing of these passages suggests how finally correct Malraux is when he applies the adjective "bizarre" only to the General's shrewdness. If the mind seems otherwise outlandish to us, it is only because it was so old-fashioned.

Its splendors, of course, can be overvalued; some of its utterances have the banality of the modern:

"I like trees. I also like woodcutters."

"No other civilization has been so powerful, none so alienated from its values. Why conquer the moon, if only to commit suicide there?"

"I didn't come to destroy capitalism. But, on the other hand, I didn't defend it."

But most of de Gaulle's ideas, like de Gaulle himself, belonged, as Malraux says, to the millennial past. Their true fascination, beyond their style of adornment, comes from his obsession with concepts that seemed outmoded to many of his contemporaries and irrelevant to many of us. What counted for the General was the permanence of nations.

"The idea of a class struggle is a powerful one," he says. "I don't deny that. But it is contrary to all that is deepest in me. I don't want to set groups against each other even to win out. I want to bring them together. . . . That's why I shall never be a monarchist whatever the agitators. There is no possibility of uniting France around the royal family. Nor is it possible to unite it around the working class, which is in the process of growing exhausted."

He wonders at one point whether Lenin knew that he had really come to reestablish Russia. "Even if Communism lets the Russians believe in Russia for nonsensical reasons, that belief is irreplaceable." The test of an idea for him then was not so much whether it was reasonable as whether it was unifying: Monarchism can no longer serve France; but Marxist-Leninism can still serve Russia.

The General's mind was set, one suspects, when he taught history at St. Cyr and there assembled in his imagination the parade of heroes that would always haunt it—the "soldier saints" on the tombs of the Middle Ages, Carnot, Napoleon, Clemenceau, even the 1870 Paris Commune because it, too, wanted to take France on its shoulders. He ought to have been less complicatedly a Man of the Right: He was an intellectual; he reached sentience when the League of the French Nation could enlist most members of the Académie Française; and his maturity was formed in a time when, as Malraux reminds him, Charles Maurras's Action Française ruled the Sorbonne. But the very antique cast of his mind made him resistant to a Right that he judged to have "ceased to have an ideology when it ceased to ally itself with the nation." That breach, it ought to be noticed, is more than 180 years old by now, having begun at Valmy where the French monarchy raised most of Europe against France; and there would thereafter be very few ancestors to people the General's imagination except men of the Left functioning as the revolutionary dictators of a nation in arms.

He would die with the collected works of Bergson in his workroom, having remained to the end in thrall to the notion of the *élan vital*. Malraux quite properly saluted him as the last antifascist leader of the West; and we can at once accept this as the most honorable appellation possible for anyone of the General's generation and recognize it as a definition of the unclubbable nature of anyone who earns it, Continental antifascism having come to seem in retrospect most curiously a kind of class treason. Class treason begins in heresy, and heresy, once having intruded in a detail, has a way of extending toward the whole: Having once dissented from the tactics of the French army, de Gaulle moved quite naturally to carelessness about the pieties of its politics.

He had welcomed the Popular Front in 1936, because "I thought: Since they must fight Fascism first of all, they will be obliged to defend France." Yet the Popular Front, try though it did to rearm, could attempt no more than a facsimile of the French Army of 1918; only Hitler's generals were open to the theories of Colonel de Gaulle. He traces his disillusionment with the Left to that experience; to the General, the only inadequacy fatal to any political theory was in military will.

His haunting by the past explains the superb effrontery of that morning in June 1940, when, essentially alone in London and setting aside his own illegitimacy in the collapse of everyone else's legitimacy, he decided that "it was up to me to assume I was France." It serves also to explain that indifference to social utility that was the most outrageous thing about him and could make him say, "[Napoleon] left France smaller than he found her, granted; but that is not what defines a nation. For France he had to exist. It is a little like Versailles; it had to be done. Don't let's sell grandeur short." But then, in the France of 1940, one could hardly have been a committed antifascist unless one was also anti-utilitarian.

But here was a vision that, as obsessions unfortunately do, tended finally to crash. Malraux is the most faithful living executor of the General's image of France; and it is useful to notice how brave and dutiful are the common people who inhabit his imagination:

"I thought of my companions in the tank—Bonneau the pimp with his wounded finch . . . Leonard the fireman from the Casino de Paris who was the star's beloved; of the men of the maquis, of the women in the black shawls each before her grave when our dead in Corrèze were being buried . . . of the prisoners of Saint-Michel at Toulouse who, when the Gestapo fellow came to our cell bawling 'Terrorists!' answered in a professorial tone, 'Tourists'; of the youngsters of Ramonchamp and Danmarie who came with their teacher in the night to plant their little flags over our first graves."

What we have here are the proletarians who charm us in the old Renoir films, the women asking no more than to stand watch and endure, the intellectuals who can command the last word in the face of the enemy, the pupils who file to their revolutionary gesture obediently behind their teacher. It is hard to be just to Malraux when the fit is upon him to reduce his myths to genre paintings of this sort. Still is there not a common message in all these images of children, pimps, professors all rendered proper by the unifying idea of the nation? To minds more mechanical than ours ought to be, they could indeed suggest the formula for national renaissance that General Maxime Weygand held out to the French along with their surrender: "God, Country, Family." And Gaullism *was* authoritarian; a great part of the General's elegance was in his cultivation of the acquaintance of ideas; still one senses that he is most approving when he watches intellectuals marching in formation.

"Desnos," he thinks, "died nobly." The memory is of a poet killed in the Resistance. "Why," he continues, "don't the intellectuals believe in France any longer? . . . Voltaire, whatever he may have thought, was more closely linked with France than with Reason."

And yet he was so much more than the General in the reviewing stand; the charm of this pair is in their contradictions; as Malraux is a very pious agnostic, de Gaulle was an authoritarian with a most distracting affection for liberty. Men obsessed by past memories of historical bursts of energy are apt, in times when no pot stirs, to think of themselves as caretakers for some burst of energy to come. "If, before I die," de Gaulle said in 1958, "I can see a new generation of French youth. . . ."

Even now he is vividly curious only about the unknown young; in the midst of most desultory talk about America, the General quickens to ask:

"Did you have an opportunity to see their great hippie gatherings?"

"I think most of them occurred in California," Malraux answers.

"What do they really want?" the General pursues.

And Malraux, deprived of anecdote, flounders for common frames of reference—existentialism, Gandhi, Che Guevara. Only the mention of Guevara stimulates the General; adventurers are a fraternity joined by the quest, whatever the goal.

The General's long watch for the new generation of French youth had, of course, both its reward and its punishment in May 1968. The young rose and formed their battalions, however transiently, and superseded his myth with their own and then departed, having left things very much as they had been not just before they came but before he came, too. The General had a professional disdain for the theater to which the young trooped in preference to his own; and he can be wonderfully ironic about those scenes:

"Revolution? *I* was the only revolutionary." (Such is his command upon our imaginations that he can almost make us forget that he, the only revolutionary, had entrusted the management of the French economy to a vice president of the Rothschild Bank.) "There were the Communists, of course; but to them the word meant seizure of power by their party. And years later, in May of 1968, their leader said to our Minister of the Interior, 'Don't give way.' "

But the larger irony may have escaped him. For in 1968 he would be rescued, if only for a little while, by Frenchmen who could imagine no grander way to celebrate their part in restoring the natural order than honking their horns to glorify the General who had set the gasoline pumps free to fuel their inane voyagings upon the road.

The Gaullists had been rescued by the Pétainists. But that has a way of happening with incarnations of the nation; different though each may be from the other, every incarnation finds his last cult in persons more interested in what can still be preserved than in what might yet be created. The need to accept is part of every impulse to incarnate; Claudel and Mauriac, Pétain and de Gaulle, those opposites, could quite comfortably be seen as successive incarnations of France. Malraux and de Gaulle were men of the Resistance, who, in their penultimate crisis, could find no salvation elsewhere than in the constituency of Acceptance. That familiar turn in a history of myths that so often begins in energy and ends in exhaustion, diminishes in no measure, of course, our fascination with the last one or our susceptibility to the next. To read de Gaulle and Malraux even here together when everything had passed them by is to understand the command that fantasy will forever be able to place upon us: Both of them are so much more wonderful than anyone real.

The New York Times Book Review, April 23, 1972

Perversities

My Last Mugging

W<small>E ARE ALL</small> addicts in various stages of degradation where I live on the Upper West Side, some to heroin, some to small dogs, and some to *The New York Times*. The heroin is cut, the dogs are paranoid, and the *Times* cheats by skimping on the West Coast ball scores. No matter; each of us goes upon the street solely in pursuit of his own particular curse.

I was plodding homeward with my *Times* at an hour no less decent than eleven on an evening in March when two figures, conspicuous through the dark for a condition of nerves frantic even for West 97th Street, came round the corner and converged upon me, one to the left and one to the right.

The one to the right was short and wore a porkpie hat of the kind one used to associate with the first account executive laid off in the agency's economy drive in the first Eisenhower recession. The one to the left was taller, sticklike, indeed, with those whitened cracks in the skin of his face that the winter of cities inflicts upon Negroes and that they call "the ashes"; and he held a knife at what I supposed to be my kidneys.

"Give us all your money," the little one stuttered. "Or we're going to cut you up right now."

"Now, be cool," the tall one said. "And just hand over your money. He means it."

Cops are said to go at criminal suspects in this fashion, in pairs, one short and mean, the other tall and protective. So here, then, were those two familiars of the station house, Jeff ravening on one side of the detainee and Mutt conciliating on the other. As jail seems to be the only institution left that can teach young black men to write, the back room of the precinct house is the last school for the techniques of negotiation. I was being accosted by ruffians who had learned their trade by losing—laboratory animals who knew nothing of the science except what could be studied while being vivisected.

The knife was, to be sure, long enough and broad enough to establish itself as the one commanding presence in the assembly; still, it was a very old knife, with no sign of any recent impulse to clean it; the hand at my kidneys had, then, quite a while ago lost either the vanity that might have shined that knife or the hope that might have sharpened it.

The mind could grasp it only as an abstraction. Courage is the product of rehearsal, as cowardice is of recollection; neither comes on call upon occasions of surprise: Surprised, one merely stands and the head wanders down paths that prove how empty the event is, since they are not even literary, only sociological—a disgraceful knife, a failure of a knife, good only for my neighborhood, a knife a man would be embarrassed to carry in the East Sixties, less a knife, indeed, than an artifact of urban decay. Where I live, we get the criminals and even the weapons of hopelessness we deserve.

"Gentlemen," I began, "I haven't got so much as a dollar. I do have some change and a subway token. But that's all I have. I'm sorry."

I took out my wallet and showed it to them with an anxiety to please that, at the moment, at least, had curiously less to do with the knife than with the recurrent sense of my own inadequacy on social occasions. I felt like a welsher. They had done their job; they had pulled a knife, such as it was, and quite enough for me; and I wasn't doing mine. Jeff was already exhausted from his contrivings of desperate aggression; and poor Mutt was left to manage the affair to its end in disillusion.

"Let's get off the street," he said. "I gotta search you." And they pushed me unzestfully into the entranceway of a building I had never before known to be other than packed with inexplicably cheerful Latins, but empty now; and there, in the bright light that illuminated how much too old all of us were for such a scene, Mutt searched me, as the police must have trained him during his service in their laboratories, all the way to the crotch.

He came up empty and reproachful.

"You look like a workingman," he said. "What you doing out in the street with no money?"

It seemed entirely proper to apologize.

"Gentlemen," I said at last, "I feel like a shit."

"Don't you think we feel like shits?" Mutt answered. "We don't like to do this kind of thing. All we're looking for is a couple of bucks to get a shot of dope."

Where I live, we are rather stiff-necked about permitting someone else to claim the moral advantage. They turned and left the lobby, with Mutt trailing the knife slackly against his trouser leg, the whole night yet before him and without the will to recover from this first mischance.

I felt the sixty cents still in my hand and called after them, "Well, anyway, take the change."

And Mutt came back and took it, and we said good night, and I went home with no sense that I had made it up to them.

For a while afterward, I dined out on this event, and everyone I told it to seemed to find it a great relief from urban tensions. And yet the experience, whose telling seems to work to lessen the paranoia of other persons, has impossibly increased my own. Not just 97th Street but nearly every other in the city has become for me a swarm of horrible shadows. I have no way even of knowing when the fear will come over me; the other day a Negro teenager approached me in a subway station and just stood there. At last he asked for a dime and, sweating, I gave him all the change I had. He had intended nothing; and yet I was his victim; my flesh could not have crawled more shudderingly if he had pulled a gun. I have thought of buying a heavy cane. Yet if I went thus armed, I should suppose that I would bring my weapon down upon the head of whoever accosted me and then beat him passionately, if ineffectually, for mere rage at this city that has taught me that I am old and a coward. For these are scenes from which it is impossible to emerge unashamed. And I am thinking of moving away to some far place where a man can keep his mask and have no need to choose between wearing the face of the victim or the face of the beast.

Playboy, December 1971

The Mafia Myth

"Gregory the Great tells us how the nun of a convent, walking in the garden, ate a lettuce-leaf without making the cautionary sign of the cross, and was immediately possessed by a demon. St. Equitius tortured the spirit with his exorcisms till the unhappy imp exclaimed: 'What have I done? I was sitting on the leaf and she ate me.' But Equitius would listen to no excuse and forced him to depart."
—HENRY CHARLES LEA, *A History of the Inquisition in the Middle Ages*

THE FEDERAL BUREAU of Investigation has yielded up to us the transcripts of its long eavesdropping upon the office hours of Simone Rizzo (Sam) DeCavalcante, boss of a Cosa Nostra Family seated in Union County, New Jersey. DeCavalcante was facing trial for conspiracy to extort; his counsel demanded that the Justice Department produce any wiretaps that might have assisted it toward the indictment; and to his surprise, and probable chagrin, he was granted the public release of his client's conversations, the private as well as the professional, all of it faithfully and indiscriminately recorded by the special agents of the FBI, and none of it, by the way, bearing upon the particular crime charged. This mass of intimacies, disjointed and expensive though it is, carries the sizable reward of providing us with more that we can trust than we have ever before been told about an American *mafioso* of executive stature.

Donald R. Cressey is Professor of Sociology at the University of California, Santa Barbara, and though we may think that *Theft of the Nation* is a title that might have better served the Sierra Club, the work itself comes to us with academic credentials more elaborate than any before offered in Mafia studies. Ed Reid began as a reporter in Brooklyn, which is to organized crime what Rome is to the Church. He won a

Pulitzer Prize for investigating police corruption more than twenty years ago. *The Grim Reapers* is at least his fifth book in the field. Yet read alongside the real life of Sam DeCavalcante, the reports of these two authorities seem astoundingly credulous, the journalist and the academic being our chief sources of social misinformation. One of the few knowledgeable persons I can imagine believing them is Sam De-Cavalcante himself; the faith of witches and of the hunters of witches survives the failure of witchcraft.

THE GAP BETWEEN such authority and the world itself begins when we set down first Dr. Cressey's notion of our general condition and then DeCavalcante's description of his particular circumstance. For example:

> The $6 or $7 billion going into the hands of ordinary criminals each year is not all profit. . . . Neither can it be assumed that the amount is divided equally among the five thousand or so members of Cosa Nostra. But the profits are huge enough that any given member of Cosa Nostra is more likely to be a millionaire than not.
>
> (Dr. Cressey)

> We got 31 or 32 soldiers. Most of them are old people who ain't making much. Those making money give me one third. Say one makes $600, then he gives me $200 and I don't split with anyone else.
>
> (Sam DeCavalcante, June 4, 1964)

DeCavalcante was describing his province, of course, a little while after his elevation to command of a Family of such modest dimensions as to be unlisted in most Cosa Nostra public registers. Then, too, he was talking to Gene Catena, whose brother Jerry was a rather more substantial figure; and DeCavalcante may have thought it wise to undervalue his estate in conversation with imperialists. For a more respectful view of the property, we have the estimate of Anthony Russo, Cosa Nostra's man in Long Branch, New Jersey: "I wish I had Elizabeth [New

Jersey] locked up like you have. . . . There's a lot of money in Elizabeth."

But it is clearly not an environment productive of millionaires. Any given DeCavalcante soldier can hardly sit in his presence without giving way to confessions of indigence:

> Frank Cocchiaro told DeCavalcante that he has money problems, as he gives his wife $50 a week, pays $125 a month rent in N.J. and $115 rent per month for his wife.

In December 1964, DeCavalcante and Frank Majuri, his underboss, meet to arbitrate a protocol dispute between Joe Riggi and Joe Sferra, two *capiregime*. "Sam, I came to you yesterday," Riggi says, "because I felt that, as an *amico nos* and a *caporegima*, I'm not getting the respect I should from Joe Sferra." Sferra's regime was the Elizabeth Hod Carriers local; his affront was in not relieving Riggi's father from carrying brick and finding him a lighter assignment.

"Sam, I had the understanding that our people came first," Riggi went on. "I think we went in and asked for the job before anybody else. I didn't get the cooperation or the respect from Joe. I have to answer for my father. . . . First I feel offended as an *amico nos*—that I can't go to my friend and get a favor for one of my soldiers. Second, even as a *caporegima*, I can't do nothing. I did what I did only because of my father, who has lived a dog's life for three years."

These are not the problems of affluence. This penury, of course, may not be typical; the legendary metropolitan Families (the Luccheses, the Gambinos, and the Profacis) could have a dividend picture closer to Dr. Cressey's gaudy colors. DeCavalcante certainly shares that impression. In January of 1965, he tells underboss Majuri: "Listen, if we don't join these big outfits and try to make a buck, we're dead. They got the money."

STILL, THERE ARE overtones in DeCavalcante's long courtship of the Gambino Family which raise doubts even about *its* majesty. His control over the Elizabeth Hod Carriers union was mainly useful to DeCavalcante for providing jobs for unemployed soldiers; and Carlo Gambino seems to have felt more gratitude at having its courtesies extended to his Family than comports with one's image of a great prince of unlimited resources. In September of 1964, Joseph Zoppo, a Gambino soldier, is laid off his job as a hod carrier; and DeCavalcante taxes the local's *caporegima* with having caused this embarrassment. "What did he run to you for?" Sferra asks. "He's got a lot of nerve."

"Joe, nerve or no nerve," his Boss replies. "You know I promised Carl Gambino that we'd treat their men better than our own people. And I want it that way. . . . You see, Joe, over here, I'm trying to build a good relationship with everybody on the Commission. Our *brigata* is small, but we could do things as good as anybody else. And I told you—as long as they are *amico nostro*, I want to keep them working before anyone else."

In the end Sferra was deposed from his regime. One culminating offense was his loss of dignity in a traffic dispute: "The [other driver] went after him like a tiger and put Joe off his feet. When he fell he broke his foot. Now is that any way for an *amico nos* and a *caporegima* to act?" But Sferra's worse sin was in neglecting his duty to provide Cosa Nostra soldiers what special favors we can imagine as available to persons seeking common labor: "I told Sferra I was saving his life by removing him; he was defying Carl Gambino." Over who gets to carry brick?

There is indeed very little evidence in these conversations that even the major Families have attained that security beyond worry about the basic necessities. "Joe Notaro [underboss of the Bonnano Family] owes me money," Joe Bayonne says. "He owes Mike Coppola money—he can't pay. He hasn't got a quarter." Joe Columbo, who inherited the Profaci Family, steals dresses from factories, two out of each lot. These are hardly either the circumstances or enterprises of captains who rule over millionaires.

The true case is rather more like the scene described in one talk between DeCavalcante and Anthony Russo, his colleague in Long Branch:

DeCavalcante: Do you know Frank [Cocchiaro] is a rough guy I have to watch. Frank would do heist jobs [armed robberies] if I'd let him.

Russo: Sammy, do you know how many friends of ours are on heists?

DeCavalcante: They can't support themselves.

Russo: Do you know how many guys are safe-cracking? What they gonna do? Half these guys are handling junk [narcotics]. Now there's a [Cosa Nostra] law out that they can't touch it. They have no other way of making a living, so what can they do? All right, we're fortunate enough that we didn't have to move around and didn't have to resort to that stuff. What are the other poor suckers going to do? Pretty soon we'll have all the mob here [in New Jersey]. Guys are coming here asking to be put on [work gambling games], and they're friends of ours, so I put them on because I can't let them starve to death. Sam, pretty soon I may have to say no to them because I got to look out for myself. I'll help your boys when I can.

DeCavalcante: My people won't starve to death. I'll feed them.

Criminal organizations dealing only in illicit goods and services are no great threat to the nation. The danger of organized crime arises because the vast profits acquired from the sale of illicit goods and services are being invested in licit enterprises in both the economic sphere and the political sphere. It is when criminal syndicates start to undermine basic economic and political traditions and institutions that the real trouble begins.

(Dr. Cressey)

No, Bob, we're doing real good here. I don't know how long it's going to last, but we're doing okay. If I can continue for two or three years, I will be able to show $40,000 or $50,000 legitimately and can walk out. Then my family situation will be resolved.

(Sam DeCavalcante)

Experts on the Mafia conceive of its legitimate businesses as disguises; Sam DeCavalcante thinks of his as an escape from the instabilities of illegitimacy. His chief licit enterprise is the Kenworth Corporation, a plumbing and heating supply house in Kenilworth, New Jersey. It is very much a Family business, having been bequeathed to him by Nick Delmore, the deceased head of what is now called the DeCavalcante Family. His partner is Lawrence Wolfson, who, if he cannot with full assurance be described as a legitimate businessman, is certainly a licensed one. DeCavalcante seems to have brought little wealth to the partnership except the weight of his name as a Cosa Nostra boss; building contractors use Wolfson and DeCavalcante to bribe construction trades labor leaders for exemption from union conditions, and reward this service by buying their plumbing from Kenworth.

Wolfson appears to have indulged this special sales technique with so much more enthusiasm than DeCavalcante ever did that there even arose complaints that he was damaging DeCavalcante's good name.

"You are known as a shakedown artist, Sam," his cousin Bobby Basile tells him. "You are shaking the contractors down! Do you think anybody would come in here and tell you this, Sam? Do you know that to the outside world your reputation is unbelievable? They dread the thought of coming in and talking to you. How come Larry Wolfson can get $150 a unit more than anyone else?"

"Our equipment and jobs are much superior," DeCavalcante answers, to which Basile gives reply, "Don't you believe it."

A FEW DAYS afterward DeCavalcante feels compelled to bring up the peril of greed with his partner. The FBI summarizes:

> Subject criticized Lawrence Wolfson for his aggressiveness in "grabbing people" on union matters. Subject pointed out the dangers of being charged with extortion if they continue this activity. He noted that he feels very strongly about jeopardizing their legitimate business. He is willing to finish whatever arrangements are now pending but has strictly forbidden Larry to start any more deals between contractors and labor officials.
>
> Speaking in confidence, subject told Larry that his purpose in

bringing Frank Cocchiaro into his business (Imperial Refrigeration and Air Conditioning) was to keep an eye on him. He described Frank as a "professional thief" who was heading for disaster as he got older.

Stealing seems to DeCavalcante an altogether less fruitful occupation than it does to Dr. Cressey, because DeCavalcante has been there. The advantage of the illicit over the licit is finally described in a conversation between Wolfson and Joseph Ippolito, a DeCavalcante soldier:

> Ippolito told Wolfson that he is making $700–$800 a week in his mason business. Ippolito claims that he is doing better at the mason business than with the numbers business he has. Ippolito claimed he lost $1300 a day and $1200 the next in paying off hits and believes that his numbers business is on the decline. . . . He would give up his numbers in a minute if DeCavalcante would let him. Ippolito says he owes $50,000 to various people and DeCavalcante will not let him give up the numbers until he repays all the money he owes. Ippolito says he sweats out all day to 6:00 P.M. when he finds out what the day's number is.

Dr. Cressey accepts that canon of Mafia studies that a numbers bank is all but guaranteed a profit. We have plainly been pursuing the wrong witches; DeCavalcante's experience indicates that when an old gypsy woman in East Harlem dreams a number, it comes up alarmingly often enough to wreck the bank. The DeCavalcante Family introduces the Twin Double Lottery to Northern New Jersey; in December 1964, Lou Larasso reports the total business down to $100 a day; in January, Whitey Danzo, as soldier-in-charge, has to confess a $6,000 loss on just one number.

"DeCavalcante," the FBI reports, "apparently intends to relinquish his one-third interest in the operation to Frank Cocchiaro as soon as he returns to Florida."

The men holding knives at the throats of American businessmen. . . .

(Dr. Cressey)

Larry explains that "we" want to sue Pako [phonetic] for selling
Kenworth inferior valves and pumps. Larry mentioned that in
addition to Pako the following firms are involved: Essex Plumbing
Supply, Janitrol and Federal Boilers. . . . Larry does not want to hurt
Essex Supply, but does want to collect from Pako. Larry feels that
Pako will settle rather than go to court. . . . Sam disagrees with
Larry.

(Special Agent Brudnicki, summarizing DeCavalcante transcripts,
September 1964)

The foreign relations of Cosa Nostra—its attitude toward outside
institutions like the businessman and the politician—constitute the
heart of the mystery and the one least reducible to the simplicities.
That is the way with international matters; when two sovereign entities
come to negotiate, it is a rare observer who can resist dividing the sides
into a wrong one and a right one. Foreign policy is invariably mythic.
Dr. Cressey's errors are those of a patriot; to him, the Mafia is foreign
and legitimate business is native. His work falls quite naturally into the
spirit of Cold War studies.

Still the changeless key of nationalism wears out all but the deafest
or hardiest ear after a while; one expatriate in Paris, after being ham-
mered upon by the Gaullist myth for ten years, said that his mind felt
like a tired piano. We commence to cry out for the opposite, particularly in moments of distaste for ourselves. The more dreadful we know
Saigon to be, the lovelier we conceive Hanoi. It would otherwise be
curious that the most popular of all examples of literature about the
Mafia should be Mario Puzo's The Godfather, a novel celebrating the
counter-myth of a Don, just, omnipotent, and in every way the moral
better of the respectable Americans with whom he deals. We want, I
suppose, in times of self-disgust to believe in Uncle Vito Corleone as
we already do in Uncle Ho.

.　.　.

BUT LONG IMMERSION in the affairs of Sam DeCavalcante does not carry with it quite enough such consolation when we surface. We can fairly compare his ethical sense to the norms prevailing in honest trade only in small snatches of his conversations with Joseph Wilf and Samuel Halpern, two builders who made him their broker with corruptible labor unions. There is here no intimation of terror on DeCavalcante's side, but considerable indication of chicanery by both:

> DeCavalcante claimed that he does not make a nickel on arranging these payoffs and that he and Wolfson are paid only by being allowed to do the heating-plumbing work on those contracts on which he arranged the labor peace.

That statement is, of course, false; it seems to be the Family custom to take half of all packages assembled for distribution to union officials. But, on their side, Wilf and Halpern are so slow to pay that DeCavalcante complains continually that he has had to lay out his own money, and is finally driven to say that he will make no payoffs "before receiving the money aforehand":

> DeCavalcante told them that he wants payoff money from them in the future and when he asks for it and does not expect to be kept waiting. DeCavalcante told them that, any time they feel they can do better with someone else to arrange their payoffs, they are welcome to stop seeing him.

His dealings with businessmen seem to have the soundly based tenor of mutual distrust familiar to the construction industry with no distinct moral advantage for either party.

In his own Family, DeCavalcante appears altogether a better master than the character of his servants deserves. Dr. Cressey expatiates at length on the Cosa Nostra code with its emphasis on "(1) *extreme loyalty* to the organization and its governing elite; (2) *honesty* in relationships with members; (3) *secrecy* . . . ; and (4) *honorable behavior* which sets members off as morally superior to those outsiders who would govern them." Dr. Cressey sounds very much the way Louis

Budenz and Whittaker Chambers used to when they were describing the iron moral fiber of the enemy, and he sustains some of the same contradictions by the facts.

Indeed, we draw that same impression of general Family delinquency which common sense ought to have led us to expect from the conduct of persons who have led the life these have. DeCavalcante's day is a fairly continuous and seldom effectual engagement with lethargic soldiers, wandering husbands, and insufficiently trustworthy lieutenants: "Louis Larasso is a cockroach" . . . "Corky can't seem to settle down. He sent me a message that he's going to start stealing again." . . . "I have to keep Danny Noto in the Family because he is a money-maker."

IN ADDITION TO his own troops, policemen and labor officials constitute the two categories of citizens beside whom DeCavalcante seems assured of his own moral superiority. The Family assumes that, in cases of arrest, the police steal your watch unless advance precautions are taken. When Angelo Bruno complains that one DeCavalcante soldier had once confessed himself a numbers banker ("No friend of ours is supposed to sign a statement with the police") DeCavalcante offers the sovereign excuse that Joe's poor wife had been caught with the numbers and that the police had threatened to take her in unless he confessed himself solely responsible.

"We're all married, Ange," DeCavalcante explains. "What man will let his wife go through an embarrassment *standing alone with detectives* being questioned?" In his youth, Bruno severely replies, the police had caught him and his wife in the same situation. "*I gave them $700 to take me alone.* I didn't sign no statement."

The unredeemed dishonor of the labor skate is taken as much for granted, although it occasionally surprises:

Bernie noted that Joe Perucci [a construction union delegate] claimed only to have received $250 all last year. Sam was astounded that he would say this because he recalled giving him $225 on one occasion at Ned's Ranch House and another $225 three months later.

But duplicity in the building trades is a habit about which nothing can be done. Sam Halpern discovers that he and DeCavalcante have each made a separate payment to an officer of the painters union for the same favor: "DeCavalcante was angered at the man for accepting a double payoff, but told Halpern not to say anything to this man, as it would be bad for Halpern to embarrass him."

"It would be bad to embarrass this man . . ."—that, you finally decide, is one of the two dominant thoughts in the night mind of the *mafioso*, the other being Angelo Bruno's reminder: *"Sam, you are a man who is watched."*

So all confrontations with persons whose morals are too much better or too much worse than one's own seem to end with the recognition that one is helpless. Sam DeCavalcante's only struggle with a force of unmixed purity comes when he intervenes in the strike of Local 1199 of the Drug and Hospital Workers against the Northfield Nursing Home in Plainfield: "This is a slap in the face to me . . . I got money in there. . . . You better watch your step where you put your feet. . . . Tell [the union president] he better not threaten people or I will wash every street with him . . . Cars overturned . . . fights in the streets . . . police beaten up . . . this sort of thing stopped in the twenties. . . . We're more educated now . . . I wouldn't want to take you to court."

After such fulminations, the union continues its effronteries as though there were no Sam DeCavalcante; and, after two days, he can only press his clients to compromise: "Everybody is trying to save face. They don't want to embarrass me and I don't want to embarrass them because we may need them again."

INDEED THERE RUNS throughout his life that same ritual pattern of threat ("Make him holler until he hears the name Sam"), followed by the revelation that the threat is without force and the weary acceptance of reality ("Remember there are situations where it is best to walk away"). Still the myth of the Mafia must be watered and cultivated, myth being the Family's main asset. Larry Wolfson flourishes it as the firm's chief article of sale: "Sam's the biggest man in the country." He is visited by Robert Rapp, a state plumbing inspector tired of petty larceny—"Five dollars a unit; that's like stealing a ham sandwich"—and wondering if they cannot all join together to "establish strong prices."

"Everybody in this area has to go through Sam," Wolfson grandly explains to him. "We can break their backs union-wise." This, of course, is just commercial puffery; in private moments, DeCavalcante is all too aware of how small a mete his rule really runs. It seems to him a signal honor to be trusted with the *private* telephone number of Tony Provenzano, Jimmy Hoffa's New Jersey delegate. Even on one week's notice, he cannot get his nephew a reservation at the Copacabana, which belongs to the Gambino Family; reservations at the Copa turn out indeed to be matters of high strategy for the agenda of Family conferences: DeCavalcante instructs Larasso that "if he goes to the Copa again and has trouble obtaining a table, he should see CARMINE and tell him he's a friend of Dr. Joe."

And, as a man who is watched, he does not seem able to expect even those routine courtesies which society accords any property holder. He needs a pistol permit to protect his payroll and calls the Kenilworth chief of police:

Hello, Chief, how are you. Sam DeCavalcante—remember me? Kenworth Corporation . . . Listen, Chief, I need a favor . . . my cousin takes care of the payroll. We'd like to get him a gun permit for this area . . . We're trying to stop crime. This is for protection. . . . We have forty men working and we pay in cash . . . A lot of people know he's carrying money and if they know he's got a pistol they might change their minds . . . He's a clean-cut kid— never had a pinch in his life . . . I'll send him down for an application. . . .

(It appeared that Sam was getting no place.)

Okay, Buddy, take care of yourself . . . I just got 25 tickets from you people. When are you going to stop coming here with tickets. . . . Listen, it's a pleasure; it's for a good cause—anytime. Goodbye.

Now a man who cannot get this small a favor from the chief of police of Kenilworth, New Jersey, hardly seems capable of getting large favors anywhere; and, after so many examples of futility, it becomes difficult not to wonder whether the Mafia is quite the majestic instrument that prevailing popular and scholarly opinion conceives it to be.

CAN ORGANIZED CRIME be described as a success in America? One great problem in assaying that question is that the existing research provides no really useful statistics. For example, Dr. Cressey says, "Estimates of the amount bet illegally each year range from $7 billion to $50 billion." Calculations of the sort that fail to fix a figure within $43 billion are hard to trust, and so are calculators innocent enough to entertain the possibility that every man, woman, and child in the United States invests $250 a year in illegal gaming.

Still there is the testimony of *The Wall Street Journal*, which in other cases has given us every reason to respect its hardheadedness:

> [The Mafia's] yearly revenues from gambling, narcotics, usurious loans, prostitution and the numbers game has been estimated at as much as $50 billion. [*The Wall Street Journal*, August 12, 1969]

But then the notion of the Mafia's infinite resources seems to be an article of faith among persons who otherwise make their living casting a very cold eye on any customer's statement of his net worth. One reason why Tino DeAngelis was able to swindle himself and other businessmen in his salad oil speculations for so long was the assumption in Wall Street that he had Mafia backing. "We figured afterwards that Tino DeAngelis must have planted the rumor that he was in Cosa Nostra," a broker who was his victim has said. "If he was backed by that kind of money, we would have known that he was good for all he owed us." It is curious that an institution of resources reputed to be so boundless would surface in enterprises as petty as those illuminated by its investigators. As an instance of underworld penetration of legitimate enterprise, *The Wall Street Journal* picks out the attempt of the Gambino Family to capture control of the knife-sharpening concession in the Brooklyn meat industry. This raid was important enough to be directed by Paul Gambino, brother of the boss and a certified *caporegima*; at the height of his dominance of the market he had attained a *gross business of $1,600 a week* and was dividing its profits among *four* sons-in-law.

The disparity between the wealth the *mafioso* is supposed to command and the risks he will sometimes take for the smallest profits is a source of puzzlement to Ed Reid. He cites the case of Nick Nuccio, one of Carlo Marcello's New Orleans lieutenants, with a $4 million a year bookie business, which by prevailing calculations should yield him more than $1 million annual profit. "Like others of the Mafia hierarchy, Nuccio could not keep his hand out of relatively minor matters," Reid says, "and thereby he provided one more look at that baffling facet of the Mafia character. Nuccio was caught in the act of burglarizing the safe of a large dairy in Baton Rouge in 1963.

"Why risk such punishment," Reid asks, "when you are already a chief lieutenant to a boss of bosses? Perhaps because most Mafiosi have a fatally flawed character. They always want more." But perhaps they want more because the revenues of "a lieutenant of a boss of bosses" are so much more paltry than we think them as to make such shifts as safecracking necessities to him.

EIGHT YEARS AGO, Daniel Bell[1] argued uniquely and persuasively that organized crime's share of the economy was shrinking rather than growing: "as an *organized* business, functioning as a chain operation across the country, with police protection, prostitution has disappeared

[1]Bell, Daniel, "The Myth of Crime Waves," in *The End of Ideology* (New York: Free Press, 1962).

from American life. . . . Gambling, which in the forties was the major source of illegal revenue, has declined considerably." Policy is a good case in Bell's point.

"I'll tell you something about the numbers," says Joseph Valachi, a remarkable witness to the insecurity of criminal enterprise.[2] "The numbers are good only when times are bad. It's poor people that play the numbers, and, if you want the truth, most of them play because they are desperate for money, and they don't have no other way to get it."

Narcotics is the only criminal staple which appears to be enjoying an increase in demand; and here, even though we can hardly believe the repeated disclaimers of the Cosa Nostra captains that they reject such traffic as immoral, there is considerable evidence that they do think it dangerous enough to be resorted to only in moments of desperation.

"Strapped for money, Valachi followed the fashion of other Cosa Nostra soldiers in the same fix," says Maas. "He went back into narcotics for a quick buck. . . . He knew a number of members who were still in heroin, took a percentage of their shipments, and made his own distribution deals with a 'couple of colored fellows.' . . . Valachi is reluctant to talk about his narcotics period. He says he only dealt in 'small amounts to get on my feet.' " Heroin, then, remains an enterprise for freebooters, inside or outside the Family, and subject to enough ambivalence to deny that central place in its distribution which we accord the Mafia when we discuss other illegal enterprises.

FINALLY, EVEN ED Reid, after more than twenty years of turning over and over the pages of the Mafia myth, begins to wonder whether these studies may not represent a lifetime of missing the point:

> Are the men of the Mafia in the thumbscrews of a power that overwhelms them? . . . Who are the suckers? The suckers them-selves or the men born to bleed the suckers white? Perhaps the

[2]Maas, Peter, *The Valachi Papers* (New York: Putnam, 1968).

answer lies in a simple concept: The mob boys have reduced their lives to such common concepts of eating and drinking and sleeping that they go on each day, doing the accepted job, but really serving as slave to bigger people about whom they know nothing, like so many ears of corn in a willing windrow ready to be chopped down at the first sign of insurrection or ripeness.

Who really bosses the crime syndicate?

Slaves they certainly are of our credulous imagination; and we go on picking over them. They are, after all, that precious asset to journalism, men who have crossed the shadow line beyond which they can no longer sue for libel and where they can thus be blamed, with impunity, for *everything*.

The New York Review of Books, September 11, 1969

The Scribblers' Choice

My BETTERS AT analyzing this sort of thing seem widely agreed that these days presidential candidates are made or broken not by the politicians but by the newspapers and the broadcasters.

This trend is another illustration of a fundamental law of social change in America, which is that every new development began as an idea conceived by criminals and then brought to fruition by respectable persons.

Las Vegas was invented by the mob and then stolen from it by its accountants. Loan-sharking used to be an underworld monopoly, but now the banks have so encroached upon the field that there are states where a finance company can charge the victim 36 percent interest a year without risk of legal penalty for usury.

A state of affairs where Americans are governed by presidents selected by the press is just one more product of this pattern. Organized crime has been governed that way for years; the Boss of Bosses dies, journalism designates his successor, and every good soldier closes ranks behind him as every good American rallies to the new president.

But now comes the case of Frank Tieri to cast the darkest of shadows upon this system of election by journalistic decree. In the fall of 1978, Tieri, a.k.a. "Funzi" and "The Old Man," was certified as Boss of Bosses of Cosa Nostra by a landslide of those press clippings that constitute the ballots in this process. There followed the customary inaugural ceremony, the serving of a grand jury subpoena; and Tieri then undertook the prime duties of his office, which were, as usual, to be indicted and tried as Unholy Roman Emperor of the Honored Society.

Jay Goldberg, his counsel, objected that Tieri lacked the physical and mental capacity to endure a trial, and the medical profession was recruited to assess the health and capacities of this titan among executives.

The U.S. Attorney's office designated as its expert Stanley L. Portnow, whose personal eminence and status as the government's own instrument should certainly free him of any suspicion of having taken a mob contract. Dr. Portnow found:

In 1977 Frank Tieri suffered a stroke that had produced organic brain damage enough to impair seriously his ability to reason.

His Intelligence Quotient is now seventy-nine.

He was asked how many pennies he would have left if he had three and gave away one. His answer was one. He was asked how much is $4 plus $5. He answered $4. He was asked the meaning of the expression: "Strike while the iron is hot" and he answered: "Press." He was asked to recite the months of the year in order and he replied: "January, February, March, April, May, September, August, June."

There was one sad revelation of the loneliness of grandeur. Frank Tieri could think of nothing he liked to do these days except play cards, but "they don't like to play with me because I keep forgetting."

Frank Tieri had his first heart attack in 1950, developed cancer of the throat in 1956, and has diabetes and arteriosclerosis. He is so wounded a pincushion for surgeons that his first remark to Dr. Portnow was that he hoped he hadn't come there for another operation.

Nonetheless Judge Thomas Griesa has ruled him fit for trial. Judge Griesa is known for his personal crotchets, and I have commended him so often when they accorded with my own that I shall not criticize him for one that seems to me to have produced a result of almost measureless cruelty.

In any case Frank Tieri, if still breathing, will be found at his post doing his duty to the code of Cosa Nostra, whose first command is unswerving service to the myths of journalism and the careers of assistant prosecutors. There is some disquiet in reflecting on the massive authority we journalists have attained in the political process when you discover that we have elected a Boss of Bosses who, a year before conquering that pinnacle, had sunk so far toward imbecility that he probably didn't even know he had won.

New York Post, September 13, 1980

Fathers and Sons

T HERE COMES TO hand *Wiretap*, a selection of Mafia colloquies that the journalist James Goode has culled from the FBI's electronic archives.

It is an irony of the Honored Society's history that the ears of law enforcement did not contrive to intrude far enough upon the private hours of its commanders and record their tittle-tattle live until their venerable institution was dying.

Crime in America is increasingly the province of aberrant and disorganized amateurs. No endeavor, however degraded, can long command our attention unless it is carried on by professionals. Amateurs are poor students and worse guardians of philosophical tradition, and these cogent, if inelegant, conversations in beleaguered garrisons serve to deepen our already pained appreciation of how much ancestral wisdom is withering away in the blight of the Mafia.

Before he went to jail, Gennaro Angiulo was the Mafia's resident commissioner in Boston, a minor trading post on the empire's frontiers. Dwellers in a civilization's backwater are apt to be the most intense keepers of the primeval flame of its old ways, and we are unsurprised to hear how faithfully Angiulo and his subordinates preserve their peasant origins uncorrupted by association with concrete contractors and theatrical lawyers.

"I wouldn't be in a legitimate business for all the money in the world," Angiulo says. It was even his illusion that to refuse to endanger his soul by mixing with respectable society would keep him outside the writ of the RICO law's ban on organized criminal infiltration of legitimate enterprises:

"We're a shylock . . . we're a bookmaker . . . we're selling marijuana. . . . Pimps . . . Prostitutes . . . we're illegal here, illegal there, arsonists. . . . The law does not cover us."

Angiulo had, of course, exulted too soon in his assurance that his infamies had guaranteed him immunity; he is now in prison for the Racketeer-Influenced and Corrupt Organizations violations he had so determinedly avoided. His refusal to trust the word of a reputable citizen had until then been so fierce and all-embracing that he was enraged to discover that his own son was allowing the dice to grow old in the crap game he was supervising.

"Don't you ever," he rasped, "[have] a pair of dice that's been used more than one and a half or two hours without replacing it with a brand new set. And that set goes in your pocket and they're thrown down the sewer . . . You ever put a deck of used cards in a blackjack game . . . and I'll kick you out of here. If I was at your Vegas night the week before, I'd know every card in that deck."

Thus spoke the sophisticated awareness of the malefactor who knows that no sucker lives who will not take advantage of any chance to cheat him. Even Jason, the son he had commissioned to deplete the wallets of the suckers, could not be relied upon not to slip toward suckerdom himself.

"You're a gambler?" he asks Jason.

"You don't want me to lie, do you," Jason replies.

"You want to gamble? Well you can't. No man that gambles can evade a problem, unless he's got a big package coming in."

But then, as our President says, the fall of great empires begins with the decline of family values. Mafia mothers of the old school remain the peasant wives they always were, and Angiulo's brother Donato can still say with confidence, "My wife has never heard from me what I do for a living and she's never asked."

All the same, the children are more and more lost to the tradition. The son of Angelo Ruggiero of the Gotti family asks for seventeen dollars and the loan of the "little car." Ruggiero yields up that benison and then says, "Hey, John, don't go to that Howard Beach." There is in that cry all the desperation of the father who recognizes that a *mafioso's* son has grown as disobedient and untamable as everyone else's these days.

New York Newsday, December 14, 1988

A Gangster's Legacy

MATTHEW IANNIELLO HAS been lost to Mulberry Street and on long-term lease to the federal prison system since 1986, and where are the scungilli of yesteryear?

Where indeed is the Mulberry Street of yesteryear?

Here is a decay that has no identifying scar more painful to the beholder than the fleckings of the paint on the Bay of Naples blue sign that used so proudly to point the pilgrim to Umberto's Clam House.

Mulberry Street's brief renaissance probably owed as much to the artistic sensibilities of Matthew Ianniello as Florence's protracted one owed to the Medicis, whose tastes weren't always inarguably superior to his. Now Ianniello is gone and the sedge has withered on the lake and no birds sing, except of course for government prosecutors in the U.S. courthouse down the way.

Much of Matty Ianniello's aura on Mulberry Street flowed from his status as a capo and resident commissioner of the Mafia. That is a splendid eminence but it comes with a stigma, and Ianniello had to do all his good works by stealth or risk having some journalist find out about them and write them down as bad.

The seventies were notable for the ascension of Mulberry Street to the elegance symbolized by restaurants like Cortile and SPQR, whose cuisines were North Italian, interiors cinquecento, and ambience altogether more Milanese upper bourgeois than Calabrian peasant.

There was gossip that Ianniello had a piece of these places, but his patronage would have been no less than wholehearted if he hadn't.

He had aesthetic standards rare even for the respectable and unique for the disreputable. The new amenities delighted him, and he did not merely approve but did his bit to inspire them. It is even said that the young architects responsible for most of the designs could count on Matty Ianniello to go along in a pinch when they submitted their plans to a dubious restaurateur, to certify their beauty and achieve immediate surrender to his superior judgment.

But at Umberto's, he breathed free of all necessities to hide his hand. It had been unconcealedly his place since it opened in 1972. On its second night, Joey Gallo, a gangster at odds with the Colombo Family, came for clams and was dispatched by gunshot, and it took no more than those six muzzle blasts to proclaim Umberto's a lasting success.

Matty Ianniello probably regarded Joey Gallo with the benignity he felt for every human creature and would have shrunk from contributing to his decease. Still, it was common knowledge that Gallo had been tipped the black spot, and even an entrepreneur less acute than Ianniello could not have overlooked the chance to invite Gallo to try the sauce and trust in luck to bring the contract's consummation then and there. And so luck did, and Umberto's would have been less immediately famous if it had staged its opening at Grauman's Chinese.

WHEN IANNIELLO WAS convicted of racketeering in 1986, the government seized his known assets, of which Umberto's was the jewel. It is now being run by federal monitors and a wayfarer stopped by to test their stewardship. The scungilli is respectable in its way but its evocations have slipped well below the Lucullan. The sauce has lost its magic; the hot tasted like the medium, the medium tasted like the sweet, and the sweet held no promise worth stooping to.

One bore away one's sorrows, taking melancholy note of the "Linguini $7.70" signs that some of the restaurants on what used to be renaissance row have been pathetically reduced to displaying on their burnt sienna walls. The rear window seat of a car parked outside

Umberto's showed a menu and a baseball cap flourishing the device, "Department of Justice, Federal Bureau of Investigation." When you destroy a culture, you cannot be fairly expected to put something better in its place, but must you put something so distressingly worse?

New York Newsday, January 26, 1990

Undertaking Roy Cohn

No MAN'S BIOGRAPHER can be so near a companion of his intimacies as the particular worm the gods choose for his devouring. There is no reason then for surprise that in *Citizen Cohn* Nicholas von Hoffman has come upon the epitome of Roy Cohn's existence in the recollections of one of the less baleful of the lights of love who hurried him to the grave with a posterior orifice you could throw a baseball through:

> So many people stole so many things from him . . . I didn't steal anything. I stole only one thing from Roy and that was his Gucci razor. This was solid silver. That's the only thing I stole.

Hardly the colors of memory that endow their object with the grandeur that von Hoffman suggests Cohn might have had and that Sidney Zion in his *Autobiography of Roy Cohn* insists he did have.

Chroniclers of Roy Cohn deserve neither to be envied their enterprise nor blamed for their failure to illuminate large tracts of a life whose ambiguities and obscurities seem almost as resistant to the strenuosities of von Hoffman's efforts as to the languors of Zion's.

Von Hoffman never met Cohn; his is the tale as others tell it. Zion knew Cohn foolishly, which is to say none too well; his is the tale as Cohn told it. Von Hoffman has the advantage of suspecting, as Zion does not, how much of Cohn's fabric was the warp of the lies to self;

but he has too disciplinedly refrained from noticing how much of its woof might have been woven from the lies others told themselves. For Cohn studies are transacted in shadowed countinghouses on dingy streets, where the teller deals across his greasy counter a coin all but unvaryingly freighted with lead.

It is of small use to complain about the little Zion and von Hoffman can show for their dig at Cohn's interior. I myself made a few stabs in that direction across the years with such meager results as to settle me in the judgment that his interior was a void from which he could draw no breath of a notion of who he was and consequently must lodge all his hope of ever finding out on the air around him and the permeations of the winds, benign or malignant, of what other people thought he was and what he appears obediently to have become.

When he was twenty-four years old and came earliest and so clamorously to our attention, his admirers called him a great lawyer and his detractors said he was homosexual. I cannot yet set him down as either at the time; all the same, he would develop into a splendid advocate, however too untidy to render steady satisfaction to his clients, and he turned out a frenziedly purposeful pederast. The prejudices of friend and enemy alike have proved themselves sounder instruments for assessing him than the sober detachment I had struggled to maintain. I have no excuse for this miscalculation beyond the surmise that the dominant chord in Cohn's being was his susceptibility to every whisper in the surrounding atmosphere, and that, since he was therefore a stranger to himself, he could only adopt whatever shape other strangers conjured up as his.

I WOULD BE a severer critic of the persistence of Zion's and von Hoffman's reliance upon reminiscences I cannot quite trust if I could be more secure about trusting my own. To remember Roy Cohn is for me the same delicate exercise in separating truth from falsehood that talking to him used to be. I knew him moderately well, which was about as far as it was safe or rewarding to go; what confounds my recollection is my extended perseverance in propagating fantasies that

I knew him better still. For, absent some willed pretense to an intimacy that would be slight cause for vanity had it been substantial, how am I to explain the long familiarity of my tongue with fables like these:

(1) That he and I sat together in my room at Washington's old Willard Hotel and watched the Edward R. Murrow broadcast that signaled more dramatically than it speeded the ruin of Senator Joe McCarthy.

(2) That he once threatened to visit one of his subpoenas upon me and was repelled by the sword of my defiance and scorn.

(1) Not so. We were not together at the Willard on that evening or any other, and I did not observe such progress as Murrow might have been making toward disturbances to a self-assurance that seldom sat comfortably on Roy Cohn anyway. But I had telephoned him earlier; and, since where reporters were the case, all was fish that came to his net, he called me back and the Murrow broadcast came up.

Cohn dismissed this aggression as a trifle. I replied that, to the contrary, I had felt it as the tolling of a bell of horrid portent for himself and his principal. Murrow might, I suggested, be one of those men blessed with the qualities of honor and courage that the high gods so esteem as to provide him with a guardian angel to protect him from employing them too hastily. Any spirit pressed by its nobility to stand up to risk is, in some curious way, insured against damaging consequences. If McCarthy had not passed his apogee and gone tumbling toward earth like a child's rocket, Murrow would not have mounted an assault that Washington took and that he, in his modest way, must have felt to be recklessly brave. We were coming to the end of the affair; McCarthy was ceasing to be a figure any longer controversial, and the act of challenging him, however sincerely conceived as bold to the point of being rash, had become the mere job of giving a hand to the waste-disposal crew.

Cohn replied that, whether I was right or wrong, McCarthy's fate was no worry for him, because he was a princeling of the Bronx Democratic organization and could rely on the Democrats on the Senate Committee on Investigations to exempt him from any punishments they thought condign for its chairman. There rose in my mind the gelid image of John McClellan, the committee's senior Democrat, ravaged by the ghosts of his dead children and too finally sacked and pillaged of all illusion about the mercies of God to be a soundly caulked vessel for mercies to his fellow man. Cohn could not have counted upon a refuge less welcoming in time of trouble. I had discovered his quite appalling innocence and would have no future reason to doubt that it lodged in his very marrow.

(2) Not altogether so. Cohn did once suggest that he might summon me to crave pardon for my dead past in the Young Communist League; but subsequent fancy has ornamented my response with flourishes as spurious as they are fustian. My answer was that I should be distinctly more confident of heavenly reward if I could recite the Nicene Creed with as little assistance from the prompting box as I would need to run through the liturgy for which he proposed to solicit the bending of my knees.

I had, I assured him, the requisite stock of hyperbole when it came to descriptions of Dark Nights of the Soul and could almost effortlessly fish my memory for the names of those who had shivered through them at my side. I would nonetheless have to decline his invitation and definitely not because it would be ignoble to embarrass, not to say traduce, old acquaintances whose original trespasses were trivial and whose lives had been blameless thereafter. Those were grounds I owed to honor; but they were a shade too high for me to be dead certain of holding to them. Life had taught me, I felt compelled to report, that anyone who stakes all his faith on high-minded reasons to keep him from doing some low-minded thing has only to exercise his wits a little while to locate an equally high-minded reason to do it. I preferred merely to say that such rhetorical flourishes as I might bring to the naming of names would be barely noticed the day afterward and quite forgotten within a week; and all that would be remembered was that I had named the names, and that my commercial future was gray enough already without being dyed blacker with a taint of those proportions.

Cohn dropped the subject as idly as he must have raised it. I should, of course, be happier if the strings of recall could be tuned to pitches more full-throated than these.

BUT THEN EVERY age gets the monsters it deserves, and Roy Cohn was about as far as the nineteen-fifties could go with the manufacture and distribution of specimens of the fearsome; and, botched counterfeit that he probably was and sodden as his time and mine inarguably was, it would take a highly combustible tongue to kindle to flame when brought beard to beard with a Grand Inquisitor who, even in those days, was commencing to look like some priapic statue incautiously bought at the flea market and left out too long in the garden rains.

In any case, the aforesaid recollections, once stripped of *post hoc* absurdities, are not inappropriate to our lugubrious pawings after human community, which on my side ran almost exclusively to lectures on the ways of the world. I could not have chosen an endeavor more hopeless. Cohn lived and died in a condition of peculiar innocence, one as disabling to those who cannot credit others with decent motives as it is to those unable to imagine that others may have indecent ones. It may be all very well to have enlisted with the infernal powers so long as you are aware of and keep a close eye out for the snares and deceits of the well-behaved; to do otherwise will serve you no more conveniently than his virtues did Prince Myshkin.

This innocence too pure to be diluted by the lessons of experience must have directed Cohn's choice of an authorized biographer no better equipped than himself to appreciate the power of conventional morality in human affairs. Sidney Zion's appetite for roguery is the glutton's and not the gourmet's; he is too greedy a gobbler of the unappetizing to notice that it can be also the undernourishing. Rascals are endurable and may, now and then, be enjoyable to the degree of their charm, but without charm they are even worse company than respectable people.

And Roy Cohn had an essence as charmless as any I have ever communed with; and, as Disraeli put it in another connection, I have read Stalin on Trotsky and Trotsky on Stalin and have known Francis Cardinal Spellman, who was so warm a friend of Cohn's that von Hoffman can hint that between them vibrated the intimations, if not the consummations, of the flesh; my own preference is for believing that what drew them close was a shared deprivation of the normal faculties for appealing to one's fellow man, and that they had the enforced fraternity of sailors starving together on an ice floe.

Von Hoffman tenders an unexpectedly substantial sheaf of testaments to the pleasures of Cohn's companionship; but their citations are too barren of examples of the feast of his reason and flow of his soul to persuade us that the fascinations of his presence had nearly as much to do with his persona as with his specious repute as mover and shaker. For the real voice, we must turn to Zion's transcriptions; and it is a stream of spite and malice unrelieved by any trace of philosophy or wit. Cohn could frequently manifest a febrile anxiety to please that now and then surprised strangers into the suspicion that he might not be by any means as bad as they assumed he would be; but that is so minimal an accomplishment that rascals even worse than he have brought it off with less exertion.

Von Hoffman appears to have started forth with the conviction that Cohn was a personage of the size appropriate for a conscientious biographer's ambitions; and he tries harder than is entirely plausible to inflate Cohn's stature among the architects of the institutions designed to enforce domestic security and enshrine official paranoia. Their trenches had been thoroughly dug before Cohn took up his post in them, and their revetments could hardly have been made more formidable with the fleeting attentions of someone as disqualified for steady work by a natural disposition as ill-ordered as his was.

Von hoffman's good sense triumphs soon enough over his early delusions that Cohn's was a figure of significant historical import; and the farther he travels, the more the subject loses the attributes that preserve authentic claims to be taken seriously, until we are left with the pitiful rag that one of the more noisome of his studs refers to as "the poor old thing," an appellation that no one would think to apply to, say, Richard Nixon, or anybody else who ever counted for much.

But Zion clings to the standard that absurdly proclaims Cohn's cosmic consequence with the steadfast will of the chronicler as fixed as the chroniclee in the creed that man's fate is the ordained result of the shifts, the sleights, and the schemes of cabals that deserve our admiration for their sovereign immunity to scruple, and that Roy Cohn lived his life at their very center. That proposition is by no means self-evident; and, as soon as Zion leaves off advancing affirmations of Cohn's skills at furthering the careers of long since obliterated unworthies and moves on to persuade us of the importance of his good will to unworthies still in being, we are powerless to resist the inference that the game has been given away.

Cohn informs us, as an instance, that Vice President Bush had been "romancing" Cohn for no end of time. But then of an evening, while Cohn's plane waited to fly off to a White House dinner, word came that all schedules were suspended until the Vice President had been cleared for takeoff. Cohn sat and fumed; and when he arrived at the White House, as timely as he needed to be and higher in dudgeon than any man of reason would think he ought to be, he rushed to tell Mrs. Reagan of this effrontery. It was always thus with Roy Cohn; you would be peaceably tending to your own business, and up he would come with some piece of shit or other.

Mrs. Reagan suggested that he write the Vice President and tell him off. Cohn proceeded to this patriotic duty with passionate intensity and back came a letter from a vice-presidential assistant conveying the sense in tones undisguisedly snotty, that, if Mr. Bush could be found, he would beyond question be desolated to learn that Mr. Cohn "felt" ill-used. The vice presidency is an office whose occupant is so conditioned to abjection and apology that we could not have imagined until now that the eye of God could fall upon a citizen of the United States whose wounded sensibilities would strike George Bush as of a moment so small that their appeasement could be fobbed off with the disdain of a mere assistant.

We bear with Zion through page after page of assertions of how much Cohn mattered and then, all unconscious, he drops this crashing revelation that Cohn mattered not the slightest to George Bush, whose office commands him to treat everything as though it mattered; and nothing remains for us to do except to say: "Okay, you two, that does it; come off it, both of you."

But then, even if we elevated the trappings of the authority that von Hoffman once believed and Zion is still convinced were Cohn's to dispense for more than the pasty gauds they were, we have grounds to doubt that they would have been what he wanted at all.

The clue to his truest aspiration can, I suspect, be found in the fevers of his exercises on behalf of Private G. David Schine. Schine had been an unpaid consultant for the McCarthy-Cohn committee until he was conscripted into the army. No sooner had he been encumbered with that indignity than Cohn rose up to extort kindnesses for him quite beyond the army's prescribed allotment of such rations to recruits; and the unbridled vehemence of those exertions brought McCarthy to ruin and Cohn too close to it.

MOST OF THE whispers about Cohn's homosexual bent had their origins in the Schine affair; his enemies then and there decided that no man could care this much about another man's ease unless he cared unnaturally overmuch about his body. Schine did indeed have the cast of countenance that too often identifies the Lily White Boy; but that was not, I think, as much the real charm for Cohn and McCarthy as his status as heir presumptive of the cluster of hotels that held out to McCarthy a continental sweep for the freeloading impulses that were the one point of concentration for his otherwise unfocused vision and that opened up to Cohn the promise of a richly endowing client for the great law firm whose star he pursued until he died with it further from his grasp than it had been when he set forth to capture it.

Cohn entered the private practice of law under circumstances un- suggestive of the auspicious. He had almost been flayed from Washing- ton and had come home trailing clouds of sulfurous excesses, maladroit chicaneries, and obsessions with the self that had made him as bad a servant as even a master so slovenly as McCarthy could have been careless enough to employ. He was widely accounted mad, bad, and dangerous to know; and yet this bundle of vices that in justice ought to be a certificate of the bearer's bankruptcy would turn out to be Roy Cohn's only inexhaustible capital.

He could flourish his disgraces as emblems of the kidney that had earned them; he could be relied upon, if for too little else, never to take up the sword without throwing away the scabbard; and every prior demonstration of his pitilessness of purpose constituted just the sort of history that commends itself to the wife or husband whose good temper has too long been tried, or the enterpriser whose conscience has known no trial at all.

When he began, his most noticeable clients were enraged spouses and ex-bootleggers like the Stork Club's Sherman Billingsley and Las Vegas's Moe Dalitz. But the prior behavior of the old bootleggers had been unseemly and the present behavior of the spouses, if anything, worse; and they were not the clientele to suit Roy Cohn's image of the corporation lawyer he really wanted to be.

What else but the desperation of his chase after this childhood dream could explain the history of the firm that never bore Cohn's name but carried to its doom no banner but "Saxe Bacon" with the penultimate addition of "Bolan"? Saxe was long dead and Bacon nearly as long retired; Roy Cohn had bought their shingle and it was worth its price for a ring like the "Cravath, Swaines" and the "Dewey Ballantines" of the great downtown law firms.

His lurches into those uniformly aborted forays as a corporate raider in the sixties could only have had their source in impulses aroused not by greed but by the yearnings of a too-tardy adolescence for retainers that had the authenticity reserved for the large and the respectable.

That was the dream that spurred him to hurl himself against corporate walls that bristled with defenders whose cunning was larger than his; and we have no way to measure the weight of resultant losses that may have been too heavy for him ever to be rid of their encumbrance.

And then he was indicted and tried three times in the federal courts and always on the testimony of fellow passengers in the shipwreck who had turned government witness and earned full absolution by swearing that he had been prime author of their failed conspiracies. He had become an insurance policy for any captain on adventure bent who had only to sign Roy Cohn on to the manifest and sail content with the knowledge that, if the ship should wreck, any prosecutor would delight in granting him immunity for swearing that it was all Cohn's doing. And oddly enough, the Cohn who so often took offense, and not improperly so, at any slight from a good citizen would take none at all from the basest betrayal by a bad one; and he once trotted docilely up the aisle as best man to a groom who could well have been in jail if he had not done his duty to common sense by testifying against Cohn a bare few weeks earlier.

It is impossible not to suspect that all these sweats and bleedings left him broke beyond recovery; and, labor though Zion may to apply the colors of derring-do to his wars with the Internal Revenue Service, there is no way to obscure those strokes that too tellingly delineate the scurryings of the fugitive irretrievably penurious.

Having been defeated in all his hopes for eminence, Cohn could only fall back on notoriety and return to being mercenary soldier for gangsters habitually disreputable or wives made transiently so by the ravenings of their thirst for vengeance. He still possessed the coin of his reputation for prodigies with extremes of the implacable and the perfidious; and the confidence that he would be ready on command was as near as uneasy spirits could get to the self-assurance that could otherwise be theirs only with the acquisition of a Mafia hit man. But, as time went on and his juices clogged, he grew increasingly languid as a servitor for the maliciously inclined; and many a recreant husband who had run shuddering to his lawyer with a letter signed by Roy Cohn would go away comforted with the information that Cohn seldom did much more these days except get off one such loud salvo and fire no longer. He had become, as von Hoffman makes plain, a careless and inattentive practitioner; and I cannot remember a scintilla of his old address at the last except once when I happened upon him on an afternoon when he was pressing the defense of some obscure hoodlum with every ounce of the acumen and penetration that used to be his when he cared; and I could only decide that he had grown so intimate with gangsters that they had come to think of him as one of their own and thus eligible for terminal measures of reproof if he should let any of them down.

Still, in those shadows, there was always Zion credulously swallowing Cohn's every pretension to glory; their talk would come to a dirty trick that had blighted some politician's career and Cohn would say, of course, that had been his doing. It was a safe enough bit of brag; no one who has done a dirty trick is excessively anxious to proclaim it; and Cohn was free to steal the credit and bemuse Zion with some fresh mark of his power, black and spurious a mark though it might be.

There has, however, been talk of one infamy that may have been the genuine work of Cohn's hand and that he never mentioned to Zion and that none of von Hoffman's informants seem to have mentioned to him. And it could well be more than talk because it was told me by a man who was close to McCarthy and privy to Cohn in his Washington days and whose wisdom, talent, and knowledge of the way the world goes has since earned him a respect amounting to veneration from better judges than either of them. His tale ran thus:

By 1957, Joe had stopped drinking and decided not to run for the Senate again. All he said he wanted was one hundred thousand dollars to buy "a spread somewhere out in the West for me and Jeanie." That was when Roy Cohn showed up with a guy who was hustling penny uranium stocks. They offered Joe a piece and he scoured up thirty thousand dollars and they went back to New York and sold batches of the stuff on Joe's name. Within two weeks Joe was worth a hundred and fifty thousand dollars on paper, and he went to the Wisconsin woods to hunt. While he was gone, Cohn and the other hustler dumped the stock and Joe came home to find that he had been wiped out. He called Cohn in haste and alarm and Cohn wouldn't take the call.

And Joe went back to drinking and it didn't take long to kill him.

That was all there was to the story; and when it was done I asked, "Do you mean to suggest that Roy Cohn blamed Joe McCarthy for ruining *his* career?"

"Of course," my friend replied.

The poor son of a bitch.

Grand Street, Autumn 1988

A Quiet, Determined Desperation

In the summer of 1960, before his every thought was a prayer and his every word a benediction, Senate Majority Leader Lyndon Johnson met Vice President Richard Nixon in the corridors of the Senate.

"Well, Dick," he said, "you boys gonna 'nigger' it at your convention this year?"

The Vice President blushed.

"We will certainly try, Lyndon," he answered.

A visitor saw him at the Overseas Press Club yesterday and remembered this occasion and all the others when Richard Nixon has endured the crudities of the powerful and, for that matter, the powerless.

Suddenly—it is a tribute to his endurance—one likes him enormously, rather more than Mr. Johnson. Say if you will that it is only lack of opportunity, but there is no record that Richard Nixon has up to now ordered the firebombing of a peasant's shack.

His smile across the room at the intruder is almost and unexpectedly beseeching. The first thought is that he is faintly crying mercy; but he must long ago have ceased to expect mercy anywhere; a man who has so doggedly followed his star without ever asking quarter from history is certainly above asking mercy from journalists. But then you understand; he is speaking on Vietnam, he has counted the heads at the Republican convention, and he knows already what the rest of us will be surprised to learn in the spring of 1968: The Goldwater people have the votes to nominate the next candidate. He must therefore make the Goldwater people believe that he is the man to stand up to Mao Tse-tung although, from what I know of his native courtesy, I would not ask Richard Nixon to stand up to the general secretary of the Communist party of Albania. He therefore needs the assistance of any friend of the Viet Cong removed enough from common sense to think Richard Nixon a screaming hawk.

So, of course: The smile is a plea for misunderstanding.

It cannot be granted, try though one will. Nixon has only to say that, in negotiations, "we must be quite precise and, by being quite precise I mean . . ." for us to know that, in his company, we are, as always, blessedly secure from the menace of the definite.

HE IS JUST back from South Vietnam; he seems always just back from South Vietnam and one is confident that by now he has established it as a bastion in Pepsi-Cola's endless struggle for coexistence.

The sad eyes looked about the room while the voice said cheerfully that he is now convinced that we can win.

On the one hand, the USSR has displaced Communist China in the affections of Ho Chi Minh, who knows that the Chinese have been after the Indo-China complex since the Ming Dynasty, but on the other a major French diplomat told Mr. Nixon that the men around Ho are more Peking than Moscow-oriented. The silence which attends such revelations of inside information fell upon the assemblage; the measure of Richard Nixon's endurance is that he could have been denied access to the daily CIA report for six years and still be able to talk with the absolutely confused authority of a man who had been briefed that morning. For only someone who believed the CIA has the experience to believe a French diplomat.

And this is a man who, say what you choose of him, came to run the course. He will, with time, be a landmark in the history of quiet, determined desperation. The years will go by and, so long as we live, Richard Nixon's name will be put forth as the only visible alternative to the especially dreadful candidate who is about to be the choice of the Republican delegates. We will end surprised to discover that we love him, the alternative having always been worse.

New York Post, September, 13, 1966

Son of Pinkerton

THE REPLACEMENT OF Allan Pinkerton, dealer in detectives for Wealth during the late nineteenth century, by J. Edgar Hoover, supervisor of detectives for Commonwealth, must be the only episode in our social history to realize Marx's prescription for the transformation of capitalistic private into socialized property. For, as Pinkerton was the only great acquisitor of the nineteenth century whose legacy has since been nationalized, Mr. Hoover's Federal Bureau of Investigation is unique among our public institutions as an example of the triumph of the socialist idea.

Its critics have often argued that socialism, once it takes power, lacks the creative impulse essential to technical development, and that, once the expropriation of private property is accomplished, the bureaucrat can conceive no device for managing it for the public good beyond those the displaced enterpriser had already invented for his personal profit. Such arguments gain unexpected force from the coincidental republication of most of Mr. Hoover's thoughts and some of Allan Pinkerton's.

STRIKERS, COMMUNISTS, TRAMPS AND DETECTIVES was Pinkerton's account of the great strikes of 1877, whose course he resisted as a spymaster for the railroad managers and whose punishment he subsequently accomplished as a criminal investigator. We had already known that most of Mr. Hoover's devices for protecting the public order were originally discovered by Pinkerton, who created the Rogues Gallery—that progenitor of the FBI's Public Enemy list—who first protected the confidential informant by assigning him a code name in his files, and who refined the undercover agent from a rudimentary workman into the skilled professional he is today.

Pinkerton would certainly have been first to use all the mechanical means at Mr. Hoover's disposal if the engineers of his time had progressed far enough to provide him with a recognizable opportunity; as it was, the employment of wiretapping would wait until thirty years after his death. In *The Masked War*, William J. Burns, almost as legendary an operative as Pinkerton and Hoover, but otherwise a much more stolid fellow, tells us that in 1912 he used a dictograph to record the conversations of visitors to the cell of a kept, but shaky, witness. In his matter-of-fact account, persons afflicted with historical imagination can thrill at the debut of the "bug."

But *Strikers, Communists, Tramps and Detectives* suggests for the first time that Mr. Hoover's debt to Pinkerton is not just for the techniques of production but for the more important ones of marketing. For, without the shadow of the Peril, who will appreciate the Protector? That remains a problem for the socialized detective almost as much as it used to be for the private one. Marketing is the mass distribution of fantasies, and it is crucial for the distributor to be caught by the fantasy he sells. To be sure of being contagious, it is safest to be infected.

Henry Ford, Lydia Pinkham, Allan Pinkerton—and who knows how many other forces for change in the buying habits of Americans?—were all half mad. To read their lives is to stand in awe of the light which broke upon D. H. Lawrence when he read *Moby Dick* and recognized how many American endeavors are described by that image of the voyage with a maniac captain of the soul and three eminently practical mates.[1] What seems senility to the congressmen who have

---

[1] What I know of the first Pinkerton's character is almost all drawn from *The Pinkertons: The Detective Dynasty That Made History* by James D. Horan (New York: Crown,

only now begun their gingerly dance in defiance of Mr. Hoover is really fantasy preserved intact:

> Never before in the history of our country had there come such a swift and far-reaching peril; nor had we record of any government being thus obliged to thus suddenly confront so overwhelming a danger.
>
> —Allan Pinkerton, 1878

> Today our country faces the most severe test ever to confront a free people.
>
> —J. Edgar Hoover, 1964

So Mr. Hoover found the tablets already engraved; no further exercise was demanded of him except some tracery at the edges. The Founder, a keen self-advertiser, published eighteen volumes running over three million words; James Horan, in his book on the Pinkertons, tells us that Pinkerton once disclosed to his son (detectives disclose while the rest of us only tell) that he had "seven writers working on my stories." Mr. Hoover must be well along to catching up with him. Who does not believe that by now there must exist at least two million words under

---

1968). The Pinkerton Agency's proprietors are not rich enough these days to subsidize an official historian; but their files retain a fascination sufficient to bemuse any journalist granted special access into a gratitude which disables him as a critic of their methods. Horan's work would certainly be more useful if it were not inhibited by his sense that he owed the Pinkertons the payment of consistently high regard for their motives.

Still, being a conscientious and morally imaginative man, Horan seems early to have discovered that The Founder was quite loony and to have at least tempered his reverence with proper recognition of that condition. Thus he reveres the institution and is appalled by the man, rather as the official historians of the Communist party of the Soviet Union must have been appalled by Stalin after he had been reduced to only a bitter thought. The result is not always trustworthy as history, but entirely persuasive as a portrait of character. Still, one feels, the reputation of all dictators must endure this posthumous parricide. Horan can afford to admire the Pinkertons while disliking Allan Pinkerton, because all Pinkerton's children seem to have hated him to varying degrees, and he would not know filial piety until J. Edgar Hoover, that stranger to his blood, came along two generations later.

his signature and very probably from his own pen, the manner being so hard to imitate?

The method of exposition is common to both, being marked by reticence about one's own methods and unbounded hyperbole about the perfidy of the enemy's. Mr. Hoover's prose is informed by an animus both broader and more deeply felt. His writing is social in purpose where Pinkerton's ran more to the commercial. Still Mr. Hoover's style exhibits a noticeable falling-off in vigor and elegance; the hacks of the nineteenth century were livelier than the hacks of the twentieth.

Mr. Hoover tirelessly labors, but he cannot bear the comparison:

> Just 100 years ago, communism was a mere scratch on the face of international affairs. In a dingy London apartment, a garrulous, haughty and intolerant atheist, Karl Marx, callous to the physical sufferings of his family, was busy mixing the ideological acids of this evil philosophy. Originally of interest only to skid row debaters and wandering minstrels of revolution, Marx's pernicious doctrines were given organizational power by a beady-eyed Russian, V. I. Lenin.[2]
>
> —J. Edgar Hoover, *Christianity Today*, 1960

After such language, with no vigor left in it except that of the distemper of its adjectives, the blood quickens when we turn to Pinkerton on the Paris Commune:

> The long restraint caused by a protracted state of siege was broken over and a period of drunkenness and debauch followed. In this condition of things the city fell an easy prey to a horde of bad men, the worst of its vile elements, and human beings so devoid of all conscience, pity or consideration, that it is hard to look upon them as possessing the least of human attributes. But this is the class, the

---

[2]The comparison of scholarship is not favorable to Mr. Hoover either. After all, if that beady-eyed Russian is not to be identified as V. I. Ulyanov, then ought he not be identified as N. Lenin?

world over, who are at the bottom of all troubles of a communistic nature. They were the *real* cause of the great strikes of '77, and their prompt and utter extermination, in this and all other countries, is the only method of removing a constant menace and peril to government and society.

This ability to evoke the horror, without the use of any epithet that does not move the narrative along, must explain why Pinkerton's customers were moved to *hire* him while Mr. Hoover's can at best rouse themselves to *applaud.*

THESE TWO PROTECTORS have a shared need to exaggerate the ubiquity of the Peril:

> They have infiltrated every conceivable sphere of activity: youth groups; radio, television, and motion picture industries; church, school, educational and cultural groups; nationality minority groups and civil and political units.
> —Mr. Hoover to the House of Representatives Appropriations
> Subcommittee, 1962

But then observe the higher imagination that Pinkerton brings to conjuring up the image of conspiracy so pervasive as virtually to overwhelm a vigilance even as pervasive as his own.

> It was everywhere; it was nowhere. A condition of sedition which can be located, fixed, or given boundaries, may, by any ordinary community or government, be subdued. This uprising, in its far-reaching extent . . . seemed like the hideous growth of a night. . . . No general action for safety could be taken. Look where we might, some fresh danger was presented.

Both Mr. Hoover and Pinkerton, of course, studied the human embodiment of the Peril in the form of its leaders; for both, of course, these figures were as contemptible as their portents were terrible. Mr. Hoover's portrait of Gus Hall, general secretary of the Communist party, aims at the appointed lineaments of disdain—"scheming, opportunistic"—but he is too clumsy to give us much detail beyond the recital of Hall's criminal record, which seems less blamable on Hall's account than on the persistence of law enforcement officers in imputing criminality to opinion. He closes with this summary:

> This then is the man—ex convict, propagandist, unabashed emissary of evil, and rabid advocate of a Soviet United States.

Mr. Hoover's enmity toward the Communists is hardly more vivid than was Pinkerton's toward the Brotherhood of Locomotive Engineers: "a huge political devilfish that feeds upon anything and everything necessary to satiate its appetite and give it power . . . animated by the vicious dictation of the Internationale . . . possessed with a greed for personal aggrandizement. . . ." But when Pinkerton describes P. M. Arthur, grand chief engineer of the Brotherhood, there is unexpected charm in his sketch:

> I can best describe him by comparing him in personal appearance with the great evangelist, Mr. Moody, and with no disrespect to that eccentric individual. Take out of Moody's face, then, the low-browed, sullen-eyed, bull-dog look . . . give him instead of a fish-like expressionless dark eye, a bluish-gray eye full of light and animation, and, at times, of jollity and merriment . . . and then give to every motion of his form and features determined, decisive action that reminds you of superb and finely-governed machinery, and you have the man before you.

This visage, otherwise so fair, of course conceals the conspirator who can tell the railroads that his engineers will help them run their trains, despite the strike, and "then secretly send [his] agents among the brakemen and firemen with orders to make such dastardly public threats against any engineer who should volunteer to take out an engine that the officers of the road became aghast at the prospect of violence."

Pinkerton's unfavorable comparison of the appearance of Dwight Moody, his century's most conspicuous messenger of Christian acceptance, with that of Arthur, one of its Masks of Anarchy, reminds us of one difference between Pinkerton and Mr. Hoover. Pinkerton warns us that "the objects of the French commune include . . . atheism, materialism, the negation of all religion." But he does not otherwise advert to such threats to God's rule on earth. Yet what is only a trickle in him has become a torrent in Mr. Hoover. ("Atheism—militant on the part of the Communists—is the common denominator of all materialists. . . . Scores of individuals who have never been members of the Communist organization contribute to the spread of the philosophy of materialism. In so doing they are adding generously to the strength of the Communist movement.")

PINKERTON, HOWEVER, DOES not appear to have gone beyond simply posting the notice to his customers that the Peril included atheism; and even that breach of conscience for the sake of commerce must have troubled him terribly. He had been a Chartist and an atheist as a youth in Scotland. Indeed, the police were searching for him when he escaped to America. Here he shed the Chartism, but he remained a bigoted atheist until he died. He was as much an office tyrant as Mr. Hoover seems to be; but the affronts that aroused his subordinates were diametrically opposite.

Once, Horan says, Pinkerton got the news that one of Moody's revivals had captured his Philadelphia employees. Mr. Hoover could hardly have been more enraged to learn that one of his operatives was living in sin with a young woman he was not assigned to investigate. "I would not have dreamed," Pinkerton wrote, "that the evil preachings spread through the US by Moody and Sankey and others would have at length come into my Agency." For the duration of the emergency, he ordered all his Philadelphia agents to work on Sundays so that there should be no danger that one of them might "in any way undertake to attend church."

When Pinkerton turns to the portrait of Robert Ammon, leader of the Trainmen's Union, his method is more contemptuous, but then he had early conceived a contempt for the Trainmen's Union, perhaps because he found it a body to which admission was so easy for any person, "no matter how low and vile," that "at the third meeting my operatives were able to become members with no trouble at all." Still, even in disposing of Ammon, Pinkerton leaves us with the sense that he has looked at his subject, something Hoover can in no way convey when he describes Gus Hall. Ammon, Pinkerton writes:

> . . . was of a most estimable Pittsburgh family [the echo is of Clarendon on *his* great enemy, John Hampden, for Pinkerton is just that stately]. . . . The son, Robert, has long been regarded by the family as an irreclaimable youth. . . . His reckless, aimless career became more marked [until] he was eventually forced into a labor which he utterly despised and became a freight brakeman . . . because the wages paid did not enable him to satisfy his elegant tastes and vile habits, he harangued the men about their being robbed; . . . he was a ranting, turbulent, trouble-provoking vagabond, with just enough assumptions to give him a certain influence and just enough brains to make him dangerous.[3]

There are considerably worse things about Mr. Hoover than the absence of even the smallest trace of the novelist in him. But when one reads Pinkerton and Burns, a certain pang about this deficiency is unavoidable. The old detectives had the gift of intimacy with the enemy. Petty gossip seemed to them at least as useful to understanding his nature as their general assessments of its dedicated malignity. Petty gossip seems useless to Mr. Hoover's method. Perhaps, for him, such

[3]Ammon's raffish charm, which is suggested by the description despite the narrator's scorn, makes Pinkerton's picture of him surprisingly like that drawn by Robert V. Bruce, a far more just and sympathetic historian, in his *1877: Year of Violence* (Indianapolis: Bobbs-Merrill, 1959). After his notoriety as a revolutionary syndicalist, Ammon became respectable, was admitted to the bar, and even convicted as a stock swindler.

trivia affront the dignity of the enemy, who must be seen as subject to no vices except the high satanic ones. Otherwise Mr. Hoover's own dignity will be affronted: Armor without a chink must confront armor without a chink. Yet Burns, lumbering though he otherwise was, rather enjoyed letting the customer know what a scoundrel he could be when the fit of the hunt was upon him.

The Masked War describes Burns's running to earth of the McNamara brothers in 1912, whose methods of organizing for the International Union of Bridge and Structural Iron Workers consisted of dynamiting nonunion contracting sites with such success that J. J. McNamara would probably have ended up emitting patriotic sentiments on the AFL-CIO executive council if he had not made the mistake of ordering the bombing of the *Los Angeles Times*.

Burns opens with a few snippets of the nineteenth-century piety, "The war with dynamite was a war of Anarchy against the established form of government of this country," but is thereafter off after the fox with not much more scruple than the fox himself. Burns failed in his efforts to catch the Anarchists he was sure had been the accomplices of the McNamaras. But the McNamaras themselves were much less well guarded by principle. They were simple labor racketeers, and their associates, when they were women, had been wronged by them; when hired thugs, had been underpaid by them; and when ordinary union officials, were anxious to get J. J. McNamara out of the way so that one of them might get promoted to his job as secretary-treasurer of the union.

Burns played upon all these motives in the most masterful fashion— because uninhibited by compunction. He brought the McNamaras down after a series of events culminating in a struggle with defense counsel Clarence Darrow for the allegiance of a key witness whom Burns had won for the prosecution with promises and whom he feared Darrow would win back with cash.

THE WHOLE STORY refreshingly brings back that time when the detective was not the Great Protector Pinkerton once was and Mr. Hoover is now, but just a shady fellow who set Thesis to combat Antithesis and then collected his fee by producing Synthesis from the wreckage. It was this image of the detective that was constructed with such high art in Dashiell Hammett's *Red Harvest*, the only manual of Leninist tactics ever composed by an American, and one who was not by the way then a Leninist but a former private detective.

Such a limited view of the self as a passionless instrument was not Pinkerton's nor is it Mr. Hoover's, both being men incapable of imagining life without order and higher purpose.

Burns saw disorder as an opportunity. So, of course, did Pinkerton and Mr. Hoover, but they also saw it as an offense against nature. Public discontent can have no source but the Hidden Hand:

> If [the Internationale's] members did not actually inaugurate the strikes, the strikes were the direct result of the communistic spirit spread through the ranks of railroad employees by the communistic leaders and their teachings. . . . At the back of the actors in the scenes I have to describe . . . will be found the inspiration . . . if nothing more tangible, of the Internationale—perhaps the identical blood-red figure who "cried havoc and let slip the dogs of war" in Paris.
> —Pinkerton, *Strikers, Communists, Tramps and Detectives*

> Some of this [Vietnam] protest comes from legitimate peace groups and others. . . . However *much* of the agitation is part of a diabolical scheme contrived by the Communist Party, USA (CPUSA), an integral arm of the International Communist conspiracy, the materialistic, godless ideology dedicated to ruling the world.
> —Mr. Hoover, *The FBI Law Enforcement Bulletin*, June 1965

To function would be impossible without guile, and one has one's methods. But since life would be empty without moral purpose, one needs to proclaim one's principles.

·   ·   ·

PINKERTON, HORAN TELLS us, opened for business with the announcement of his *General Principles*, which still exists, Horan says, "not only as an historical document but also as the guide rules for the modern agency." "The agency will not report union meetings unless the meetings are open to the public," and "they will not shadow or investigate . . . trade union officers or members in their lawful union activities."

But Pinkerton practiced both devices and even bragged about them. The main purpose of his guidelines was, then, by their mere exhibition, to rebut all assertions of sneaky conduct. Mr. Hoover has his laws, too, and their letter is regularly cited by him as final proof that none of his agents could possibly have done something imputed by his agency's enemies. The only reference to wiretapping in Mr. Hoover's newest chrestomathy is his affirmation of how seldom he does it.

Last of all, the need for moral purpose in life required that neither Pinkerton nor Mr. Hoover could ever refer to one of his own victims without portraying him as the victim of The Enemy.

When the Brotherhood of Locomotive Engineers threatened to strike the Reading Railroad, one of his clients, Pinkerton selected those of its members to be fired, found replacements for them, and saw to their being generally blacklisted. Afterward, "these misled men had reached a condition of abject want and suffering." And what was to blame that so many of them "had lost their homes, had had their families broken up . . . were forced into becoming tramps and vagrants"? Only the "recklessness" of the Brotherhood of Locomotive Engineers.

Mr. Hoover can come close to the note thus pitched for him by Pinkerton.

The great majority of American youths are genuinely convinced that they would not fall for the Communist bait. Many never would. But there are others who might never know they were "hooked" until the enormous tragedy of their loss of faith dawned after bitter years of fighting the American way of life, almost unwittingly, as dupes of the Communists.

These objects of his pity are, of course, the same young upon whom Mr. Hoover sets spies, whose dossiers he shares with the local policeman, whose conversations he sets the college telephone operator to monitor. But the Great Protector never forgets that he is the guardian of even those who suffer from him. Even as he afflicts them, they remain for him victims only of The Enemy.

The New York Review of Books, May 20, 1971

The Knights of Labor

NEW YORK'S LABOR leaders gave another rub to eyes awakening from the long slumber of their social indignation Friday and gathered near Washington Square at the site where 146 working women died in the Triangle Shirtwaist fire 78 years ago.

The AFL-CIO had sponsored this pilgrimage as the inaugural ceremony for what it projects as an annual Memorial Day for those killed in the workplace accidents whose costs the public records assess at 7,000 lives a year.

The backdrop of the speakers' platform was a long streamer bearing the device "Pray for the Dead and Fight Like Hell for the Living." Those words go back almost as far as the Triangle fire and have for years and years lain buried with it in the graveyard of things judged obsolete and then forgotten.

Joyce Miller had come from Washington to represent the National AFL-CIO's executive council and to lead her two-thousand-member audience in the unfamiliar shout, "an injury to one is an injury to all." That slogan is also an antique, having been cast by the Industrial Workers of the World seventy-five years ago.

Our labor professionals seem suddenly to have been pressed into an archaeological dig for relics of the spirit of class rebellion that they had for twenty-five years united with the rest of us in dismissing as irrelevant. Having lapsed too long from the awareness that might have inspired them to come up with fresh expressions of clamorous defiance on their own, they must make do with the words of the Wobblies.

We would do well to bless every sign of their awakening to the proper business of rebels against injustice. Better wages and more decent conditions of labor are splendid objectives, but the greatest prize at the disposal of union leaders who care is the gift they offer to ordinary people of the sense that they can have some degree of control of their own lives.

That may be an illusion, but it is a divine one, and like most such, born from disillusionment. The rhetoric of Friday's speakers was especially striking for its bitter thoughts about the price labor has paid for its too protracted dependence on the social conscience of the political class.

Thomas Van Arsdale, president of the city's AFL-CIO council, pointed out that New York State's workers' compensation law sets three thousand dollars as the death benefit to an employee killed at the work site and dying without dependents.

He asked, as he was clearly entitled to, whether that was a fair compensation for any human life, however lonely. Some of us may also be entitled to ask, without disdain, where the unions have been while this condition obtained. Legislators and governors pull the forelock to their lobbyists, and yet workers' compensation boards go on skimping the victim.

That, of course, happens to be a function prescribed for workers' compensation boards; employers accepted them with special grace because they were a guarantee against encumbrance by expensive suits for damages.

The victim of an occupational injury has no avenue for his claim except the workers' compensation board. Negligence suits are debarred. The unions could not help their members more immediately than with a strenuous campaign to persuade the legislature to allow the negligence lawyers their shot.

It is one of the ironies of our social history that most of our too slow progress in the direction of industrial safety has lately been owed to the negligence lawyer. We should as an instance still be choking on asbestos fibers if a battery of negligence lawyers hadn't sued Johns-Manville.

They labor, to be sure, under some imputations of greedy motives.

But what else works these days, even sometimes for the common good, except greed?

Still, brotherhood might help too, and we are to be heartened by increasing evidence that this suspicion has occurred to the AFL-CIO. Its appreciation of reality seems, however, still trapped a little too far back on the trails of a memory scarcely evocable on the scene that has erased the building where 146 seamstresses died at their machines or on the pavements to which they leaped. Out of the ashes a piece of New York University has risen, and its young walked gaily in Friday's sun.

The unions could have served their refreshed conscience more fitly if they had moved their ceremonies a few blocks east to Stanton Street, where poorly tutored children play on streets pocked like the craters of the moon and amid trash piled like Pelion upon Ossa.

In that case, we would have been called not just to remember the bad old days but to see how like them these good ones are.

New York Newsday, April 30, 1989

A Gentleman Betrays Himself

K<small>INDER?</small>

Gentler?

George Bush?

We have no fair claim to the suspicion that last weekend's rabbling of Anita Hill was inspired and commanded by the President of the United States. We are, however, at liberty to assume that George Bush enjoyed it.

There have been too many other occasions when, tempted to do whatever may be useful to the politician, he has proceeded unblushingly to do what disgraces the gentleman. His posture in such moments has too often suggested the pleasurable savorings of the distasteful that identify the man who might think it worse to be dismissed as a wimp by the boorish than thought a cad by the refined.

His every seizure by some fresh partisan fit fortifies the impression that George Bush is somehow ashamed of having been brought up by a mother who was a lady and taught by headmasters who had a fine hand with manners if not with Greek and Latin.

These lapses from the good breeding his childhood provided him could not be so distressing were it not for the position he occupies. The President's will is by now powerful enough to stifle the Congress and mold the Supreme Court; we would not go too far if we said that, with the possible exception of Abraham Lincoln, America has not had a ruler this close to absolute since the thirteen original states were

George III's colonies. A president has at last been exalted to the station of a monarch. The most, and it is by no means a small thing, that can be said for monarchs is that, in the better instances, they can be thanked for setting the proper tone for their subjects. The most deplorable aspect of this president's tone is that, instead of resisting, it seems almost to cater to the vulgarity that permeates the atmosphere of our national discourse.

Now and then, to pay its way, CNN would interrupt the Senate Judiciary Committee hearings for a trailer soliciting our patronage for a movie in which Danny DeVito seems overweeningly proud to incarnate every shade of the bestiality Anita Hill may have been unjustly imputing to Justice Thomas's larynx. We were presumably expected to laugh at this sort of thing; and, if we don't, we must nonetheless resign ourselves to tolerating it.

One irony of the new and redeemed-for-community-standards Supreme Court is that crippled women may have to worry about their Social Security disability checks but that pornographers have little cause to worry about their commerce. Filthy T-shirts have befouled our streets with impunity ever since the old court confused public nuisances with the rights accorded dissent by the First Amendment. The new court shows no disposition to redress such indecencies, being, we may suppose, too busy restoring suspended licenses to abuse the poor.

It could not have been accident for Anita Hill's detractors to evoke the image of the *Fatal Attraction* antiheroine who was the very crest of a misogyny so rampant in Hollywood that we can scarcely hope to see a movie unreeking with the smokes and biles of its screenwriter's resentments of his alimony bill.

No loss of patience with the excesses of organized feminism can excuse the hatred of woman as woman whose epidemic proportions revealed themselves in Anita Hill's treatment by those licensed bullies, Senators Alan Simpson, Arlen Specter, and Orrin Hatch, Bushites all. She could not with propriety demand to be believed; but she came with and deserved to keep an overriding claim to be respected.

Men and women are condemned to live together; and, taking its consequences all in all, I have no reason to complain of the sentence. Those who attempt to divide men from women and women from men are enemies of courtesy and concord; and George Bush ought to be infinitely more ashamed of the vice of enthusiastic enlistment on one side of this repellent quarrel than anyone should ever be of the virtue of a gentleman's breeding.

New York Newsday, October 18, 1991

Stupidity Does Not Discriminate

FEDERAL JUDGE KENNETH Conboy has forbidden City College of New York further to violate Professor Michael Levin's civil rights by subjecting his "controversial views . . . about race, feminism and homosexuality" to special scrutiny and possible sanction.

The Constitution's protections of freedom of expression are beyond dispute so universal as to shield both Michael Levin and Leonard Jeffries. But neither's opinions are exempt from critical assessment by the rest of us.

Newsday recently printed a Jeffries and a Levin speech in full. Of the two, Levin's is the more useful to engage, simply because it at least attempts an argument by reason.

Levin posits a white citizen, who is peaceably traversing the streets and becomes aware of the approach of a young stranger of color. What does he do? First he reminds himself that the crime statistics indicate that one in every four black males has gone to prison for a violent felony.

He is then "entitled to turn on his heels and flee," since there is a 25 percent chance of immediate danger of assault. To be persuaded by statistics is, of course, to free oneself from the realities of human experience.

If statistics were the only measure, Levin would be underestimating the peril of black criminals to white pedestrians. In at least one out of two instances of violent felony, the offender escapes being arrested at all. If we extend Levin's method of projection, the odds that a black stranger is a dangerous criminal would then approach 50 percent; and we would be well advised not to go out on the street. But the fact of life is that we do; and the fact of experience is that we seldom feel either impulse or necessity to turn on our heels and flee.

We have learned to be cautious as rational beings must. But to suggest that we respond to every inference of alarm with ungainly flight is to demand that we make a habit out of abandonments of personal dignity. To decide that we cannot live except by conduct this abject is to settle for the worthless life. With every affectation of the airs of logic, Levin is directing us down the road toward paranoia, which happens to be the destination of reason's final dislodgement.

What appalls in such stuff is not that it is bigoted but that it is stupid. Levin holds a professorial seat in a department of philosophy where Morris Raphael Cohen was shining scarcely half a century ago. Cohen embodied the philosophical temper whose very opposite this dolt incarnates. And yet he was in a position to complain, with perfect truth no doubt, that City College's persecutions had forced him to decline at least sixteen invitations from scholarly journals and campus audiences.

Jeffries's opportunities for self-display are even richer because he has a livelier touch with malignities. The college lecture circuit has become an endowed freak show.

What we are witnessing here is the terminal degradation of the academic dogma. Set aside Levin and Jeffries and contemplate the once great educational establishment that employs them. Jeffries plunges into one extreme of nonsense and Levin swims more delicately in the opposite extreme. City College is embarrassed by both; but its curious notion of fairness forbade it to trouble one without troubling the other.

Still, Levin and Jeffries are only conspicuous boils on a diseased body; they would not be where they are if college administrators did not hold their students in contempt. What in the end is a black studies department except the consignment of students of color to a separate and unequal system of education, with standards abysmally inferior to Tuskegee's and with a teacher like Jeffries who owes his eminence to college administrators who think him no worse than his classroom deserves?

We have to concede that the constitutional ideals of liberty adjure us to leave these two where they are. But if there is a Heaven, Morris Cohen can only look down on Michael Levin and weep with the angels.

New York Newsday, September 8, 1991

Unsentimental Education

WE MAY SUPPOSE that failure was the first thing Luis Soto learned in school. Maybe he withdrew into himself, maybe he struck out at others. It scarcely matters whether he was too distracted or too distracting for the classroom norm. We have said enough when we identify him as one of those children who are marked and mocked as "retards" as soon as their schoolmates mature enough to know the language of cruelty.

The Board of Education has no remedy for inconveniences like Luis Soto except in the facilities for emotionally disturbed or learning-disabled students it clusters, higgledy-piggledy, in its special education programs.

He was consigned to the Manhattan School of Career Development; and last November, he found out just how special his special education could be. Robert Eichler, Career Development's dean, came to Luis Soto's classroom, collected him and nine other boys, and told them to come with him.

Luis Soto's counsel has sworn by affidavit that the dean who thus conscripted these wards of his keeping did not tell them where or why they were going.

A police lieutenant from the nearest precinct had asked to borrow ten boys to flesh out the lineup around a youthful Hispanic robbery suspect. We have every right to expect a dean of special education to remember that his charges happen to be children peculiarly vulnerable to feeling in the wrong. Instead, this one herded them together, watched them arrayed on the precinct stage holding numbered cards on their chests, and staring, as commanded, at the blank wall behind which the victim sought to pick out the putative offender.

Luis Soto and comrades under draft had no way to tell whether they were not themselves under arrest; and its managers stopped the process only when one of its exhibits began to cry. Luis Soto remembers only one apology and it was tendered, unsurprisingly, not by his own teacher but by a cop.

Luis Soto was paid ten dollars for his yet-to-be-forgotten pains. He came home haunted by the sense that, without knowing why, he had put himself in too much trouble to tell his mother. He finally dared to tell an older sister. She told their mother, whose response, rarely familiar in her son's experience with the world, was to visit the blame on the school instead of him.

Carmen Rodriguez is bound to a wheelchair and untrained in English. But, all the same, she is of the stuff that lodges in heroic natures. Dean Eichler's parade distressed and humiliated nine other families; but only Carmen Rodriguez has pressed her protest until it has finally brought her to sue the Board of Education for damages. But then it must take the strongest sort of parents to live through their child's protracted treatment as worthless and still believe that they themselves are worth enough to be much use in braving the world for him.

By March, Luis Soto was still damaged and afraid to go back to Manhattan Career Development. Over the summer, the Board of Education at last yielded to his mother's pressure and transferred Luis and his sister to Bronx Career Development.

Those two arrived there when the schools opened this week and they shrank almost immediately homeward. "Those kids," Luis Soto's sister said yesterday, "looked just too rough."

These children had been sent alone, in their shaky state, to bear the shocks of a strange new school with no adult company to ease their passage. But then special education probably doesn't offer escort services gentler than those drovers give to herds.

Stephen Greenberg, the plaintiff family's lawyer, introduced its members to the press yesterday and thought it unsafe to allow more than one question to Luis Soto. It was "How do you feel?" He answered that he was scared and stopped and bowed his head in the withdrawal that wishes the floor would open and hide the person.

He had failed again. He won't always. His parents are in his corner, bearing him up, and fighting to keep his chances alive for the time when he is up to using them.

New York Newsday, September 13, 1991

Rollcall

WHAT FOLLOWS IS a four-item selection from the city's ever-expanding catalogue of human infamies:

· Summer 1986. A landlord incensed by the complaints of a cheated tenant hires two street bravos to exact his vengeance. They execute the contract with razor slashings down both sides of the tenant's face. Irradicable scars remain after repairs requiring 150 stitches. The victim is a model whose career was in early bloom and henceforth must depend for survival on such work rations as the market affords for disfigured celebrities. Public attention: clamorous. Disposition: landlord and his two hired hands, all, five- to fifteen-year prison terms.

· Summer 1990. Another model, seventeen and new to the city, is slashed in the face while walking on the Lower East Side. An emergency-room resident does what he can with sixty stitches. There is further resort to plastic surgery, but the prospects remain uncertain for a modeling career barely begun. Public attention: invisible. Disposition: putative assailant awaiting trial with a reasonable expectation of a two-and-a-half- to five-year sentence.

· Summer 1989. A band of up to thirty youthful males goes reveling at night through Manhattan's best-known public park. Result: three violent assaults on entire strangers, the most savagely used of whom was raped, beaten unconscious, dragged naked one hundred twenty feet and left for dead. Public attention: again clamorous. Disposition:

three youths sentenced to five to ten years, the maximum for juveniles, and others awaiting trial.

• Summer 1990. A group of six or seven adult males drive to another recreation area, less well-known but cherished by its regular visitors, jump from their car, slash one stranger from ear to chin, beat another sorely, and then make a failed effort to throw him in the Hudson. Public attention: again invisible. Disposition: one boastful confession that earns Ronald Canaby a three- to five-year sentence; and a diminishing likelihood of successful prosecution of the other defendants, because the victims are reluctant to testify.

The model in the first example, is of course, Marla Hanson, who is famous for reasons all else but her choice. The model in the second is unknown and would prefer to stay that way, because his assailant took or mistook him for a homosexual and told police afterward, with just a touch of pride, "Yeah, I slashed the fag." The park victim is of course the Central Park jogger. The also unidentifiable recreation-area victim had just arrived with two friends at the Christopher Street pier in Greenwich Village at two in the morning. As leader of the assaulting pack, Ronald Canaby announced, "I just got out of jail, I hate faggots," and emphasized his point with razor slashings of face and arms.

Here are four instances of mayhem, all unprovoked unless we are to say that Marla Hanson's insistence of what was her right and due was an asking-for-what-she-got. Two of them arose in the utterly random impulses of a mob and a third in a passerby's sudden whim. They are essentially alike in the viciousness of the deed and the irreparable damage to its object's person. And yet we know about everything that happened to Marla Hanson and the Central Park jogger and nothing about what happened to those two presumed homosexuals whose treatment was close to as cruel as theirs. But then, violent criminal acts truly stir those portions of our hearts where pity and terror reside not by the degree of their depravity but to the extent to which we can identify with their victims. The wrongs that outrage our sensibilities are those visited upon people like ourselves; the rest are only statistics. But, until we the comfortable begin to cry out against the inflictions that have become routine for persons different from us, we will be blithering in the wind no matter how loudly we say how much we care.

New York Newsday, September 14, 1990

Autumn in New York

THE LOVELIER OF New York's days have a curious way of bobbing up on the mornings after the eviler of her nights.

Such was especially the case Friday on Ward's Island, where Carlos Melendez was hacked to death and eight other homeless men sent to the hospital by a costumed gang of Halloween revelers.

Ward's Island is as close an approach to Eden as the East River's landscape has to offer. There is, however, a significant difference between this and the first of all gardens. Adam and Eve were expelled from Eden to wander everywhere else, while most of its overnight lodgers have sunk into Ward's Island after wandering and been all but expelled from everywhere else.

Ward's Island's only historical importance has been as a chosen spot for quarantines. The nineteenth century used it for a potter's field, for a refuge for destitute aliens, and for the New York Asylum for the Insane, which is now called the Manhattan Psychiatric Center and would be the last public building left on the island except for sharing that dignity with the Charles H. Gay Volunteers of America men's shelter.

The streets of New York have been the reefs where a great part of a whole generation of men have been shipwrecked, and they wait to do the same for the boys who are those men's children. We might go too far if we said that the young who murdered Carlos Melendez were striking not at some Other but at a part of that Self they are in exigent risk of becoming in middle age. But how, after all, did these nine unlucky men offend this mob if not by incarnating the future that hangs like a sword over so many of its members?

W. H. Auden once reminded us that we must love one another or die. The soft beauties of Ward's Island's ruin served to start that thought on Friday, but the harshness of its reality fairly shouted the insistence that we cannot love one another and that therefore we will die.

Ward's Island is an Eden gone to weeds and sorrows, but its charms are somehow heightened by the ghosts of misfortuned lives that whisper in its breezes. Some of its functioning structures have columns and one has pediments, and their suggestion of the Old South is enlarged by the sight of wooden buildings long abandoned and now tumbled down to look like the wake of Sherman's march through Georgia.

Ward's Island's single prideful ornament is the stand of fine trees at the foot of the bridge that was the cutting floor for Wednesday's Halloween celebration. This grove's trees were planted long ago and in a wide variety of species, each identified by its own metal label and with its leaves turned Friday to its particular fall color.

A visitor walks through high grass along dirt trails and now and then meets a homeless man and shudders from old alarms more ridiculous than usual, because here is not the dangerous but the endangered. Our encounters are as those upon a rural path, and the airs around its foliage bring whatever scents we might suppose to lie where the woodbine twineth.

The intimations of the Old South have on short order become so inescapable that the imagination can barely resist hanging black bodies on these trees. These thoughts would be pleasanter if they had no place except in the imagination. But they have come too near to where we live.

The South has given up rabbling the helpless, and New York has taken over. Judge Lynch has changed his venue, and the mobs that are his enforcement squad belong to us. Howard Beach, Central Park, Bensonhurst, and now Ward's Island were each and every one a lynching bee.

It seemed probable Friday that the mob that fell upon Carlos Melendez and his fellow strayed innocents would be in police custody before the weekend was over. Predators for no gain but the trophy of their prey always get caught, because they do it for bragging rights and they can't shut up.

After a while it seems useless to try to explain things that cannot possibly be excused. It is, as an instance, often said that the lynch spirit draws its fires from fear and hatred of the Other. And yet, whenever a derelict is beaten or set afire in this city, his assailants generally turn out to be children whose own pinched existences are not far from the edge their victim has crossed and fallen over.

The police are already all but certain that Carlos Melendez was butchered by young men from the East River Houses, a project whose residents come in the main from the same class of the working poor that is the lost origin of most of the homeless. When the police complete their arrests, they are unlikely to find a single suspect who does not have a cousin or an uncle or even occasionally a father whom the world has as far wounded and brought so low as Carlos Melendez was.

New York Newsday, September 21, 1990

A Klondike of Ironies

THE MOST ENTHUSIASTIC reception for any speaker at last week's convention of the National Association of Black Journalists was reserved for Army General Colin L. Powell, who is a man of color and President George Bush's designee as chairman of the Joint Chiefs of Staff.

Every delegate stood up to welcome him to the Manhattan Hilton's grandest ballroom with the enthusiasm that is never so resonant as when it is evoked by a figure whose achievement is made larger than himself because he incarnates the otherwise so frequently delusive promise that, in America, opportunity has no ceiling.

Colin Powell reminded his audience that he would not be where he has arrived if it had not been for "the sacrifices of those black soldiers who served this nation" in the Revolution, on the plains of the West, and on San Juan Hill. He had, he said, been raised up "on the backs of those who went before me" and he knew that there are "still more rivers to cross."

He had never forgotten Langston Hughes's injunction that "to save the dream for one, it must be saved for all." His job as a soldier is to defend that dream; and he was so far from sure of its accomplishment without the inspiration of black history that he had once gone on pilgrimage to the Martin Luther King, Jr., Center in Atlanta, and Coretta Scott King had sent him home with the parting gift of a portrait of her husband.

General Powell hung it in his conference room; and the first sight that meets his eye when he sits down at the head of the table is Martin Luther King, Jr.'s, image with the inscription, "Freedom has always been an expensive thing."

Lech Walesa knows that truth, and so does Nelson Mandela, and so do the Chinese students, Powell said, and so ought the military appropriations committees of the Congress because "we must never send our soldiers forth" underprepared and unequipped. The gospel of Martin Luther King, Jr., had been distilled into "Freedom is an expensive thing/the Stealth bomber is an expensive thing/therefore freedom is the Stealth bomber."

We had been brought not too comfortably close to a poster of the prophet whose most tangible memorial is a Center for the Study of Non-Violence and he is pointing his finger above the martial cry, "Martin Luther King, Jr., wants you."

The irony of this reflection carries with it no want of respect for Colin L. Powell. He is both a soldier and a man of color and free of preference for one identity over the other. But, proud as he is of black history, he reads it with a soldier's eye and finds his progenitors in the Buffalo Soldiers whose job it was to defend freedom by stripping the Indian tribes of theirs.

For, if he is sincerely aware that he has risen on the backs of the black soldiers who came before him, he also knows that the words may be Frederick Douglass's and Langston Hughes's but they are to be marched to the tune of all the Joint Chiefs who have come before him too.

We do not lift our strivers as high as he if they blow any trumpet other than the one the supply sergeant issued them on the day they were sworn in.

The mass of the troubles and the fragments of the triumphs of persons of color are rooted in 350 years of American life; and their history endlessly fascinates. It is, after all, so much their country's that the rest of us ought long ago to have recognized how much easier it is to learn about America with an all-else-excluding concentration on the history of Afro-Americans than it has ever been to depend on histories that scarcely mention them. Black history is also the more appetizing because, however often its protagonists make us ashamed of ourselves, they don't often impel us to blush for them.

And then black history is especially to be cherished for the richness of the lode it offers for diggers in the vein of the national ironies. Even General Powell was not quite so precious a specimen as the Feasts of the Prodigal Father the newspaper publishers lavished upon these black journalists whose elder brothers couldn't get a seat at a typewriter, let alone a heaped up dinner table, in a time not thirty years gone.

My own revered employers snared Powell; and the Gannett papers weighed in with a luncheon dedicated to the memory of W.E.B. Du Bois. The eye could not see that name without being flooded with the puzzle of which Du Bois our masters proposed to salute. Was it the Du Bois who sits with small company on the peak where there abide those who have supremely described the world?

Or was it the Du Bois who assembled the evidence that got poor Marcus Garvey, the black nationalist, in jail for mail fraud? Or was it perhaps the Du Bois who strayed too far in the direction of Marxism-Leninism to be tolerated by the National Association for the Advancement of Colored People, was expelled from the editorship of *The Crisis*, the NAACP magazine he had founded, was harried by grand juries, and died at last self-exiled in Ghana, scarcely noticed and even less mourned by the organs of enlightenment that polished his laurels yesterday.

But such is black history, a Klondike of ironies, mostly its nation's but often its very own. Of course. It is American.

New York Newsday, August 20, 1989

Fatal Attraction

BOBBY EDMONDS WAS seldom hard to locate. His days had the regularity his habit dictated. They would begin and trail out in a heroin shooting gallery on Harlem's West 121st Street. The cops could count on finding him there when the time came for using him, and so could the Vigilantes when the time came for killing him.

Bobby Edmonds was a terminal junkie. Wherever he went, he carried with him a scent that Detective James Bratton still remembers as "like a sewer. His abscesses were acting up; you get that deadlike smell."

He had once served the Vigilantes by hustling the brand of heroin that is the symbol of the monopoly they enforce on Eighth Avenue from 116th to 121st streets. But he had failed even at that, and he was simply a slave without function on the October night in 1982 when next he saw Nookie Sweeper, who had been boss of his sales crew.

He recalled later that he had seen Nookie and two other Vigilantes firing their pistols upon McKinley Freeman, a mutual acquaintance, until Freeman was satisfactorily enough defunct to be eligible for Nookie Sweeper's ritual farewell of the kick in the head.

Bobby Edmonds was not yet far enough round the bend to run to the police, but he seems to have been incautious with gossip; and a day or so later, he was roused from his slumbers at the 121st Street shooting gallery, informed that he had been heard to talk too much, and worked over with a brick.

Edmonds finally confronted and recognized Nookie Sweeper as a creature even more degraded than himself, and he drew the line at last. With his mouth and eye still bleeding from the brick, he hobbled to the 28th Police Precinct and turned Nookie Sweeper in. Detective Dennis Mulcahy would later recall a stench about Bobby Edmonds's person so pervasive that it was necessary to keep the door open while his statement was being taken down.

That statement did not merely complain that Edmonds had been beaten by Nookie Sweeper but went on to affirm that Edmonds had seen Nookie Sweeper shoot McKinley Freeman to death.

At that point, Bobby Edmonds was disinclined to compound Nookie Sweeper's wrath by putting his own name on a formal assault complaint against him. He agreed, however, that, with the requisite assurance of advance secrecy, he would testify against Sweeper if the Freeman homicide ever came to trial.

Detective Mulcahy sent him back on the street. The police knew Edmonds well enough by then to assume that, in case of need, they could always run into him "either in the gutter or in the shooting gallery." Detective Bratton had been pursuing the Freeman murder and went off at once unsuccessfully to check the gutters and the galleries for this new witness.

Eventually he found Edmonds in a New Jersey hospital, and brought him before a grand jury impressed enough by his testimony to indict Nookie Sweeper for murder.

Jury selection for Sweeper's trial began last November; the time was close at hand when acting Supreme Court Justice Myriam Altman could no longer avoid releasing to the defense the name of the prosecution's main witness. Certain precautions for Edmonds's well-being had by then become advisable, and Detective Bratton hunted him out at the shooting gallery.

He found his man so sick that the District Attorney's office agreed that it would be best to take Bobby Edmonds to a hospital where he would be fairly safe and where his sores could get enough treatment to make him reasonably presentable for the jury.

Bratton took him to Harlem Hospital and left him there on the presumption that he would be admitted as a bed patient.

Harlem Hospital was content to bandage his abscesses and turn him away for reasons never explained. When Bratton found out what had happened, he could only go back to the shooting gallery, where he found Bobby Edmonds "out of it."

"[The hospital] wouldn't take me, man," he said. "I'm in bad shape. I'll be here all day. But I'll be straight tomorrow."

Tomorrow was the morning appointed for Bobby Edmonds to take the stand as a witness against Nookie Sweeper, and it was by then an appointment well known to the Vigilantes. Detective Bratton departed and eight hours later, a person still unidentified walked into the shooting gallery and shot off the back of Bobby Edmonds's head.

In the indignant words of acting Justice Altman, "no steps whatever [had been] taken to safeguard [him]." Self-destruction is so much the destiny of junkies that it can almost be thought of as willed, and perhaps Bobby Edmonds was satisfied to die. But, low as he had fallen, he had at least chosen to go to his end with a measure of honor, which is more than we can say for the public institutions that are responsible for healing the sick and doing justice to the wicked and that did less than the Vigilantes but more than they should to help him toward his grave.

New York Newsday, December 9, 1984

Pride and Prejudice

ALL THOSE WHO may still adhere to the half-forgotten if not quite abandoned cause of fair housing will have to wait a week before they learn whether Richard Nixon will have a place to lay his head.

It is no easy business to be your country's most conspicuous and enduring symbol of martyrdom to prejudice, which may explain why our lost president is always seeking new quarters. Misfortunes like his engrave the sense that anywhere else might be better than where you are.

Last year, Nixon approached the 61 East 72nd Street Corporation with the requisite $1.8 million purchase price for an apartment. When we speak of this building as an East Side co-op, we identify it as representative of our most powerful evidence for the conservative doctrine that there are few worse tyrannies than unrestrained rule by a democratic majority.

The warmth of his initial reception was tempered by requirements for admission not altogether consonant with a former president's dignity. The building's negotiators stipulated that his Secret Service attendants "be at all times dressed in business suits, i.e., coat and tie, or coat, vest and tie, and at no time loll about the couch or chairs in an ungentlemanly manner." Any police officer assigned to post by the city would be forbidden the premises unless he confined himself to the small office beside the vestibule.

This great historical figure, who had upheld his country's interests through protracted bargaining sessions with the loftiest of its allies and antagonists, seems to have surrendered his own prerogatives, let alone those of the secretary of the treasury and the police commissioner, without a moment's hesitation. He dared to bargain with Brezhnev and Mao, but he knew better than to try to bargain with an East Side co-op.

And even then, having fairly scuttled over the last mile, he could not yet find peace. Jacob M. Kaplan, an owner-tenant, wrote his fellow directors to express alarm at the "unsubstantiated rumor" that Richard Nixon might be their neighbor. Kaplan is over ninety and rich from the pressings of Welch's grapes. He is also a fervent and pitiless liberal Democrat. He enclosed the Columbia Encyclopedia's summary of the applicant's career: "Indications of pervasive corruption."

"We would be forced to ride with Nixon and his entourage in the elevator; curious crowds might gather in front of the building in order to get a glimpse of him," Kaplan protested.

"The substantial and potentially catastrophic consequences" he foresaw included a potential decline in the dollar worth of any apartment at 760 Park Avenue. The threat to real estate values has, of course, always been a staple of the resistance to persons of color aspiring to move in.

Kaplan went to court to enjoin the sale and relented only when the directors agreed to meet and discuss it. They met yesterday while the journalists waited outside. Seven-sixty Park Avenue's canopy leaks; the gilt leaves that form its entrance grate have not lately been polished; and when the superintendent appeared now and then to berate those tormented by the rain, it could be noticed that he was not wearing a coat and tie and that his manner was all else but gentlemanly.

But such is the way with fair-housing controversies: The object of prejudice is always neater and better behaved than those who bar his way. In due course, word came that the directors had approved Nixon with one dissent. Now, he must face the judgment of all the other tenants, including one woman who says she won't vote for him because she doesn't like him.

Who else in America except the tenant of an East Side co-op has a license to lock somebody out for no better reason than his fancied unlikability? Oh well, perhaps Nixon suffers for the best. If this nonsense continues much longer, the new Civil Rights Commission might at last find a case of discrimination worth its attention.

New York Newsday, December 5, 1984

The Shame of *The Washington Post*

THE FRONT PAGE of Sunday's *Washington Post* had room for just one reference to the doings of President Reagan and no space at all for those of Pope John Paul II, Leonid Brezhnev, and Alexander Haig. The cosmic had been displaced by the domestic, because of the *Post*'s distraction by the transgressions of Janet Cooke, whose "Jimmy's World" had brought her paper the transient reward of a Pulitzer Prize and herself the lasting disgrace of being exposed as a fraud the very next day.

The *Post*'s explanation and apology was, if here and there short on chivalry, indisputably long on honor. It was also obtuse. If I may be personal, the *Post* is my favorite newspaper, present company excepted; I rather long ago gave up withholding my affections from some institution or other for no better reason than my finding it obtuse. We are all of us obtuse.

Like all of us, the *Post* looks everywhere except under its own nose for the cause of its shame. The overriding fact is that the *Post*'s editors can blame their gullibility and Miss Cooke's opportunity for self-disablement on the conditions that even that best of newspapers appoints for the black members of its staff.

Miss Cooke can hardly be excused for faking her credentials, but the *Post*'s account makes it quite clear that she wouldn't have been hired if she hadn't. According to the *Post*, she attached six samples of her work to a resumé that included the fiction that she was a Vassar Phi

Beta Kappa. In normal circumstances, you would think the work samples would be the most relevant test of a candidate's worth. But Executive Editor Benjamin Bradlee, who was happy to get black reporters and women reporters, was happiest of all with a black woman reporter from Vassar.

Having made her entrance by inflating her social eminence, Miss Cooke was assigned to the District Weekly, the *Post*'s ghetto. The *Post* has three area weeklies, one for Virginia, one for Maryland, and one for Washington itself. Since Washington is 70 percent nonwhite, its District Weekly deals largely with black achievements. Miss Cooke worked earnestly and well under a black editor; her sin was a consuming ambition to advance to the Metro section, where she could cover breaking local news.

The *Post*'s tradition of separate and dubiously equal facilities seems to have a smaller but not insignificant place in the operations of the Metro section. Milton Coleman, city editor for Washington proper, is black, while Metro's suburban editors are, of course, white. Judging from the *Post*'s account of Miss Cooke's road to ruin, we can assume that the black reporter gives satisfaction to the District Weekly by celebrating black success and earns his ticket to the higher precincts by retailing black disasters.

Miss Cooke did this quite thunderingly by inventing an eight-year-old heroin addict whose name was Jimmy. When she was struck down, she was busy contriving a fourteen-year-old black prostitute. She was, in other words, delighting her editors by bringing them back tales from a zoo.

But Miss Cooke's white editors, in the astronomical reaches above her, were untroubled by doubts. As one of them said, they took it for granted that, if the Jimmy story were a fake, Coleman would have detected it. Coleman was, after all, black too. It never seems to have occurred to anyone that blacks come in no end of varieties, and the jungle Miss Cooke was describing is a world as closed to a black city editor as to a white one.

All in all, it is remarkable how much the *Post*'s explanation makes even the finest newspaper sound like an antebellum plantation. Miss

Cooke is a young black woman who came and went without having worked under any supervisor who was not black too. Mightn't the *Post*'s ombudsman at least have suggested that its editors bus their black reporters to Maryland and Virginia every now and then?

New York Post, April 21, 1981

The Meritocracy of Labor

THE MOST PUBLIC life Ernest Green is ever likely to know is now not quite seven years back in his past. He is only twenty-three now. Ernest Green was the first Negro to be graduated from Central High School in Little Rock, Arkansas. He was for a while a subject for all the news photos, a thin child with glasses walking through the crowds in the fall of 1957, and then still a thin child in a black robe with his classmates in the spring of 1958, a graduate, thanks to the protection of federal troops.

He was one of 601 seniors at Central High School. Just 14 of them wrote their good wishes in his class yearbook.

"I really admire you, Ernest," the secretary of Central High's student government wrote under her picture. "I doubt if I could have done half so much if our positions were reversed. May you achieve all your goals and they be the best."

THE FIFTIES FOCUSED on the special Negro, and his story was always inspiriting. Now the sixties are confronted with the ordinary Negro and he has almost no story at all.

Ernest Green departed the South to complete his education at Michigan State University; and few of the strangers who saw him in his singular high school year can have thought much about him since. The other day I went to Brooklyn, from some small curiosity about the ordinary Negro, and came upon Ernest Green. He has found his goal in the Bedford-Stuyvesant area, which is Brooklyn's Harlem. He spends his days trying to find jobs for young Negroes as plumbers, electricians, and carpenters.

It would be too much to say that it is as hard for an ordinary young Negro in New York to be taken on as an apprentice in a skilled trade as it is for an extraordinary young Negro to be admitted to a Southern university. But it would not be a great deal too much to say.

In 1958, the year of Ernest Green's high school graduation, the New York State Commission Against Discrimination made an ethnic survey of the apprentices in the state's construction industry. Apprentice training is the only means of entry into those building crafts which have always been the best general opportunity for comfort and pride available to the young whose education ends with high school. In 1958, the State Commission Against Discrimination estimated that perhaps 2 percent of New York's 15,000 construction apprentices in training were Negroes.

That estimate may have been generous. We have lived since through seven years of innumerable protest demonstrations by Negroes and frequent if seldom effectual responses in plea and intervention by government. And after all these efforts at remonstrance and conciliation, no responsible agency can yet assert that more than 12 percent of the construction apprentices now in training are Negroes.

The skilled-job market has, of course, always been controlled by a company of trade unions which have been the only medieval institutions in the city, being hierarchic, feudal, and frequently consanguine. Apprentices, more often than not, have been connected by blood or friendship with full members of these guilds. The tradition of the job as property to be bequeathed or given away has done as much to bar the Negro as any lively prejudice against his color. There were three thousand union plumbers in Brooklyn a year ago last August; nine of them were Negroes, none of whom held the "A" membership card and earned the $4.10 an hour wage that rewards survivors of the apprenticeship stage.

Last spring the State Commission for Human Rights found Local 28 of the Sheet Metal Workers Union guilty of discriminating against Negro applicants. Local 28 had and has 3,300 members, none of whom was or is a Negro. Some 26 of the 30 applicants accepted for the local's apprenticeship program in July 1963 were related to union members. A journeyman fitting the standards of this guild earns up to $6.15 an hour. Under pressure of court orders, Local 28 has agreed to give up selecting its apprentices by family bond and to subject all applicants to an aptitude test supervised by New York University next month.

A construction worker's certificate as a skilled craftsman may at last be coming to depend less on favor and more on objective standards. Last year, the Taconic Foundation made a grant to the Workers Defense League to seek out young Negroes to take these tests. The League set up its apprenticeship program headquarters in the most impressive building on its shabby block on Fulton Street. Ray Murphy, holder of the master's degree in clinical psychology, which is so much easier for a Negro than a plumbers union work permit, is its director and Ernest Green is his assistant.

THEY HAVE PERHAPS 150 young Negroes on their rolls as prospective applicants to any apprenticeship class a union opens up. None of them can remember schools remotely as good as Central High in Little Rock. They had no chance against the barriers of custom; and now they do not have a greatly improved chance under the test of merit.

Their common problem is illustrated in the case of Arthur Harris, nineteen, a graduate of Thomas Edison Vocational High School in Queens, where he was selected above all his fellow seniors as laureate in the plumbing award of the ladies auxiliary of the Master Plumbers Association. In April 1964, Arthur Harris tried to follow the bent indicated for the best plumber in his class by applying to the apprenticeship training program sponsored by Brooklyn Plumbers Local Number One. Local One did not answer his letter; Ray Murphy intervened and in October the education committee of Local One agreed to let Arthur Harris take its aptitude examination.

The new merit system for neophyte plumbers administered by

New York University is not one of rigid intellectual standards. An applicant, to be eligible for apprentice training, need only show himself above the level of the bottom quarter of the average American high school senior class. Arthur Harris could, then, have passed with a score of 100 out of a possible 400. He scored a 63; and, at that, may have done no worse than a majority of the other applicants, all of them white graduates of New York City schools. No more than 20 of the 60 testees seem to have achieved what is no more than a 25 percent passing grade.

Arthur Harris scored 5 out of a possible 100 in the category of "mental alertness"; 7 out of a possible 100 in mechanical reasoning; and 5 out of a possible 100 in numerical ability.

Ray Murphy guesses that a young man who had mastered the elements of the ninth grade would pass this test. There can be no sensible quarrel with the honesty of the academicians who conducted it. We can only conclude then that the best prospective plumber in a New York City vocational school had been equipped by his teachers to rank less than a point above the *lowest 5 percent of American high school graduates* in alertness, mechanical capacity, and skill with numbers.

Arthur Harris has dropped from sight since this disaster; Ernest Green is afraid that he has given up. Most of the young Negroes who sit in Bedford-Stuyvesant are like Arthur Harris and other graduates of vocational high schools, which means that they belong to a category of persons trained for no vocation at all.

We can assume, however, that if the Taconic Foundation and Ray Murphy and Ernest Green are patient enough, the building trades unions will have to yield their privileges and accept their apprentices on objective merit. But even that surrender is by no means imminent; most of Ray Murphy's day is spent in the continual interventions necessary to persuade or press union officials to give his charges a chance just to take their tests.

There is the case of Emmett Washington, a member of the maintenance division of Local Three of the International Brotherhood of Electrical Workers. In June of 1964, Local Three sent out letters to its members asking if they had any sons who might like to be apprentices to its construction division. Emmett Washington wrote back that he had no son but that he himself was a member of the union still young enough to be an apprentice. He got no answer; Murphy inquired further on his behalf and was told that the local had decided not to hold a class this year.

"I took one kid down to Local Two of the plumbers union to see a man named Kearns who is secretary of their joint apprenticeship committee," Murphy said. "When we got there Kearns came out and said that Kearns wasn't in. We had to go back again before he'd give him an application. I'm still not sure when he will take a test.

"I took two kids to Local 40 of the iron workers last October and they told us they weren't interviewing applicants unless they were accompanied by two sponsors who were union members. They had promised two years ago that they would no longer require sponsors. I got in touch with the secretary-treasurer and reminded him of some of these things and he called back to say that it had all been a mistake and we should apply again.

"We went back down and while we were waiting, one of the white applicants said we could go in first because his *sponsors* hadn't gotten there yet. Anyway, we were finally able to make an application ten days ago."

STILL, THE TESTS are coming; the problems that cannot be righted by any pressure at Murphy's command still have much to do with the unreadiness of the tested. When we think of the ordinary Negro, we recognize that the New York school system has settled into a mold as segregated in class as anything we have deplored in European education. The South, of course, traditionally drew the distinction of race; the academic public high school was for white children; the industrial or vocational school was for Negroes. New York has unconsciously drifted into a system which, in essentials, ends with the same result.

A child's pattern is set when he is thirteen and ready to enter the complex of city high schools. He may, if he can pass its tests, enter an academic high school and hope to go on to a municipal college, where the tuition is still free and open to any high school graduate with an average of 85 in his academic subjects. Short of that, he can try for a technical high school, where the academic standards are also excluding and where he can learn a trade. Failing all tests, there is no place for him except the vocational school that teaches almost nothing and serves no purpose beyond the requirements of compulsory school education.

On the bulletin board in Ernest Green's office, there is a clipping from *The New York Times* telling the story of Michael Stewart, the first Negro apprentice to be accepted by Local 40 of the iron workers union. " 'His father, Malcolm Stewart, writes technical manuals for Sperry Rand,' " Ernest Green read from the *Times*. "Now there's a working-class background."

Sheet Metal Workers Local 28 sent out word last week that on February 13, it would conduct its objective test for apprentice applicants as prescribed by court order. Murphy and Green think they might have as many as sixty candidates; Dr. Kenneth Clark has agreed to hold classes for them at the Northside Center for Child Development and, in the little time remaining, do whatever private tutoring can to repair the damage public education has done.

"You know, five of our kids did pass the electricians' apprenticeship tests on Long Island," Ernest Green said. "Of course, three of them were college students. They were overqualified. Maybe I'll take the sheet metal test myself."

He is the graduate of a Southern high school and a Midwestern university. It does not seem that attainments significantly less impressive will soon give a Negro a chance to work at a skilled trade in New York.

The New Republic, February 2, 1965

Sexus

WE HAVE BEEN told again and again that the criminal justice system can only be redeemed when every citizen begins to care; and the exhilarating tide of public response seems at last to rise.

The trial of the dentist, Marvin Teicher, for sexually molesting his patients in the course of their "gentle arousal" from sedation was only a day old when Acting Supreme Court Justice Dorothy Cropper felt impelled to move the proceedings to a larger courtroom and accommodate the multitude of the civicly conscious doing their duty toward the injunction that an informed public is a cleansing instrument.

The time arrived yesterday for Justice Cropper to inspect a video-tape of Teicher at his ministrations, produced by the New York City Police Department and featuring a straight woman provided by the Westchester County Sheriff's Office.

The four hundred spectators bulged every pew in the courtroom, and included two judges, both of whom professed themselves burning to learn more about videotape as an evidentiary instrument, and what appeared to be the whole company of the Legal Aid Society, no doubt convened in assembly to be instructed in the art of cross-examination by Professor Henry Rothblatt, of the New York Law School and counsel for Teicher.

The solemnities of the wait were almost universally occupied running the infinite set of changes offered by the off-color.

There is no more mysterious delusion than our notion that sex is funny. It is, in fact, a dreadful curse. Heterosexuality, being the most pervasive, is the most destructive of mankind's deviations, and has been the cause of more murders than whiskey, more embezzlements than gambling, and, for all I know, more wars than politics. It is a thing whose beauty cannot be mentioned without paying due respect to its terror.

Take the instance of Dr. Teicher. He has the wave of white hair and the healthy complexion of one of those all-purpose actors equipped for any character part from the benevolent to the malignant.

There is no means of saying whether his is the face of guilt or innocence; and yet, if guilty, he is the victim of his fantasies, and, if innocent, he is the victim of the fantasies of young women.

Either way, there is great cause for sorrow somewhere around such premises; yet we deal with it by looking at the sufferer and cracking wise.

And even he seems to collaborate in our conspiracy to reduce the awful to the trivial, carrying about the scene with him as he does a smile so wide and so unforced as to suggest the enjoyment of some extreme of either the pure or the loose.

Given jokiness's insistence upon intruding into the business, it was rather a relief to have a judge named Dorothy Cropper.

There is something about the subject of sex that sets masculine judges to winking and leering about man the frail vessel and woman the hammer that smashes him.

Put a male on the bench and bring before him an injured female and she can hardly stammer out the details of her wrong before he rises in facetious outrage and commences to conduct himself as though the worst offense a sinner can commit is to be young and reasonably attractive.

Still, it could not escape notice that, even though there is no jury and Justice Cropper is the only party whose inspection of the video-tape could have any social function, she had nonetheless arranged to have two TV consoles set up facing the audience so that no unfranchised repository of public moral sensibilities would be cheated of his kicks.

When sex is on the judical calendar, light-mindedness seems unisexual.

This particular electronic overload proved too much for the court's technicians and they fiddled for hours yesterday afternoon without producing a picture that suggested Teicher had committed any worse malpractice than pulling a policewoman's wisdom tooth in a blinding snowstorm.

They went away to fiddle in private; and the court had to make do instead with a sound tape. It lasted twenty-eight minutes, contained no sounds of lust or ecstasy, reached no emotional pitch higher than the noise of Teicher's drill, and offered little of probative value beyond its evidence that, as aphrodisiacs go, radio station WRFM doesn't.

For at least this visitor, that appeared to end the afternoon; and he departed, only to learn much later that the court's technicians had repaired their disarray and managed to play the videotape after all.

Not having seen Teicher at his healing arts was a lapse of duty of which I am duly ashamed; still, the delinquency of having shirked the uttermost invasion of privacy exerts no small claim to be forgiven.

New York Post, June 8, 1978

A Triumph of Democracy

MARILYN MONROE'S ADDRESS book fetched $4,250 at yesterday's Swann Galleries auction. Anyone present with as long a purse and haughtier standards for the dignity of history could have spent $75 less and gone his way with a package of autographs and letters, from Napoleon I (two), Franz Liszt, Sarah Bernhardt, Eleanora Duse, Charles de Gaulle (two), Madame de Pompadour (two), Louis XIV, George III, Joseph Goebbels, and the Marquis de Lafayette.

Still, Marilyn Monroe was often foolish but never deplorable, and that affectionate judgment is as well-deserved by a sense of cultural proportion that rates a scrap of hers six times more valuable than two letters from the Pompadour, who found more stability as a king's mistress than Marilyn Monroe did in three marriages.

If the autograph market reflects our taste, democracy rides triumphant over grandeur. A letter from Douglas MacArthur sells for $70, and an autographed photograph of the Marx Brothers for $600. Those of us who, however despondently, cling to some figment of the socialist dream should be grateful that there was nothing from Karl Marx to embarrass us with the revelation that he is worth half a Groucho.

And yet who can repine at so much evidence that the authoritarian personality is a fading commodity and that what comes from below shines in its place? The Nazi items fell consistently below Swann's expectations, and even Hitler's signature is down below $1,000 at last.

And, as the Nazis decline, great figures from black culture rise in the market: Photographs of James Weldon Johnson, the poet, and Louis Armstrong, the great river, sold for twice what the auctioneers had anticipated, and the massive script of Haiti's Henri Christophe was knocked down for more than the combined signatures of four kings of France.

It seemed odd that Marilyn Monroe's address book should have been the most coveted of all these riches. The green and gold of its cover has little more majesty that would comport with the aspirations of a lunch-counter cashier, and the inside seems to have been infrequently touched by a human hand and almost never by her own.

The only entry indisputably written by her is "Clifford Odetts" [sic] and, in the lining, there is a scrawled note to remind her of lunch with "Clifford Oddets." Clifford Odets was one of those great contemporaries of Arthur Miller's, upon whom she was trying to get a handle; but then the poor girl's grasp was never quite secure.

All the other addresses seem to have been written down by her secretary and—except for those of her in-laws—they are impersonally utilitarian: directors, studios, beauticians, couturiers, doctors, and other appurtenances necessary to a great star. There is a note to "call Jack at 11 o'clock" that has set the gossips to imagining the beat of great wings overhead; but, since the year was 1957, the odds are that this Jack was only her hairdresser.

All this seems poor stuff indeed to be valued twenty times more than Duse writing her agent to complain about his neglect of her career and ten times more than the Pompadour telling her mother how glad she is that her niece is a plain girl, because "a transcendental face . . . only serves to make you the enemy of the entire feminine sex."

There are no intimacies to match these in the Marilyn Monroe address book. But then that may be why she still holds us so much; there was something about her that seemed always to offer and never to have. The address book works in its way to bring us closer to the emptiness in her life: here is the intimacy of deprivation. Inside the cover there was an envelope addressed to "Norma Jean Dougherty"; it had been sent by her mother in 1946. You think of her carrying it around for eleven years always meaning to answer.

All of a sudden, after so long venerating those who could cope, we assign the highest price to the memorabilia of someone who couldn't.

New York Newsday, September 30, 1983

A Walk on the Wild Side

I
T IS SLIGHTLY more than four years since Mark L., a young man of no very fixed purpose, was standing outside Greenwich Village's Ramrod café when the coin telephone rang nearby.

He answered and the caller was, of course, a stranger. He put the question; and Mark L. replied that he was "hot," a term of art referring to the subject's charms and graces rather than to the calorific measure of his passions.

This assurance won him an invitation to a birthday party catering to appetites for cocaine and "water sports." Mark L. had been bidden to festivities that promised their summit with his employment as a public lavatory, a prospect to which he seems to have looked forward with an enthusiasm that might seem curiously placed in any civilization except this one, where no taste for outré enjoyments can go unslaked so long as its possessor is street smart enough to make a random call to a pay telephone strategically located.

When Mark L. arrived at the address appointed, he entered the inner chambers of the Andrew Crispo Art Gallery where, he swore yesterday, he suffered indignities altogether less pleasurable than the dousing he had bargained for.

Now Mark L. is witness-in-chief at Crispo's Manhattan felony court trial on charges of kidnaping, sodomy, and rape. It is his claim that he was bound, menaced with a pistol, and threatened with murder by Crispo and Bernard LeGaros, his putative attendant thug. Mark L.

testified yesterday that he had begged for his life and promised that, if they would let him loose, he would lead them to somebody else—apparently his roommate—whom they could kill instead.

After four and a half hours of travail sufficient to cure all but the most powerful addiction to pleasures of the sadomasochistic variety, Crispo displayed an autographed portrait of Roy Cohn—"I was quite impressed"—and told him that, if a word were breathed about the doings of this night, the Mafia would track him down wherever he sought to hide.

Having delivered this stern injunction, Crispo said, "I'd like you to go to dinner with us." Mark L. said he would if he didn't have to pay; he had drawn the line at the ultimate outrage and Crispo agreed not to inflict it.

They went to a restaurant where Mark L. found tenderness unexpected for anyone in his circumstance, because its prima donna—"a wonderful black woman"—sang the Cole Porter song he recalls as "Down in the depths on the 90th floor."

"It's about being at the height of wealth and yet being all alone. A very New York song; and Andrew said, 'That's the way I feel all the time'" and gave way so far to sentiment that he took Mark L. to the washroom and gave him a toot of cocaine. Mark L.'s memories were mellowing; and there had begun to enter into his tone some suggestions of a developing case on Bernie LeGaros, who had turned out to be a fellow graduate of cinema studies. But then Bernie went off in pursuit of a girl; and the waiter refused to accept Crispo's Diner's Club card and Mark L. put up the cash and Crispo paid him with a check.

There are no perfect evenings; and there are often distinctly imperfect mornings like the one when Mark was informed that Crispo's check had bounced.

In the afternoon, Mary Shannon arose to cross-examine Mark L. for the defense. Were you not, sir, she asked with the strokes of a hammer, an illegal alien, a tax evader, a swearer to imaginary Social Security numbers, a contriver of fake addresses? Mark L. mustered a not-before-suspected dignity in conceding each and every one of these imputations. Until then one observer had despaired of understanding people

like these. But now they were commencing to look comfortingly familiar; they pass bad checks, they dodge their taxes, they hide out from
the Immigration Service and act upon a fundamental moral sense just
about as normal as that prevailing for a lot of the rest of us.

New York Newsday, September 29, 1988

Tender Mercies

T HE TRIAL OF Stella Valenza on charges of hiring three mechanics to rid her of her husband, Felice, is stuff to lift the hearts of those of us who had despaired of ever finding a domestic hearth where the fires of mutual passion still burn hotter than when they first took flame.

Felice and Stella Valenza were married six years ago and are plainly crazier about each other now than ever before.

He was a witness for the prosecution in Queens Criminal Court Friday and singularly unequipped for the job. It has been well and frequently said that the husband is the last to know. By common account, his wife was so compulsive a shopper for contract killers in the spring of 1986 that all Bayside seems to have resounded with her inquiries.

And yet, when Felice Valenza was fallen upon by unknown parties with baseball bats a year ago last May, he carried his wounds home from the hospital still convinced that he had been had at by hypercompetitive brothers in the fraternity of landscape contractors.

In June, when Stella had barely begun to apply her tender mercies to his convalescence, he tried the air of his front yard and was shot six times by a .25. Even then, he does not appear to have suspected that the heart of these uncomfortable mysteries might lodge in the inflamed bosom of his wife.

But then husbands are notoriously inattentive to the nuances and forgetful about the routine occurrences of the family round and, when

Bert Koehler, Stella's counsel, asked if Felice had ever put a pistol to her head and demanded that she serve the cravings of his flesh on short order, he replied, "I don't remember."

There is much that is admirable about any sentiment that has kept its warmth long past the time when it cools for souls more conventional than these, but he who is possessed by this fixed a passion runs the risk of taking any excess in its display as an exercise too normal to be worth the bother of recollection.

And Stella's obsession was a match for Felice's. We have all known and enjoyed the company of those women who cannot spend five minutes of conversation without pulling some reference, generally fond, to their husbands out of the blue sky.

But, if we are to credit the witnesses against her, Stella was incapable of talking about anything else. It is the prosecution's theory that she schemed to have Felice killed because she wanted to collect on his $93,000 of insurance.

No notion so crass can do justice to the apparent selflessness of her commitment. A woman gave witness Friday to the afternoon in April when she and a friend had been driving with Stella to the Valenza home to look at an apartment for the friend. Stella's companions asked about the cost of the rent and the size of the security deposit, and the witness recalled that their hostess had replied that ". . . we shouldn't have to worry about security and rent because she was gonna get her husband taken care of."

So, if Stella Valenza so spoke, would have spoken the woman who had her mind on higher goals than greed pursues.

Her milieu and Felice's was the society of Queens landscape gardening and, unlikely ground for the hiring halls of qualified assassins though these bosky circles might be, Stella seems to have confined her market research to them.

Paul Turchen remembered that one afternoon he and his partner were installing a shrub and Stella Valenza stopped her car and said she needed to find a killer for Felice. He suggested that she might more fitly take her problems to a priest. Even after that sound demurrer, the force of her insistence drew him to a meeting at Garden World, where among the earth pots and leafy branches, she offered to give him five hundred dollars and her car to do the office.

He felt that "she was getting a little offhand" and declined the tender. In June, their cars passed again and she stopped to say that she must hurry because "I have to meet the guys who are going to kill my husband and pay them more money."

They parted, and Paul Turchen drove off and thereafter kept his silence about this revelation, as he thought, he explained, any "young gentleman ought." Stella Valenza had already found richer soil in his brother Peter.

Peter Turchen testified that he and Stella had met at Francis Lewis High School, the academy where both had flourished from the seeds of cultivation. She asked if he knew anyone who might kill her husband and he replied that he might. In a day or so, he put the question to a friend and got the answer, "Sure."

At intervals in his witness, Peter Turchen would smile rather charmingly, and it could be seen how cool he was and how casual was the whole memory. In him, Stella had found a vessel as empty as she was overfilled. Peter Turchen had a poor eye for head-hunting; his recruits tried the bat and tried the bullets and botched the job with both. If Stella Valenza was as bent on the final consummation of her bond with Felice as her prosecutors contend, she would have done surer and better if she made the work her own. Such things ought not to be done but, if they are, they are best left to those who really care.

New York Newsday, November 13, 1987

The Uses of Neglect

I

Finche ch'e la morta, ch'e la speranza.
—*LAMPEDUSA, Il Gattopardo*

So LONG AS there is death, there is hope? That is a sentiment so singular and so rooted to its place of origin that, if you found it upon a shard in the farthest desert, you could guess that someone had tarried there who had spent most of his life in Sicily.

There is no part of Sicily less Sicilian than Ortygia, the last extremity of its southeast corner. It is all the flower and none of the thorn. And yet nowhere else does the odd notion of death as man's last best hope press a stronger claim. For here is the most wonderful city that any of us is ever likely to see and a great piece of its wonder is that it is dying.

ORTYGIA IS THE island fortress of the old Greek Syracuse from which the new Syracuse has fled. In its abandonment it cries out to the portion of us all that cherishes its fellow creatures and deplores their aspirations. It achingly and joyously reminds us that the blessings of the modern arrive in the company of two curses: Nothing speeds decay like progress and nothing preserves except neglect.

Aeschylus staged *The Persians* in Syracuse. The tyrant Dionysius called Plato here as instructor in the arts of government and repaid him with so valuable a lesson in the nature of governors that only an unceremonious debarkation for Athens saved him from sale into slavery. Pindar was inspired and Cicero edified here. Archimedes glared across these seas and employed their sun and his mirror to set Roman ships afire. Syracuse had broken Athens and sent the Carthaginians limping away; and, this time round, she and Archimedes came close to beating back Rome herself.

The Syracusans were moderate in their moments of aggression and implacable in their hours of resistance. Ortygia has been violated again and again, and always it has outworn its conquerors and restored its own inviolable self. And always, when the Syracusans turned at bay, their last asylum was this little island a hundred feet from their mainland.

Naturally then, the huge and formerly swarming Hôtel des Étrangers stands empty, the once-arrogant crimson of its façade paled and chastened by the sun. The tourists are no longer a force in occupation; dying, Ortygia has outlived the last of its barbarian invasions.

The grandeur of the names in this great history seems rather beside the point now, because Ortygia owes so much of its command over the sensibilities for being a monument to anonymous artisans. By no means the smallest of its charms is the refuge it affords from distraction by certified masterpieces.

ASIDE FROM ITS Greek coins, Syracuse possesses only two works eligible for notice in college surveys of the history of art. They are the "Venus Anadiomene," which could dangerously ignite the libido of a Capuchin who had lain for a century dead, and the ravaged "Annunciation" of Antonello da Messina. And, with perfect tact, Syracuse has spared the visitor the perturbations of awe by sending both on voyage, the "Venus" to Canada and the Antonello on a ramble about Sicily before being dispatched to America as part of the exhibition of a master whose work, since Sicily is the sport of foreign conquerors and alien tastes, seems far more Flemish than Italianate.

We must then happily make do with the comfortable companionship of masons and stone carvers whose names long ago were mixed into the dust toward which their buildings are exquisitely sinking. Few of them were allowed the pretension of calling themselves architects; Luciano Ali, who designed the superb Benevantano del Bosco palace, is identified merely as "a local master mason." Still he has left a name that has endured for two centuries, and that is a distinction unique for his class and his kind. The workmen who rebuilt Ortygia after the 1693 earthquake are otherwise almost all unknown gods; and yet they have left everywhere behind them the mark of their pride of craft and their recognition of the law that cities live or die according to the opportunities they offer to those who glory in work. Ortygia never erected a palace for some Spanish proprietor without reserving its ground floor for the shops of artisans.

All those artisans are gone now and they have left no descendants, because it has been more than a century since Ortygia has had any function except to enchant the beholder and stifle the inhabitant. The Church of Rome was its last major employer; when the eighteenth century ended, this island that a laggardly wayfarer can walk all the way around in forty minutes held twenty-two parish churches, fifteen monasteries, and eleven convents.

In 1861, the new and anticlerical kingdom of Italy nationalized the monastic properties; and this triumph over superstition was followed by one of those cataclysms for the life spirit that serve to teach even the most radical temperament that it cannot keep touch with reality unless it keeps a few reactionary ideas firmly in place.

THE MONASTERIES HAD been the chief labor market for Ortygia's lay population; and, as they declined, there was less and less use for the old skills, and the old craftsmen left when they could or withered away when they stayed. Ortygia has quarters that have lost three-fifths of their population in the last fifteen years; and, in a while, there will be no one living there except those who would rather live anywhere else if poverty had not stranded them in warrens so tortuous that appellations like *via* for street and *vicolo* for alley are inadequate to describe the extreme limits of their constriction. Ortygia's street plan is singular for needing recourse to the word *rione* to designate passageways that are too narrow for the shoulders of any National Football League linebacker.

To wander past the all but empty palaces and to peer through the poor garments hung out to dry in the fifteenth-century courtyards of this bleached, airless, but still most seigneurial of slums is to reflect how hateful to the dweller a place so lovable to the visitor must truly be and to understand that the flight to the salmon-colored cement blocks of modern Syracuse across the bridge has been the desertion of poetry in the cause of common sense.

From time to time, over the last hundred years, one or another cloud conqueror has given way to the vision of dragging Ortygia into the modern age, if only to the extent of renaming its streets Via Cavour or Via Nizza or Via Vittorio Veneto or Via Trieste, as though its inhabitants might feel at one with a greater Italy if they walked past signs affirming their community with personages and places so distant from themselves as to seem inscriptions in some foreign tongue.

The Italy of fascism undertook the last of these ventures into salvation by destruction; and its scars survive in the terrible swath where Benito Mussolini's engineers made hecatombs of palazzi to create an avenue fit for the local branches of Alitalia and UPIM, the department store chain. It is only one more instance of Ortygia's endless capacity for absorption that this Corso Littorio, the name Mussolini chose to celebrate his newest battleship, is now called Corso Matteoti as a tribute to the socialist parliamentarian murdered by the fascists.

Post-Mussolini Italy has been uniformly subject to the ministrations of governments with a philosophical commitment to leaving bad enough alone; and they have been conscientious about resisting most temptations to rescue Ortygia.

II

WHATEVER IS NEW on Ortygia's walls is most often a reminder of death. When a soul departs, those it has left behind signify their sorrows with broadsheets plastered about the streets or, in the cases of more penurious circumstance, notepaper-sized placards on the doors of the bereaved. They run from the humble ("My Dear Husband") to the grand ("The Marchesa Ada Gardella de Castel Lentini, 26 May, in Rome"). Of course: *Marchesi* may give up the ghost in quite dreadful ambiences; but they don't die in birthplaces the world has since forgotten.

Occasionally an eminence passes who is more locally familiar, and then the walls flower with memorial testaments: "The Communists of Syracuse remember the intense social and civic involvement of Comrade the Attorney Salvatore Di Giovanni." And right next to that affirmation of a faith that has no need for God, the wife, the sons, and the daughter of this deceased Bolshevik have certified a more intimate grief on a placard bordered with lilies and crowned with the head of Christ in thorns. Sicilians are Italian only for being part of a shared community of divided souls.

One day there was a new sheet on the walls and, for once, it had to do with life, if only, Ortygia being Ortygia, with life whose liveliest claim is upon the historical memory: The next offering of the Syracuse Tourist Agency's cultural program would be a concert by the Romano Mussolini Quintet.

Romano Mussolini is the third and youngest son of fascism's founder. He was, one has to think, more the fruit of policy than of passion, since Mussolini was obsessed with the acceleration of Italy's birthrate and felt it a leader's duty to teach by example.

Romano Mussolini was only thirteen when his father lurched into the Second World War; and, in less than three years, his family was expelled from the Rome that had felt complimented to leave its name at his christening font. His public debut as a jazz pianist returned him to transient notice twenty-five years ago; but it did not seem a career option that held much promise or was worth much attention. He had come old to his apprenticeship and had brought there a taste even more obsolescent than his name; when he began, by all accounts, time had stopped for him where it did for the New Orleans Rhythm Kings, somewhere in 1925 in the exhausted vein of "Tin Roof Blues" and "The Original Dixieland One-Step." Still Syracuse is the attic of the world; and there could not have been conceived a more proper place to find one of history's discards at work on a selection of jazz's.

The visitor was then drawn across the bridge to mainland Syracuse's archaeological park by the same irresistibly unsavory impulse that used to carry the crowds to watch Lola Montez in her cage or Joe Louis at Caesar's Place; and nothing could have been less to be imagined than to have this discreditable pilgrimage end with the discovery of a piece of flesh that is Italy's only inarguable repudiation of every vestige of the fascist spirit.

THE STAGE HAD been lit for the Mussolini Quintet in the open-air amphitheater whose vegetation has immured and softened most traces of tyrants dead twenty centuries ago. Romano Mussolini would play with his back to the altar of Hieron II, a pile of stones no longer capable of evoking their original function, which is just as well, because Hieron, an otherwise temperate ruler, was accustomed to celebrating his and Syracuse's prosperity with the annual sacrifice to Zeus of upward of 450 oxen there. The conjunction of relics of despots, varyingly benevolent, and 2,200 years apart, could have served to inspire fashionably ironic reflections if Romano Mussolini had not so startlingly turned out to have nothing whatsoever to do with that sort of thing. He was found at the soda wagon beside the gate, drinking a can of the orange pop called Fante. *Fante* is also the Italian word for "infantryman," and there can still be seen in Palermo a fascist construction flourishing Benito Mussolini's slogan: "The *fante* is the bud and victory is the flower."

Romano Mussolini has let his figure go most agreeably, and his countenance is rubicund, humorous, and forever immune to his father's itch for the display of the self as counterfeit of iron. The peaceful and the pleasant sat upon him as comfortably as the old coat over his shoulders. Somewhere back on the road, his mother's genes had ex-pelled his father's; and here was the proof of her victory.

He had, he said, found his path when he was a little boy, and his inspiration had been his brother Vittorio, who is ten years older. "My brother," he remembered, "was one of Italy's first jazz critics. He used to contribute articles to the university reviews. I was only ten when he gave me a big picture of Duke Ellington."

Most of what his visitor had known about Vittorio Mussolini before then had been that he had been a pilot in the Ethiopian war and that, afterward, he had published a reminiscence that included this image:

> One group of cavalrymen gave me the impression of a budding rose unfolding as the bomb fell in their midst and blew them up.

But now it had become possible to wonder whether some fascist hack had not conjured up this atrocious picture and whether Vittorio Mussolini had not just signed without reading it, and turned back to Jelly Roll Morton. The brothers Mussolini were coming to sound like children whose tastes were enough better than their father's as to make them fortunate that he came home too seldom to notice where their minds were tending.

Suddenly there arose the fantasy of some secret life of fascism in its terminal writhings: the Anglo-American fleet lowering upon the south-ern coast of Sicily, and, in Rome, at the Villa Torlonia, Benito Mussolini upstairs abed under assault by his ulcers and intimations that it might all be coming apart, and downstairs little Romano listening to Count Basie on the American Armed Forces Radio and rejoicing that its signal was growing louder and louder.

"DUKE ELLINGTON CAME to see me in 1950, the first time he got to Rome after the war." There have been better years than 1950 to be a Mussolini in Italy; and his recital of that memory summoned up all his loneliness and the renewed recognition that, in Duke Ellington, Amer-ica had raised up its only purely perfect gentleman.

Then it was time for Romano Mussolini to go about his business and he set to arranging the microphones. There was no telling him from any other workingman who, having taken his ease, is now about to return to the task he loves. If only for a little while, the spirit of its ancient artisans had come back to the neighborhood of Ortygia. After which, there occurred as the ultimate surprise the revelation that Romano Mussolini is a very good workman indeed. There were barriers to the fullest expression of his best, to be sure; his drummer and his trombonist are both Argentine imports and, to speak as kindly as possible, rather too stuck in the primeval, the one too clumsily intrusive in any vein except the Afro-Cuban, and the other too much the victim of what Henry James once called "the demoralizing influence of lavish opportunity," in this case the open horn.

But there arrived occasions even so when Romano Mussolini worked alone with Julius Farmer, his contrabassist, and only then could there be heard vivid suggestions of high possibility.

Julius Farmer is twenty-eight and was born in New Orleans, a city that Romano Mussolini cites as the founding capital of a vast territory with the same fervor that his father brought to his invocations of imperial Rome. But Farmer does not work in the New Orleans tradition; his line is like Tommy Potter's or Curly Russell's, lean, spare, and thrifty of notes.

When their companions rested from their clutter, bass and piano worked alone with the entire intimacy that is the particular marvel of jazz; and there came a moment on Ellington's "A Train" when Romano Mussolini left Julius Farmer on his own and sat there, his fingers off the keys, looking at the soloist as though this young man had some secret that he himself proposed to go to his grave pursuing, and as though this was one of those nights that bring the belief that some day he will find it.

The Mussolini family's African empire had shrunk down to one young black American, and that one not subject but comrade. Trajan's legions could hardly ever have marched across richer possessions than those these two were sharing then.

· · ·

NEAR THE CLOSE Romano Mussolini confessed himself so happy that he could not resist singing, and he stood up and hoarsely chanted that most dignified statement of emancipation from all forms of false pride: "All right, hokay, you win. Honey honey come back to me."

Between whiles, he explained the music, and told jovial anecdotes about life on the road, and held a contest with a free record as prize for the first scholar to name the composer of "Honeysuckle Rose." By then there was the most honest sweat upon his forehead and the dark blue tails of his sport shirt had worked their way free of his trouser belt and he was talking beguilingly with his hands.

He was the incarnation of all the Italy his father had tried to harden into something fierce and stern; when Benito Mussolini sought an adjective to describe the sort of Italian who most roused his contempt, he settled for "picturesque"; and that is just what his son Romano is and no less serious a man for it.

Afterward his visitor remarked, by no means insincerely, that he had detected echoes of Art Tatum in the style. *"Magari,"* Romano Mussolini replied. *Magari* is an all-purpose Italian word which the dictionaries define as meaning both "maybe" and "even," and then collapse in despair before the whole spectrum of its nuances. In this instance, we may take *magari* to have meant, "If only. . . ." His father's dream was to be Julius Caesar; and his is to approach, in time, the level of a blind, black piano player. We old men are wrong: Taste does not necessarily deteriorate from generation to generation.

History has set Benito Mussolini down as an inattentive parent. And that may have been the best gift he could have given his children; how otherwise could he have left behind a son this utterly unfascist? Ortygia turned out, after all, to be the most appropriate of places to come upon Romano Mussolini. They are both splendid examples of the sovereign uses of neglect.

The New York Review of Books, April 14, 1983

Invisible Cities

W HEN JOSEPH CONRAD distilled the elements of human existence into the blessing of illusions and the curse of fact, he anticipated
the Soviet history whose epitome The Museum of Modern Art provides with its freshly opened exhibition, "Architectural Drawings of
the Russian Avant-Garde." The Modern's show runs from 1918, when
the Soviet Revolution was newborn, through the scant sixteen years
that were enough for it to swell into the pomposities of middle age.

REVOLUTIONARY HISTORIES HAVE a habit of beginning where every
attuned spirit knows that the future is glorious but has no tangible idea
of what it will look like. We ought not to be surprised, then, that the
earlier works in the Modern's display have none of the disciplines of
scale and line we associate with architectural draftmanship. The project
that Vladimir Krinsky labeled "Temple of Communion Between Nations" is an abstract drawing that the artist could have as plausibly
called "Study in Form and Mass (3)." "Communal House" suggests
nothing so much as one of those old French towns whose roofs and
frames Georges Braque used to heap together and then send running up
a hill.

Illusion has willed away fact. The architect has no need to plan,
since this communal house is not yet a building and will never be. It
is a house of Krinsky's imagination and yet so solid in its maker's mind

that he has conjured up structures settled and grown old together so long that the only eyes that can see them in a new way would have to be a Cubist painter's.

Krinsky did not approach the drawing board as an architect but as an adept pupil of the Russian Constructivist school. Until now Constructivism had seemed to some of us only a starveling country cousinship to Braque and Picasso; but here it takes on a far grander pathos with our recognition that Constructivism is the art of those with no chance to construct.

THE SOVIET ARCHITECTS began with modest and rather homely ideas and were soon conscripted to bulging with grandiose ones, and in few cases did any get built at all. The fault at the beginning was less in the revolution's narrowness of vision than in its circumstances.

Catherine Cooke points out in the catalogue that splendidly accompanies the Modern's show that civil war had depleted the Russian construction industry of most skills and all materials except timber and concrete; and that, as late as 1926, the Soviets had nothing to gain from European modernism because they didn't even have plate glass. When materials fit for the dream of the New came to hand in the thirties, prejudices for the Old had embedded themselves too deeply for change.

Lenin's distaste for the bourgeois had not taken him forward but back, to the ducal style. A preference for other centuries seems inevitably to carry the mind to earlier and earlier times until Lenin's preference for Renaissance palaces was succeeded by Stalin's for Pharaonic monoliths.

The Soviet vision of monuments that their revolution deserved would remain mostly unrealized. The sketches bravely dashed off when there was no stuff available for the works progressed to elaborate submissions of architectural drawings to juries that didn't know what they wanted. The architectural competition had replaced the materials shortage as cause for non-building.

The Palace of the Soviets and the Commissariat of Heavy Industry are here embalmed as perspectives of grand vistas with a future existence no more real than that of Krinsky's Communal House. The only difference was the loss of charm and proportion and the arrival of confusions so disorderly that the Palace of the Soviets' jury seriously considered a replica of the Doge's Palace in Venice before accepting a pile crowned with a statue of Lenin "the height of a twenty-five-story skyscraper" and with an index finger twenty feet long. What must henceforth be must be gigantic; and, as usual with the revolution, it would never be at all.

The New York Review of Books, August 16, 1990

Hostage to History

THE VISITOR WHO carries to Moscow even a scant familiarity with the lights and shadows of its revolution's history is soon surprised to discover how much more he knows than the run of even aware Muscovites have been allowed to.

One visitor's final conversation was with Alexei Adzhubei, the journalist whose vast sophistication was deepened by the intimacy of his years as Nikita Khrushchev's son-in-law.

Their talk turned to the old days and the comments of his guest indicated a knowledge of detail that, skimpy as it was, must have struck Adzhubei as uncommonly informed and he asked, "Are you a Sovietologist?"

That question had been asked before, and the visitor answered as he had learned to a while ago:

"To me, the only Sovietologist who is always up to date is Anton Chekhov."

Adzhubei laughed, and there passed across his face the knowing smile of someone to whom that thought had already occurred and not infrequently. Only the day before, there had been an exchange of similar cast with Sergo Mikoyan and, when it was over, Mikoyan had lit with just that knowing smile.

None of us could be so bold as to advance a particular Chekhov story as the greatest of all but "My Life" would be a splendid candidate. At one juncture, its hero marries a young woman of wealth, who is transiently possessed by an itch to go back to the land. They go off to convert her estate into a working farm and spend a horrid few months until, disgusted by the crafts and coarsenesses of the peasants, she abandons all lofty notions and flees to London to study singing.

From there, she writes to ask for a divorce and to report that she has bought herself a ring engraved in Hebrew, "All things pass away," and that it would be her talisman against future infatuations. And he reflects:

"If I wanted to order a ring for myself, the inscription I should choose would be, 'Nothing passes away.' "

And nothing seems ever to pass away in Moscow. Russian history asserts itself there as all but immutable and immovable, and so it asserted itself for Chekhov in 1900. The on-again, off-again harryings of Andrei Sakharov and Boris Pasternak would have been for him the oldest of tales.

He could have recalled the year when Maxim Gorky, the novelist, was voted into the Russian Academy of Sciences and had his election nullified when it was remembered that he had been arrested for violating Article 10.35 of the czarist penal code, which made it a crime to agitate against the state. Article 10.35 or its equivalent endures as Soviet law today.

Gorky's treatment provoked Chekhov into writing the chairman of the Academy of Sciences "to beg you most humbly to be relieved of the title of honorary academician." He was almost alone in his protest and his resignation, and so were the all too few academicians who stood with Sakharov and Pasternak.

The czars will never be back but, after seventy years, their style of command has yet to pass away, perhaps because tradition is so stubborn in Russia that the techniques of journalism, wondrous as they are, come to appear so inadequate for dealing with her development year by year, let alone day by day. Journalism's engagement is with what is happening, and here so little happens that a good deal of what is taken for important may be insignificant and what looks insignificant may be quite important indeed.

The other day, as an instance, the Soviet Supreme Court announced the acquittal of four distinguished Bolsheviks the Soviets had executed as traitors fifty years ago. Legal scholars will be put to some pains to discover what available evidence of their innocence is any stronger than the stuff that served to prove their guilt, and addicts of irony may be enlivened to take note that the ashes of Andrei Vishinsky, the prosecutor who staged that frame-up, are still interred in the Kremlin wall.

All the same, this gesture, empty as it looks, is not without implications of some consequence. One prime article of the Stalinist creed was that men did not disagree because they were mistaken but because they were evil; for the czars and far more spitefully for the Soviets, to dissent has until now been to betray. Given that history, the formal concession that the defendants in the Moscow trials may have been foolish but were not treasonable can be looked upon as no small advance in the direction of enlightenment.

But it has taken terribly long and been arrived at through incalculable torments of interior quarrel. Long ago, Karl Marx said that the philosophers had described the world and that it was up to man to change it. Now the Soviets are finding out that many things have changed the world—one of them the failure of their revolution to change itself or Russia—and that it is up to man to describe it. For the workers to arise and break the chains of capitalist oppression was unexpectedly easy work in 1917 but those chains were gossamer compared to the cast-iron shackles of a Russian tradition that has so far outworn every idea of the new.

New York Newsday, June 19, 1988

The Zionist Tragedy

"Hanna Siniora, editor-in-chief of the East Jerusalem daily *Al Fajr* . . . was questioned
for five hours about his recent call for Palestinians to boycott Israeli cigarettes and soft
drinks—which gained little support—and released on a $1,300 bond."
—*JONATHAN C. RANDAL*, *The Washington Post*

A CIVILIZED SOCIETY cannot reasonably be asked to grant the
ruled a sovereign right to throw rocks at their rulers. But can a society
long feel assured of its civility once it has taken to arresting men who
did no worse than urge the ruled not to buy the coffin nails and
bellywashes sold them by their rulers?

Israel need not apologize if it is no longer as concerned to be a light
unto the nations as of old. Its problem is distinctly more intimate: It is
ceasing to be a light unto itself.

Harsh treatment of violent extremists is repression, which is unattractive but has some show of excuse. Harsh treatment of moderates
is oppression, which is far more unattractive and without a plausible
excuse.

Hanna Siniora has been a moderate. Israel now thinks him a danger
to the peace. It did not think him such five years ago. Something has
changed. Perhaps it is Israel that has been changed in the course of the
conduct that has finally carried it to the logical, which is almost always
the wrong, conclusion that every conspicuous Palestinian who objects,
however peaceably, to twenty-one years of occupation is a danger.

Or perhaps Hanna Siniora has changed and arrived at a sympathy
with extremism that he could not have imagined before now? In that
case what could have changed him except the events of two decades
when all available options belonged exclusively to the conquerors?

Israel did not take over the West Bank and Gaza in 1967 with the slightest notion of being there in 1988. Now its occupation has settled into a condition of at least semipermanence; and the West Bank's identification as Judea and Samaria, which used to be the slogan of a political sect, has of late emerged as an official ideology. The formal procedures of the West Bank's custody are pretty much as they were when the Israeli Defense Force installed them. The cruel difference, all but inevitable for occupations, is they are now so much more morose, more callous, and infinitely more alienated from the occupied.

The Israelis have frozen themselves and their situation and engraved it with every appearance of inalterability. But people are not inalterable; you can put off the process of changing your situation; but you cannot escape the process that this postponement works upon you. There is a look that has to come upon a soldier's face when he frisks an Arab laborer for the 175th time and it is not the look of the human in company he thinks quite as human as himself.

The voice Israel now raises from the isolation of its beleaguerment at the United Nations strikingly defines the difference of what it is becoming from what it used to be.

When Israel lurched into Lebanon five years ago, Yehuda Blum, its ambassador, spoke for the defense at the UN Security Council. It could be argued that he made too much of his facts; but every one was a fact beyond challenge. That used to be official Israel's way; its interpretations were open to dispute, but you could count on the truth of every citation.

But who can give rational credence to the words of Israeli ambassador Benjamin Netanyahu when he echoes the sheriffs of our own old South and blames a pervasive rebellion on alien agitators? Conjuring this sort of thing is not quite up to the wild fancies common to Iran and Iraq; but there is enough scent of the rhetorical excess of the Middle East to make the listener wonder whether the Arabs may be on their way to beating the Israelis after all, because they have at least corrupted the Israelis into sometimes talking a language like theirs.

And then there is the coldness of the occupation, an indifference no less to the elementary needs of the Palestinian refugees than to their grievances. Yesterday there could be found in the racks of the UN press office a message from Giorgio Giacomelli, secretary-general of the UN's refugee relief agency, announcing new emergencies in Gaza and the West Bank. What is called for, Giacomelli said, is "immediate relief: improvements in water quality, sewerage, roads, etc.; housing."

Twenty years ago, Israeli troops came to Gaza representing a people unique for their generosity and found this tragedy of the hitherto innocent. They have their own problems and might not be expected to help solve this subject people's; but it would seem unlike them to hinder. And yet, when Giacomelli summed up the last year of his agency's work, he reported that the occupation force was still promising to provide permanent shelter for fourteen families whose houses it had demolished in 1971. Israel had arrested thirteen of the agency's caseworkers. In fairness, Israel had also contributed $296,000 worth of supplies for refugee relief, which is approximately 40 cents a head.

To read the Old Testament and come upon the pitch of some prophet's outrage is now and then to think, "Unhappy is the nation that needs a Jeremiah." Israel may or may not be an unhappy nation; but it looks very like needing a Jeremiah.

New York Newsday, January 17, 1988

Never-Never Land

ONE SMALL LOSS in an existence more and more deprived of the joys of the harmlessly ridiculous is the shortening supply of Westerners who have seen the future and think it works.

The days have seemed all but gone when newspaper publishers came glowingly home from Mussolini's Italy and when theologians returned to report so much bread in Stalin's Soviet Union that the state groceries were giving it away free, and when social scientists mapped new paths taken in Tanzania, Cuba, Nicaragua, and all the other elsewheres full of chances for illusion to do the work that is better but less contentingly done by eye and touch.

And then yesterday, the UN Correspondents Association club rooms lit up with the presence of eight residents of the United States just back from a peace mission to Kim Il Sung's Democratic People's Republic of Korea (DPRK).

They had looked for signs of poverty and repression, and found so little of either, that Ben Dupuy, a Haitian editor in exile, could say with assurance that "there is no comparison between Haiti and the DPRK." Somehow one could think of compliments more expansive even in the currently depressed market for imaginary paradises. Perhaps the same thought occurred to Dupuy's fellow delegates and summoned them to the heroic flights into the unlikely that followed.

The DPRK is a "material, cultural and social triumph." It has eliminated the income tax and property rent. It has built a hotel almost as tall as the Empire State Building and grander than the pyramids. The media is, of course, "limited." Still there is no evidence of discontent like the student unrest that so incessantly abrades the government of South Korea.

"The only concern in the minds" of DPRK's students "is their divided country." They also have "environmental visions" that they can realize because "one of the very few places where students have a voice is Korea."

One visitor asked whether the exaltation of Kim Il Sung might have suggested certain excesses in the direction of the cult of personality. The response was the familiar reminder that it is a mistake to look at such phenomena "according to our own cultural standards." The DPRK used to be "colonized, backward and feudal" and Kim Il Sung is the symbol of the material achievements of its redemption, and his public's response is not "worship but love and devotion."

It had been an hour rich with satisfaction for those of us homesick for the nonsense about the People's Democracies of Eastern Europe that used to be ladled out not just in modest precincts like this but on the heights from which President Richard Nixon once scattered rosebuds for Nicolae Ceaușescu's Romania.

For both the left and the right share an addiction for countries of the imagination. The difference is that, even if the left displayed more common sense than these pilgrims to Kim Il Sung had on hand yesterday, it would scarcely matter because we are governed by the right anyway.

We are thus free to laugh at the illusions of the left and bound to shudder at the illusions of the right because they ordain our history. Once the right had its imaginary Iraq and our State Department referred to Saddam Hussein's abuse, and worse, of the Kurds only for purposes of mitigation and excuse. Now the right is at last aware of the real Iraq, and President George Bush reels back in by no means premature shock to cry out to the United Nations General Assembly against the "genocidal poison gas war against Iraq's own Kurdish villagers," which our government scrupulously neglected to notice when it was happening in 1988.

But countries of the imagination are too important for us to throw one away without resupplying ourselves with another. And so, for our discarded fantasies about Iraq we have substituted our fantasies about Syria, steadfast ally in the struggle for rule by law. The only self-delusion that truly harms is the kind afflicting personages with the power to act on its commands.

New York Newsday, October 3, 1990

Standards of the Trade

ROBERTO RODRIGUEZ WAS nine days away from arrest on July 10 when the Drug Enforcement Administration's wire mechanics picked up his complaints against "El Negro," a middle manager decreasingly reliable.

Rodriguez's executive wrath reached its crescendo at ". . . don't let him touch not even a kilo."

Not even a kilo? Not long ago, a kilogram of cocaine or heroin was a quantity of considerable worth. Barely ten years are gone since Nicky Barnes was straining against the fetters of maximum security imprisonment to consummate his last drug deal by arranging the transport from Philadelphia and the sale in New York of a kilogram of heroin.

Barnes was a giant in those days, and Rodriguez has walked all else but tall among his successors. But all the same, he could do what Barnes never could do and speak of cutting off an offending subordinate with "not even a kilo" in the contemptuous tone mean-spirited husbands employ when they tell their lawyers that they won't give their wives a dime.

Rodriguez is a modest entrepreneur by the standards of his trade. The criminal information lodged against him and twenty of his lieges defines his imputed commercial market as four square blocks in the Hunts Point area of the Bronx, although it does allow the inference that he adventured far enough to have established a drug boutique catering to Parkchester.

Even so, he has managed to farm his constricted patch so intensively that the DEA agents assess his gross as high as $30,000 a day. In the nineteen-seventies, Nicky Barnes bestrode Central Harlem like a colossus, and yet his annual revenue might very well have been less than what this obscure cocaine wholesaler seems to have been collecting at the end of the eighties.

New York has progressed just that far in the mass distribution of the implements of mortality. Narcotics may indeed be the last flicker of the American capitalist spirit that founded its growth on the principle that, if it produced more and priced it for less, its market would ever grow.

Drugs are the one commodity whose executives have held the line against inflation. Heroin and cocaine cost scarcely more on the street than they did twenty years ago, which is why cocaine, a luxury item in the sixties, became stuff for general use in the seventies.

Halfway through the present and mercifully departing decade, the industry faced the crisis of a supply glut, and its enterprisers recognized that they had more cocaine on hand than middle-class consumers could use, responded with the alacrity that seems lost everywhere else, and came up with crack, which is cheap enough for purchase by the most deprived of citizens.

We have been no less generous in putting firearms within reach of the poor.

Twenty years ago, having a gun, if only as an appurtenance to one's uniform for parades, was a qualification essential for membership in the Black Panther party. That talisman was so difficult to find then that one Panther went scouring all the way to Baltimore in search of a rifle reportedly available there.

Our post–world war youth gangs went forth to battle with zip guns. Now adolescents on the street kill each another with semiautomatic weapons. One young woman on Long Island decided to put out a contract on her father and had only to go next door to find herself a hit teen, and we may assume that she could have met her felt need with even smaller trouble in Hunts Point.

Sermons on moral decay are as tedious for civilized sensibilities as they are life-enhancing for politicians, but all the same, it would be pleasant to look forward to a mayor who might be genuinely outraged by the condition of a city where poor babies die for want of proper medical care and their mothers and fathers and brothers die from an abundance of those two deadliest of substances, guns and crack.

New York Newsday, July 26, 1989

Ralph Ginzburg: Panderer

With all sympathy to Ralph Ginzburg, who will go to prison for five years as a pornographer, it should be said of him, almost with admiration, that he has a far broader and more sensitive instinct for profiting by appeal to the baser passions than the Supreme Court imagines. He is really a dangerous, though not indictable, man.

Eighteen months or so ago, there came to my office a postcard which, if memory serves, bore no more than a sentence saying approximately:

> If you have ever had the experience of distortion by *Time* magazine, please write and tell us about it at the address below.

The address below was *Fact*, followed by a post office box address.

Now, the man who conceived this postcard could have sent me a page from *Fanny Hill* day after day and never have come close to the depths beyond decent expression that he had plumbed within me by the mere mention of *Time* magazine. My hatred of *Time* is my one unbridled lust. If the pornographic impulse is an obsession with the contemplation of a debased object, then I have a dirty mind about *Time*.

For example, I could not imagine myself participating in an obscene telephone call except in response to a polite inquiry from a gently nurtured young lady identifying herself as a *Time* researcher. Young men from *Time* are the only ones I meet on a story whom I automatically identify as enemies rather than as colleagues. As a slaughterhouse of moral integrity, *Time* is the Verdun of the young. Its agents greet you, be you Gus Hall or Robert Shelton, with the announcement that they are on your side against their bosses. This, for some reason, is supposed to make you believe in their honesty.

I remember hearing a Kluxer in Little Rock call a young man from *Time* a liar because he had gotten an interview on the plea that the North needed to know the Klan's side of the story and then the Kluxer had read the result. I do know what special places in hell are reserved for editors who will encourage innocent youth thus to place itself at a moral disadvantage to a member of the Ku Klux Klan.

But let me cease this public surrender to thoughts of which I am ashamed by saying that, if I were conscripted to execute the Central Committee of the Chinese Communist party, I would trust myself to do the job with solemnity and sorrow, yet I would machine-gun the entire board of editors of *Time* in a fit of laughter. That is the only orgy with any appeal to my fantasies.

So this postcard had no need to identify itself as to source; it acted upon me as a note from a sailor would have upon Hart Crane in a bar near the Navy Yard. Say *Time* to me and tell me to answer with a letter in a tree in Lafayette Park and I would run slavering through a hundred vice cops to get there. Still I forgot to answer, being as indolent in this, my last sex mania, as I am in all things.

Then the months went by and I discovered that Ralph Ginzburg, with his special genius, had found my perversion. He had started *Fact* and had decided to lead its first issue with some comments on *Time*.

Ginzburg's first cover was emblazoned with something like: "What *Time* did to me" and a list of victims detailing their experience. The authors included James Gould Cozzens, Bertrand Russell, David Merrick, P. G. Wodehouse, Dwight MacDonald, Mary McCarthy, John Osborne, Eric Bentley, Tallulah Bankhead, Senator John McClellan, Conrad Aiken, and Igor Stravinsky.

Now this is an extraordinary author's list for a new magazine. It is possible that some of these people would not write their children unless a stamped self-addressed envelope were sent in advance; being professionals, they work only for pay. Yet Ginzburg got them all for free and writing from the inmost reaches of the heart, just for a postcard offering them a shot at *Time*. Now there's a man who knows how to exploit perversions.

New York World-Telegram, March 16, 1966

Bronx Wisdom

POLICE OFFICER ARNO Herwerth carried a face stricken with loneliness away from the Bronx courtroom where he had stood yesterday
to be arraigned for the criminally negligent homicide of Mary Mitchell
last November 3.

Shouts of "murderer" and inquiries as to how he could sleep at night
beat at his back from the spectator benches. The time is not long gone
when a cop with troubles like Arno Herwerth's could at least count
upon emerging from the courtroom to be welcomed with the encour-
aging cries of other policemen gathered to buck up their beleaguered
colleague.

But no such fraternal assemblage awaited Arno Herwerth yesterday.
And the Bronx district attorney expressed his thanks to the internal
affairs division of the police department for helping to make the case
against him. Whether or not Arno Herwerth escapes a felon's taint and
punishment, he hasn't much chance of staying a policeman.

Herwerth's counsel will probably think it politic to eschew his right
to a trial by jury and leave the facts for and against him to final
assessment by Supreme Court Justice John Collins. By now the conventional wisdom holds that ordinary citizens of the Bronx so hate their
law officers that no indicted policeman can hope for fairness from one
of their juries.

There is also the unconventional wisdom that expressed itself in the
outcries of spectators dead sure that Herwerth had shot Mary Mitchell

not in criminal negligence but with premeditated intent. Wisdom, whether conventional or otherwise, inclines to neglect the complexities of the divided soul.

The circumstances of Mary Mitchell's death make both sorts look rather too simple quite to satisfy. Herwerth and his partner were brought to Mitchell's apartment by a telephoned appeal for help from a member of her family.

The most plausible account of the events that preceded this call for police assistance has been provided by Maxine Brown, Mitchell's niece.

Two days after the shooting, Maxine Brown told *New York Newsday*'s Mitch Gelman that Mitchell's daughter Tiffany had confronted her mother with a cane and said, "This is the night you're gonna die." The two had fought a few nights before and Mrs. Mitchell had come out of the encounter with a broken arm. On this night, Mrs. Mitchell had picked up a knife and Maxine Brown thought it time to call 911.

Her outrage at Herwerth's subsequent excesses did not alter Maxine Brown's conviction that he had good reason to be where he was. "He was called to help," she told Gelman. "And not to murder."

What burns through this judgment is the ambivalence of those Bronx poor who at once dislike police officers and know that after dark they have no one else to depend on. The cop is at one and the same time the incarnation of the peril and the rescue from peril. Herwerth had been sworn to a vocation sometimes ugly and sometimes noble; and he was unequipped for the uneasy balance of coarseness and delicacy that the cop needs for his trade.

At this stage in his case, it is not for us to say that Arno Herwerth killed Mary Mitchell when he had no cause to fear for his life; but his superior officers plainly think he did.

Tiffany Mitchell was absent from the arraignment, having been excluded by the Reverend Al Sharpton, master of all ceremonies of protest. But wherever she was, she no doubt wore a countenance of sincere bereavement for the hugeness of a tragedy in no way felt as any fault of hers. She hadn't really meant what she said about November 3 being her mother's night to die.

All the guilt belonged to that Other, the cop. But then perhaps

Arno Herwerth can console himself with the image of his own Other, the troubled poor on his beat. In that case both will have found their refuge in that unconventional wisdom of the Bronx to which paranoia is simply common sense.

New York Newsday, January 4, 1991

Thugs and the Man

ANHATTAN DISTRICT ATTORNEY Robert Morgenthau yesterday defined the status of 322 West 22nd Street as "converted to a
nine-unit co-op or condominium." Balzac once observed that behind
every great fortune stands a great crime and, behind a good deal of
Manhattan's gentrification, there would seem to stand the thug.

Until the fall of 1980, 322 West 22nd Street was home to five elderly
men of pinched resources. But then, a grand jury has asserted, its
owners leased the services of Morris Lender and Hardmon Perry Lambert, who seem to have been pioneers in the discovery that New
York's vast surplus of hookers and junkies can be transformed into a
real estate asset.

Lambert commenced by firing the old superintendent and replacing
him with Barry Stukes, who, by Morgenthau's account, at once displayed his kidney by threatening to throw downstairs an aged tenant
who wondered about the heat and hot water.

By then the loneliness of these old parties had been alleviated by the
distribution of three hookers and some eleven drug addicts in the
vacant apartments around them. The indictment of Lambert avers that
he once observed that "to get tenants out of a building, 'a bunch of
[blacks] together is like a pot of gold.' "

Even those of us most reluctant to impute ethnic prejudices to these
poor old men would have to concede that, if such existed, the conduct
of their new neighbors was calculated to reinforce them. In three

months, all five of these ancients had quietly departed, and 322 West 22nd was ready for social improvement.

If we are to believe the district attorney, the building's purgation had been effected by the gentlest of the techniques that Lambert and Lender had coarsened so refinedly that they commanded a $100,000 fee from any owner who called them in to purify his premises.

The property at 1729 First Avenue, now a luxury rental, was a harder case. Lambert and a 'Vicki' took a first floor apartment themselves and scattered thirteen other denizens of their bizarre labor pool around the other vacancies. One of Vicki's labor skills was to revile one tenant's daughter as "a [black] bitch." When this style of contumely proved inadequate, the family was burglarized and thereby encouraged into agreeing to take $2,000 and get out.

The proprietor of the laundry downstairs gave up her lease after being twice flooded to the ruination of the clothes in her custody, and, as she recalls, being told by Lender that it was dangerous to work alone in New York, and then being won over with $5,000 for becoming the last occupant to surrender.

Their indictment suggests that Lambert and Lender provided employment free from the vicissitudes of the seasonal layoff: No sooner had their crew triumphed at one work site than it was carried off for the conquest of another.

The vocation contained a variety of crafts. Sid and Toni Melvin seem to have provided the requisite complement of noisy children and noisier radios. A "Babaloo" is identified as author of the burglaries, a powerful incentive for the stubbornest tenant to take his $2,000 and depart.

Louis Tirado is accused of exercising his superintendent's function to stuff up the toilets, seal apartment locks with toothpicks, and warp the front door so as to lay 332 West 19th Street open to any predator silly enough to imagine that the army in occupation had left anything worth stealing unstolen. Antonio Nova is alleged to have been contractor on call for taking out staircases and leaving third-floor tenants stranded.

The oddity is that enterprisers this ingenious did not invariably succeed. The occupants of 446 West 19th endured floodings, burglaries, and a drug parlor for six months, and most of them remained so adamantly in place that the siege had to be lifted. If these charges are correct, then the only experience more painful than a Manhattan residence managed by Lambert and Lender could well be the search for somewhere else to live.

New York Newsday, May 2, 1984

The Confusions of Conscience

THE COUNCIL ON Economic Priorities yesterday celebrated the publication of "Rating America's Corporate Conscience," a consumer's handbook for those of us who, if we can't carry enough cash to the marketplace, would like to think we come there pulsating with the juices of social decency.

With their guide to the corporate conscience in hand, the morally scrupulous will be on the alert, in the words of Council President Alice Tepper Marlin, to "pass up the spaghetti sauce [Progresso] made by a major weapons contractor [the Ogden Corporation]." The Council "prefers Campbell's Prego." In this instance, as in too many others, one wishes life were simpler.

There seems to be something to be said for Prego's proprietors, but unfortunately there does not seem to be significantly less to be said for Progresso's. We all have the bundle of prejudices we too generously call our social philosophy, and my own, while bizarre, may not be untypical of the difficulties presented by "Rating America's Corporate Conscience."

I have the requisite distaste for weapons, although, thanks to the attentions of the Internal Revenue Service, I contribute far more to the Pentagon's food and lodging than I do to my own. I also happen with almost as much despair but with rather more of my own free will to vote Democratic. Progresso's Ogden sends 85 percent of its PAC contributions to Democratic candidates.

I am also a committed, if too often delinquent, union member. "Rating America's Corporate Conscience" informs us that, in 1981, an Ohio State Legislative Committee found that the pickers harvesting tomatoes for Campbell were working twelve hours a day for low wages. Although the matter was resolved last year to the satisfaction of the AFL-CIO, Campbell appears to have maintained its deafness to reproach throughout a period when I might have been eating Prego all unconscious that I was savoring the blood of the toilers.

How then strike a balance? On one side Progresso, which contracts weapons and supports the party of the common man. On the other Campbell, which treats women fairly, indulges a number of charities, and had to be persuaded quite forcibly to stop contracting child labor.

One might, of course, opt for woman and for charity, but the second criterion loses considerable force with the discovery that the highest percentage of profits given to charity is registered by the Dow Chemical Company, which, as the Council reminds us, has been fiercely resistant to alarms over dioxin. The choice becomes too much an agony to linger with further; there is no way to keep the conscience clean except buy my sauce from one of those Village grocers who bottle it at home and to pray never to find out that he has locked an undocumented alien to the vat in his cellar.

The Council deserves our sympathy for attempting to grade American corporations for a conscience that for them, as for the rest of us, turns out to be a mixed bag.

Sara Lee is a striking case in point. Here is a company that not only delights our palates but allots 1 percent of its profits to programs "for the economically disadvantaged." And yet it had no sooner taken over the Hanes textile plants when it found itself in stubborn conflict with the Occupational Safety and Health Administration. Four years after these complaints were resolved, 89 percent of the Hanes workers sampled in a poll judged it a worse workplace. An impressive sacrifice for charity to the economically disadvantaged had come from others of the economically disadvantaged.

But then, the more delicate the calibrations, the worse the confusions in the measurement of conscience. There are many things to be said in conscience's favor and not least as an instrument of convenience. Of all the distractions that oppress us, it seems to be one of the easiest to lay aside.

New York Newsday, January 21, 1987

Rot and Ruin

CHARLOTTE STREET IN the South Bronx has fallen out of the fashion it enjoyed when it was almost as universal a symbol of New York's urban blight as the Coliseum is of the grandeur that was Rome's.

The ruins of Charlotte Street used to be the most familiar of backdrops for presidents and those who would be presidents, come on pilgrimage to affirm their determination to rescue our cities from decay. The site still stands, an offense preserved intact, but the actors left its stage so long ago that cynics might surmise that organized society never really cared.

That is by no means the case. If organized society had not cared about Charlotte Street, Fred Neuberger would not have been able to move to Sutton Place in Manhattan and still be man of substance enough to afford a $1-million bail bond after pleading guilty to grand larceny.

Neuberger is the former president of Wedtech, which began as the South Bronx's only story of success and has now ended, as its other stories generally do, in sack, pillage, and wreck.

Wedtech began as Welbilt Electronic Die, the creation of John Mariotta, a welder, as a machine shop with a labor force recruited from jobless residents of the South Bronx.

John Mariotta was a splendid production manager shrewd enough to understand that he did not know how to run a business and misapprehending enough to hire Fred Neuberger to do it for him. Neuberger had until then been a teacher of managerial techniques to aspiring minority enterprisers.

He had been barely installed as Welbilt's vice president for marketing when he recognized that the image of John Mariotta was its most attractive article of sale.

Mariotta's Hispanic identity qualified him for federal loans and contracts as a minority business enterpriser. And, since he had assembled his work force from persons until then deemed all but unemployable, he incarnated some promise of a renascent South Bronx.

It took Neuberger ten years to harvest the crop from these special advantages, but he reaped it so handsomely that by 1982 Welbilt was earning $20 million a year as a favorite ward of the Department of Defense.

In 1983, Welbilt was reorganized as Wedtech Corporation with an issue of 6 million stock shares.

By then, Neuberger had brought on board three fellow officers, all Mariotta's betters in financial sophistication and distinctly his inferiors in morals, and the new team seems to have set about almost at once to loot the Department of Defense with false invoices totaling no less than $6 million and squirreling the spoils away for themselves.

Somewhere in the course of these depredations, Mariotta was squeezed out of his managerial functions and stripped of his stock holdings, and only heroic exertions in the influence purchase line appear to have held at bay the suspicions of the Small Business Administration's loan agents that Wedtech was no longer a minority business enterprise eligible for their blessings.

But the game was up, and in December Wedtech filed for bankruptcy and laid off the last of its 1,400 employees.

And Neuberger and friends are spending this month taking their pleas. Their treatment in Manhattan federal court last week was conspicuous for the exquisite courtesy reserved for sinners who promise to turn in more famous sinners.

Former Wedtech vice president Mario Moreno confessed to having bribed public officials, filed false invoices, and stolen "in excess of $500,000" for himself. When he brought off this affectation of shame,

Assistant U.S. Attorney Mary Shannon hastened to ask the court to grant Mario Moreno leave to go to Florida. He can be trusted to return and do his duty and serve up a congressman or so.

To hell with congressmen; they are only takers. Neuberger and his friends are gougers; they stole in the name of the poor, and they have cheated the poor of one of their scanty few hopes. They belong in jail until they rot like Charlotte Street.

New York Newsday, February 6, 1987

The Gonof Theory of History

"Gonof, gonoph, gonef: A thief, esp., a skilled pickpocket."
—ERIC PARTRIDGE, *A Dictionary of Slang and Unconventional English*

"He's as obstinate a young gonoph as I know."
—CHARLES DICKENS, *Bleak House*

T HE TOWER COMMISSION'S report on the errantries of the National Security Council is distinguished by a high tone of reference to various philosophies of statecraft; but its analysts have regrettably failed to make use of that most splendid of interpretative tools, the Gonof Theory of History.

Lieutenant Colonel Oliver North did not wander lost in the maze of Iran for want of a guide. The Virgil to his Dante was Manucher Ghorbanifar, a rare and exotic specimen from the illustrated catalog of the Gonof Theory of History.

Ghorbanifar was an Iranian who was attempting to repair fortunes that had crashed with the shah by establishing or anyway pretending to have established confidential friendships with the mullahs.

In 1984, he essayed his first entry into cosmic affairs by suggesting that the CIA hire him as middleman for paying Iran cash ransom for American hostages held in Beirut. That was too coarse a proposition at the moment; but Ghorbanifar was back a year later with merchandise more appetizing.

He returned as part of a consortium with Jacob Nimrodi and Al Schwimmer, two Israeli arms dealers; Amiram Nir, Israeli Prime Minister Shimon Peres's adviser on counterterrorism, and Adnan Khashoggi, the Saudi enterpriser. Together they had devised a plan to sell weapons to Iran in exchange for American hostages.

A trusted source informed the CIA's Charles Allen that "profit was certainly a motive but the group did see its efforts as leading toward stability in the region."

Ghorbanifar had acquired his license as North's cicerone. In August of 1985, Israel shipped 508 TOW missiles to Iran and thus, by Ghorbanifar's account, won release for Benjamin Weir. That was enough to put North in thrall; and by December, he was inditing NSC memos to the effect that "while it is possible that Ghorbanifar is . . . simply lining his own pockets" he is nonetheless "irrefutably the deepest penetration we have yet achieved into the Iranian government."

He had decided to trust an intermediary defined by National Security Adviser Robert McFarlane as "a person of no integrity" and by CIA Director William Casey as "a fabricator and wheeler dealer."

And yet did North cling to him. There was no abundance of alternatives; the other available guides to the Middle East appear to have been exhibits in demonstration of the Gonof Theory scarcely less formidable than Ghorbanifar.

In January of last year, North recorded a conversation in which Nir, an Israeli official, said that "Ghorba" had indeed wangled a $10,000 per TOW missile price from the Iranians and "that Gorba probably lied to Schwimmer [his partner in the deal, mind] and that Schwimmer had probably lied to Nir about how much was available." The next day, Nir reported that Iran hadn't paid the full $10,000 a TOW price, but "whether this is because Schwimmer pocketed the rest or whether there was a kickback [to someone in Tehran] neither Nir nor I know."

Still the Americans had started to learn the Gonof Theory if too little else and were schooled in the uses of extortion as freedom's shield. On April 7 of last year, North told the NSC's director, Iran would transfer $17 million to an Israeli Swiss account. The Israelis would take a $2 million fee. The CIA would then procure a consignment of HAWK missile parts for Iran. They would cost $3.65 million and be delivered to Teheran with a $13.35 million markup.

North would then allot $12 million of this windfall for lethal aid to the Nicaraguan counterrevolution. By now, the murk of the scoundrelly has so suffused these transactions that there is no secure knowing whether the $15 million ever reached North's designated Swiss bank or where it went thereafter. Ghorbanifar was, in any case, of no further use. He had borrowed $10 million from Khashoggi to finance this last and grandest deal at the interest rate of 20 percent a month felt due so signal a service to Western civilization.

Ghorbanifar was unable or disinclined to meet the loan's terms and had grown increasingly distant in the hiding place into which he swore he had been forced to avoid being killed by his creditors for the $22 million insurance policy they had, as a business precaution, taken out on his life. He was a burnt-out case; and North dropped him from operations with a vague promise of $4 million severance.

Khashoggi has been wailing for his $10 million ever since; and his creditors are assiduously plastering him with their liens and foreclosures. Now that the game is up for North, there is some irony in noticing that, having set out to bring down all manner of evil empires, the only one he helped overthrow was Khashoggi's.

After all these rascalities, it is refreshing to learn that Robert McFarlane brought a chocolate cake baked in Tel Aviv as a house present to his hosts in Tehran. At least one thing in this business was kosher.

New York Newsday, March 1, 1987

O Lucky Man

ALBERT HAKIM SEEMS to have traveled through life with a pair of needle-pointed elbows; and there may be those still scarred enough from his passage to be surprised to be informed that he is a man of sentiment.

They ought not to be. There were few elements in Hakim's testimony before the Joint Congressional Committee on Contrayatollah more plausible yesterday than his affirmation that he had contrived to disguise his business accounts so cunningly that he didn't understand them himself.

No one who can bear that triumphant a witness to his own sinuousity could fail to appreciate the commercial value of an occasional surrender to tender and lofty impulses.

Hakim took his oath as a new citizen of the United States in 1984, and was thenceforth inspired to serve his country with frenzies of patriotic endeavor that earned him $6.85 million in less than two years.

He had trusted America and America had handsomely rewarded him. By last August his gratified affections had found their incarnate symbol in Lieutenant Colonel Oliver North of the National Security Council. North was Hakim's ideal of the selfless patriot, which is, of course, the one useful to the selfish; he had been patron saint of a $9 million profit for Hakim and his partners.

Hakim had begun to worry about Oliver North's future. He was, he said, troubled by how often North talked about the stresses and dangers of his duties, the enforced neglect of his family, and the prospect that he might die young and leave his children too poor for college.

Hakim carried his tender alarms at length to Major General Richard Secord (Retired), his partner in enterprise. He told Secord that, "I thought it would be wise to set aside $500,000 as a benefit for Ollie."

Secord's response was a reproof. Hakim had, he said, no conception of lives different from his own.

"He made a remark that . . . I have no understanding of what a soldier's life is, and that there are benefits that the government provides."

Hakim would have to do his good works on his own; and he proceeded about them in the mysterious ways of habit by setting up one more dummy corporation and depositing a $200,000 reserve fund for North in its account. The code name he chose for North was "Belly Button." North's prior style in code names had been in the key of "Blood and Guts" and "Steel Hammer"—and diminished in resonance though it sounds in comparison with the others, "Belly Button" was the only one that ever offered North the promise of a score.

There is good reason to doubt that North ever knew of the promise and every reason to be sure that it was never kept. Hakim made one essay at seducing Mrs. North with the offer of what he insisted would be presented to her as the gift of an anonymous donor. She seems to have been bemused enough to travel to Philadelphia for an interview, but nothing came of it because Hakim was still trying to find a suitably cunning disguise for his boon when his good intentions were overtaken by the events of November.

And so Oliver North has been lucky for the first time in quite awhile; his reputation for honor, if not for containment, remains substantially intact.

It is impossible not to surmise that he owes its preservation to Richard Secord. What could he have meant when he told Hakim that he had no understanding of a soldier's life if he were not speaking most of a soldier's honor? Hakim could hardly be taxed for not understanding the soldier's honor; he had been buying soldiers for a good part of his life.

But Secord knew about honor because he had so carelessly lost his own. At one juncture when short of cash, he had engaged in a private transaction with Edwin Wilson, who had since gone on to such multiple infamies that the mere odor of their prior intimacy cost Secord his military career. He had been ruined by a hustler and here came another hustler with designs of benevolence to Oliver North.

When someone like Hakim spoke of concern for North, Secord heard only calculation. He was damaged goods and so was Tom Clines, Hakim's other partner. Only North, its essential instrument, was still undamaged and thus a security risk as collaborator for the likes of Hakim.

Life has not been kind to Secord nor has he been kind to himself, but he cherished better days and a better self and he knows the price of letting a bad man get a hold on you. The fallen may have fallen, but they have their principles. It would take a hooker of very bad character to be accomplice to the seduction of a virgin to her trade.

Oliver North can thank Richard Secord for all too little except one great thing. His virtue was preserved from all temptation, and Richard Secord had been its preserver.

New York Newsday, June 4, 1987

The Confidence Man

THE CLOSER THE years draw toward one's own appointment with the Recording Angel, the stronger swells the claim of duty to be gentle with the pleadings of one's brother sinner. All the same, the eleven pages Michael Milken has spent crying mercy from his sentencing judge present a considerable trial to the patience.

This sodden screed is at once as false and as sincere as any junk-bond prospectus its author ever distributed for Braniff or Memorex Telex. The self-absolving Milken is the unaltered junk-peddling Milken. He remains an essentially honest fraud; and the chances are that he cannot even yet tell any lie that he hasn't told himself first.

STYLES IN AUTOBIOGRAPHY seem somehow dictated by vocation. Former presidents sound alike, and there is no detectable difference between the tone of one retired ballerina's memoir and another's, perhaps because they all share the same writer. That rule seems to obtain so rigorously for the grand swindlers that to read Milken's prose is like coming upon some unapologetic apologia left behind by Charles Ponzi.

Ineptitude in matters of grammar is a common mark of the honest swindler. "Life," Milken reminds his judge, "doesn't allow one to take an eraser out and erase mistakes they have made." No mere confidence man would ever be that careless; his work is camouflage and demands attention to small points, since he is always conscious that the slightest misstep can bring his ruin.

No worry so trifling afflicts the sincere swindler's serene assurance that his every felony is a public benefaction. Thus Milken can say and seem still to think that his career at Drexel has "resulted in a tremendous increase in the value of American enterprises."

Painful though it is to give the lie to honest faith, we need do no more to recognize such stuff for its portentous nonsense than read the complaints of the Columbia Savings and Loan Association in its suit for a share in what flotsam and jetsam still float from the wreck of Drexel Burnham Lambert.

As of December 1989, Columbia held a portfolio of Drexel-underwritten junk bonds with a book value of $3.998 billion. It has since sold as many as it could, at a loss of $198 million, and is stuck with the rest. The book value of Columbia's holdings has declined at least $1 billion; and the $2.9 billion assessment of the remainder is well beyond the best that could be hoped for it in the market. The Federal Deposit Insurance Corporation rates the worth of Drexel-inspired investments at just about half their original cost to the bankrupt S&Ls in its custody.

So much for Michael Milken's stimulus to "the tremendous increase in the value of American enterprises." And his means were as coarse as their end was disastrous.

By the government's account Drexel made of its virtual monopoly of junk-bond issuance the sword that overbears and the honey that deceives. Its brochures were "materially false." It refused "to provide underwriting services unless the issuer purchased Drexel bonds." When some piece of junk turned sour, Drexel warned its favorite customers to sell out in time and left the others to take the fall. It withheld the equity warrants that were due the customer as part of his junk issue and gave them to the Drexel Partnerships for a killing sometimes as high as five thousand times the original investment.

A frequent Drexel device was to persuade the customer to double the junk-bond issue he needed and spend the surplus proceeds on other Drexel bonds.

The catalogue of Michael Milken's sins runs on and on; and the blacker his copybook gets, the more fervor he puts into a fresh dismissal of each felonious blot as just another mistake. However we may despair of ever touching the infinite, we never so sense its presence as when we contemplate the sincerity of the swindler.

New York Newsday, October 18, 1990

The Floating Life

PETER COHEN'S FALL from his summit as CEO of Shearson Lehman Hutton fortifies the impression that career plunges may be growing as precipitate for our master of business administration class as they have been for the communists in Central Europe.

There are, of course, degrees of difference in the harm done in power's exercise by MBAs as compared to communists, since MBAs just damage our economy while communists ruin theirs.

The marks of kinship are otherwise striking. Both enter the world of work certified by schools of the sort that stuff their students with theory while protecting them from every contagion of familiarity with practice. A Marxist-Leninist Institute degree may be a worse credential for productive service than a Wharton MBA, but the distinction is not broad.

The communist capacity for accelerating social decay is, to be sure, inarguably superior to any so far displayed by the MBAs, whose contribution to the wreckage of a dozen or so American corporations seems quite pitiful set next to the incomparable accomplishments of the communists in producing a Poland without sausage and a Russia without kasha.

Still, the MBAs do what they can with their limits. In the period when our hospitals were getting worse and worse, the Bureau of Labor Statistics generally recorded the highest percentage of increase in any job category as "Hospital Administrators," few of whom could have got their chance for mischief without an MBA as ticket of entry.

The United States has fallen measurably and the Soviet bloc almost immeasurably behind Japan, Taiwan, and even South Korea in rate of economic growth, and those who credit this achievement to the freedom of these nations from encumbering communist bureaucracies might also notice that none has a business school.

The MBAs will, to be sure, need to carry us much farther into industrial ruin before we rise up and try to get rid of them. That has already happened to the communists in Eastern Europe, and we can't be sure they're gone yet. We tend to forget that the Eastern European regimes were in power for nearly forty years, which is to say that most of their subjects who have arrived at middle age grew up knowing that offices of comfort and managerial responsibility were reserved for communists.

A young man making his way had no sensible option except to join the party, absorb its unserviceable teachings, and then be mistakenly judged fit to direct his country's business. An MBA diploma has been our closest approximation of an East German party card, and those who flourished either are curiously alike in speaking the language of an undifferentially hollow militance, the communists with their slogans and the MBAs with the martial imagery so peculiarly attractive to draft dodgers.

And the MBAs will survive their discomforts and the Eastern European communists their disasters, because once a young man starts out committed to making his way above all others, he can never find himself completely in the discard. Overthrowing the Eastern European communists looks easier than dislodging them.

The power monopoly they held for four decades has left no trained managers except themselves. The very mechanics who snarled the machine have turned out to be the only ones with the slightest experience at running it. Lenin's theory has failed them, but there's always another for the theory junkie and the communists are clutching at Milton Friedman, who is like Marx in his megasized talent for observing and minuscule gift for predicting.

These communists may have had to discard most else in Lenin, but they stay true to his lesson about times when it is necessary to take one step back before you can take two steps forward. The middle managers of the old order in Eastern Europe have taken three or four steps back, but don't count them out in the race to step forward. Don't count Peter Cohen out either. Communist bureaucrats and MBAs are of the stuff that does not sink but only dives and will come up again.

New York Newsday, July 1, 1990

The Truth About Machiavelli

"Perhaps Leonardo was only the greatest of cranks."
—*BERNARD BERENSON*

I**T IS HARDLY** revolutionary to suggest that, if to be modern is to be of any use at all, we must attempt to cast the same cold and common-sensical eye even upon the Renaissance that Berenson did even upon Leonardo.

Unfortunately, Professor Giuseppe Prezzolini in his new book, *Machiavelli*, cannot serve as that eye. He is the Italian guide before the Bernardo Luini grandly and charmingly running on about *sfumato* and *contraposto* while all the time we wonder why the object of so much enthusiasm is so dark and blurred in line. From such guides one just has to flee to other sources if not from the museum altogether.

The puzzle about Machiavelli is not the obloquy which so long attended his name and is here so laboriously catalogued by Professor Prezzolini. That was long ago explained by Voltaire in his disenchanted observations on *The Anti-Machiavelli* of Frederick the Great: "If Machiavelli had had a prince as disciple, the first thing he would have recommended to him would have been to write against him."

What is much harder to understand is the persistence of that image of Machiavelli as the first modern political mind, *and* as the great realist about statecraft which has been magnified through four centuries until Professor Prezzolini can now offer him to us as our contemporary.

We know now that the Renaissance was more closely tied to the Middle Ages than the nineteenth century liked to think it. And Machiavelli is certainly closer to the Middle Ages than to any period of scientific inquiry. He had precisely the weakness for myths about military adventures that the monks had for myths about saints. His thought was closed, formalistic, and committed to history as a lesson in repetition. The man liberated from credulity about griffons was still chained to credulity about Cesare Borgia.

And yet these very qualities do rather strongly argue for Machiavelli as our contemporary in one special way; if he was the son of the Friars Minor, he was also the father of our Academicians Major. For the real Machiavellian is not the statesman but the scholar who would assist the statesman. Servants and not masters are Machiavellian. What is most current for us in *The Prince* is not its teachings about statecraft but its purpose as a prospectus for a job with, or failing that, a study grant from the state.

"I have composed a little work *On Princedoms*," Machiavelli wrote his friend Francesco Vettori:

> . . . By a prince, especially a new prince, it ought to be welcomed. . . . There is my wish that our present Medici Lords will make use of me . . . even if they begin by making me roll a stone. . . . And, through this thing, if it were read, they would make use of me, they would see that, for the fifteen years I have been studying the art of the state, I have not slept or been playing.

So then, it was not Machiavellian of the Central Intelligence Agency to endow the Center of International Studies at the Massachusetts Institute of Technology; it was Machiavellian of MIT to accept the grant. The instructive Machiavelli experience was to have got in trouble with the Medicis because he had served a republic and to have died in trouble with the next republic because he had served the Medicis. For Machiavellianism is above all else the commitment to serve the secular arm whatever it may be. The disillusion of Professor Eric Goldman, the stubborn illusion of Professor John Roche and not the devices of Lyndon Johnson, their master, are what are contemporary in the Machiavellian experience.

Even so there endures the image of Machiavelli as the master and not the victim of circumstance. Professor Prezzolini deplores Cesare Balbo's epithet about "the elegantly indifferent mind of Machiavelli" and properly so: Machiavelli was wildly romantic. If he ever wished for elegance, it was denied him; and it was with extreme difficulty that he managed, even so infrequently as he did, to be philosophical about, let alone indifferent to, the circumstances of his time.

Yet what admiration he evokes still is dependent on our illusion of his detachment. It is not difficult to understand how the notion of his detachment could persist in those who read him translated across the Alps; what is much harder to conceive is how Balbo, an Italian, could have yielded to it.

You and I read, to take a case, this letter to Guicciardini: "For a long time I have not said what I believed nor do I ever believe what I say, and if indeed sometimes I do happen to tell the truth, I hide it among so many lies that it is hard to find."

In translation we can feel ourselves in the company of a man, a little weary certainly, but all the same assured of his control of events and the impenetrability of his mask.

But an Italian reads this:

Da un tempo in qua io non dico mai quello che io credo, né credo mai quel che io dico, e se pure é mi vien detto qualche volta il vero, io lo nascondo fra tante bugie, che e difficile a retrovarlo.

Professor Allan Gilbert's translation (*The Letters of Machiavelli*, p. 200) is accurate beyond any powers of mine; yet am I wrong in the suspicion that what is lost in any translation of this sentence is its melancholy, its confusion, its suggestion of a voice that has told so many lies so long as to have quite mixed them up and to have become itself unsure of finding the truth among them any longer? Such disorder was inescapable for any man living in Florence after 1494, the year which Guicciardini fixes as the last one in which "those who held power stood in little danger of losing it."

"But, when the French came to Italy, they introduced such efficiency into war that up to 1521, the loss of a campaign meant the loss of a state."

We have not often, since that period, been safe in saying whether Italy's circumstances have been rendered hopeless by her politicians or whether her politicians have been rendered hopeless by her circumstances.

Machiavelli entered the service of the state in 1494 and was driven from it in 1512, never to return with any real authority. If reading him did not teach so well the dangers of mechanical devotion to historical analogy, we might be tempted to think that living in Florence at the end of the *quattrocento* was rather like living in the Weimar Republic. Certainly there is a Bert Brecht in Machiavelli, held in check though it generally is, even in his familiar correspondence, in which, since most of what survives was written to his betters, he seems to have exercised special care with the refinements expected from a gentleman and a snob.

But *La Mandragola* shows how harsh and spiteful he could be in the vernacular. He says in its prologue that he is a man who respects no one in all the world, though he will be the lackey of anyone who wears a better cloak.

Machiavelli failed as a statesman, of course; but the circumstances made it impossible for him to succeed. What surprises anyone dependent upon his writings to judge his wisdom is that, in those cases where he had power to act, Machiavelli was a very shrewd servant of the state indeed. He did more than any civilian to win the Pisan War, a victory whose chief use was to put an end to one of the least sensible distractions in Florentine history. When it became plain that Italy would be the province either of France or Spain, Machiavelli's counsel, surprisingly un-Machiavellian, was for Florence to avoid choosing sides until the issue of battle became clearer. Florence chose instead to stand loyal to her traditional French alliance and, while doing very little, did just enough to bring down upon herself the arms of Spain and the vengeance of Pope Julius when the French evacuated the peninsula.

With the Medicis installed again, Piero Soderini, standard-bearer of the Republic of Florence, fled to Dalmatia and the better than Christian mercies of the Turks. In January 1513, the terminal moment in that connection with real decisions of state which he was to finish his life struggling to restore, Machiavelli drafted a letter to the only one of his masters who had given and would ever give him serious attention.

How is it, he would wonder to Soderini, that "he who does not know how to fence overcomes him who knows"?

> [Hannibal] with cruelty, treachery, and lack of religion kept his armies united in Italy and made himself admired by the people, who to follow him rebelled against the Romans. [Scipio] achieved the same result in Spain with mercy, loyalty and piety; both of them won countless victories.... [The] reason why different ways of working are sometimes equally effective and equally damaging I do not know, but I should very much like to know.

Machiavelli could only conclude that Fortune holds all men under her yoke.

That observation is the best sort of warning against the doctrine that humanity is always the same and that to know the ways great men controlled the events of antiquity was most of what any statesman needed to know. Machiavellianism can hardly be an instrument of real precision once the historical examples begin to contradict one another.

Now, one perplexity of Machiavelli studies must be that the poor man, whether for pleasure or from necessity, was almost continuously an actor. Even, perhaps especially, in his private letters, it is seldom possible to know whether he meant what he said. To tell Soderini that he had been unfortunate rather than the Milquetoast Machiavelli thought him would have been certainly tactful—as Machiavelli always is—and rather generous—as Machiavelli seldom is—in approaching a master unlikely ever to be of use to him again.

But Machiavelli does not seem to have dispatched this letter, a fact which argues to me at least that it may have been composed as much to himself as to Soderini. Political disaster does concentrate—this is, usefully confuse—the mind; and, under its weight, Machiavelli does seem to have a better grasp of political reality than he would subsequently show in the exposition of political realism.

His sense of reality had never been all that strong. There are, from the very beginning, signs of that dangerous rigidity of the intellect which impels men to follow their ideas to their logical conclusions, one of the worst mistakes possible in human affairs.

Consider his famous comment on Pope Julius's rash expedition into Perugia and on the contemptible weakness of Giampolo Biagone, its tyrant, who, with the Pope at his mercy, collapsed into superstitious awe and ultimately yielded the city:

> People of judgment could not understand why [Giampolo] did not, to his everlasting fame, crush his enemy with one blow and enrich himself with the plunder, for the Pope was accompanied by all his Cardinals with their jewels. They could not believe that he refrained on account of any goodness or any conscientious scruples, for the heart of a wicked man, who committed incest with his sister, and destroyed his cousins and nephews so that he might rule, could not be accessible to any feelings of respect. So they came to the conclusion that there are men who can neither be honorably bad or perfectly good, who do not know how to go about committing a crime, great in itself or possessing a certain splendor. That was the case with Giampolo; he who thought nothing of incest and the murder of his kinsmen did not know how, or rather did not dare ... to perform a deed which would have caused everyone to admire his courage and won for him an immortal name.

For all the quaint charm of this passage, it entirely neglects that men are not that logical: A villain already damned for incest and murder might still vividly quake at the hellfire reserved for anyone who would sack a church. More proper statesmen than Giampolo decided to bomb Hiroshima, in disregard of its women and children, and to spare Kyoto out of deference to its shrines.

Machiavelli's place in political thought is owing most to the credit given him for the discovery that politics is an art separate from Christian doctrine. That could hardly have seemed a discovery to the Italians. Cosimo de Medici had said, before Machiavelli was born, "It needs something more to direct a government than to play with a rosary." The politics of Machiavelli's adult life were successively controlled by a Pope Borgia, a Pope della Rovere, and two Popes Medici, none of whom seems to have wondered for a moment whether politics had anything to do with religion.

Machiavelli's error was to notice the displacement of one doctrine and thereupon conclude that it had been replaced by its direct opposite. But notions of absolute logic have a common weakness; to rule by the illusion that all men are wicked is at once less attractive and no less disabling than to rule by the illusion that all men are pure. There was an absolutist doctrinaire in him that could not be repressed. One suspects that, if you asked Machiavelli what to do, his immediate answer would be as sensible as could be; but, tell him to sit down and indite a report and he need but take up his pen to become at once the prisoner of historical absolutes.

When he set down his recommendations for the treatment of the people of Valdichina after the suppression of their rebellion against Florence, he could not resist the either/or remedy: The Romans, he asserts, always said that the only way to govern conquered peoples was "either to benefit or to kill them." This has a grand sweep to it, and to announce it has the use of avoiding the more subtle problems of government. Still there does remain the difficulty that in the area between blessing and cursing lie most solutions to puzzles which are hardly easier to engage with the doctrine of either/or than with the fingering of rosaries.

Then there is his report to the Florentines on how Cesare Borgia had his mutinous lieutenants strangled. "The Means Employed by the Duke of Valentinois, etc.," is the literal translation of the beginning of Machiavelli's title. What enchants him in this case is the nicety of Cesare Borgia's procedure, which began by deceiving and ended by murdering. *"Del Modo Tenuto"*—"The Means Employed": These are aesthetic expressions, and the purity of the object has small reference to its necessity. One wonders continually whether his concentration on the beauty of the means had not too much diverted Machiavelli into exaggerating their necessity for the ends. It remains hard to say whether Cesare Borgia would have been more effective if he had been less terrible and absolutely impossible to say whether there would not have been a Roman republic, as Machiavelli insists in the Discourses, if Romulus had lacked the good judgment to murder his brother.

But Machiavelli could never escape his weakness for the downright.

That may have been the medieval mind in him; having so few living examples to admire of the kind of heroic virtue which he himself would not dare, he settled for examples of heroic infamy of the sort he would not dare either. We see this in his attitude toward the two politicians he observed most directly—Borgia, whose strength remained for him the model for every prince and Piero Soderini, whose feebleness remained for him an object of lively contempt.

Some of the distinction in his mind accords to be sure with the distinction in the social position of these two men. Machiavelli had the best of excuses for being sensitive to social position; his own political career was always handicapped by the rumor that his father had not paid his debts, in Florence the mark of low birth hardest of all to erase. Borgia was a Duke and the *arriviste* in Machiavelli loved a Duke; Soderini, although a gentleman, had only a republican title. What may be more to the point was that Soderini had recognized Machiavelli's talents; and the *arriviste* in Machiavelli cannot always have found it easy to respect a man who would take *his* advice.

What seems curious about these examples, Borgia who met the formula, and Soderini who failed it, is that each died in exile fumbling with schemes for his restoration. Borgia was beaten because Alexander VI died and he himself became ill at just the wrong moment. Soderini was beaten because he listlessly yielded to an internal conspiracy. Borgia, then, was the victim of Fortune and Soderini of his own lack of Virtue. The trouble with that estimate is that the rebels unseated Soderini only when the Spaniards were at the gates of Florence. Had Soderini been Cesare Borgia he might have strangled his internal enemies, in which case Florence would have been conquered by the invader in a matter of hours anyway. Borgia was strong and unfortunate; Soderini was weak and would have been just as unfortunate if he hadn't been weak.

You end up respecting Machiavelli even though you do not like him. He is the more appealing for the very deficiency that makes him of so little real use. He misread his own time just because of his possession by nostalgia for a time he had not known and which was clearly better. What ideals he had, Spartan rather than Athenian, were survivals from medieval Florence. Bored as he was, and we remain, with his *Florentine Histories*, he was more sustainedly romantic there than anywhere else. Perhaps that nostalgia is enough to get his worst judgments forgiven.

Professor Prezzolini has struggled through everything written about Machiavelli since his death; he drags up the names of scholars so long forgotten that the reader can only abase himself before any other scholar who has ever even heard of them. Even so, there remains a small unease about the quality of the minds to whom Machiavelli has seemed useful. That doubt increases when we check the index for references to men who for all their differences, would, I think, be accepted as the most illuminating observers of the nineteenth century.

For Alexis de Tocqueville, there is no listing at all; apparently he did not bother to notice. Under Karl Marx, there is essentially no more than this: "Actually Marx and Engels did not pay much attention to him." Still he will go on being taught in the schools, having the appeal of always seeming up-to-date, without ever being either relevant or prophetic.

The New Republic, March 11, 1967

Main Events

Bessie Smith: Poet

"Woke up this morning when chickens was crowing for day."
—*"Young Woman's Blues"*

WOKE UP YESTERDAY morning where there is not a chicken to crow for day and remembered that on September 27 next Bessie Smith will have been dead for fifty years.

She was killed a few miles from Clarksdale, Mississippi. The gods could not have selected a more appropriate place to close her epic, because Clarksdale is not very far from the railroad tracks where the Southern used to cross the Yellow Dog and where Miss Susie Johnson's Jockey Lee had gone.

September is a while away. But what fitter day for filing an advance notice of this special occasion could there be than July 4, which is sacred to the falling-short but undiscouragable pursuit of happiness that is most of what the works of Bessie Smith are about. Most but, as usual with great subjects, by no means all.

The rising sun ain't gonna set in the East no more.
                                        —"Hard Time Blues"

To distill a complexity into the sparest of direct statements and still preserve intact its paradox was among the subtler of Bessie's arts. We have no way to know the source of most of her lyrics; she must have picked up a good many in the carnivals and others were written for her by hands more practiced. But a lot of these words have to be her very own and they bring us the sense of being in the company of the last of the Anglo-Saxon poets. There are, as an instance, those lines in "Lost Your Head Blues" that have been authenticated as pure improvisation: "Once ain't for always and two ain't but twice." I have puzzled over them off and on through my conscious life and am yet to be sure precisely what they mean. All that I know with certainty is that they are entirely beautiful.

> *If I ever get my hands on a dollar again,*
> *I'm gonna hold on to it till the eagle grin.*
> —"Nobody Knows You When You're Down and Out"

Or "My heart's on fire but my love is icy cold." No generation is long enough to produce more than one writer who can bring off this cadence so perfect that, when you think you remember it and look it up, you find that you were wrong because you had allowed some bit of dross—say an adverb—from your own literary baggage to intrude and spoil the rhythm and taint the purity of the original. Those of us who learned to write from the blues are to be envied, and those of us who have since forgotten the lesson are to be pitied.

> *Thirty days in jail and I got to stay there so long.*
> —"Jailhouse Blues"

"Jailhouse Blues" was her first record and the first of hers I ever owned, which is to say that it was the one I have played most and thus the one I have loved most, because the record of Bessie's you have heard most often ends up the deepest in your heart.

I also saw and heard her once at the old Howard Theater in Baltimore in 1933, and was too overwhelmed for any coherent recollection. Witnesses to the apparitions of creatures from another world are seldom useful for details. I have only two memories. One is the shock of the recognition of how faintly even her records conveyed the immensity of her actual presence.

The other involves one of my companions, who was far from having conquered his baby fat and was indeed huge enough to be the most conspicuous figure in the house except of course Bessie herself. At one point she descended from higher things to "One-Hour Woman," one of the requisite dirty songs her grandeur somehow always kept from being quite disgusting, and then she noticed Freddy and, like giantess calling out to giant, she began singing that she had found in him her one-hour man.

He turned turkey red and fled the theater. Long afterward I ran into him and wondered as tactfully as I could if he remembered the afternoon we had gone to hear Bessie. He replied that he had and that, even though dozens of women had since bruised his heart, it was the supreme regret of his life that he had not held his ground and heard the whole set.

"Is it true," he asked, "that she sang 'Muddy Water'?" I answered that she had and his sigh had resonances of sorrow and loss not unworthy of her own. We would still have no more used for her any name except the bare and stately "Bessie" than we would have spoken of Juno as Mrs. Jupiter. Goddesses do not have last names.

Awhile back I fell into one of those tiresome discussions where the other party says you take Julius Erving and I'll take Larry Bird and you take Sarah Vaughan and I'll take Ella Fitzgerald. There was no disposing of such nonsense except to observe that the years have taught me to be grateful for having them all, but I had to say that Sarah Vaughan is the greatest jazz singer I have ever heard. "What about Bessie Smith?" a bystander inquired. I could only answer that I had concluded that there could never have been a Bessie Smith; the molds where they stamp out human beings are just too small for stuff of those proportions.

New York Newsday, July 5, 1987

The Genius of Mussolini

I

"In a quarter of the city which was inhabited only by mechanics and Jews, the marriage of an innkeeper and a washerwoman produced the future deliverer of Rome. From such parents Nicholas Rienzi Gabrini could inherit neither dignity nor fortune; and the gift of a liberal education, which they so painfully bestowed, was the cause of his glory and untimely end. The study of history and eloquence, the writings of Cicero, Seneca, Livy, Caesar, and Valerius Maximus elevated above his equals and contemporaries the genius of the young plebeian. He perused with indefatigable diligence the manuscripts and marbles of antiquity, loved to dispense his knowledge in familiar language and was often provoked to exclaim, 'Where are now these Romans—their virtue, their justice, their power? Why was I not born in those happy times?'

"In the death, as in the life of Rienzi, the hero and the coward were strangely mingled."

—*GIBBON ON COLA DI RIENZI*

ECHOES RESOUND NOW and then in the history of every nation; but for Italy's they roll forth in unbroken succession. Thus: "In a small house outside the village of Predappio, the marriage of an innkeeper and a schoolmistress produced the future conqueror of Rome."

Denis Mack Smith's style in *Mussolini* seldom reaches for the key of ironic majesty even when the object of its engagement has been some ghost he admires; and in Mussolini's case this preference for the downright tone is fortified by the disdain that any man of Mack Smith's sovereign common sense is bound to feel after emerging from the middens of florid and counterfeit paper through which he has burrowed to extricate his trophy.

All the same, no contrast in manner of presentation can quite obscure the common import of Gibbon's material and Mack Smith's. Gibbon reminds us that Petrarch assigned to Rienzi "the name and sacred character of a poet." When Pirandello saluted the conquest of Ethiopia, he said of Mussolini: "The Author of this great feat is also a Poet who knows his trade." Even those of us who are sure that Rienzi deserves better from history—the shade of Mussolini has a dog's chance of finding its Wagner—can only be confounded when we contemplate a culture so perdurable that 582 years go by and one grand master employs the very metaphor for his triumphant *duce* that an even grander master summoned up for his fallen tribune.

MACK SMITH'S MUSSOLINI is a portrait in every way admirable; but if it does not manage to be as wonderful as his awesome industry ought to have made it, we can only blame that falling short on its deafness to the echoes. After a while there arises the suspicion that he has almost willfully stuffed his ears. An unclouded appreciation of reality is not often among the rewards of a great love; and Mack Smith has a love for Italy that can only be called great, and that I would be the last man alive to think misplaced. To him Italy is a lifelong mistress, which means that he cannot conceive her affair with Mussolini except as one of those freakish escapades that a restored lover can only dispose of by rendering the severest justice to her seducer and the uttermost mercy to herself.

We need to go to other quarters to discover how many untarnished vessels of the national culture intermittently overflowed with enthusiasm for fascism. Mack Smith identifies Arturo Toscanini as an early fascist, a lapse excused by its brevity. And yet, if Toscanini was the first genuine ornament of the Fascist party permanently to recoil from it, he had nonetheless been one of the twenty candidates the party offered in the National Assembly elections of 1919, by which time it had already made clear on the streets of Milan that thuggery was a political expression that suited its preferences infinitely more than parliamentary rhetoric ever could.

Mack Smith passes over this evidence of how much Toscanini was

able to swallow before final revulsion, and avoids mentioning Bene-
detto Croce until it can be noticed that he "utterly repudiated the
movement in 1925." Utter repudiation is a flatter description than
Croce's ambiguities entirely deserve: As Pirandello donated his Nobel
Prize medal, Croce served up his own Senatorial medal to be smelted
into some weapon for the Ethiopian war, which makes our own intru-
sions into Vietnam seem almost high-minded.

Shortly before his death in 1923, the revered economist Vilfredo
Pareto adjured the freshly anointed Premier Mussolini to be "merci-
less." The scientist Marconi, the composers Mascagni and Respighi, and
even the young Enrico Fermi all felt honored to be members of the
Fascist Academy.[1] To overlook Mussolini's ability to addle heads as
august and subtle as these is to undervalue his not implausible claim to
have been the most creative and consequential figure in mankind's
political development since 1920.[2]

OUR CENTURY HAS come up with too few improvements in the way
it manages to govern, but it has marvelously advanced, while coarsening, the techniques for controlling the governed; and Mussolini is to this

---

[1]For these examples of the susceptibility of intelligences so far above the norm, I have
needed to resort to Alastair Hamilton's *The Appeal of Fascism* (New York: Macmillan,
1971). They suggest Mussolini's powers for bemusement more forcibly than Smith cares
to concede and far more tellingly than the tributes of Shaw, Gandhi, Trotsky, and de
Gaulle, because what can tourists know?

In fairness to these high guardians of the Italian spirit, Giovanni Gentile was the
only one of them who did not, at least now and then, fall away from Mussolini; the
others were generally more apt to be put off by the vulgarity than by the brutality of
a regime whose reigning symbol once told his waiter that punching "is an exquisitely
fascist means of self-expression."

[2]The *bizarreries* of Anthony James Joes's *Mussolini* (New York: Franklin Watts, 1982)
conclude with this assessment, which may be an indication that the myopic sometimes
bump into truths that the clear-eyed refuse to see. Joes sees in Mussolini the inspiration
for the governments of a sizable segment of the General Assembly of the United
Nations, and, in an oddity extreme even for him, seems to regard the resemblance as
a compliment to his hero.

dreadful science what the Wright Brothers were to aviation and Colonel Tom Parker to rock and roll.

Any day's passage through Rockefeller Center suffices to convince us that Mussolini's aesthetic taste is our century's dominant one. He does not deserve to be saddled with all the blame; the style of public building has been so dominantly totalitarian for so long that it could well be argued that Borromini was the last purely antifascist architect. Mussolini clearly read the case as such, since, Mack Smith tells us, the Rome he envisioned as his monument would have razed "all the 'filthy picturesque' houses of 'the centuries of decadence' (which in his book included the baroque and the Counter-Reformation) so that the Colosseum, the Pantheon, the Capitol, and the Tomb of Augustus would stand alone in imperial majesty."

Figures or anyway figurines cast from his mold are all over the landscape. Qadhafi is, of course, almost a replica, but that was to be expected; the posturings of their overlords are dangerous contagions for colonial children; and Qadhafi's bearing probably owes as much to his mother's awe at some sight of Italo Balbo, Libya's last Italian governor general, as a Ghanaian justice's wig does to the Old Bailey. Still, when Mack Smith notes the fallen Mussolini's prediction that fascism would "still prove to have been the dominant ideology of the century" he is citing the one promise springing from the Duce's vainglory that was not a delusion.

We cannot truly appreciate the pervasive realization of this prophecy unless we remember that "fascism" is a word whose connotations can embrace both left and right. The sheaf and the axe served as emblems of the Sicilian proletarian and peasant strikes thirteen years before Mussolini adopted them. They are simply recalls to past national glory, in this instance the Roman Republic; and their name has no more tangible meaning than OVRA, the title Mussolini selected for his secret police on the solid presumption that this parade of initials which stood for nothing whatsoever had just the ring needed to sound the proper note of omniscience and threat.

.   .   .

MACK SMITH HAS no trouble convincing us that, beyond the *bastone*, the phantasm of the all-seeing leader, and a windy bellicosity, there was no such thing as a fascist philosophy. By the standard of its own professions we cannot even describe it as an operative system. The "corporate state" was never more than an expensive myth; it served only as a feeding ground of otherwise unemployable fascists and, says Mack Smith, "its functions were not clear except that it cost a lot of money and sometimes acted to clog the wheels of industry." In 1940, when Mussolini succeeded in hurling Italy into the war he conceived as its prime purpose for existence, its infantrymen were worse equipped, worse led, and smaller in numbers than the armies that took the field in 1915.

But then we do Mussolini's genius an injustice if we subject what were only slogans to the tests applicable to hypotheses; as political scientist, he never extended his teaching range beyond the means for taking and holding power. "I put my finger on the pulse of the masses," he once wrote, "and suddenly discovered . . . that a public opinion was waiting for me, and I just had to make it recognize me through my newspaper." It is useless to judge a thinker by the ideas he grasps from the vagrant air; Mussolini's was one of those talents that prove themselves not by the quality of the catch but by the instinct that dares to grasp.

That supreme Italian bourgeois, Pietro Nenni, used to retail an anecdote that he likely invented—because Mack Smith is both the most tireless and the most scrupulous of scholars, which means that he could not have missed and would not have omitted it if it deserved belief.

Nenni and Mussolini had been close socialist comrades in the Romagna until the First World War divided them; and Nenni was even said to have been Edda Ciano's godfather; and he might well have been if both he and her father had not been febrilely anticlerical and if, for that matter, Mussolini and his Donna Rachele had been married at the time. In any case the vestiges of ancient companionship remained assertive enough to induce Mussolini, when he got around to arresting Nenni, to consign him to the island of Ponza, the pleasantest of his holding pens. After his unfrocking in 1943, his successors transported

Mussolini to Ponza; and he arrived just when Nenni was preparing to depart as beneficiary of a general amnesty for antifascists.

As Nenni told the tale, he was on his way to embark for freedom when he met the beached Mussolini marching toward internment. Nenni was disinclined to social converse; and the overture fell to Mussolini.

"Ah, Pietro," Nenni used to say he said, "you go. I come. Who cares, so long as it serves socialism?"

So fascism will forever endure if only, as Huey Long acutely noticed, in the name of antifascism. Now and again, Mack Smith informs us, there "were moments when it was hoped that Stalin might be moving towards corporativism and 'state capitalism' and possibly might be becoming something akin to a fascist." In 1937, the fascist censors cleared for publication a study by R. Butoni, whose title was *Russia: Trionfo del Fascismo.*

Mussolini held, in Mack Smith's summary, that "the masses ... did not want discussion or debate; they preferred to be commanded, and he admitted that his attitude here was the same as Stalin's."

Contempt for the governed is, of course, among the fundaments of fascism's set of values; that much if no more of Mussolini's assessment was shared by that great refiner of systems for manipulating a free electorate, our own Richard Nixon. The first reference to a "silent majority" came, if not from Mussolini's own lips, at least from those of his incense bearers.[3]

IN HIS GUESS that he and Stalin might be approaching cousinhood if not twinhood, Mussolini was nearer the mark than the run of his contemporaries; but then he had the advantage of a common experience, since

---

[3]Contempt for the led deserves to be thought of as more a philosophical concept than a moral defect in those who hold it. Nixon lacked the fascist temperament, the essential test for authenticity in these matters; and it may have been our salvation that his kinship with Mussolini's outlook was only an intellectual and thus a feckless one. There is, to be sure, a further resemblance: Both collapsed in final crisis largely because each one's will had been eroded by a succession of escapes from emergencies that were usually the result of their own follies.

both were revolutionaries who had in quick time accomplished the journey from enthusiasm to imposture. As a general rule, any revolution calling itself socialist and revering a leader who seems to sleep in his uniform is an expression of the fascist spirit. Tito and Mussolini both commissioned themselves marshals, which is all we need to know to understand that Tito's workers' councils doubtless inhabited the same realms of the imagination that Mussolini's corporations did.

Castro is singular for having held absolute power for twenty years and avoided becoming a much worse man in the process. But however more conscious of Garibaldi as model and inspiration Castro may be, those pictures of him cutting sugarcane evoke the bare-chested Mussolini plunged into the battle for wheat. Communism and fascism are not theories of government, but ways to police.

And yet, club, spy, and detention camp aside, how does such awfulness not just hold its sway but even command a measure of admiration in the society it abuses? There had to be a side of Mussolini that Italy found appealing; and, if Mack Smith's distaste debars him from wondering what that might have been, his material offers rich ground for credible surmise.

Although Mack Smith disdains Italian Fascism's boast of direct descent from Mazzini and Garibaldi, that assertion is not unpersuasive once we set aside the lofty character of those progenitors of Mussolini's fancy. We are, after all, dealing with a country of nationalists with no reason for assurance that they lived anywhere that they could yet confidently identify as a nation. Even those of us who look at the statues in the Villa Borghese and rejoice to have found a land where Toscanini will always be Pope must sympathize with those Italians who felt that the Risorgimento had to be something of a cheat once it had been concluded with the ascension of a crude and upstart Piedmontese dynasty with little more entitlement to veneration than dukes of Tuscany or even kings of the Two Sicilies. And, since they knew themselves swindled, Italians understandably gave way to the illusion that merely to swell the country meant to overcome the multitude of doubts about its reality. In his decrepitude, Mack Smith reminds us, Mazzini cried out for "a patriotic war to secure Italy's 'natural frontiers' of language and race." Croce and Pirandello also thought that they did not yet have a nation and imagined that real estate would give them one; and so they cheered on colonial wars while far less refined citizens of other countries had sickened of them long before.

THE OTHER ITALIAN disease for which Mussolini arrived as an infection pretending to be a serum was the same itch to be modern that curses the Third World. That would explain his temporary affinity for the Futurists, who, in their discontent at being stranded in a society that in some sectors had but recently entered the age of steam, sought to leap, without intervening pauses, directly into the age of the diesel.[4]

Mussolini the plebeian could not have become Mussolini the god if he had not made his assault upon an Italy equally dosed with reverence for *La Patria* and contempt for the country. For the ravages of this contradiction, we need only look at Giovanni Giolitti. He had been five times premier of Italy and, at eighty-two, did not abandon hopes of a return until Mussolini had been in power for a year. By then the parliamentary system was in process of destruction and Giolitti knew that Mussolini had ordered his telephone tapped. And this old liberal's only comment was that in fascism the Italians at last got the government they deserved.

Hypochondria was the prescribed response for every wise man who

---

[4]Futurism, in its revolt against a culture that had lain but half awake through Impressionism and Postimpressionism, could bring itself up to date only by jumping, like Soviet Constructivism, all the way to Cubism, whose poor country relative each became. Still it is hard to avoid a deplorable affection for the Futurists. Of course Marinetti contemplated the countenance of Mussolini and there discovered: "Massive, rocklike head, but the ultradynamic eyes dart with the speed of automobiles racing on the Lombard plains." His nonsense had its elements of divinity all the same: He had been a soldier in the First World War and there had learned everything he needed to know about the consequences for anyone who obeys the commands of an Italian officer of field grade. Nonetheless, at sixty-one, he volunteered for what could only be the inescapable doom of service on the Russian front in the winter of 1942. Mussolini quite naturally abandoned Futurism once he consolidated his power; revolutions are a passage from the fraternity of the avant-garde to the narcissism of the monumental.

examined the health of the state, and its pervasive symptom was an outsized alarm whenever there was the feeblest stirring from below. Such fears were fascism's capital. Its chaos was barely noticed because it was mistaken for the order that had saved and still protected Italy from Bolshevik chaos. Mack Smith has little trouble disposing of that misconception; and no one moderately familiar with postwar Italian communism will be surprised that it was easy work for him.

Italy's greatest anarchist could never have been as admired as he became if he had not been a Malatesta da Rimini. The communists themselves are so acutely aware of Italy's class wall that their leadership succession seems almost a reflection of continual struggle for social acceptability. Their general secretaries have all come from Sardinia: first Gramsci, like Machiavelli, the son of a small bourgeois impoverished because accused of embezzlement; then Togliatti, the lawyer scion of a more secure middle-class family; and now Berlinguer, a count.[5]

Mussolini must then be assigned his place among the dominant majority of statesmen who get their chance not because they fit the needs of their time but because they are particularly suitable repositories of its misapprehensions.

II

IF MACK SMITH'S portrait seems in some vague way finally unsatisfactory, we can only blame, even while admiring, the defect of a standard for human virtue that inhibits intimate engagement with a character so

---

[5]There is a story that when he had to imprison the anarchist Malatesta, Mussolini hastened to the cell with the promise that he would do his utmost to make it certain "that Your Highness will be comfortable." I remember only one audience with Togliatti; its none too comfortable progress was interrupted by the introduction of a Sicilian fisherman who had earned the honor by winning a Party competition in soliciting subscriptions for the Palermo version of *Paese Sera*, its daily newspaper. Togliatti addressed his visitor as *"compagno"* and the response was invariably *"Dottore Togliatti."*

rascally. Not many personages enter history unless their contemporaries to some degree suspend disbelief; and no chronicle can be as rich as it ought to be without a pinch of that credulity. Whenever a biographer sets out to deal with a protagonist who disgusts him, he is off on a heroic but unpromising adventure. We will be continually too conscious of the ten-foot pole.

But if Mack Smith's scorn debars him from a vivid enough evocation of Mussolini, it is most serviceable in explaining his peculiar force. To deny him pretty much every other talent is to isolate and thus highlight his singular genius, which was that "he was probably the best popular journalist of the day."

HE FOUND HIS way after trying and failing on several others. He began as a teacher; and the end of each school year was the signal for him to begin scouring for a classroom in some other town because his appointment had not been renewed. The causes of offense were invariably the same: His private life was raffish and his teaching style was tyrannical. In due course, his students would have their vengeance; he had first started threateningly gazing upon his Donna Rachele when she was his seven-year-old pupil; and she repaid him by bullying him throughout the last twenty-five years of their marriage.

He cast off the discouragements of these rude academies for the vocation of full-time socialist functionary; and, given his subsequent history, we are less surprised to be told that he was languid in matters of organization than we are to learn that he was in no way charismatic as a street agitator. He was like Grant in Galena when he got his liberating chance as a subeditor of *Popolo*, a forum for Italian irredentist discontents in the still-Austrian provinces of Trentino.

"Though it lasted only a month," Mack Smith says, "his experience of working on a daily paper was excellent training. He remembered how it taught him many tricks of the trade, including how to invent a news story and how to write a whole article about some nonevent without arousing disbelief. Few other lessons of his life were to be more useful."

He had at a stroke happened upon the debased principles of a certain kind of journalism that served as his philosophy of government for the rest of his career:

> He had discovered that readers liked extreme views and rarely bothered much about inconsistency. If he appeared successively . . . as socialist and then conservative, as monarchist and then republican, this was less out of muddle-headedness than out of a search for striking headlines and a wish to become all things to all men.

> The technique that he recommended was to be always "electric" and "explosive." He took pride in being able to write on either side of any subject and in adopting a simple but always forceful line; there was no point in rehearsing all the arguments on an issue, because the object was to sweep readers off their feet, not to provide them with the material for a continuing debate.

> One of the valuable lessons he had learnt as a journalist was that the public was easily deceived and an editor could change his views without most readers worrying or even noticing.

I should suppose that only those of us who have reveled in the guilty pleasure of employment on an especially outrageous newspaper can know the full mixture of amusement and horror at the thought of a government controlled by a mentality like its publisher's. The catechismic style of Stalin's speeches reminds us of what can happen when a former theological student is let loose upon those he considers the enemies of light and truth; and Mussolini's administrative practices underline the results of giving his head to a truly inspired, which is to say lunatic, editor.

By 1930, Mack Smith reports, half Italy's cabinet ministers and half the members of the Grand Council of Fascism were journalists.

> Twenty other newspapermen had become senior diplomats and sixty-eight were in parliament. Mussolini commented that they were among the best in each field of public life. In the early years, he once told an assembly of newsmen that they perhaps carried a

marshal's baton in their knapsack, and the reference was apt because they were the nearest equivalent to Napoleon's marshals.

In democratic societies journalism is often a branch of government; but in Mussolini's, government was a branch of journalism. Mack Smith seems rather to skimp the connection between Fascism's catastrophe and this curious reversal of the normal arrangements of nature and reason. He has the excuse of having done that office most handsomely in *Mussolini's Roman Empire*. We can fully respect the honor of any chef who refuses to reheat an old meal's leftovers for mixture in another one; but his latest dish might well be more nourishing if he had.

In *Mussolini's Roman Empire*, Mack Smith defined the Fascist objective as in essence "to create belief and enthusiasm rather than to make people actually do anything." Such, of course, is the appointed function of newspapers in wartime.

> At the same time as he needed the reputation of being a great war leader and organiser of victory, [Mussolini] also by instinct saw the usefulness of creating the impression that he could win easily and without great disturbance to the ordinary life of the nation. . . . Fascism continued to think it a matter for boasting that so little was demanded from Italians and that there was no general mobilisation. To put this differently, resources were considered to be less usefully spent in war production than in fuelling the great propaganda industry that was trying to convince ordinary citizens that all was well. The monthly supplement of Mussolini's personal paper, the *Popolo d'Italia* weighed over [three pounds] in May 1940, and its issue of November 1942 . . . was still over [two pounds] despite all the talk about paper shortages.
>
> [His] was an essentially unserious world, where prestige, propaganda, and public statements were all that counted; and it is hard to avoid the conclusion that this was the central message and the real soft core at the heart of Italian fascism.[6]

[6]Mack Smith, Denis, *Mussolini's Roman Empire* (New York: Longman, 1976), pp. 239, 247, 252.

III

GRAHAM GREENE ONCE remarked that Haiti is a tragedy with banana peels. The same incongruity of the fatal and the farcical runs all through Italian Fascism's history. Dreadful as he was, there is a certain element of the engaging in any *Übermensch* who threw away his collection of bowler hats after noticing "that in American comedy films (for which he had a passion . . .) they were no longer worn except by his favourite stars, Laurel and Hardy."

The uses of permitting oneself an occasional withering smile are richly demonstrated by *Mussolini Unleashed*. MacGregor Knox's researches are hardly less formidable than Smith's and his narrative posture has the greater lissomeness for being able now and then to unbend and amuse us. *Mussolini Unleashed* is limited to the year and a half between September 1939, when the Second World War began, and March 1941, when the succession of his disasters in Greece and North Africa had reduced Mussolini's destiny to helpless dependence upon Hitler's. The descent from clouds of grandeur to the hard rock of surrender needed only the ten months after June 1940, when Italy entered the war. That short span occupies most of Knox's compass, and quite suffices to illuminate the true character of a concept of statehood whose fair test and final proof could, Mussolini often said, come only in battle.

Knox's chronicle of these months makes plain how useless it is to study Italian Fascism as though it ever possessed the elements that any scheme of social management must have before we can call it a system. Its founder was not an architect but an avatar. "A hearty manner in dealing with his generals," Knox says, "masked a secret inferiority complex that inhibited him from much questioning of their technical advice."

This unaccustomed diffidence becomes stranger still when we remember that here was an ex-corporal whose chores had ended after he was wounded by a grenade thrower that blew up during a training exercise. That should have been enough to teach him that, whether its business were planning, procurement, or combat management, Italy's command staff was barely second to any declared enemy's as menace to the limbs of its soldiers.

But then Mussolini's genius was the journalist's, and it was no less deep for a narrowness walled against the lessons of anyone's intimate experience, even his own. He had begun with the quite bad enough experience of thinking like an editorial writer and he ended with the worse one of thinking like a publisher. Whenever Knox deals out one of those cocksure banalities Mussolini dropped like beer cans on his road to ruin, the mind automatically clicks back, "Up to a point, Lord Copper." Henry Luce probably talked like that; Beaverbrook certainly did. Triumph at making hordes of people swallow nonsense is reserved for men who have voraciously swallowed it themselves.

It is the identifying mark of minds like these that their self-assurance and timidities are quite misplaced. The Mussolini who instructed philosophers, attuned musicians, and corrected novelists was the minister of defense who dared not argue with generals. He was so pretentious as to announce himself the master of all the arts that are mysteries, and at the same time too abject to contradict career soldiers whose craft happens to be one so free of mystery that it can only botch matters when it overlooks some rule of common sense.

THE WORLD WOULD indeed be a happier place if we could speak of unrequited gullibility as often as we must of unrequited love. His generals gulled Mussolini everywhere this side of catastrophe, and he gulled them into that.

The true progenitor of his style as leader may have been Napoleon III, who executed a not unsimilar ascent from *carbonero* to emperor. He was still Louis Bonaparte when Tocqueville described him as one of those men who mistake their good luck for genius; and that happens to be an enormous, although transient, asset, because it is infectious. Luck is a kind of talent; when anyone comes to power cutting as mangy a figure as Hitler's or as ridiculous a one as Mussolini's, his bearing is all the more apt to overcome the observer because it looks so inappropriate: He could not have come to this great stage if the gods had not appointed him.

Thus, in Knox's words, Victor Emmanuel III "harbored an almost pathetic belief in Mussolini's luck (*'lo stellone'*) that had held through so many difficult moments since 1922." Even Pietro Badoglio, chief of general staff—the most prudent because most timid of Italian commanders—could not help surrendering his cautions to his faith in Mussolini's star. When he announced the decision for war in May 1940, Badoglio soothed his alarmed subordinates "by saying that, even though preparations were abysmally defective, Mussolini could be relied upon to make the right decision at a moment when only a minimal effort was required for victory."[7]

EVERY NOW AND then, in the course of great events, the elements of tradition and innovation ally themselves and each one's weakness supplements the other and together they achieve the perfect debacle. Fascist Italy was such a fulfilled conjunction of professional soldiers who put all their trust in politics and a politician who put all his trust in war.

In its sedate way, Knox's treatment of Italy's high command affords an abundant ration of sport. There is General Ubaldo Soddu, undersecretary of war, who was accustomed to say, ". . . when you have a fine plate of pasta guaranteed for life, and a little music, you don't need anything more." The transmutation of the soldier's creed into this comic aria armed Soddu against every reversal in life. He was not just an artist of survival but its preceptor and so persuasive in that role that he first induced Victor Emmanuel III to yield to Mussolini his own constitutional prerogatives as commander in chief with the argument that the king's abstention from responsibility would leave his prestige intact if things went badly; and then he convinced Mussolini to admit Marshal Badoglio to a share of this new power with the argument that he could blame Badoglio if things went badly.

[7]Mack Smith, *Mussolini's Roman Empire*, p. 208.

An intriguer with such refinement of address generally earns the misfortune of getting his opportunity for glory; and Soddu rose to theater commander in the war with the Greeks and there restored his serenity amid bouts of panic with the collapse of this salient or that by composing soundtrack music for films.

There was General Pietro Maletti, "the old wolf of the desert," who was spearhead of Italy's only offensive against the British in Egypt, and, having forgotten to take along his Arab guides, contrived to get his brigade lost while it was still in Italian territory. There was the chief of staff of the "Wolves of Tuscany" who "accidentally sent back to Berat a truck containing the only available topographical maps," and thus assured the destruction of untrained and freshly landed troops assigned to relieve the pressure of the Greek advance with a counterattack across ground their officers had never seen.

MOST OF ALL there was Marshal Rodolfo Graziani, viceroy of Ethiopia, army chief of staff, and last and most lamentably director of the war in North Africa. Any opera that ends by casting its protagonist into the fires of hell is opera *seria* rather than *buffa;* still, Fascism's libretto is more Da Ponte than Boito. And, if Soddu is its Don Basilio, Graziani was its Bartolo. His gifts as buffoon were almost entirely verbal, since his nature was too immobile to execute the pratfalls that a really rounded clown brings to his performances.

Graziani was instead one of those rare masters of the absurd who get their effects from single-minded concentration on one device. He never spoke except to pronounce. A solemn ponderosity established his comedic character as those crossed eyes did Ben Turpin's; and Knox has only to disinter some utterance of his to raise the echo: *"Tutta Sevilla conosce Bartolo."*

When the general staffs convened for the last time before they went to war, he played the "rough soldier" and dismissed the trepidations of his colleagues with the blithe declaration, "When the cannon sounds everything will fall into place automatically." Then he was off to North Africa, where 37,000 British Commonwealth troops were all that stood between his 167,000-man force and the conquest of Cairo. No one else alive better knew how unfit the army was, since he had been the chief of staff primarily responsible for its decrepitude; and he trembled with every intimation that cannons might sound.

This indisposition for battle finally aroused Mussolini to insist on action; and Graziani could comply only after washing his hands in his diary: "It is against the most elementary logic [and] prudence. . . . For whatever evil may occur, I, before God and my soldiers, am not *responsible.*"

In this high martial spirit, Graziani essayed an uneasy advance to Sidi el Barrani, a negligible sandpit that the British abandoned with no more regret than it deserved. There he rested with the relief of having for a while slaked Mussolini's thirst for "the sudden striking deeds in every communique," for which, his police chief advised him, the Italian public was impatient. A month later Mussolini again disturbed Graziani's peace by summoning him to Rome and ordering that he forthwith proceed with the invasion of Egypt.

Graziani cunningly exuded a confidence in the enterprise he in no way felt, and said that it required only consultation with his staff to become absolute assurance. Having thus effected his escape back to Libya, he then informed Rome that the state of his command made it impractical to resume the offensive immediately. This demonstration of the agility that was easier for him in engagements with his commander in chief than in confrontations with the enemy won Graziani back his ease; and he was found languidly paltering with the plans he prayed he would never have to execute when the British assault broke upon him three months later.

This crisis found Mario Berti, Graziani's most important subordinate, in Rome visiting his mother and being treated for piles. In two days, his Tenth Army had been obliterated. Graziani's reaction was to turn the cannons of his rage on Rome:

> I consider it my duty, rather than sacrificing my useless person on the spot, to go to Tripoli [and] if I succeed in getting there, to keep flying on that citadel at least the banner of Italy. . . . Let this be said

as my last will and testament, and in order that everyone assume in the light of history the responsibility for what today is occurring here.

He then beset Mussolini himself with a telegram that was a litany of reproaches, the most heartfelt of them: "You did not give me the recognition due me upon my return from Ethiopia."

We cannot render entire justice to Mussolini's capacities as conductor of his nation's destiny until Mack Smith brings us to July 25, 1943, the morning after the Grand Council of Fascism had withdrawn its support and Mussolini arrived at the Palazzo Venezia with "an emergency plan to resolve the situation" by appointing Marshal Rodolfo Graziani as general chief of staff.

But, like so many others who have advanced themselves by tireless exercise of the hectoring tone, he was prone to being cowed by anyone else equipped to sound it. His daughter, the Countess Ciano, has indeed offered the surmise that:

> My father launched himself into political life so as to have an excuse to be absent from home a good deal of the time and thus be spared my mother's jealous scenes, to which he preferred the beatings of the police and his adversaries.[8]

IV

BUT IT WAS rather more critical to Mussolini's final fate that his conditioning as a journalist left him helplessly susceptible to the imbecilities of Giulio Douhet and everyone else who peddled the doctrine that war's objectives are achievable at a blow. When his armies were floundering in Greece, his remedy was to suggest that 500-plane

[8]Ciano, Edda Mussolini, *My Truth* (New York: Morrow, 1977), p. 50.

bomber raids against Athens and Salonika "[could] produce enemy political collapse." When his air chief of staff intruded upon this vision with practical objections, Mussolini replied, "You forget that I am conducting a lightning war like the Germans in Poland."

That is the authentic voice of the gallows bird. Even so we cannot quite dismiss him as the mere shoddy adventurer that is most of what he was to Denis Mack Smith. *Mussolini Unleashed* offers good cause to credit him with larger and even more horrid proportions; it is Knox's argument that beneath the charlatanry and beyond the lunges to the improvised, Mussolini had conceived for Italy a grand design for whose purposes these devices ought to be regarded not as aberrational but as essential. He had to have his war, Knox contends, because he knew no other avenue to the realization of his aspirations both for the Italians and himself. The risks did not really bother him, because he was too bedazzled by the promise that victory would bring fruits otherwise beyond his grasp: "Externally Italy would rule a vast empire; internally he would remake 'the Italians' into a cruel and domineering master race under his own unchallenged control."

This savage ideal was not entirely out of key with the spirit of his country's culture. Gramsci once took note of the "very harsh character" of the class struggle in Italy and commented that "cruelty and absence of sympathy are two characteristics peculiar to the Italian people."

As brutality of action identifies the despair of the deprived, brutality of thought identifies the despair of the comfortable. And yet this is a brutality of thought whose expression sounds more often than not as though it had been arrived at across the flat plane of the intellect rather than risen from the viscera. The iron will such people elevate somehow comes off as an abstraction; we feel ourselves in the unpleasant company of a mind whose logic has led it to decide that sloth and gluttony so pervade its surroundings that they can only be expelled by savage doses of official violence. And then we take pause and are cautioned by the recollection that when he was a civil servant Machiavelli was careful to avoid the extremes he leaped at as a philosopher.

We cannot, of course, deny that there were aspects of Mussolini's temperament more suited to the armed robber than to the statesman;

Arnaldo Mussolini once commented that deep down in his brother's character there was a deplorable streak of delinquency. He was all the same enough of an Italian intellectual frequently to succumb to the illusion that to have pronounced the word was to have done the deed.

If Italian Fascism failed to match the Nazis in ultimate criminal excess, we can be grateful for a saving grace of indiscipline in the Italian nature, which shows itself on the one hand capable of the brutality that originates in impulse and on the other unable to completely consummate the brutality prescribed by what has been a process of reason, however deplorable.

IN THEIR *Vichy France and the Jews,*[9] Michael R. Marrus and Robert O. Paxton provide a remarkable and surprising account of the resistance the French and Germans met from Mussolini's soldiers whenever they attempted measures against the Jews in the eight departments of France allotted to the Italian occupation. The Italian zone became so crowded a sanctuary that by 1943 its Jewish population had tripled. In one instance Italian troops forced Vichy to free five hundred Jews it had gathered for deportation to Germany. By 1943, Nice had "become a Jewish political and cultural center." This tolerance and indeed benevolence from representatives of a regime officially committed to anti-Semitism cannot be assigned to the bribable disposition of some of them. The Germans finally persuaded Mussolini to dispatch a southern police chief to extirpate this infamy; but, far from removing these obstacles to the will Vichy shared with Berlin, this Fascist official reinforced them and went so far as to inflict upon Vichy the humiliation of a reproving contrast between the Italian search for "a human solution" with the severities of the French and Germans.

Italians could accept Mussolini's image of "a cruel and domineering master race" as a theoretical conception of how great nations conduct their affairs; but some disabling kindness of nature seems all too often

[9]Marrus, Michael R., and Robert O. Paxton, *Vichy France and the Jews* (New York: Basic Books, 1981).

to have asserted itself and reduced to inanition one or another effort to translate declared policy into reality.

MUSSOLINI LOOKED OUT at the world and it looked back at him as though he were an absolute ruler; but he was galled by the limitations of his writ. He had always to accommodate to powers smaller than but still independent of his—the Vatican, the king, the industrialists, and even the armed services. All of them—even the Vatican, with its Italianate Sacred College—shared his dream of a great empire; but since they were far from adventurous, they quaked at any risks its accomplishment required.

He labored then under the necessity of circumspection in leading them to the slaughter. His generals and admirals were more inclined to admire the cunning of the jackal than to emulate the recklessness of the lion; and their faith in him was usefully strengthened when they learned that, after Germany, France, and Great Britain had been at war for six months, he had told the Grand Council of Fascism that his fondest hope was that the "lions tear each other to pieces until they leave their tails on the ground—and we, possibly, can go and scoop them up."

Such a précis of their own military philosophy was all the insurance they needed before following wherever he beckoned. The king could have stopped him; the generals could at least have slowed him down; but his command triumphed over them with the skill that made them think that his was a mind running on the same track as theirs. He could not have wrecked them if he had not so adroitly bemused them with the prospect of the safest of voyages.

But then the first rule for successfully telling a lie is to tell it to oneself first; and Mussolini may have half believed that he was the cautious pilot of a policy that guaranteed every gain without the smallest pain. Yet this view of himself as some Cavour was as abstract as the vision of themselves as cruel and domineering which so polluted the waters where the Italian intellectuals swam as to infect even Pareto and Pirandello.

For Mussolini did not want ease and safety; he wanted a war of blood, iron, and sacrifice from which the Italians would emerge hardened to granite and accountable to no master except himself. He got it all, blood, iron, and incredible sacrifice; and when he was done, he had not hardened the Italians but so softened them that, say about him what you will, he can still be thanked for the comfort of the knowledge that it will be a long while before they again take up the duty of affirming themselves a great nation. It is distressing to notice that nobody seems to have devised a pleasanter method than his for teaching that valuable lesson.

I REGRET THAT I must decline any attempt to engage Professor Anthony John Joes's *Mussolini*. There is no way to deal with a scholar who persists in bowing down before a legend nearly two generations after the events that exposed it as a myth. This is work fit for an intelligence like John Hinckley's while, fortunately, being too bland to inflame his fantasies further. Professor Joes teaches at St. Joseph's University of Philadelphia, an institution whose basketball teams have given me so much pleasure that I would rather cherish what goes on in its gymnasium than think about what seems to be going on in one of its classrooms.

The New York Review of Books, October 7, 1982

The Roosevelt Revolution

J OSEPH ALSOP'S *FDR* is one of those conjunctions of its author's charms with his subject's that are so close to perfect that they nearly numb the critical faculties. Even so, when we reluctantly take our leave of its delights, the old question still teases: How far did these worlds we miss for so many good reasons go to bring us to the world that so afflicts us now?

Henry Adams complained that President Jefferson governed his White House dinners by the protocol of "pell-mell" and Alsop's memories of Franklin D. Roosevelt's table sound very much in that key—a company "haphazardly mixed—old friends, high officials, the odd distinguished foreigner, members of the family, often one or two of the waifs and strays Eleanor Roosevelt had a habit of picking up here and there on her trips."

One of those waifs and strays was Joseph Lash, then young and radical, and subsequently a demonstration in proof of Mrs. Roosevelt's shrewd eye for the better picks in that lot. When they met, Lash was executive secretary of the American Student Union and he and she shared a high faith in the Popular Front. Then Lash jibbed at the Nazi-Soviet Pact and the communists drove him from office and left him alone except for his great patron. Mrs. Roosevelt was never one to run out on her mistakes and she continued to lend her benevolence to counterfeits of purposeful youth like the post–1939 Student Union and the American Youth Congress even after their managers had forfeited every claim to dignity by shifting from vociferous antifascism to fever-ish pacifism when Joseph Stalin announced his treaty of nonaggression with Hitler's Germany.

Even after most of its fronts had deserted her Popular Front, Mrs. Roosevelt continued to manifest the "patient Griseldaism" which Alsop recalls as among the nobler of her qualities and which she herself seems to have deplored as her most demeaning. The Youth Congress had become a thorough nuisance by February of 1940 when it assem-bled in Washington for a national convention monopolized by the slogan "The Yanks Are Not Coming." In the face of these affronts, Mrs. Roosevelt persuaded her husband to meet and reason with the Youth Congress's leaders in the basement of the White House. His guests turned their opportunity into an occasion for defiance and contumely that reached its peak in a hectoring lecture by Gilbert Green, executive secretary of the Young Communist League. "And FDR just sat there," Lash remembers, "with his cigarette holder pointing to the ceiling and the harsher the speeches got, the more his smile gleamed."

MOST OF WHAT is unforgettable about Roosevelt abides in the wither-ing good humor of his smile. It was read as friendly by those who loved him and contemptuous by those who hated him; and yet neither impulse was the prime source of its majesty. He beamed from those great heights that lie beyond the taking of offense, because the of-fender, struggle though he may, can never rise to being worth the bother.

Those of us who were born to circumstances less assured tend to think of, indeed revere, this demeanor as the aristocratic style. That is an image which embarrasses Alsop. He is writing, after all, as a kinsman, and some of his most beguiling recollections of their friendship come from the hours when Alsop dined at the White House less because of his own distinction than because his grandmother had been close to Roosevelt's mother.

He is especially engaging for his anxiety not to be caught taking on airs, and cites with approval Mrs. Archer's observation in *The Age of*

Innocence: "Don't tell me . . . all this modern newspaper rubbish about a New York aristocracy. . . . Our grandfathers and great-grandfathers were just respectable English or Dutch merchants. . . ." This is one of those statements whose accuracy is only formal. Alsop's evocation of Roosevelt would not be nearly so touching if the pair of them had not had in common a governance by assumptions that if we cannot call them aristocratic leave us bereft of any other useful adjective. There were differences of temperament to be sure: Roosevelt maintained his cheerful disposition by sunny indifference to the intellectual ferment of his time, while Alsop has now and then darkened his by too fierce contention with its nonsense.

But all doubt that the true aristocrat defines himself by his arrival at being the entire democrat has been resolved for anyone who has had the luck to observe the egalitarian fraternity with which Joseph Alsop reminds the waiter that their shared duty to the standards they are sworn to preserve requires that the hollandaise sauce be carried back and thrust under the cook's nose. Our Dukes of Orléans are Philippes Egalité or they are not dukes at all. And yet Roosevelt's elegance was an element that so pervaded his accomplishments that our appreciation of them is particularly served by a chronicler as homesick as Alsop for a time when America was ruled by gentlemen and ladies.

Roosevelt must have been the first president since Lincoln who awoke the capacity of society's castoffs to look above them and find someone to love. All the same, the tastes of and a taste for his own secure caste survived every expansion of his social horizons; and the New Deal was disproportionately framed with the help of carpenters drawn from the class that came most to dislike him.

MY OWN EXPOSURE to the relics of the Roosevelt cabinet was limited to a scant acquaintance with Frances Perkins, his secretary of labor; and her conversation was marked by a habit of judging the actors on the stage of her memory by the presence or absence of good manners. The deal of good she had done for the workingman had in no way improved her familiarity with his customs and habits. She looked at the tumults of her time through eyes conditioned by a life so sheltered from the harsher winds that, when she expressed regret that the New Deal had done so little for the Negro, she blamed that oversight on a cultural deprivation general in her milieu. "After all," she pointed out, "we had always had white servants."

She remembered Dave Beck with a wry affection because, when he was rising in the Teamsters union, he was noticeable for his alacrity when the time came to carry her briefcase. It was Mrs. Perkins who first explained to me that John L. Lewis made his way in the early councils of an administration whose grand antagonist he was to be because his bearing was so lordly. "You know, of course," she reminded me, "that Mr. Lewis's wife was an FFV"—an expression so obsolete in Virginia even then as to suggest the insulation of the old friends in the grand army that Roosevelt brought down to the Potomac. The claims of class exacted their authority: what the Lower East Side's Belle Moscowitz had been to Al Smith the Upper East Side's Henry Morgenthau would be to Franklin Roosevelt.

The Second World War at once stimulated a national urge to unity and the president's natural solidarity with the sort of persons who had, until then, misconceived him as a renegade. He reached out to the fortresses of commerce and the temples of enlightened Republicanism for recruits like Henry L. Stimson, Colonel Frank Knox, and Edward Stettinius.

Harry S. Truman, for all his plebeian pretensions, was oddly elitist in matters of state, and, except for a regrettable fling with the egregious Louis A. Johnson as secretary of defense, continued to trust the extension of the national destiny to servitors of genteel origin, established dignity, and essential indifference to party. Starting with Roosevelt, and speeding up under Truman and carrying on through Kennedy, government by the Democrats, in larger affairs at least, became government by what William F. Buckley has nicely called PLUs, or People Like Us.

THE ROOSEVELT REVOLUTION ended, as such things usually do, with the triumph of the conquered. The flaws inevitable in the estate he left behind give us all the more reason to be grateful that Alsop has used his budgetary resources to spend prodigally on Roosevelt's presence and to skimp on the works. Six pages are enough to dispose of the economic measures of the first New Deal and seven are required to trace the pains and passions of the young and out-of-office Roosevelt's too perilously requited love for Lucy Mercer. It is a skewing richly rewarded. For Roosevelt's attachment to Lucy Mercer was of that special order we must assign to threats to a great destiny that can only be escaped through disappointment. These were persons even grander on the domestic stage than they would end up being on the cosmic one.

Mrs. Roosevelt discovered Lucy Mercer's letters to her husband and told him that their marriage could continue only if he broke off the affair, and that, if he refused, "she would give him his freedom." Roosevelt chose Miss Mercer. They told his mother, the stern tower of a generation infinitely more tolerant of adultery than divorce. The senior Mrs. Roosevelt coldly announced that she would disinherit her son if he persisted in his resolve. Roosevelt's fixed purpose overbore this prospect of ruin; he would have Miss Mercer as his wife if she would have him as her husband. But she would not; her soul was saved and his star preserved on its course by a simple Catholic certainty that to marry a divorced man was to burn.

"The really striking aspect of this moving and sad story," Alsop observes, "is the behavior of the three principals when the climax came. Franklin Roosevelt was ready to sacrifice both fortune and career to love. Eleanor Roosevelt did not choose to keep her husband against his will. Lucy Mercer was guided by deep religious faith and strong principles. All met this crisis in their lives, in fact, in the grandest style—to a degree that one can only admire nowadays, although their vision of the grand style is likely to bewilder all too many persons in the 1980s."

Franklin and Eleanor Roosevelt and Lucy Mercer had all acted as the rules dictate for each lady's and each gentleman's condition of circumstance; but Franklin and Eleanor Roosevelt went on to engrave their distinction in that small company by being forever disinclined to be quick to reproach those who didn't. As a politician Roosevelt could now and then be light-minded about the gold standard; but as a man he was inalterably serious about personal standards.

It seems odd that their chance should have come to a pair who were so close to obsolescence even sixty years ago. That chance was owed to the Depression, which did their country the signal service of transiently diminishing its veneration for the newly rich. By 1933 every climber was pretty much tumbling in the heap with the poor souls he had climbed over; and the old, slightly shabby, aristocratic elegance had its time of authority once more.

THAT ROOSEVELT WAS the democrat that great gentlemen always are in no way abated his grandeur, and, in the photographs Alsop distributes through his text, he looks like a swan most affably touring a duck yard. This majesty had its notes of condescension to be sure; and Alsop has included one photograph of the new president on inaugural parade in a silk hat, his hands clasped overhead, eyes as goggly as a monster's, a smile that is near to a predator's ecstasy—a mixture of the regal and the ridiculous to fit our imagination of Ubu Roi. All the other portraits explain why Roosevelt was loved; but here is one that powerfully suggests why he was hated; and it does great credit to Alsop's sense of justice that he declined to pass over it.

The manner may have done as much to make him the Depression's particular hero as his measures did. The exuberance that was his nature's only excess might in time have led people to think him careless and inconsiderate if it had not been redeemed by the lofty distinction that exactly suited the taste of the prostrate country whose command he had assumed.

In bad times men cherish the elegant and in good ones they exalt the raffish. The symbol of the busted thirties was Fred Astaire, and the Rolling Stones were the archetypes for the spoiled sixties. But elegance becomes an affront without the companionship of compassion: It is the combination that adds up to true majesty.

Roosevelt was lucky for a time whose techniques were primitive by the standards of our own. Radio was his only instrument for universal communication; and radio brought his voice from the remote sphere where only the high gods seem to reside. By now television has made domestic intimates of our presidents; and, starting with the clumsy self-importance of Lyndon Johnson, passing into the insinuating ungainliness of Richard Nixon, and ending with the frozen diffidence of Jimmy Carter, they have all ruined themselves as guests in our living rooms.

Roosevelt had the advantage of distance; and that is very likely why the New Deal's spirit never arrived at proper definition until 1947 when Tennessee Williams had Blanche DuBois say that she had always depended on the kindness of strangers. It was at once her *envoi* and the epitaph for Franklin D. Roosevelt's America. He was the kindly stranger, and that kindliness brought our last necessarily remote president closer to us than any successor has been since. And yet would our nostalgia be as aching as Alsop makes it if to be a great presence had by itself been enough to be a resistless force for permanent change?

"A GREAT PRESIDENT," Alsop affirms, "is above all a great teacher of his people; and all of us still repeat, albeit unknowingly, the lessons we have learned from each of our great Presidents from George Washington onwards."

Washington, Jefferson, Lincoln, and Franklin Roosevelt bear names that unquestionably belong on any list of great Americans who were also presidents. Each was, in his way, a considerable instructor; but only Lincoln and Roosevelt can, with entire persuasiveness, be credited with having done most of their teaching when they were presidents. Washington offered his most useful lessons as a warrior; and Jefferson's two terms had aspects sufficiently un-Jeffersonian to make him a richer source of inspiration out of office than he managed to be in it.

Even the cases of Lincoln and Roosevelt remind us that, when we identify great presidents as great teachers, we had best resign ourselves to the recognition that, even when great men are not necessarily the bad ones Acton thought them, they almost always do better service to their own times than future ones allow their ghosts. They tell the student body more than it cares to absorb. And so Lincoln saved the union and preserved it as an estate for no heirs more appetizing than the proprietors of the Gilded Age.

Alsop's assessment of the America Roosevelt left us is endearingly exalted:

> The essence of his achievement, at least that part of his achievement which gave the whole true grandeur, derived in differing degrees and in hardly perceptible ways from the combined impact of all his domestic reforms. On a very wide front and in the truest possible sense, Franklin Delano Roosevelt included the excluded.

This affirmation cannot be denied its elements of historical fact even by those of us who might find its cadences a trifle overstimulated by our national impulse for always going a yard or so too far. Roosevelt left his country an immeasurably more comfortable dwelling place than he found it. A great part of that comfort was owing to his sealing upon the public consciousness the sense that men were indeed equal; and, through all the subsequent vicissitudes of politics, a want of social concern has never since been quite respectable in a public officer. Whatever else he might do, President Reagan could never speak in the icy tones of Calvin Coolidge or the numbed ones of Herbert Hoover.

The hatred Roosevelt inspired spewed forth streams of *ancien régime* ravings to be sure; but had it not been for his example, we could hardly look back, with almost as much admiration as amusement, at those two remarkable resources for the ironist—General Douglas MacArthur, pausing occasionally to revile the liberal Democrats during his employment at reconstructing Japan on the New Deal model, and Senator Robert A. Taft, that most intellectually vigilant captain of the resistance, making himself author and champion of the federal programs for aid to education and public housing that were just about all the Truman years had to show in the way of social advance.

Alsop remembers the path to the 1932 Democratic convention as a journey both sinuous and hazardous and is heartily grateful that Roosevelt arrived at its prize, because, if he had faltered and failed, "the country would then have had to choose between another four years of Herbert Hoover or a Democratic candidate . . . wedded to the ways of the American past."

We are used to assigning MacArthur and Taft to Alsop's category of "past thinkers" and yet, even as both scorned Roosevelt's baton, each was to some degree forced to move to his measure. But then Roosevelt was and remains so large a figure that to have lived through and survived him was an experience that compelled even his contemners to look back and see this enormous bulk standing between them and all prior history, and, in dislike almost as much as in affection, bend their heads in its shadow. A national preoccupation with looking backward at Roosevelt lasted a full decade after his death and is the most plausible explanation for the long disablement of his natural political heirs. It became their delusion that he had not merely begun but had completed the great change. When his ghost achieved the last of his five electoral triumphs over Herbert Hoover, they felt sure that their reign was permanent and had established the perfect balance of economic progress and social justice. There was nothing left to be built; and even after General Eisenhower upset the complacency of their assumption of permanent office, this chastening in the particular did not deplete their self-satisfaction in the general.

For it would not be the least lasting of Roosevelt's accomplishments that he had overborne the liberal capacity for the kinds of questions that go to the fundament. He took command of a society clamorous with quarrel about the basic equities of its economy; and when he died, he had left social inquiry such a wasteland behind him that ten years went by before a Commerce Department economist grew curious about the distribution of income and was surprised to discover that its inequality had persisted almost unchanged from Hoover, through Roosevelt and Truman, and after Eisenhower and into Kennedy.[1]

Only then when he had long since blazed and burned out in our heavens could it be suspected that Roosevelt's had not been a revolu-

---

[1]See Herman P. Miller, *Income of the American People* (New York: Wiley, 1955) and *Rich Man, Poor Man* (New York: Crowell, 1964, revised edition, 1971).

tion but a restoration; in lifting the nation from the pit, he had raised the parvenu class higher than it had ever been and yielded to the muckers the sword that would bring the gentlemen low.

His modest elevation of the lives of the millions may be less to the point in real history than the opening he gave to careers of no very tasteful sort; here we are at his centennial and when we cast about for a living monument, we can only settle on John Connally, the last New Dealer, bred in the bone and scheming still in the flesh.

IT DOES NOT matter. Alsop cannot be entirely correct; but he is right all the same. He is himself a man of the lost cause and so was Roosevelt in the end. We ought to think of his life as belonging, like Jeb Stuart's and Prince Rupert's, among those who threw away the scabbard and, smiling still, lost their wars to larger battalions of men more cautious and calculating. Not as relevant to history as we would like to think perhaps but splendidly eternal for romance.

Somehow though, cruel as it is to think of an America deprived of Eleanor Roosevelt, there is a fugitive fantasy that together he and Lucy Mercer had sacrificed her immortal soul at his own high destiny. There these two will endure in the imagination, growing old together, say near Newburgh, he languidly farming and dimly drawing wills and litigating country quarrels and she stealing now and then into the dreary little church to grieve a while for the spiritual loss that had bought their happiness. The Depression is hard on him; but, when he dies, he has managed to recoup by selling his remaining acres for a postwar housing development. His obituary is exactly the size the *Times* metes out for former assistant secretaries of the navy who had been nominated for vice president of the United States in a bad year for their party.

She lives a long while afterward, is restored to the Church, and works in the library and always thinks of him tenderly. They would, we may be certain, have brought it all off far better than the Windsors, and hardly anyone would have known they had.

The New York Review of Books, April 15, 1982

The Trouble with Harry
(and Henry)

"I put on some Red Russian army song records for Mrs. Roosevelt and also some Russian rural songs. She seemed to like both. Also I put on several Spanish records. Mrs. Roosevelt put in most of her time knitting a sweater, which was nearly completed and which was very well done. Apparently she has rather unusual facility as a knitter."
—*THE DIARY OF HENRY A. WALLACE*, November 20, 1943

"The night Stalin was host I had some very nice conversations with him. I liked him. I didn't like what he did, of course, but I liked him. . . . He was just like me about Chopin. He liked Chopin. Churchill didn't."
—*HARRY S TRUMAN TO MERLE MILLER*

THE GHOST OF Franklin Roosevelt rises unexpectedly when we consider Henry Wallace and Harry Truman. For how can we think about these two without Roosevelt's shadow upon them? Their place in history was appointed by his will, the first discarded, the second raised up and now with the rays of apotheosis around him. Great historical presences are continually intrusive; we read about these two creatures of Roosevelt's will and we wonder why he disposed of Vice President Wallace and elevated Vice President Truman, and thus, having commanded his own twelve years, set with his dead hand the course of the next eight.

He could not, one suspects, have acted in this situation without making a fundamental choice. Roosevelt seems to have presided over two national tendencies, irreconcilable except under his scepter, the one swampy, the other stony. The commercial triumph of Merle Miller's version of his conversations with former President Truman is evidence of the continual appeal of the stony to our imaginations; and yet John Morton Blum's selections from former Vice President Wallace's diaries entitled *The Price of Vision* might make some of us miss the swampy rather more.

THE SWAMPY MIND suffers, of course, for seeing a great deal that is not happening, but its very capacity for absorption lets it take in a great deal that is happening. The stony mind, being conditioned for rejection, at once repels fantasies of the vaguer sort and facts of less immediately apparent force. Wallace had a confused consciousness and Truman a decisive one; one nature was spongy, the other granitic. Reading the thoughts of each, you come to think of them as representative of the halves—the one called idealistic, the other called practical—that have contended if not for the soul at least for the franchise of historic American progressivism for decades.

Neither Wallace nor Truman was an entirely satisfactory representative of the best of either; still they are useful exemplars of the contrast. Their difference is nicely demonstrated by the visions the Soviet Union inspired in the mind of each.

For Wallace, to think of Russia was to hear the folk at their singing. Before he went there, he could quote with approval the view of the Mexican ambassador to Moscow that "people do here every day what people in the United States only talk about on Sunday"; and, in Siberia, an Eden which must force a considerable draft on the most abounding utopian imagination, he drew back from a gentle theological dispute with his Soviet guide with the ecumenical blessing that "I am willing to grant that your religion is doing good."

MR. TRUMAN'S MIND had no room in it for such collective abstractions, being so focused on the personal that it saw Russia only as Stalin, and the issues that separated them as matters for bargaining power to power, politician to politician. Wallace's was the sort of innocence that is apparent immediately, while Truman's was of the kind that takes a little longer to recognize. Still you cannot long avoid noticing how large a part credulity plays in minds that dedicate themselves to purely practical calculations. Mr. Truman began his presidency by asking Harry Hopkins if you could talk to Stalin and was assured you could; in Potsdam they had "some very nice conversations." Even in 1948 he could still emit the casual campaign comment that "Old Joe is not such a bad guy"; and, near the end, he could tell Merle Miller, "I liked him. I didn't like what he did . . . but I liked him."

This is a singular current of accommodation to run through a nature whose tolerance of different ways and different men does not very often rise above designating President Eisenhower as a son of a bitch. There are different sorts of foolishness, but we can be fairly certain that on the whole we have been damaged less by politicians like Wallace who vaporize human events into some "millennial and revolutionary march toward manifesting here on earth the dignity that is in every human soul," and who dream of peoples singing to peoples, than by politicians like Truman who concretize all problems into formulas like "Dean, we got to stop the sons of bitches no matter what," and who dream of dealing as Number One to Number One. Perhaps this is because it has always been our national habit to cede the ultimate opportunities to politicians with Truman's cast of mind.

BUT WHATEVER THEIR differences in merit as instruments of public policy, Wallace in these diaries is an altogether more useful resource for historians than Truman in his talks with Merle Miller. He has, to be sure, the advantage that belongs to the chronicler of immediate experience. When Truman talked to Miller he was seventy-seven years old, and his vanities and his resentments had hardened into caricature.[1]

[1]He was well on his way to becoming the embarrassment he could often be to the pure in heart. Three years or so after his conversations with Miller, Truman was taking his morning walk in New York with his accustomed train of reporters. One of them asked him what he thought about the prospects for an increase in racial intermarriages. The *Times* man came back to the office to report that Truman had replied: "Would you want your daughter to marry a Negro? . . . You'll edit the man she goes out with. I did. And mine married the right man." The right man, of course, was the managing editor

Wallace's diaries begin in February 1942, when he was Vice President of the United States and they end when he was cast out as Mr. Truman's secretary of commerce in September 1946. They cover a span between the time when he had genuine administrative authority as secretary of agriculture and the time when he too was driven into caricature as the 1948 Progressive party candidate for president. We see him then at what must have been his best, since on the one hand he had no real power to make policies and thus could spare us the excuses that men with power have a compulsion to inflict upon us, and, on the other, he still retained enough access to the way policies were made to provide us with most intimate and valuable observations. To take a case, here is Wallace on Truman just after Roosevelt's death:

> Truman was exceedingly eager to agree with everything I said. He also seemed eager to make decisions of every kind with the greatest promptness. Everything he said was decisive. It almost seemed as though he was eager to decide in advance of thinking.

And here is Truman's assessment of Wallace:

> You take a fella that carries on too much about the pee-pul—it's like what I told you about folks that pray too loud. You better get home and lock the smokehouse, and that's the way I always felt about Henry Wallace. I didn't trust him.

It is difficult, on these two styles of portraiture alone, not to decide that Wallace's eye was the keener, although as things turned out not the shrewder, and that he is the witness better able to stand cross-examination. Falsities in the commerce of public men generally have

---

of *The New York Times*, which was by no means reluctant to publish the compliment but was confused that Truman should have spoken of "editing" his son-in-law when he might more precisely have said that he had checked him out. It seemed sensible to call the old man and ask him if his remarks had been accurately transcribed. "Sure," Truman answered, "I asked this fellow whether he'd want his daughter to marry a nigger, etc., and etc."

long histories. Still, the priority of betrayal in the Truman-Wallace relationship seems to belong all to the survivor. On January 22, 1944, Vice President Wallace made this entry in his diary with what seems unlikely to have been forethought:

> Senator Truman came in to say . . . that he was eager to support me for Vice President again, that he and I had seen things just alike, etc., etc.

There is no evidence that this pledge was ever implemented even during its fleeting tenure. In July, Senator Truman came to the Democratic Convention openly campaigning for Director of the Office of War Mobilization James F. Byrnes and he departed with Wallace's job.

BUT MR. TRUMAN'S image was bound to become more tender in the national memory because it fits two fundamental articles of the American faith: An unremitting profanity of speech is proof of the honesty of the speaker; and the mere word of the machine politician is worth more than the signed and notarized contract of the ideologue. Truman's account of the history of his times, being straightforward only in its vulgarity, thoroughly disproves the first tenet of folk wisdom. Wallace's experience with professional politicians effectively disposes of the second. All the archons of orthodox democracy treated him with every courtesy and even professions of fraternity when he was vice president whom fate might make president. Then they united when the chance came to snatch him out of the line of succession, and having assisted at the deed, most of them—including Kelly of Chicago and Hague of Jersey City, two of his assailants who had nothing to lose by being recognized as his enemies—automatically dispatched to him their denials of complicity in his fall.

In most transactions Wallace seems to have been clearly more honorable than either President Roosevelt or President Truman. This judgment, of course, does not acquit him of personal guile—any more than the fascination of his diaries denies the certainty that their author must often have been a tiresome and now and again a nagging companion. Yet he seems to have been much shrewder than the vagaries of his manner suggested. Just as he was rather more sportsmanlike about his disappointments than the bitterness that afflicted his ultimate disillusionment led us to think. He turns out to have been unexpectedly sensitive to the problems of the men who betrayed him.

EVEN IN 1946, when he had pushed himself into open dissent from Truman's policy toward the Soviets, he remained flexible enough to suggest that the President allow him to remain as secretary of commerce. To present the voters with the spectacle of a Democratic administration openly quarrelsome but still a family could be, he thought, the only hope of getting through the congressional elections.

> I told Truman that he was looking at the whole situation in too much of a negative light—that the emotions and interest aroused would help get out the vote. . . . I said the practical thing for Truman was to work with the progressive element during the election months, *remembering that he would have to live with the reactionary Southerners after the election was over.* I said he could not hope to win the election unless he went way over to the left not merely with the words but with the tune. [Italics added.]

We could not easily find a more compact statement of the prescription that rescued Truman from what appeared to be his terminal political illness in 1948. Wallace deserves a more generous assessment of his political senses than his taking leave of them for his aberrant voyage with the 1948 Progressive party had led us to assume. It is true that he lacked social gifts; we cannot credit much talent for personal accommodation to any man who presided over the Senate for four years and made so few friends there that he could be confirmed as secretary of commerce only by the tie-breaking vote of Vice President Truman. But bemused as he occasionally was into taking Soviet rhetoric as descriptive of Soviet reality, he was generally clearheaded about the ground on which he stood. After fourteen years of consequential government positions, he was a veteran and unexpectedly pliable practitioner of the compromises government makes between what it says and what it does. He was accustomed to seeing the left start most of the arguments and lose them all—the left had lost a clamorous argument with him over payments to sharecroppers when he was secretary of agriculture. Losing was an experience that did not often surprise or ever quite offend him.

ROOSEVELT GAVE HIM grander titles if not measurably more majestic powers than generally fall to vice presidents; he was successively chairman of the Supply Priorities and Allocation Board, the War Production Board, and the Board of Economic Warfare; still Roosevelt was careful to advise him to avoid "the hurly burly of actual administrative details."

Even so, the war was a consuming enough cause to inflame the not small part of his nature that liked to scold. He saw self-absorption and want of zeal all around him; and there was indeed enough of both to arouse a fancy less susceptible than his. His pacifist habits seem to have given way entirely to a New Model Army bloody-mindedness: He pressed the necessity of bombing the Japanese mainland, he found himself "jumping on" Secretary of the Navy Knox for not getting the Japanese out of the Aleutians, he seemed troubled that Attorney General Biddle would not prosecute the publisher of the *Chicago Tribune* for undermining the national morale. He pressed Roosevelt for an "everlasting" bomb attack on Germany. If his rhetoric was no worse than the sort civilians usually oppress us with in wartime, it seems startlingly at variance with the pleasantly squashy operations of his mind in more normal times.

This conviction of his unique position as total warrior spurred the long struggle his Board of Economic Warfare fought and lost against Secretary of Commerce Jesse Jones for control of the import of strategic materials. It was a fight between the zealot who insists on the priority of the present and the banker who sees himself as guarding the future. Their quarrel became an open scandal in June of 1943 when Wallace told a hostile Senate that his efforts to increase imports of scarce materials were frustrated because Jones's Reconstruction Finance Corporation insisted on haggling indefinitely over the terms of its loans to foreign producers. The secretary of commerce, Wallace said, cared for nothing so much as the RFC's profit picture, while he, the Vice President, cared for nothing except to win the war and save lives.

The facts, granted some hyperbole in their statement, seem all on Wallace's side. But his disabling flaw was less in his judgment than in his persistent disrespect for conventions about property. This was enough to get him thought of as a radical. "The State Department, the Army and the Navy are interested in winning the war," Secretary of State Hull told Elmer Davis. "You and the Vice President are interested in winning the war, but even more than that, you are interested in producing world-wide revolution even at the danger of producing revolution in the United States."

WALLACE HAD AN uneasy enough time keeping himself in domestic employment, and he was early on barred as an article for export. The State Department forbade distribution of his "Century of the Common Man" speech in Cuba because, among other misunderstandings, it "might result in additional unrest among labor factions in [that] country." When a strike of Bolivian miners threatened wartime tin supplies and Wallace suggested that a portion of the increased prices the United States was then paying for tin might usefully be "allotted to the workers in the form of food," Jesse Jones replied that "we ought to avoid any action that would make people think we were engaged in social reform of any kind."

Almost as soon as he and Jones began slanging each other in public, Wallace lost; the Board of Economic Warfare was abolished and he was bereft of even the shadow of authority. His chief employment for the rest of his tenure was as wandering preacher to those elements in Roosevelt's constituency that we loosely identify with Mrs. Roosevelt, a task he undertook with considerable philosophy and more than common shrewdness about the master, who had now begun to dangle and would soon enough drop him:

> The fact that the President himself read my entire speech more carefully than he has ever read any of my speeches and made several minor changes in his own handwriting suggests his usual technique of being very nice to a person he has just got through hitting. However it must also be said that he is really fond of me except when stimulated by the palace guard to move in other directions.

Within a year, he would become that least fortunate of nuisances, the one who can be mistreated with impunity because the risk has passed that he might inherit the property. In their last meeting before he disposed of Wallace, Roosevelt did say that he intended to make his fourth term "a progressive one" and that he proposed to get rid of those subordinates "who were thinking only about their own money." But it is not easy to find in these expressions any impulse beyond nostalgia for the rhetoric of his first term and some seigneurial care for the sensibilities of a progressive he was about to drop over the side. After all, its poetry once granted, the basic measure of the New Deal revolution is a simple one: When Roosevelt took office in 1933, 1 percent of the population owned 28 percent of the wealth; by the end of his second term, 1 percent of the population owned 30 percent of the wealth.[2]

As WITNESS, WALLACE has the one-eyed man's claim to testify about the doings of the kingdom of the blind. If he did not see what was happening whole, he at least sensed its shape better than anyone around him. He helps us to judge the process by his occasional notice of such persons as were making their way while he was tottering

[2]See Robert J. Lampman, *The Share of Top Wealth Holders in National Wealth, 1922–1956* (Princeton, N.J.: Princeton University Press, 1962).

toward his fall. In 1942, he observed to the President that Louis Johnson, our minister to India, had very quickly made himself *"persona non grata"* there. Roosevelt answered that Winston Churchill "had personally requested him to see that L. Johnson did not come back." Louis Johnson returned home to become president of General Dyestuff, a confiscated German enterprise that had become a patronage resource for Leo Crowley, the Alien Property Custodian; he would bob up again as Truman's Secretary of Defense.

Wallace's diaries echo with the noise of the hammering and the crafting of the America that would arise after the war. At dinner one evening, he outlined to Assistant Secretary of Commerce William A. M. Burden his proposal for an international authority to control postwar air traffic. "I found that Mr. Burden was very much disturbed. . . . He wants to preserve private initiative." As early as August of 1942, he was beginning to recognize that the civilians had surrendered control of procurement to the army—"which has the money." The synthetic rubber program had already sunk into a squabble over the future between the oil and the alcohol companies. Wallace was then grieving over, without being able to resist, Roosevelt's order to suspend antitrust prosecutions throughout the war.

By November of 1942, he was beginning to visit his reproaches on the President:

> Many officials were putting out the story . . . that men in uniform were going to run the country for the next ten years. Businessmen in Commerce and their kindred souls in State Department were increasingly getting the idea that big corporations were going to run the country. . . . It was common gossip in Wall Street that the President had gotten over his foolishness now, that he had settled down, and that we were now headed toward the kind of world in which Wall Street felt comfortably at home.

Even when he was at his best, Roosevelt's replies to such remonstrances were disturbingly vague; and, near the end, he seems to have slipped more and more into the embarrassing tendency that some aging men have to sound like their mothers. After the 1944 Democratic Convention, he assured Wallace that "I could have any job I wanted in the government with one exception. The exception was the State Department. He said Cordell Hull was an old dear and he could not bear to break his heart." In one of his last visits, Wallace expressed his discontent with the depressing array of assistant secretaries of state the President had just nominated, in particular Will Clayton, a Texas cotton broker. "Will Clayton is not so bad," Roosevelt replied, "and his wife is a dear."

Wallace could feel confident that he was himself the subject of similar endearments; even so he had to shame Roosevelt into making him secretary of commerce; and the loss of this whimsical patron could even seem to him for a while a gain for his prospects. Truman was agreeable; Wallace seems to have spoken out more often at the new President's cabinet meetings than he had lately felt encouraged to do at the old ones.

BUT HE WAS irrecoverably damaged goods. It is curious that a man could be dismissed and distrusted as a radical who believed as devoutly as Wallace did that tax incentives were the sharpest spur to increased production, and who was so diffident about the inflationary perils of large-scale public works. But still there was that swampy mind, restored to all its native pacifism, and thus, to stony minds, the symbol of everything that must be repelled.

His first experience with the treatment his rhetoric had earned him came at a September 1945 cabinet meeting whose subject was the peacetime development of atomic energy. Secretary of War Stimson opened matters by citing the conviction of most scientists that the secret of the bomb could not long be kept and, given this circumstance, the United States might just as well offer to exchange its scientific information with all the other United Nations including the Soviet Union.

"Stimson then," Wallace says, "entered into a long defense of Russia, saying that throughout our history Russia had been our friend . . . [that] our relationship with Russia during recent months had been improving.

President Truman agreed to this. The President then called on Dean Acheson who indicated that he agreed with Secretary Stimson."

Secretary of the Navy Forrestal entered the most strenuous objections, and then Wallace responded with an argument that was little more than an elaboration of Stimson's. Two days later Wallace had the unlovely surprise of reading in the press that he had expressed himself, as Forrestal later put it, "completely, everlastingly and wholeheartedly in favor of giving [the A-bomb secret] to the Russians." None of the accounts seems to have suggested that Wallace had been anything but alone in this position; there was no mention either that he had spoken only as echo of a venerated secretary of war or that he had been joined in his opinion by Acheson, by Secretary of Labor Schwellenbach, and by Postmaster General Hannegan.

We tend to think of the Cold War as prodigal with its victims. And yet its unconscious turns out to have prompted a pretty strict economy of sacrifice. Sometimes one victim was enough to instruct persons of his bent that there was no future in his company. The trial and condemnation of Robert Oppenheimer served to remind the scientists of how dangerous private and personal reservations could be; and in the case of Wallace the politicians were similarly reminded. The process of his separation from the flock had commenced by the fourth month of Truman's tenure; and yet no more than Oppenheimer was he a man who wanted to be alone with his conscience. Two months after Wallace's punishment for having fellow traveled with Henry Stimson, Secretary of State Byrnes was telling the cabinet how much Roosevelt had cherished Chiang Kai-shek. Contrary recollections were intruding upon Wallace's memory, and he was repulsing them.

> Perhaps I should have spoken up, but I didn't say a word. It seemed as though the President and Secretary Byrnes had made up their minds as to the course they were going to follow and that any effort to speak about the true situation in China would be misunderstood.

Even when he was impelled to public dissent, he seems to have assumed that a place in government could remain for him, unlike Ickes and Morgenthau, who were long gone. By the spring of 1946, when he was showing Truman the draft of a speech to a Russian War Relief dinner, he could say to the President, "Now, if you get into any trouble or embarrassment as a result of this speech, don't hesitate to repudiate it in any way you want."

When they had their last long conversation, "I said [to Mr. Truman] that the people didn't believe him to be as progressive *as I knew him to be at heart.*" When their talk was over, Wallace agreed to make no more speeches on foreign policy until Secretary of State Byrnes could get peacefully through the belligerencies of the Paris Peace Conference, and he seems to have been almost resigned to the prospect that he might have to keep silent for the indefinite future. After all those hints of restored complaisance, Truman fired him as secretary of commerce two days later. It cannot be an insignificant fact in the history of the left in America that Henry Wallace, its most notorious symbol, did not secede from government but was expelled.

Some prevision of the loneliness and the humiliation that attended his final divorcement reduced Wallace, we must finally suppose, to telling himself over and over again that Truman was not as bad as he sounded. The Truman recorded by Merle Miller demands, in charity and common sense, some of the same discipline from the sensitive. Wallace's Wallace comes to us as a reproach; but Miller's Truman is simply an embarrassment.

Yet the balance between them was by no means as uneven as we might think if we had no evidence beyond these two books. It is not fair that Wallace should be judged by his best and Truman by his worst, even if it is a worst which the editor of *Plain Speaking* and hordes of its readers seem to insist on thinking attractive. That we are ashamed of ten years of toughness that failed is a very poor excuse for rendering ourselves so suddenly homesick for a toughness that we can imagine as having triumphed.

PLAIN SPEAKING IS as powerful an argument for measured and restrained discourse as *Deep Throat* must be for long underwear. It is a *catalogue raisonné* of the vulgar and the trashy. Its tone is a monotonous litany of scurrilities. The speaker forgives no one and regrets nothing; his enemies are dragged past us as images of the most threadbare invective: He remembers how MacArthur kissed his ass at Wake Island; he unearths all the gossip about Eisenhower's wartime romance as a prelude to the assertion that he saved the reputation he now labors to destroy by shredding the evidence in the Pentagon files; he calls former Supreme Court Justice Tom Clark the dumbest son of a bitch he has ever known; he says that Ike just sat on his ass like if (sic) he didn't know what was going on; and he calls Nixon a shifty-eyed goddamn liar and, of course, a son of a bitch.[3]

Even the Truman whom Wallace remembers turns out to be much more appetizing than the Truman his old age wanted us to remember. Here is Miller on Truman:

> If there was one subject on which Mr. Truman was not going to have any second thoughts, it was the Bomb. . . . The Bomb had ended the war. . . . That was all there was to it, and Mr. Truman never lost any sleep over *that* decision.

Here is Wallace on Truman:

> [At the cabinet meeting of August 10, 1945], Truman said he had given orders to stop atomic bombing. He said the thought of wiping out another 100,000 people was too horrible. He didn't like the idea of killing, as he said, "all those kids."

[3]What Truman gives us of his notions of the dignity of history and the complexity of man is hardly improved by an editor who has suspended his normal detachment and sensitivity to swallow them whole. Miller's historical footnotes are slavishly accepting. He reminds us, for example, that Eisenhower yielded to the pressure of Senator Joseph McCarthy's incense bearers and excised from a 1952 Wisconsin campaign a complimentary reference to General George C. Marshall. "So much," Miller comments, "for [Eisenhower's] respect for freedom." Not quite so much; the balance is not that simply on Truman's side. Real history would not leap so blithely over their Supreme Court appointments: Truman, Chief Justice Vinson. Eisenhower, Chief Justice Warren. Truman, Justices Minton, Burton, and Clark. Eisenhower, Justices Brennan, Harlan, and Stewart.

[At the cabinet meeting of July 25, 1946], the President spoke very vigorously in one part of the meeting about the necessity of cutting down on the askings of the Army and Navy. . . . But within half an hour he was saying that after the last war we had cut our Navy too much; that we had to be careful not to cut our Army and Navy; that if we had not cut our Army and Navy after the last war there would not have been World War II. I was utterly amazed that he could go two different directions within the hour. It reminded me of Tuesday when within the hour he spoke about being patient with Russia to me and then at the cabinet luncheon agreed completely with Jimmie Byrnes in a number of cracks he took against Russia. I suspect there never has been a President who could move two different directions with less time intervening than Truman. He feels completely sincere and earnest at all times and is not disturbed in the slightest by the different directions in which his mind can go almost simultaneously. I say this realizing that he has always agreed with me on everything.

There had been, then, a divided mind before it turned to the stone that was Truman's final pride. We cannot say, of course, that Wallace's mind might not have turned to stone too. But then it is a waste of time to wonder what sort of president he might have been. He could not have been. At the end, tired as he was, Roosevelt had too keen a vision of what *our* future would be.

The New York Review of Books, April 4, 1974

The Underestimation of
Dwight D. Eisenhower

"He was a far more complex and devious man than most people realized, and in the best sense of those words."
—*RICHARD NIXON, Six Crises*

T HE FULL MOMENT of revelation about the great captains may be possible only for one of the casualties they leave behind them. Richard Nixon was writing in hospital: Just once, the resentment whose suppression is the great discipline of his life breaks through and is taken back with that saving clause about the best sense of the word, of course. Yea, though He slay me yet must I depend on Him.

Dwight Eisenhower was as indifferent as Calvin Coolidge, as absolute as Abraham Lincoln, more contained than John Kennedy, more serpentine than Lyndon Johnson, as hard to work for as Andrew Johnson. Historians seem to accept most of these qualities as necessary for greatness: certainly none of them diminish it. But, then, most are accounted sinister by the great mass of civilians, and to confuse civilians and to keep them off his back is the soldier's art. Eisenhower, who understood everything, seems to have decided very early that life is nothing unless it is convenient; to show the living flesh of greatness to one's contemporaries means to show one's face in combat and to be argued about: The only convenient greatness is to appear as a monument.

The most precise description of Eisenhower was rendered in another connection by Edward Lear:

> On the top of the Crumpetty Tree
> The Quangle Wangle sat.

> *But his face you could not see,*
>   *On account of his Beaver Hat*
> *For his Hat was a hundred and*
>   *two feet wide,*
>   *With ribbons and bibbons on*
>   *every side*
> *And bells, and buttons, and loops,*
>   *and lace,*
> *So that nobody ever could see the face*
>   *Of the Quangle Wangle Quee.*

Innocence was Eisenhower's beaver hat, and the ribbons grew longer and more numerous until his true lines were almost invisible. It took a very long watch indeed to catch the smallest glimpse.

"He told Nixon and others, including myself, that he was well aware that somebody had to do the hard-hitting infighting,[1] and he had no objections to it as long as no one expected *him* to do it," Sherman Adams says.

It was the purpose of his existence never to be seen in what he did. When he fired Sherman Adams, his chief of staff, as a political liability in 1958, Adams thought it was Nixon's doing. While he was coldly measuring the gain or loss from dropping Nixon as his 1952 vice-presidential candidate, Nixon thought it was Thomas E. Dewey's doing.

When this gesture proved insufficient, Eisenhower accommodated to what was inevitable, if transient, and even offered himself up as battle trophy for Goldwater's brief triumph at the San Francisco convention. It was a situation where, the surreptitiously neat having failed, the heroically messy could hardly succeed. The useless employment of further resources would have been an affront to that superb sense of economy which made Eisenhower a soldier successful just for being so immune to notions of glory and to pleasurable anticipations of bleeding.

"He is the most immoral man I have ever known," one of Nelson Rockefeller's captains said not long ago. He was probably wrong: There

---

[1] Definable to the Democrats as the dirty work.

is always the danger of going overboard in moments when the watcher
thinks he has found Eisenhower out. To be absolutely immoral is a
perilous excess: Being moderate in all things means, after all, being
moderate in the expenditure of immorality.

No thought was to be uttered undisguised: The face had as many
ranges, indeed as many roles as there are sins to commit, because it was
an instrument for hinting without ever quite saying. Even the syntax
was an instrument. When things were at their stickiest in the Formosa
Strait, James Hagerty, his press secretary, told the President that the
best course would be to refuse to answer any questions at all on the
subject if it came up at his press conference.

" 'Don't worry, Jim,' I told him as we went out the door. 'If that
question comes up, I'll just confuse them.' "

Those press conferences, his highest achievements as craftsman in
masks, seem certain to be half the sport and half the despair of historians; they will give up, one has to assume, and settle for the judgment
that he was a man hopelessly confused, it being so difficult to confess
that anyone, across so many years, could still so superbly confuse you.
The mask he contrived for his comfort has already become the reputation. Generals like MacArthur and Montgomery, as proud of their
intelligence as he was appalled by their weakness for theater, seem to
have thought him stupid, as he certainly thought them a little dippy.
The other presidents already evoked most often for comparison with
him are General Grant and James Buchanan. But still there abides the
mystery of why he never left the country ruined by his laziness, as
Buchanan did, or himself ruined by his friends, as Grant did.

The difference in both cases was partly Eisenhower's intelligence,
partly his appreciation of those occasions when self-indulgence can
produce worse inconveniences, and partly that chilliness of his nature
which protected him from ever indulging others.

"I could understand it if he played golf all the time with old Army
friends, but no man is less loyal to his old friends than Eisenhower,"
John Kennedy observed when he was a senator. "He is a terribly cold
man. All his golfing pals are rich men he has met since 1945."

"In the evenings when he had no official engagements or on week-ends," says Adams, "the President liked to spend his time with old friends whose faces were often seen at Gettysburg—Bill Robinson, the entertaining George Allen, Cliff Roberts, Pete Jones, Bob Woodruff, Al Gruenther, Slats Slater, Freeman Gosden ['Amos' of the famous radio team of Amos and Andy], Sig Larmon."

These Sigs and Petes and Slatses could hardly have been more stimulating than his old Army comrades—of whose intelligence he *does* seem to have entertained the lowest opinion—and, when one member of a salon is granted special distinction as "entertaining," his fellow inmates must be dreary indeed.

But the Sigs and Petes had one substantial advantage: They earned his affection as Casanova made *his* conquests: They were men who paid.

Once, Eisenhower remembers, he had a few days' rest in Scotland on a state trip; and someone, thinking he might be lonely, suggested that he call a few friends to fly over for golf and bridge.

"The idea," he says, "struck me as intriguing, in certain respects the brightest I had heard during the entire trip. Forgetting the time differential, I picked up the telephone and within minutes was talking to Bill Robinson in New York. My call got him out of bed: In New York it was two o'clock in the morning. Without a moment's hesitation he accepted my invitation and a few hours later he and 'Pete' Jones were on their way. I was indeed fortunate to have friends who were such light sleepers."

He lived among strangers; his protective coloration was the appearance of being amiable and innocent. Very seldom does he give himself away: Once he said that, when he was president of Columbia, he never went for a walk at night without carrying his service revolver with him. There is surprising hauteur in this image of the most eminent neighbor at large in Morningside Heights; but there is also the grandeur of a man whose dedication it was never to experience a moment of confrontation without the proper weight of means; to him all life was a matter of logistics.

He is revealed best, if only occasionally, in the vast and dreary acreage of his memoirs of the White House years. There he could feel safe in an occasional lapse of guard. For one thing, political history is the opiate of Democrats and he had spent eight years grandly erasing any suggestion from the minds of anyone else that anything he might ever say could be remotely interesting. He had concealed his marvelous intelligence from admirer and critic alike; by now, there was little danger of its being noticed even if confessed; he could be as secure in his memoirs as in his private diary.

The Eisenhower who emerges here intermittently free from his habitual veils is the President most superbly equipped for truly consequential decision we may ever have had, a mind neither rash nor hesitant, free of the slightest concern for how things might look, indifferent to any sentiment, as calm when he was demonstrating the wisdom of leaving a bad situation alone as when he was moving to meet it on those occasions when he absolutely had to.

Of course, we think: That is the way he wants us to see him; he is still trying to fool us; but he won't get away with it this time. And so he has fooled us again, for the Eisenhower who tells us that he never makes an important mistake is telling us for the first time about the real Eisenhower.

There is the sound of trumpets, the fog of rhetoric, then for just a moment the focus of the cold intelligence.

The President-elect goes to Korea.

"We used light airplanes to fly along the front and were impressed by the rapidity with which wounded were being brought back for treatment; evacuation was almost completely by helicopter since there were no landing fields for conventional planes in the mountains. Except for sporadic artillery fire and sniping there was little action at the moment, *but in view of the strength of the positions the enemy had developed, it was obvious that any frontal attack would present great difficulties.*"

All else would be conversation; one look had decided Eisenhower to fold the war.

Iraq's monarchy has been overthrown, Lebanon's government is collapsing, the British are otherwise committed; President Eisenhower will have to send the Marines.

The basic mission of United States forces in Lebanon was not primarily to fight. Every effort was made to have our landing be as much of a garrison move as possible. In my address I had been careful to use the term 'stationed in' Lebanon. . . . If it had been prudent, I would have preferred that the first battalion ashore disembark at a dock rather than across the beaches. However, the attitude of the Lebanese army was at that moment unknown, and it was obviously wise to disembark in deployed formation ready for any emergency. As it turned out, there was no resistance; the Lebanese along the beaches welcomed our troops. The geographic objectives of the landings included only the city of Beirut and the adjoining airfield.

And, thereunder, he appends this note of explanation:

The decision to occupy only the airfield and capital was a political one which I adhered to over the recommendations of some of the military. If the Lebanese army were unable to subdue the rebels when we had secured their capital and protected their government, I felt, we were backing up a government with so little popular support that we probably should not be there.

There was French Indochina, now of course Vietnam, and this cold intelligence looks upon the French with all the remote distance it would always feel from the romantic poetry of war:

The President is told that the French propose to put ten thousand troops in Dien Bien Phu.

I said, "You cannot do this."

"This will bring the enemy into the open," he said. "We cannot find them in the jungle, and this will draw them out where we can then win."

"The French know military history," I said. "They are smart enough to know the outcome of becoming firmly emplaced and then besieged in an exposed position with poor means of supply and reinforcements."

Never thereafter could he contemplate the war in Indochina except in the frozen tones of a war college report on a maneuver by officers who can henceforth abandon all hope of promotion. The French, he instructs Foster Dulles, have committed the classic military blunder. In Geneva, Dulles is said to have hinted that the United States might use the atom bomb to save the French; there is no evidence that he would have dared transmit that suggestion to a President who plainly would not have trusted him with a stick of dynamite to blow up a fish pond.

Dulles, unhopefully, does pass on a French plea for United States bomber support of the Dien Bien Phu garrison; Eisenhower does not even seem to have noticed it. He had already made up his mind about that:

> There were grave doubts in my mind about the effectiveness of such air strikes on deployed troops where good cover was plentiful. Employment of air strikes alone to support French troops in the jungle would create a double jeopardy: *it would comprise an act of war and would also entail the risk of having intervened and lost.*
>
> [Sitting with Undersecretary of State Bedell Smith,] I remarked that, if the United States were, unilaterally, to permit its forces to be drawn into conflict in Indochina, and in a succession of Asian wars, the end result would be to drain off our resources and to weaken our overall defensive position.

The French went down; Eisenhower blamed them and the British, who, of course, blamed Dulles.

Then, in his utmost refinement, there is the Eisenhower who supervised the C.I.A.'s U-2 reconnaissance flights over the Soviet Union:

> A final important characteristic of the plane was its fragile construction. This led to the assumption (insisted upon by the C.I.A. and the Joint Chiefs) that in the event of mishap the plane would virtually disintegrate. It would be impossible, if things should go wrong, they said, for the Soviets to come into possession of the equipment intact—or, unfortunately, of a live pilot. This was a cruel assumption, but I was assured that the young pilots undertak-

ing these missions were doing so with their eyes wide open and motivated by a high degree of patriotism, a swashbuckling bravado, and certain material inducements.[2]

Then Francis Powers' U-2 was shot down, and Eisenhower, of course, ordered the announcement of the "previously designed 'cover story.' "

Upon which, "Mr. Khrushchev, appearing before the Supreme Soviet once more, announced what to me was unbelievable. The uninjured pilot of our reconnaissance plane, along with much of his equipment intact, was in Soviet hands."

The State Department was still lamely adhering to the cover story. That seemed totally irrational to Eisenhower, who at once ordered a full confession, altering its draft "to eliminate any phrase that seemed to me to be defensive in tone.

"In the diplomatic field," he explained, "it was routine practice to deny responsibility for an embarrassing occurrence when there is even a one percent chance of being believed, but when the world can entertain not the slightest doubt of the facts, there is no point in trying to evade the issue."

And there we have, in Dwight Eisenhower of all unexpected persons, the model of that perfect statesman of Voltaire's ironic dream, the one who could learn nothing from Machiavelli except to denounce Machiavelli.

The precepts are plain to see:

---

[2]One of the confusions making difficult the full appreciation of Eisenhower's subtlety is the condition that he seems to explain himself in anticlimactic series. For example: "As president of Columbia, I became deeply interested in the educational, financial, and public relations aspects of the job." Normally one would expect a college president to be more interested in education than in public relations, and the succession seems anticlimactic. But, with a little thought, one understands that Eisenhower knew he was at Columbia as a public-relations man. In the same way, normal rhetoric would assign the climactic role in the readiness of a soldier to sacrifice his life to "high degree of patriotism": Eisenhower, with perfect understanding, gives the emphasis to "certain material inducements."

1. Always pretend to be stupid; then when you have to show yourself smart, the display has the additional effect of surprise.

2. Taking the blame is a function of servants. When the orange is squeezed, throw it away.

3. When a situation is hopeless, never listen to counsels of hope. Fold the enterprise.

4. Do nothing unless you know exactly what you will do if it turns out to have been the wrong thing. Walk not one inch forward onto ground which has not been painfully tested by someone else.

5. Never forget the conversation you had with Zhukov about how the Russian army clears mine fields. "We march through them," Zhukov had said. It is a useful instruction if applied with the proper economy. Keep Nixon and Dulles around for marching through mine fields.

6. Always give an enemy an exit.

7. Never give an ally his head.

8. Assume that your enemies are just as sensible as you are. ("Personally I had always discounted the probability of the Soviets doing anything as 'reaction.' Communists do little on impulse; rather their aggressive moves are invariably the result of deliberate decision.")

9. Lie whenever it seems useful, but stop lying the moment 99 percent of the audience ceases to believe you.

10. Respond only when there is some gain besides honor in meeting the challenge or some serious loss from disregarding it. For example, when Eisenhower was the first candidate for President in memory who indicated that he was unable to pronounce the word "injunction" when discussing the labor problem, I suggested to one of his admirers that he seemed extraordinarily dumb.

"If he's so dumb," was the reply, "why is he such a good bridge player?"

Like all defenses of Dwight Eisenhower, it seemed silly at first; but, with thought one understood its force. Eisenhower spent the twenties as an officer in garrison; his friends were civilians in towns like Leavenworth, Kansas. He learned to play bridge well because his pay did not cover losing money to civilians. He is equipped to respond to any challenge which seems to him sensible.

He was the great tortoise upon whose back the world sat for eight years. We laughed at him; we talked wistfully about moving; and all the while we never knew the cunning beneath the shell.

I talked to him just once. He was in Denver, getting ready for the 1952 campaign when he would have to run with Republicans like Senator Jenner who had called General Marshall, the chief agent of Eisenhower's promotion, "a living lie." I had thought that anyone so innocent as Eisenhower would be embarrassed by this comrade and proposed to ask what he thought about what Jenner had said. It seemed cruel to spring any such trap to anyone this innocent, so I told Hagerty that I intended to ask the question.

The time came and I asked, "General, what do you think of those people who call General Marshall a living lie?"

He leaped to his feet and contrived the purpling of his face. How dare anyone say that about the greatest man who walks in America? He shook his finger in marvelous counterfeit of the palsy of outrage.

He would die for George Marshall. He could barely stand to be in the room with anyone who would utter such a profanation. The moment passed while the enlisted man in garrison endured his ordeal as example to the rest of the troops; and suddenly I realized that in his magnificent rage at me, he had been careful not to mention Senator Jenner at all.

Afterward Hagerty took me aside and the General offered the sunshine of his smile; there was not the slightest indication that he was thinking that there was anything for him to forgive or me either. It had simply been the appointed ceremony. I was too dumb to understand him then. It would take ten years before I looked at his picture and realized that the smile was always a grin.

Esquire, September 1967

Romans *(with James Ridgeway)*

"Robert Frost wrote fifty years ago, 'nothing is true except as a man or men adhere to it—to live for it, to spend themselves on it, to die for it.' We need this spirit even more than money or institutions or agreements."
—*JOHN F. KENNEDY*, November 18, 1963

B Y SATURDAY NIGHT, even the television seemed worn out by attempt and failure and ceased to comment and gave over to a succession of photographs of the columns and the windows and the corners of the White House and of the shadows of the great Lincoln head in Springfield and to a voice reciting "Oh, Captain, My Captain." It is to be, then, the grand style. But the ship has not weathered every storm; Mr. Kennedy is not Abraham Lincoln; not because he is more or less, but because he is a remembered physical presence and Mr. Lincoln an image of the plastic arts. One's own time is personal, not historical. Just how long will it be before many of us will want to read a book about the day Mr. Kennedy was shot?

THE NEWS OF the President's assassination was given by a taxi driver to three gentlemen as they left a hotel on Arlington Street in Boston. They turned right around and hurried back inside to attend to their investments. Packed with students and businessmen a shuttle plane from Boston to Washington waited for permission to take off when the captain came on the intercom: "Folks, up here on the flight deck we've been listening to the news and the President is dead." There was only time to hear one woman say, "How dreadful" before three men went back to discussing plan specifications. A college student reading *Agamemnon* paid no visible attention. One of his notes read, "love-in-hate."

The plane took off, the stewardess collected the money and started to serve drinks. Then the captain was back again. They had been listening to more news, that is trying to listen to news because their real job was to hear flight control. There had been a gun battle in Dallas; a patrolman was killed; the police had taken a man in a movie theater. Vice President Johnson was now the President. The talk of business went on through this, and stopped only when the captain again interrupted to say that the new President had been sworn in aboard an aircraft. A few laughed.

THEY ASK TOO much of us when they ask us to act up to the grand style. We are not an emotionally affluent people. And yet some of us always complained that Mr. Kennedy did not seem quite emotionally committed enough. But now someone remembered with special affection a moment late in the 1960 campaign. Mr. Kennedy was in a motorcade and the Democratic governor who was with him said how wonderful it was to feel the love with which these crowds pressed forward to feel the touch of their candidate. "Oh, dry up," Mr. Kennedy said. It seemed now somehow a special grace in him that he used only the real in emotion and abstained from fabricating the expected. He had too much respect for the grand style to counterfeit it; how much truer to him might we have been if we had come down in scale and if the many of us who must have remembered the lines from *Cymbeline* had thought them proper to speak:

> Fear no more the heat of the sun/Nor the furious
>   winter's rages.
> Thou thy worldly task hast done/Home art thou
>   and ta'en thy wages.
> Golden lads and girls all must/As chimney sweep-
>   ers come to dust.

Cymbeline is a Roman play. The Kennedys are a Roman family; America seems only a Roman crowd. For us alone in it, there is only a terrible irritation with God and with self and with every other face that is left.

Friday night caught most of the President's Cabinet away from the city. All that could be collected from his official establishment came to Andrews Air Force base to meet the dead man come back from Dallas.

Everything mechanical intruded as it would intrude all weekend. The lights were vagrant, savage, and aimless; the planes came and went on distracting, irrelevant missions. The face of Undersecretary of Commerce Roosevelt seemed the ruin of his father's. Every uncared-for lank of Senator Dirksen's hair, every fold under every chin, seemed for the moment our own fault.

For we had lost in the instant the hope of beginning again. Reason might argue that the sense of a new start was already gone. The main story in the morning's *Washington Post* had detailed the exculpations of a congressman who had made a 1,000 percent profit from the stock of a company which had enjoyed his good offices with the Internal Revenue Service. The very Senate which dissipated in shock at the news from Texas had just before been waspishly disputing the privileges and emoluments of elective office. For weeks it had been hard to remember anyone in Washington talking about anything except who was getting what from whom. Mr. Kennedy seemed to be wasting in his city and to be nourished only by the great crowds in the countryside. The films from Dallas, painful as they were, reinforced the feeling that he was his old self only away from Washington. It could be argued then that we would see a time when we recognized that all that promise had been an illusion; but you need only look at hope lain dead to know how easy it is to look forward to regret. It had been less than three years since Mr. Kennedy had announced that a new generation was taking up the torch; now old General de Gaulle and old Mr. Mikoyan were coming to see the young man buried.

The great red and white plane of the President of the United States came to Andrews at last bearing all the transition in one horrid, large, economy-size package. There was a portable yellow elevator to bring Mrs. Kennedy and Attorney General Kennedy down with a casket that looked like a ship's chest. Half of Lyndon Johnson could be seen waiting in the open door behind them. Mrs. Kennedy's weeds as a widow had to be what some said was a strawberry and some said was a raspberry-colored campaign suit. Everything mechanical that did not intrude functioned badly; the elevator seemed to stall; Mrs. Kennedy tried a door of the ambulance, which did not work, and the attorney general, with a deliberation unbroken as hers was, found one which did and she was gone at last, the high Roman figure that she would be all weekend.

So Mr. Johnson came on, tall as ever but wearing the glasses which his image of himself has always thought unsuitable to state occasions, emptied by his misfortune of all his vanity, small and large, and of almost everything else. His lips seemed wet, his chin uncertain; there was a fear that he might be a man who would cry in public and who there was enough his better to blame him? He said something into the microphones that was identifiable only as being hoarse, broken, and undeservedly apologetic, and then his new household gathered around him. And the eye as cruel to everyone else as the heart was cruel to self, focused and saw only the hearing aid of an undersecretary. The next morning, Mr. Johnson had repaired his interior and left off resenting himself, as all of us had better do if we are to get about our business.

As THE PEOPLE waited the passing of the cortege on Sunday some of them squabbled over who was to stand on the stepladder and shoot the first pictures and at what speed and at what lens opening. A mother trying to tune up a transistor radio said to a pouting child, "I want you to understand one thing. This is very important to me." Amidst the people came a teenager with a portable tape recorder. He stuck out a microphone and said, "Sir, on this day of national mourning how do you feel?" Coming away from the Capitol after viewing the bier, a man with a camera slung over his head said to another man with a camera, "Did you get any good pictures?"

ONE SAT IN the Senate press room away from the rotunda on Sunday night and read a wire service report on the tributes paid to the patriotism of Jack Ruby by the master of ceremonies of Mr. Ruby's strip parlor. There was a story about the good fortune of the Dallas citizen who had been in at the death with his movie camera and had sold the films to *Life* for $40,000. The National Football League had played its full Sunday schedule; every seat in Yankee Stadium was filled with mourners. One thought with respect—it was not possible to be grateful to anyone—of Randall Jarrell for having known enough soon enough to have written a book and called it *A Sad Heart at the Supermarket*.

Then a man spoke up and said:

"She came in with the children this afternoon when the rotunda was first opened and she was standing and waiting and the kid looked up at the dome and began to walk around, and she bent over and touched him and he looked up and she straightened her shoulders to show him how to stand at attention, and he did it for about ten seconds. You know, I wish it was a dynasty and the kid was taking over and she was the regent."

Monday was sunny and for those to whom life is a picture, the Capitol was the best and largest color television screen anyone could hope for. A boy sat on his father's shoulders and his father told him to use the number one setting. The band began "Hail to the Chief," the boy raised his camera and instructed his father not to move. Behind them a woman put a child on her shoulders; the child must have tickled her because she kept laughing, comfortably, and this pleasant distraction continued until the coffin could be detected from its flag to be coming out and she left off and pointed her finger and said with undiminished gaiety, "See, there he is." One left and walked past a girl clutching a paperback. Then suddenly there was one man kneeling with his hands over his eyes and his hat on the sidewalk, and it was impossible not to stop and put a hand upon his shoulder and not to begin to hope that a chain might be put together again.

In front of St. Matthew's the crowd was quieter.

THE BANDS AND the soldiers went by, the pipers last; and then, like thunder, there was Mrs. Kennedy with the senator on one side and the

451

attorney general on the other and ramrods up their spines. And behind them, the powers and potentates of the earth; the Kennedys were marching with all of Madame Tussaud's in their train, as though Charles de Gaulle had been created a Marshal of France and Haile Selassie I the Lion of Judah only for this last concentrated moment. The powers and potentates waited; Mrs. Kennedy, for the moment made flesh again, gathered her children. Cardinal Cushing came down, under his mitre, looking, to his credit, a trifle irritated with God; we could be grateful for the Catholics and grateful to them for providing one cardinal who looked like a Prince of the Church.

And the children in their sunny pale blue coats began walking with their mother up the stairs, the little boy stumbling only at the vestibule and then they were gone. We had lived awhile with old Romans; now the doors were closing and we must make do with ourselves.

The New Republic, December 7, 1963

The Achievement of Lyndon B. Johnson

I THINK THAT, when all but one of us is gone, the last one of us will be telling children about the speech Lyndon Johnson made last night and that, in such a moment, he will be proud again of his people and of himself.

There cannot be anyone alive who knows the names of all the children who carried us and Mr. Johnson to the place where he stood last night.

There was a little boy named James Gordon, who lived right by Clay, Kentucky, and traveled twenty miles to school because Clay would not take Negro pupils. In the fall of 1956, he heard on the radio that Negroes had been taken in the Sturgis School, twenty miles away.

"Mommy," he said, "if they can go to school in Sturgis, why can't I go to school in Clay?"

His mother thought awhile and then she answered:

"If you got the guts to go, I got the guts to take ye."

And so he and she walked down to the school on Monday morning and were turned away by men in overalls with guns. They came back on Tuesday morning.

Harry Briggs was an eight-year-old boy in Clarendon County, South Carolina, in 1949 when his parents, along with those of thirty other Negro children, petitioned the county for a better school. They went in the end to the Supreme Court and Harry Briggs, Jr.'s is the name of record on one of the 1954 cases ordering the integration of schools. He grew up, of course, to be graduated from a Negro high school. Two years after the Supreme Court decision, his mother was instructed that she would lose her job as a motel chambermaid unless she took her name off the integration petition.

"They axed me what I wanted," she remembered, "and I said I only wanted for our children what every child in America was getting. So they said I'd have to leave, and I said, 'Do you want me to go today?' And they said yes unless I wanted to go down to that lawyer and make a statement taking my name off. And I said, no, I can't and I haven't worked since. Heck, we been on that petition for seven years."

That petition was just about all they owned.

In May of 1961, the cooks and maids of Montgomery, Alabama, were sitting in their First Baptist Church while the federal marshals struggled with, and the local police looked benevolently upon, a mob outside. Those domestics were singing the song that was then called, "We Will Overcome," fighting to believe against all the evidence around them.

But who could have believed that, only forty-six months later, a President of the United States would be hollering "We Shall Overcome" across the well of the House of Representatives.

Julia Aaron was a freedom rider that spring and had been beaten when she got off the Greyhound bus at Montgomery. Even so, she and her companions insisted on going on to Jackson, Mississippi, and the Alabama Guard commandeered the bus on which they had tickets and convoyed it across the state to be met by the Mississippi Guard. It rained at the border while they were changing the guard and Julia Aaron looked out the window at the Mississippi soldiers standing with their bayonets.

"That's terrible," she said very seriously. "Those poor men having to stand there and get wet."

She got off the bus at Jackson and went straight to jail.

I have always thought of them as part of my own history of the United States. But, last night, Lyndon Johnson put the great seal of the President of the United States on their lives and their words and they belong to the history of all of us now.

We have had a few presidents who bent down to be kind to these people. But last night for the first time we had a president who looked up and saluted them. May God reward them for what they have done to make him what he was last night and us what we may be tomorrow.

New York Post, March 16, 1966

The Triumph of Martin Luther King, Jr.

O F ALL THE memories of so many brief encounters with Martin Luther King, Jr., the best is of an afternoon sitting on a porch in Montgomery seven years ago in May.

The Freedom Ride to integrate the interstate buses had come to its crash there. The riders had been bombed in Anniston and set upon and beaten in Montgomery; and now they had stopped and wondered whether they should go on to Jackson, Mississippi, and jail if they were lucky.

Martin King had not been on the ride; he had come there after the trouble, as he always did in any trouble, to draw fire. He and his friend, Ralph Abernathy, talked a long while about whether their children should go on to Jackson. There was the assumption then that to go meant to be killed. Another friend, the attorney general of the United States, was exceedingly anxious that the riders stop where they were with their wounds; the majesty of the United States of America could not protect them in Jackson; the reputation of the U. S. might suffer if the worst happened. But Martin King did not talk about that.

He turned to Wyatt Walker, his executive assistant.

"Wyatt," he said, "go back and tell those young people that I don't want them to go. I will go, and Ralph will go. But I was not put here to send children to get hurt."

They had fooled him, of course, going down one by one to buy their bus tickets in the night. And when he and the adults got up the next morning to go to the terminal, these children were there waiting for him, and off into the unknown they went together, as they always did, since, in those days, they would do anything he asked except turn back from sharing the risks he wanted to take all by himself.

AFTER THAT, I do not need the Nobel Prize Committee or the flag at half mast over the Capitol to remember that Martin Luther King, Jr., was a great man. A great man is one who knows that he was not put on earth to be part of a process through which a child can be hurt.

Martin King was an ambassador, a reproach indeed, from the older America of country churches and poor people so embedded in our history that they could enter and leave its great stages entirely unselfconscious and always saying just the right thing.

He belonged to the maids and the porters, the people who worked in kitchens to send their sons to college and then saw them come out porters too, and then began to dream for their grandchildren. He came to them after all those years at Boston reading Hegel, different from them in every way except the essential one.

I saw him first in one of those churches, when he was only twenty-six, and I was surprised at how much he looked like the young Charlie Parker, the least appropriate of presences. But if he seemed in any way unusual to them, I suppose, it was as a sudden embodiment of all they had dreamed their children might become, the son who went off to study, who had the whole world before him and who came back home to be with them. Those nights, he never talked to us but only to them; and he worked in the ancient ritual of his affirmation and their responses; he did not speak for them but with them; if we wanted to listen to him, we had to listen to them too; they accompanied him into history.

HE DIED ASSERTING the dignity of garbage collectors. And he died at a moment when his ideas had never seemed quite so unfashionable. We have been very sick; a country is sick when the second thought in everyone's mind with the news that a Nobel Peace laureate has been murdered can be the fear that his death is the signal for violence and arson and that his first memorial must be children fleeing from a burning tenement.

And yet at the very moment when the irony of his failure was being marked in smoke and fire, you understood that he had won. He had proved the uselessness, the malignity of violence, the emptiness of riot. Men do not weep, nor do they make revolutions breaking into liquor stores. Never before so much as in these spectacles had quiet people been so recognizable as the only people who count.

He lived to teach us; in death he had taught us too. He died for us. We were sick, and alive he could not heal us. Suddenly, in the shock of what we have lost, there is the sense that we commence to heal. Pray God that today he is being buried with the coming of spring.

New York Post, April 9, 1968

The Decline and Fall of the Democratic Party

THIS IS A memoir of the Democratic Convention of 1968 from a participant who knows infinitely less about a great deal of it than any American who owns a television set, being the report of a delegate from the Twentieth Congressional District of New York.

But it is also about the infinitely more I know now about the political process than I had ever known before or will ever know again, because the week before I was only a journalist commissioned to describe politicians, and I can feel myself already becoming only that again.

I ought to commence by saying how I happened on this scene. "I am, and my father was before me," John Ruskin began, "a violent Tory of the old school—Walter Scott's school, that is to say, and Homer's." I then am a violent Whig of the old school—Lord Byron's school, that is to say, and St. Thomas Aquinas's, being for whatever is the opposite of Ruskin's most sincere love of kings and dislike of everyone who attempted to disobey them. I am for Doctor Spock against the Department of Justice; and I am for Ernesto Guevara—or anyway his ghost—against the Central Intelligence Agency.

But, just because I have been thus cursed by the violence of the part of me that thinks, I have always tried to be blessed by the passivity of the part of me that acts. Mine has for years been a life dedicated to no civic activity except striving to protect this country from being managed by persons like William F. Buckley, Jr., and myself.

I was called from this quietude by a national contagion and a private pique. We are likely to remember the last four years of our history most for having been shaken by persons ashamed of their country, in movements with symbols as diverse as Barry Goldwater and Eugene McCarthy, George Wallace and Martin Luther King, Jr. We live among union men who no longer listen to George Meany, Democrats who no longer listen to President Johnson, Negroes who no longer listen to Roy Wilkins.

The humiliated-citizen part of me turned to Senator McCarthy because he stood for the Commons against the King when no one else in the Commons would. And the part of me that gives way to private pique turned against Senator Robert Kennedy, whom I had liked almost more than any public man I have ever known. My reasons were all those of the time and circumstance in which he declared for president. In my rage, I quite forgot how much I liked him; and now I can only say that my judgment in this case seems to me correct but not right, a profound difference.

I was asked to run as a McCarthy delegate from the West Side of Manhattan. I should not have accepted if the chance had not offered itself to run against both President Johnson and Senator Kennedy. Then Senator Kennedy was murdered, and I did not care any longer whether I won or lost, being only ashamed of all rages at anyone. But Senator McCarthy moved his mysterious way upon the waters; I was elected; and, after a while, the thing began to matter to me again. And at the convention I learned to my surprise that, if Robert Kennedy had lived, he could have been the nominee and I should have voted for him. To you who saw it, the convention must have seemed terribly squalid; to me, knowing no more of it than a soldier on patrol would know about his campaign, it seems instead a tale of high romance lacking only the one ingredient high romance needs, a romantic hero.

It happened to my surprise that my way of finally discharging my duty as a delegate was to be discharged as a bailee from the Central Police Station in Chicago. A sergeant said that evening that he hoped that being arrested hadn't been too bad.

"No, sergeant," I replied, "I haven't had as much fun as I've had this week since I was ambushed in the Philippines."

It began with finding the New York McCarthy headquarters and asking Sarah Kovner, the executive director, where I should go for my delegate's credentials. Mrs. Kovner answered that I was to find Frank Rossetti, the New York County Democratic leader, who was receiving visitors and distributing credentials in Room 2143 upstairs in the Sheraton-Chicago.

It was, I said, always fun to talk to Frank Rossetti.

"Now, look here, Murray Kempton," Mrs. Kovner said. "You could be funny yesterday. You can be funny next Friday. But you're not going to be funny this week. You go right up there and all you say to Frank Rossetti is that he is dead as a leader if he doesn't vote for McCarthy."

I had first met Mrs. Kovner as Sarah Schoenkopf perhaps eight years ago; she had been a copy girl on one of the too many journals that have bought my bread. My feeling for her then and since may be described as one of increasing affection and decreasing condescension. She was a Reform Democrat then and remains one; although the life of struggle against the regulars has softened her tongue, it has not diminished her determination. But all the while, in our different lives, my friends, such as they were, had been among those who had the political jobs and hers among those who wanted them, which does after all describe a fundamental difference between senior reporters and copy girls.

But Sarah had never had the physical proportions or the psychological disposition to be any sort of shrew; and, with the years, I had grown rather fond of her without taking her very seriously. But now all that was changed; Sarah was my leader, and I knew she ought to be. And so I went upstairs and, feebly to be sure, told Frank Rossetti that he was dead as a leader if he didn't vote for Eugene McCarthy.

A week or so before, I had said a carelessly admiring word about Richard Nixon, and my wife had said, "Murray, you are not a serious man." I had been indignant then, but now I knew she was right and I was indignant no longer. I thought of writing a postcard just to say: "You are right, my love, I was not a serious man. But I am this week at least. I am taking my orders from Sarah Schoenkopf." But that would have seemed to her another poor joke.

Sarah had instructed me that I was free until the New York McCarthy delegates caucused at eleven o'clock that evening. So I could be an observer for a while and see what the world was seeing of the great stage of history. I went, with my son David, who is seventeen, to a candidate's forum and looked down from a great distance upon Senator McCarthy. I learned only that his hair is thinning at the top and I had great trouble explaining why he meant so much to me, not knowing then how well the next four days would explain it for me.

And then it was time for the first caucus of the New York McCarthy delegates.

It ought to be explained how we felt, many of us, there at the beginning, if only because such thoughts seem such strangers to me now. Before Senator Kennedy's death, the New York Democratic Party had been made up of many regulars, a few liberal insurgents, and a very few leaders who were Kennedy loyalists but otherwise regular in all things. When their great chief died, the leaders of his home guard had chosen the allegiance that seemed best to each: John Burns, the Democratic state chairman, had declared for Vice President Humphrey, and John English, the party's Long Island chairman, had declared for Senator McCarthy, bringing himself and perhaps six other delegates.

Now, it might theoretically be assumed that the McCarthy delegates should have been grateful for any allies we could get, but in fact the more sophisticated among us commenced with no more, and in some cases less, trust for a Kennedy delegate on our side than we felt for a Johnson delegate against us. The more sophisticated you were (sophistication at the start of a national convention being very little more than the ability to identify some other delegate's county leader), the more reasons you imagined for distrusting John English.

I for one thought that the Kennedy people could bring nothing but quarrel and recrimination with them, and that we should all be better off if they would just draw in their pickets, dismantle their artillery, and retire to the passive rectitude of their great wound. And there were less intimate reasons why we New York delegates who had always been for Senator McCarthy should seem inimical to John English and the troops he had brought with him.

Just our presence was a revolutionary affront. Of New York's 190 delegates, 123 are elected in party primaries, the other 67 being picked by the state committee—that is, the party leaders. Senator McCarthy had elected 65 delegates in the June primary. His had not been a cause to attract practical men of experience; so many of our delegates—and I include myself in all important respects—had only the vaguest notion of how the party system functions, seven of our number even being divines of variant ordinations.

Such upthrusts of the ignorant bring wild alarm for property holders. No regular leader had been more rudely jostled by our irruption than John English. Eugene Nickerson, his Senate candidate, had lost the primary to our Paul O'Dwyer; all his delegate candidates had been beaten; he had been further affronted when Allard Lowenstein, the earliest organizer of the McCarthy disturbance, had won the congressional nomination in one of English's own districts.

McCarthy's primary showing had, of course, given his followers the excuse to demand that their power be recognized by the regulars in selecting the 67 delegates-at-large. The party leaders of the metropolitan counties were the only ones who needed even to listen to that claim; together they had given us twenty-one delegates-at-large, most of whom could call themselves supporters of Senator McCarthy while being otherwise loyal to the county leaders in all things.

And so I sat down at this caucus of my fellow travelers, where too many of those I assumed I could trust were strangers to me and too many of those I felt I ought to mistrust were all too familiar. In those circumstances, I was grateful at least to see as presiding officer Paul O'Dwyer, New York's Democratic candidate for the Senate.

I have often meant to ask Paul O'Dwyer whether in early youth he had come across some teacher who had expounded Roman virtue, but I would probably have learned nothing, for I suppose that the wax has long forgotten the seal.

He was the brother of William O'Dwyer, mayor of New York (1946–1950). William O'Dwyer's career was shadowed at its end by the sort of scandal that is more gossip than matter. Paul remained so proud of his brother that once, years after the fall, he jumped to his feet, said, "That's all, sister," and ordered a reporter out of their office just for asking William O'Dwyer if he thought history had now vindicated him.

The memory of this breach of Paul O'Dwyer's deepest habit—which is his manners—was still vivid in her mind a few weeks ago; and I could answer only that we had all admired Robert Kennedy for being so loyal to his brother, but that anyone could be loyal to John Kennedy and it took a great gentleman to be not just loyal but so fiercely loyal to a brother in whom strength and weakness were as mixed as in William O'Dwyer.

Paul O'Dwyer had chosen to be a reformer in New York City politics, with all the general misfortunes a man must endure when he puts principle above convenience. He got reform nominations of two sorts: those for secure offices that were beneath him, like a seat in the City Council, and those for offices that seemed beyond the power of any rebel to reach. His nomination for the Senate by the McCarthy group came under the latter job description. When he won, those who had cherished him for years awoke—at just the same time as those who had never heard his name—to discover that he was someone to be taken seriously as a politician.

And then he did what I should think no sensible—by which I mean ordinary—politician would do when luck had cast up to him an opportunity so eminent. He simply informed the Democrats that he would not forgive Mr. Johnson his war or support Mr. Johnson's candidate in November. So he was with us still, when he should in common sense have been with those regulars whose help he needed.

The caucus commenced with the platform. Allard Lowenstein detailed the floor fight we were to make for the Vietnam war plank that had been agreed upon by Senators McCarthy and McGovern. A while later, Eleanor Clark French, our representative on the party platform committee, escaped her labors to tell us cheerfully how nice it was to be back with people from New York, and that she could not believe that there were such reactionary people as there are on that committee.

Somewhere early on, David Livingston, president of District 65 of the retail and wholesale workers' union, captured the floor to say that the Vietnam plank did not go far enough, and that we must stand for what we really want, which is to tell the convention that the war is brutal and horrible. Livingston had summoned up the key and the tone that used to signal the appearance of the Stalinist in the public debates of my boyhood. Professor Sidney Hook had informed me by Multilithed letter that Communists were scheming to capture the McCarthy movement; and now—though it has been a long time since I exercised the smallest dependence on Professor Hook in my struggle for the light—long-forgotten warnings and buried animosities stirred as Livingston sat down. First the clergymen, then our share of the Kennedy legatees, then the snobs, and now perhaps the Stalinists: Lighten our darkness, we beseech Thee, oh Lord, and by Thy great mercy, defend us from all perils and dangers of this night.

Beyond all the mischiefs to be imagined from the workings of such sects within, there was the innocence of the whole body without. Some of us still seemed to think it possible for any one of us to arouse the National Convention of a great political party just by finding a microphone and shouting, "Mr. Chairman, on this question . . ." Even those of us who knew more than that had not yet crossed the shadow line that separates those who have a part to play, however mean, from those who only watch. When we talked to each other, the subject was usually one of those rumors that wander on the outskirts of conventions and do the service of raising illusions in the audience that the thing that is inevitable is only one of several possibilities and that the audience should therefore keep watching to see whether what has already happened is going to happen. Mayor Daley of Chicago had made his contribution to these exercises that afternoon by adjourning the Illinois caucus and announcing that he would not announce its choice for president until Wednesday. Now, in our meanderings, a delegate demanded that we resolve to protest the security system which threatened to make the convention hall a jail; and Robert Silk, my alternate, answered that any protest like that would affront Mayor Daley, upon whose kindness we might be able to depend when the roll call came. I remember thinking how sensible that warning was, sure as I was that we should be very careful of Daley's feelings, which solicitude from the rebels was probably what the mayor had in mind when he announced delay and allowed us to infer hope.

At last, very late, we moved from the many things about which we could do nothing to the few about which we could do something, although naught to our profit. That night New York's delegates could be roughly distributed as: Johnson Party, eighty-six; McCarthy Party, counting bequests, from the Kennedy estate, eighty-six; parts of the Kennedy estate that had fallen to Vice President Humphrey, eighteen. Kennedy's bereaved household troops represented less than a sixth of the whole state delegation; still their twenty-nine votes, properly deployed, could control its organization in alliance with either faction they chose. Having no present, they cared only about the future; State Chairman John Burns wanted therefore to be elected chairman of the delegation, and John English to be elected Democratic national committeeman from New York, the essential outpost for keeping a guerrilla force in being until 1972 and the only long-term office at the delegation's disposal.

John English needed all eighty-six McCarthy votes to assure the Kennedy estate the tenure on this property; and, as I sat down remembering all the spite between us, if there was one gift to which I was determined not to contribute, it was this one to John English. Delegate Alex Rosenberg came over with an escape device. It was a disgrace, he said, that the Democratic party did not have a single national committeeman who was a Negro. He proposed to nominate Percy Sutton, borough president of Manhattan; would I second him? I agreed with enormous relief. If your only reason for opposing a candidate is a personal one, it is necessary to announce a high principle, and what defense can a white man offer when another white man accuses him of not being colored? Percy Sutton's name was thereupon put in nomination, and it was at once announced that he would decline in favor of John English. I had been afraid so. Percy Sutton is a person of considerable parts and elegance and he is constantly being offered either nomination for a job no Democrat can win or a chance to lead minority factions hoping to confuse the majority by forcing it to crush a charming Negro. No man in our politics therefore knows how more swiftly and courteously to elude swords pointed in his direction and honeyed as nominations.

Someone then nominated Eugene Nickerson, Nassau County Executive, who also declined in favor of English. Sutton persisted in his graceful evasions, and, writhing, we turned to Allard Lowenstein, who had already offended John English by defeating his candidate in a congressional primary. A search for Lowenstein was approved.

By now there was no one left on the floor but the middle-aged. We have read a long time about the Communist device of capturing organizations by coming to their meetings early and staying on after everyone had gone home. But I know now that this is not a tactic but a habit; I and these memorials of my youth had long ago abandoned everything about the Communist life except its inertia; we always stay late, because we are, on the one hand, people who never leave so long as anyone is left to listen to us, and because, on the other, it takes us so long to make up our minds. We would wrangle on until dawn and then accept John English.

Lowenstein could not be found; someone suggested that he ought to be nominated anyway. But now I was looking at John English, standing at the side, his hair brush-cut, his broad face as agreeable as if he had slept all night, so different from us yet now so surprisingly acceptable. The motion to draft Lowenstein just lay there; and we gave in; we McCarthy delegates had given the Kennedy estate the only office in our power. His heirs and not ourselves would lead the long war inside the Democratic Party that would begin when this battle was lost. And it did not seem a bad idea at all.

We were in bed for three hours and returned to consider the punishment of John Burns, who wanted to be chairman of the delegation, but who had announced his support for Humphrey. State Comptroller Arthur Levitt, by contrast, had sworn himself uncommitted and promised to be fair to us: The recommendation was that we support him. I rose to object. I did not, I said in effect, know any man who would not declare himself fair if you asked him, and I wondered whether we would not be better off with Burns, whom we knew at least and to whom we would not need to be introduced if an emergency came. My objection was dismissed, and we all went upstairs to the Grand Ballroom and the whole New York State caucus.

I was not again to take the floor for the rest of the week except once when I was asked and once when there was no one to speak for me. For I was becoming a delegate, a function too utilitarian to have much room even for habitual self-display; and, thereafter, if I had what seemed to me a sound idea, I would try to find a good speaker to present it. For my normally languid nature was beginning to be possessed by the coldness of the fanatic, the clarity of the tunnel-visioned, the concentration on the immediate that may or may not be possible only to a man who knows on Sunday that he will be hanged on Thursday—all the virtues that are alien to my normal self. In short, I was going a little mad and I could understand the clear minds of the mad; I knew now that, although Don Quixote may have been deluded when he thought the windmills were giants, he must have fought them coldly and alertly, as a soldier with a lance has to fight a giant.

Madness is not an attractive virtue. That would be my last real caucus with the New York McCarthy delegates; another would be called for Tuesday, and I would go to sit down and see some stranger, no doubt perfectly reasonable, in the chair explaining how to demonstrate on the floor. "Who's that jerk?" I asked my neighbor. "That's my father," he answered, and I mumbled some fragment from my former sanity and departed, having learned that to be mad is also to be bad and dangerous to know.

After my strictures on Levitt, my son said that it was extraordinary what close attention everyone paid when I spoke. He had been sitting too close to me to know the reason: Those fixed gazes had not been attending to wisdom but only straining to hear a voice that is inaudible beyond the first two rows. Upstairs, in a little while, this disability would prove of strangely comic service.

[Monday]

THE NEW YORK caucus room was impassable with wives, children, and seekers for the void that generally lies at the core of secret meetings, and other inadmissible bodies. John Burns had commenced to look like the host at midnight who has a sick child upstairs and is too polite to mention it. He said first that the caucus was closed to all except delegates and alternates, then tried a roll call, surrendered, and at length requested that the room be cleared so that we could all start over again and have our credentials checked.

I was sitting on the steps waiting for this process to thin, and Herman Badillo came over and made me a proposal. Badillo was one of the two New York members of the credentials committee, whose charge it is to hear the complaints of persons claiming discrimination in the selection of delegates from the several states. The committee's fundamental task is to adjust the Democratic party's egalitarian pretensions as conveniently as it can to the rights of property holders.

The managers of the convention were directors of a bank in whose vaults were stored those myths that the Democrats so desperately hope are not yet too worn to pass one more time as currency. One of those myths is the notion that used to comfort us all—that the Negro has a full voice in the politics of the North and none at all in the politics of the South. The dramas of the credentials committee are therefore played out against a chorus of outcries of southern Negroes attesting themselves deprived of their fair place in party affairs. In Georgia, for example, the credentials committee had to choose between a delegation chosen by Governor Lester Maddox, plainly the legal proprietor, and Julian Bond, whose moral posture was as blinding as his position in law was dim. The committee majority had sought its balance by proposing to seat half the delegates sent by Lester Maddox, the lawful owner, and half those brought by young Bond, the moral claimant.

With the proper mix of piety in such violations of reason, the credentials committee can expect awards as hilarious as this judgment from a historian in attendance:

DELEGATE FIGHTS
TRANSFORM PARTY
Democrats Ousting Bigots
and Beckoning to Youth

By MAX FRANKEL
—*The New York Times*, August 28

Since the credentials committee is the official complaint booth of the powerless, it is the custom of advanced and progressive parties like New York's to allot their places on it one to a Negro and one to a Puerto Rican, just as advanced and progressive labor unions always appoint a Negro director of their civil rights department.

Chairman Burns had appointed to credentials Mrs. Hilda Stokely, a Johnson Negro, and Herman Badillo, a Kennedy Puerto Rican. Mrs. Stokely is an old-fashioned lady of the sort that only the old-fashioned Negro community seems any longer capable of producing in the mass; she accepted what the committee majority wanted.

But Herman Badillo is a conspirator. He is a paladin of Puerto Rican politics in New York. He had voted with the minority of the credentials committee that wanted to cast out all the Maddox Georgians and also to seat a group from Texas that claimed that Governor John Connally's regular delegation had too small a quota of Negroes and Mexicans. Now he sought New York's vote for his position.

"Will you make the motion to support the Texas protest?" Badillo asked. "You're not in politics and you don't have to worry about reprisals from the President."

Rational objections poured forth from the ruins of my reason. I told Badillo that he knew as well as I that the only case against the Texas regulars was that only 9 percent of their delegates were Negroes or Mexican-Americans, two groups that together constitute 27 percent of their state's population. Neither of us had any reason to doubt that as good a case could be made against Illinois, let alone New York; and I could not, with any imitation of conscience, stand up and move the application of a standard for Texas that no one would demand of Illinois; and then, without pausing for breath, I told Badillo that I would make his motion.

By now the aisles were clear, and Badillo opened the business by asking New York to support Julian Bond against Lester Maddox unanimously. And Julian Bond appeared, vividly evoking the tenderness of that time when we had all loved the Student Non-Violent Coordinating Committee, until Stokely Carmichael proclaimed how much he hated us: Of all Julian Bond's obvious virtues, none seemed more compelling than the simple one of his not being H. Rap Brown. He had carried us back to that Arcady of the fifties when life offered us no choice more complicated than whether a young Negro of impeccable mien should be admitted to the University of Alabama. At the sight of him, ingrained respect for the property rights of other regulars quite abandoned our minds; Stanley Steingut, the party leader in Brooklyn, took the floor to move, "out of sense of honor," that New York do anything at this convention that young Mr. Bond might ask of it. The caucus acclaimed itself of that mind. We had arrived at one of those high moral moments in northern political organizations when someone need only say, "The black and Puerto Rican delegates demand that we endorse cannibalism," and the regulars would give him the resolution, so long as it carried no provision for bodies.

The time came for Texas. Herman Badillo served forth his poor case and nodded to me, and I moved that New York support the protest against the Connally delegates, having enough vestige of grace to commence with, "It is a complicated question but . . . " and enough of propriety to be certain someone on the other side would have the sense to object. But they all sat there exhausted from excessive indulgence of virtue and unable perhaps even to hear me; and the New York Johnson delegates sat unanimously pledged to vote against Johnson in the President's own state.

We could move then from the trivial business of the sacred to that essential business of the profane, the election of the officers of our delegation. Comptroller Levitt, having won all our eighty-six votes, could not find a single vote among the regulars who constituted his own family, and had to withdraw. John Burns was therefore elected chairman by semi-acclaim.

At last, then, the convention hall. Its managers had placed New York (too much McCarthy) and California (much too much Kennedy) at the back of the hall where their schismatic yawpings would not disturb too much the orthodox congregations to the front. From where I was, the formalities were accessible only in broken fragments: Very early the anticipation that I could really listen had to be abandoned, even though now and again some expression, either outrageous or inspiriting, would pass from the platform into my subconscious and then burst upward to stir me to outrage or approval. That first night a voice said, "Four years ago, our platform promised. . . ." and some bell within me signaled that some confession was coming, and I roused vaguely to recognize Secretary of Urban Affairs Robert Weaver, who was proceeding to testify that we Democrats keep our promises; and the interior monitor turned off, and I was deaf again and thenceforth.

Senator Daniel Inouye of Hawaii appeared a dimly embodied distant shadow, and commenced his keynote speech, and I ventured to depart these torpidities in search of a beer and ran into Secretary of Labor Wirtz, that cherished survivor of a more attractive time. "How do you like Danny's speech?" he asked. I said I took it as one more piece of evidence of my experience that the one political institution likely to be to the right of a conservative party out of power is the liberal party in power, at which the secretary looked so wounded that I hastened to   • the pressroom to find and read Senator Inouye's speech. Its text confirmed most of my prejudices, but a few graceful sentences, standing lonely like willows overlooked by a bulldozer, suggested that Secretary Wirtz might have been the father of some first draft horridly mutilated. I was embarrassed, and, more than that, surprised that the old words like "commitment," "dissent," "the true dimension of the challenge," limped across the pages like convict strangers, hoarsely attempting to communicate with me. Had I so lost my feeling for the great issues that I could no longer even understand the great clichés?

So back I went to that killing floor: Governor Hughes was up and ready to deliver his credentials report. Jesse Unruh moved on behalf of California that the subject be laid over until the next afternoon so that Julian Bond could prepare himself for the debate. The chairman rejected that suggestion and made plain management's determination to entertain no delays; Unruh appealed and the first roll call was ordered.

"Jesse's just trying to mess up the convention," Richard Goodwin explained happily. Herman Badillo suggested that Julian Bond would expect New York to vote for postponement. But now, though, the regulars had begun to understand that they were out of step with the dancing master; Mayor Daley's Illinois voted 118 to 0 against the Unruh motion, and they knew that, trivial as the issue was, there must be some outrageous deception if Daley had voted one way and they were committed to vote the other. Chairman Burns was beset by regulars demanding their right—having voted once, drunk with virtue, to vote again sober with realism.

"This is procedure," Frank Rossetti growled. "We didn't promise him anything on procedure." In the silence that followed this definition of the difference between matters of mere substance and matters of real consequence, John Burns turned to Monroe Goldwater, the New York organization's legal counsel. What, that old gentleman wondered, was the degree of our commitment to Julian Bond? Absolute, the McCarthyites replied; and absolute it was; in the flight of Stanley Steingut's hyperbole we had so bound ourselves that Julian Bond need only send a request that New York immolate itself upon the floor in his cause, and we could have no option in honor but to send for the matches and the gasoline cans.

I, being of no further service in the chorus of mutterings for justice, commenced wandering the floor again, coming upon Mayor Daley just as he woke up former Senator Paul Douglas to cast his vote. I returned to find Monroe Goldwater talking to Julian Bond, who had come to thank New York for its useless but ornamental gift.

"On this business of delay," Mr. Goldwater was asking, "did you want us to vote for that?"

"We didn't care about that much, one way or another," Bond replied.

And then at once, as though from the very floor, there sprung up the two Negro regulars in the delegation, short men and heavily circular ones, and they began pushing young Julian Bond. "Boy," said one, "don't you do that again. You keep in touch with us, do you hear? You better straighten up, do you hear?"

Julian Bond brilliantly abstained from saying "Don't call me 'boy' "; he looked straight at Mr. Goldwater:

"Mr. Goldwater, I'm very sorry about the misunderstanding. I'm sure we can find ways to be sure that it doesn't happen again. I don't think New York has been very much hurt."

Mr. Goldwater smiled and said he didn't think so either. Gentleman had called to gentleman across the doorkeepers; the thick black hands fell away from Julian Bond's jacket. Mr. Goldwater observed that now it was time to vote on Julian Bond's demand for all the Georgia delegation; did it seem to him that New York owed him 190 votes for that, too?

"Mr. Goldwater," Julian Bond answered, "I can't say whether it comes within your commitment or not." And then he explained his case, and said he was sure New York would know what it ought to do, gravely said good-bye, and shiningly departed. Mr. Goldwater turned around and told John Burns that we were committed to give Julian Bond all of New York's votes.

George Miller, a supporter of President Johnson, asked how we could have been so low as to pull anything like this off on them.

"But, George," I replied with sudden illumination, "if my second serve comes into your court and you put it in the net, that's not my ace; it's your error."

I had learned something I had never known. Politics is a game like weekend tennis, and it is decided not by its placements but by its errors.

All delays having been voted down, first Texas, then Georgia, was put to the question, and the evening's last roll call began. The crash of the great state organizations came down on Julian Bond, and, at every intonation, you could feel the infinitely long night falling at last upon that Democratic party whose rule over our affairs we had come to take for granted as permanent. There is a moment in our politics when a faction takes command of a major political party before carrying it to catastrophe; and, when it does, its signal is to assert itself as a majority for what is loosely called reactionary.

Julian Bond had a dubious claim indeed on all the Democratic party's seats for Georgia. But rights and wrongs aside, our voters do cherish the myths of liberalism. Then the announcement of sentence went up at last: Georgia regulars, 1,413; Julian Bond, 1,041½. It was a little closer than we had a right to expect; still, Humphrey was going to be nominated.

California began shouting "No, no"; then there began the chant of "Julian Bond, Julian Bond," in hoarse tones imitating portent. When the chant was picked up by New York, it did not seem my own kind of theater and I was silent.

But then my discontented eye fell upon Monroe Goldwater—thrusting his hand forward and chanting "Julian Bond, Julian Bond, Julian Bond." Mr. Goldwater is eighty-two now, and he was the law partner of Edward Flynn when the Bronx was as rigidly Flynn's as Ciudad Trujillo was ever *trujillista*. This night he had voted for a complainant Negro against an owner of property, a thing he could hardly have done often before, since that side of that kind of case does not often come to his office. Mr. Goldwater stood there—at three forty-five in the morning back home—and he growled the defiance of the lost cause and the fallen flag.

To the many, conventions must seem a very squalid chore; but to the few, if they wait long enough, conventions can bring those special moments of epiphany that Webster defines as "a manifestation, especially of divinity." Monroe Goldwater, oldest of all the regulars, had come to his epiphany. I left it to him who had deserved it to serve out the chant "Julian Bond, Julian Bond," and went home.

[Tuesday]

THE TRANSCENDENT OCCASION of Tuesday's caucus was to be the appearance of Humphrey and McCarthy and McGovern in competition for our already closed minds; but they had gone to California, and they would never get to our part of the field, because we fought there most of the day, having no time to pause and pass in review before our commanders, being too busy—on one side the regulars in order of battle, on the other we, scuffling at once to bleed them and to stay in being another afternoon. It was not a battle about which anyone except ourselves was ever likely to know.

The caucus's first business was to elect a national committeeman, the only trace we could leave behind us, and therefore one the regulars were determined to obliterate. They moved to postpone that selection until Friday, when the Vice President would be the Democratic nominee and his wishes would be New York's duty. Our side objected and the roll call began, the decisive test of whether John English would survive in the hills. If the election were held that day, he would win; just as surely, if it were deferred until Friday, he would lose. My name was called to vote early, and I wandered over to sit among the regulars with William McKeon, who used to be the party's state chairman.

McKeon voted to elect the committeeman this day, and then he said, "You'd better win this one, because I have to switch on the next." Billy McKeon was a Kennedy legatee fallen to Mr. Humphrey; he was sworn to vote for the Vice President's choice for national committeeman; he could do no more than give John English his only real chance. At the end of the roll call, an immediate decision had been decreed—by just 15 votes and inestimable subtleties in minds like Billy McKeon's. John English was thereupon nominated and elected, 108 to 80½, with Billy McKeon faithful to the forms of his new allegiance, but all other Kennedy legatees announcing for English, and even a few regulars indulging the opportunity to imply their independence by supporting the winner in a case where their votes against him would be useless.

And then the Johnson party brought up its guns: There would be

476

no chance to hear the candidates today; even so, it was moved that, without waiting for them further, the delegation be polled and its choice recorded at once and the Vice President's 104–86 majority officially revealed.

It was a device promising Humphrey no important gain and us McCarthyites no particular loss except whatever small headline the delegation remained capable of producing; and it was directed more at the Kennedy heirs than at us, the phantom of Senator Edward Kennedy being the only shadow left across Mr. Humphrey's path.

But it had become essential to us to buy all the time we could before that phantom had to be laid to rest. Clarence Jones moved to table any immediate roll call on presidential candidates. That seemed so useless a gesture that Congressman William Fitts Ryan was already at work on another resolution saying that, in mere courtesy, we should delay choosing among the candidates until we had heard them all. Ryan's motion to delay a vote seemed to have no more plausible chance of prevailing than Jones's bare motion to table, although it did have the ornamentation of an argument. We seemed to have no resource left except to use up all the delays provided by procedure.

The tally on the motion to table opened among these gloomy reflections; and, while it pointed toward its patently inescapable end, Jerry Bruno came over to see William vanden Heuvel. Jerry Bruno had managed Senator Robert Kennedy's upstate office: he had fallen, after the disaster, to Vice President Humphrey's troop, and he was committed to vote with them now. Still, he said to vanden Heuvel, he had a contract with three upstate county chairmen to give him a vote apiece on any one roll call he asked for it on; did vanden Heuvel think that this was a time to call all that in? Vanden Heuvel thought it was, time being all he had. Jerry Bruno went back to his side of the hall: And I was mildly surprised when three votes normally alien to us were called out on our side. Secretary Ben Wetzler announced that we had voted 96½ to 92½ to put off the roll call on candidates one day more, and by then we could feel the depletion of the regulars' heavier pieces. We could come down from the hills, briefly and safely reckless, and engage them on the Vietnam plank.

Both the majority and the minority had made those concessions designed to appease the great middle body. And the differences between the two positions were not startling, although Theodore Sorensen, for the minority, made a cogent effort to make them seem so, as Wilson Wyatt, for the majority, made a painful effort to make them seem not. It was a curious debate. Jules Feiffer drew hair on the head and chin of Mr. Humphrey on one of Mr. Humphrey's brochures, wrote "Che Lives" under it, and, laughing, we passed that around.

But a silence had descended upon the regulars; no professional among them would care to speak out for Mr. Johnson's war; his defiant spirit had life and echo only from Tom McSpedon, a delegate from Yonkers: "Why don't you stand up for America? You got no guts." The regulars did not stir or even seem decently ashamed of not stirring. After the debate ran down, Matthew Troy asked me to vote for the antiwar plank. Matthew Troy is the city councilman from Queens and the Patrolmen's Benevolent Association, although it has always been hard to believe so while looking at him: The standard-bearers for unpleasant people are quite often rather pleasant themselves, an irony of experience to which I owe some of my failed seriousness. Still Matty was the prime organizer of those "Support our Boys" displays that are unique among our ceremonials for being the only parades in which the marchers beat up the bystanders; and now he was soliciting my support for the creeps, the Congs, and the mincing epicenes. But the wild interior laughter at his apparition could hardly be heard in the crush; the vote for the antiwar plank was 116 to 24, and we rose and cheered.

"I just cast one vote my wife and children won't complain about," said Moses Weinstein, the Queens leader. And so, I answered cheerfully, had Matty Troy.

And then I knew what had happened. It was not we who had won but the ghost of Robert Kennedy. All we had done was faithfully, even commendably, play our parts in a novel that had been robbed of its hero. And, without that hero, we had provided nothing more consequential than a momentary embarrassment to what was established and would be preserved to collapse before Mr. Nixon. Every little surprise of the day—the calling to the letter of contracts held in reserve by the

Kennedy people, the timely evasions of the spirit of contracts assumed to be held by the Johnson people—was the way in which these things are done, and they all had been done for a Robert Kennedy who would never be there. This was just the way it would have happened: All over Chicago, delegates turning desperately—whether at Damascus or Waterloo, who could say?—the old men going down, the revolutionary hero rising up. The hero is not that perfect piece of goods that alone suited my old self. I used to complain that Robert Kennedy contrived so well to suit both the blacks who hate the whites and the whites who hate the blacks, being, I would say, at once the backlash and the black-power candidate, the beloved of all who cry harshly and gesture wildly. But now I understood how helpless we were without him—this candidate of Matty Troy and Julian Bond, this healer who wounded, this pacifier who outraged. And this was when he would have taken control; I sat in a room filled with every element of his nomination except the nominee; I see Batista, I said to Billy McKeon, but we have no Castro.

There would be nothing more for us beyond that afternoon; we had, as so often before, won victories of a strange and almost portentous splendor, and they would be followed tomorrow by the triumph of the conquered.

I felt as though I had come from a village to some huge, unfamiliar city. At lunch most of its inhabitants complained about Senator McCarthy, who had failed to ignite the California caucus. I could not, at the moment, think about McCarthy—he seems about that time to have stopped thinking about himself—last night having been for credentials, tonight being for the platform, and any thought of tomorrow being only a distraction from today. Did the mind of the slate-fitter on the roof of Chartres run much to God or the Virgin or the Saints, let alone Blanche of Castile? I felt removed from all cloud conquerors and even more removed from that self that would too soon return to nice, scornful appraisals of their style of flight. I clung just this little while to my village, to its obscure quarrels and unnoticed resolutions, to all that was left to me of a time like the one for which Robert Oppenheimer confessed himself "homesick"—the transient but unforgettable occa-

479

sion of "artists concerting their skill, and of men of learning content with anonymity."

The convention gathered again that evening for seven and a quarter hours of dedication to the most grave and ancient of things: chaos, night, and dullness. I had promised to give up my delegate credentials awhile to Robert Silk, my alternate, so I wandered among the bazaars off the floor, coming across Robert Boyd of the Knight newspapers, who said that his publisher had seen Senator McCarthy that afternoon and that the senator had said that he could not possibly win, and that the Chicago *Daily News* would be proclaiming this concession within the hour. A girl bystander put her head against a door and began to cry; nothing in my mulish insularity came up with either the impulse or the words to console her; crying, in the first place, was for Wednesday and, in the second, my only thought was that McCarthy had been honest a day or so too soon; the vote on Vietnam was coming up that night, and we might have gained a vote or so from the pretense that Mr. Humphrey had an opponent still on his feet.

Miss Aretha Franklin opened our proceedings by singing "The Star-Spangled Banner": A young man in our train said that, if *he* were black, no one could get him to sing that song in public; and I growled back that, if he were black, he wouldn't be that stuffy about anything that paid union scale. A Negro is somebody who gets one chance at a job for every three we get; he doesn't have our options.

It turned out to be a night for me and the convention to wander to no detectable purpose; around midnight I came upon the mayor of Chicago. Adlai Stevenson III was kneeling beside him in earnest converse, looking the way bond servants must have when they wanted passersby to know that they were, anyway, tutors. Peter Lisagor of the Chicago *Daily News* introduced us. The mayor asked how things were in New York, and I told him in all the petty detail that no one else had cared to listen to all afternoon; I had finally come upon someone as incapable as I of resisting accounts of inconsequential intrigue. There began to stir in me intimations of awe, for this was someone mad for the rest of his life while I was mad only for an occasion; he was the permanent of what was only the transient in me, my coldness a trick of the will, his the marrow of his bone. I congratulated him for having made so good a soldier of Paul Douglas; and he laughed effortlessly and freely, knowing it to be a compliment; the mayor is a rather pleasant-looking man when things are going as he wishes. And I understood that we were only sports and that he was history; Stalin must, I suppose, have had much the same effect on Communists.

"What do you think you all will do on the platform?" I wondered. Mr. Johnson's draft platform had just been distributed. The mayor picked it up and concentrated on the cover, which said: THE PLATFORM OF THE DEMOCRATIC PARTY, AS PRESENTED TO THE DEMOCRATIC CONVENTION, CHICAGO, 1968, in silver letters. Then he turned it over and looked with the same care at the back cover, which was blank. Then he laid it down. "I think we'll go with it as it is," he said, and after a while I arose and excused myself from history.

Back at New York we waited for the platform, and the evening exhausted itself with the dispute over the credentials of the Alabama delegation and labored off to some nonsense about granting the Young Democrats the recognition their generation deserved. "They're trying to wear us out," one of our young men complained.

"They want us to vote on the platform at two in the morning when nobody will see it on television." The notion that anyone on any side knew what he was doing was too outrageous to let pass without some objection; it was we, after all, I said, who had insisted on all these credentials fights; and it was the last of our credentials fights that had consumed the session with a roll call both interminable and fore-doomed; our error was nobody else's placement.

At last poor Hale Boggs blundered onstage, smiled tentatively upon the beasts awaiting, and made ready to introduce the platform. It was well after midnight; we had two hours before us, but I remember hoping very much that we would do the business now, television being in another country and the only issue left to me being some assurance that its allotted evil be confined to each day. How the rest of us felt I do not know; I left one delegate crying out a demand that the debate on Vietnam be deferred not one minute longer, and I returned in two minutes to hear him shout, "Let's go home." In any case, at our distance any shout of ours was irrelevant; Hale Boggs had retreated; and, in his place, Mayor Daley rose up to rasp that the galleries were trying to take over this meeting, and that he was ordering the delegates to go home. And I saw all at once how repellent history is, and silently rejoined the resistance to it and went home for three hours of sleep, not knowing at the time that this was just about all I should have in Chicago.

[Wednesday]

MY GRANDFATHER HAD engraved on my grandmother's gravestone: SHE HATH DONE WHAT SHE COULD, and I remember my aunt laughing many years later about what a stiff compliment that was, great as was the love it tried to express. This morning it seemed the grandest compliment in the catalogue. Our odd lot of the innocent and all too knowing, of the untried and the damaged, had indeed done what we could; and now nothing practical was left.

When Matty Troy asked me to vote for the antiwar plank, I had replied that I was bound to vote for it if no one else in the room did, sent as I had been by the only congressional district this side of Albania where the name of Joseph Stalin still evokes some reverence. I did not say this to mock my constituents, but only to set them stiffly apart from Matty's; there was, in truth, growing within me a sense like holy obligation to them and beyond them to the institution of the convention, this butt for the derision not just of all observers but of its own and very self. A little while ago Mayor Daley and I had laughed about how easy the poor beast was to manage, the mayor and I, Olympian slob and attendant slob, indulging together the vice of gods, which is contempt for men. For two days I had seen delegates prodded, pushed, stopped, and all but frisked by security guards, almost never protesting, no more able than Mayor Daley to recognize themselves as members of a parliament, a curious parliament to be sure, but enough of one to render their persons, if not sacred, at least above continual stoppage by the king's men. What remained of their dignity had this morning become oddly precious to me, just because there was so little of it. This was the day we were going to lose, and I began to think of voters of the Twentieth Congressional District—or more precisely to imagine them—sitting all those miles away feeling themselves cheated, and I knew that my duty ran not just to my ballot but to some gesture of their reproach and their promise to return and try again.

Then it turned out that packages as curious as the one in which McCarthy had been conveyed to this convention carry unexpected resources: Theodore Bikel volunteered to lead us all in song after we lost the vote on the antiwar plank, and that settled very comfortably the conflict between my nature and what I thought I ought to do.

Coming into the hall, I saw John Burns at our standard, touching my sympathy even more than usual; I saw the prospect before him, the appalling embarrassment of our deportment, the weary effort to protect us from the wrath of the guards. I said to him that I would not boo or cry out but that I had a contract to sing with Bikel. Then I sat down, as insurance of my good conduct, next to Benjamin Buttenwieser, limited partner of Kuhn, Loeb & Company, who was reading *The Wall Street Journal*. I had never known Ben Buttenwieser—while revering his wife, the lawyer Helen, as shield of the outcast—and there existed, on my side at least, the eternal diffidence between the debtor and the creditor class. If there was anyone in our company who could be trusted to be as stuffy as I wanted to appear for the occasion, Ben Buttenwieser was my model.

Hale Boggs began reading Mr. Johnson's Vietnam plank and paused a moment, overcome possibly by the horror of what his wife and daughter would say to him at dinner; and from our seats delegates started to arise, and, leaning fiercely forward, brandished rags painted STOP THE WAR and began to chant. I winced and looked at Ben. He reached into his pocket, pulled out his banner, climbed on a chair, and chanted too. He sat down to meet my stricken eyes. He said something like *damned war; even our plank is inadequate; we ought to get out now and pay these poor people indemnity.* Ben, I said in sincere alarm, think of the Establishment; his answer was a growl about whether Helen ever thought of the Establishment and he climbed back on his chair and went on chanting.

So now I was all alone; the model for my manners had been carried away from me and was wriggling, so far as a Kuhn, Loeb partner can be said to wriggle, in *his* epiphany.

Alone, I broke my contract with myself and John Burns. Something on the platform said, "Thank God for Mayor Daley," and then I booed. I did not know what Mayor Daley was doing, being cut off in my village from the great city outside, but instinct cried out that if it were something that could be praised along with the war in Vietnam, it must be quite awful indeed. I asked someone who the speaker was, and he identified Congressman Wayne Hays of Ohio.

Now I had covered Wayne Hays with some attention when he was harrying Adam Powell, and I reflecting that Adam Powell gets the enemies he deserves. But I had no more recognized Hays than I had recognized Inouye; you could not tell the faces on the platform without the sort of checklist of sins and virtues the Recording Angel must have learned by now to use; these were types, Humours, with only the last feature on each face that the caricaturist would have had to leave—the neck of Daley, the slack mouth of Wayne Hays, the engravement of all the occasions of tragedy announced on Pierre Salinger, the wound to his self-esteem that his Democratic primary had done to Wayne Morse. I did my best to follow what they were saying; still I was surprised to find, when I came upon various limbs of it embalmed in the *Times* a while afterward, that it had been quite a brilliant debate. No matter that; its end was appointed.

While we waited for the secretary to announce the roll call, the mayor's band played the Air Force hymn, the Marine hymn, the artillery hymn, and all the rest, making Mr. Johnson's point with an emphasis that Mr. Johnson's speakers had not often dared give it. There was one omission in this medley to stir the blood of patriots; and I sent Bikel the suggestion that, when we began to sing, we should open with "The Eyes of Texas Are Upon You." Then the vote was proclaimed, and there rose from the left of me the music of "We Shall Overcome" and I understood why the choice was Bikel's by right: The professionals do not make jokes.

I first heard "We Shall Overcome" so long ago that I remember it as "We Will Overcome" because, in the beginning, it was sung by persons not noticeable enough for a grammarian to explain to them those nice distinctions of conjugation between "shall" and "will." But I had sung neither version, at least in company, for reasons of decency taught me by another worldly man. *When Pope Pacelli was dying at Castel Gandolfo, an Italian count went about his daily water-skiing in the lake below the papal residence. Coming ashore, he was met by journalists putting as much reproach as they could into their respect for his rank. "Gentlemen," he answered them, "it is not fitting for a man who has lived his life as I live mine to take part in prayer for the Pope."* But now I sang the song, not as my own, but as the song of young men in jail against the war, and of other young men on corners, the song of the scorned and the humiliated, mine for this once and then only on a credential from all the lost constituencies. A sweetness strange in me and as strange in this place seemed to hang all around; I floated and swayed in hazy summer air, reaching for Ben Buttenwieser's hand as I would have reached just this once for Mark Rudd's, this being a moment not of defiance but of promise. Then those long, dreamy five minutes were over and I left and went upstairs where New York was finally caucusing to register its votes on presidential candidates.

I walked up with Moe Weinstein. "Did you see who was singing 'We Shall Overcome'? Matty Troy! And when I think what that guy's friends have done to me in my district!"

The caucus voted 96½ for the Vice President to 87 for Senator McCarthy, with a few scattered to Senators Kennedy and McGovern. Now that we could no longer do them even paltry damage, the regulars had begun quite horridly to hate us. Congressman James Scheuer exerted a special privilege to complain of scurvy treatment by the Chicago police and introduced a resolution demanding reforms in procedure that would guarantee that no Democratic delegate be treated this way again. "No, no, no," the regulars cried, hideously. "Support your local police," Theodore Bikel cried mockingly. And we all disbanded with averted eyes as if from some cheap hotel, guilty haters turning out to be as furtive as guilty lovers. Afterward I said to Stanley Steingut that I thought Scheuer's motion might have been better served if he had just looked at the regulars and said to them: "Gentle-men, how many of you can be sure that one of your children is not out there being hit by a policeman?" Stanley Steingut answered, "If any kid of mine got hit by a cop, I know it would be his fault." Now, if there is one thing I know about Stanley Steingut, it is that he would do his feeble best to strangle any adult who touched a child of his.

I remembered having one more contract to offer. It had occurred to me, somewhere back in our lost innocence, that the properly contained gesture of the McCarthy delegates might be to wait, each in his particu-lar delegation, until his vote had been cast, and then leave. By now I knew that it was no more possible to make a dignified and noticeable exit from this place than it would be from the Vincennes, Indiana, bus terminal. Still, there survived a vestige of this image reduced in propor-tion but inflated in grandeur: Arthur Miller and Paul Newman were delegates from Connecticut. What if they would walk out once their state had voted and I could find, say, Sander Vanocur and suggest that it might be worthwhile for him to interview them for NBC on the way out? So I found Arthur Miller and braced him with the contract. He answered that he had not yet made up his mind whether or not it remained his duty to work within the system; I accepted this as a polite but just estimate of my notions of theater, and we drank beer, filling me with the discovery that the best companions have the tragic sense of life.

My comrades and I had come to my village of New York at least with some sense of place, many of us having consorted or disputed with its regulars well before this; a man can make his way, however mod-estly, in villages he can persuade himself he grew up in. But the doings of Arthur Miller's Connecticut had been far beyond any experience of his. Nobody there even seemed to know who he was. No mythic figure alive is, of course, less inclined than Miller is to bring his godhead into the conversation. I thought with pity and sadness of all our other delegates who must be sitting as helpless strangers all around the hall. But even in his isolation, Arthur Miller had developed a kind of fond-ness for his Connecticut neighbors, and one of his reasons for not staging a grand exit was not wanting to embarrass them.

On the first television screen I saw outside, there was the sight of Delegate Alex Rosenberg, my neighbor, being thrown by two guards out of my own quarter of New York, summoning me back to the room I had just quitted. Whatever was happening on the street outside was seeping its baleful infection inside to all of us; we had become, I am afraid, quite hysterical.

What was public about the rest of the evening is lost to me. We spent it reading bulletins brought in from the streets, and wandering out to caucuses, past television sets lurching with images of clubs and heads. We held meetings to exchange unformed and hysterical recommendations, once passing a resolution to proceed at once downstairs and set up so barbaric a yawp that Chairman Albert would have to entertain a motion for a roll call on adjourning until the next day. That last seemed to me the worst idea I had ever heard or even thought of. We were taking part in an obscene movie calculated not just to degrade but actually to inflame its audience, and the less we did to slow it down, the sooner it would end, the screens go blank, and an incitement to riot and slaughter be removed. But the resolution to disrupt appears to have been forgotten by the time we returned to the floor; some guardian angel had been obliterating every bad decision we made all week, before we had time to act it out to disaster. So the business got done, with minimal nuisance from us. I had meant to walk out as soon as New York was called; but then Mr. Humphrey was proclaimed the nominee, and I realized that, at some point in the mingling of our private nightmares, my vote had been announced and I had not even heard it.

Back then upstairs in the caucus room, we listened on the loudspeaker to Senator McCarthy talking to the reporters downtown. All I remember about that was the pride and gratitude I felt for someone who had come to pitch nine innings and whom we had taken through fifteen, talking at the end not about himself but about the wounded. Richard Goodwin and Allard Lowenstein talked about our future in speeches that were remarkably moving, just for being so contained and so passable when parsed. Then—the beat of hysteria being exhausted by now—it was suggested that we march past Mayor Daley's house and on to the Hilton, carrying candles as a silent reproach. By the time we were out of the hall, a representative of the city of Chicago was waiting outside to tell us: 1) that there was a city ordinance against parading past the mayor's house; 2) that the Hilton was eight miles away; and 3) that buses were waiting to take us to some place "outside the riot area," from which we could walk to the Hilton. We got on the buses. "Remember," said Patrick O'Neal, "if they hand you a bar of soap and say it's a shower, don't take it." A policeman clambered up to say that our route had been changed again "because of riot conditions," and I surrendered to the vision of being dumped in Gary, Indiana, and to thanks to the Lord for Mayor Richard Hatcher.

But we were deposited, rather decorously, at Michigan and Randolph, very close to the Art Institute, and stood with our candles, as chaste as seniors singing their farewells in the twilight; it was starting to occur to me that, when a man commits himself to demonstrating for one day in his life, he had best know the risk that he might have to demonstrate *sine die* and indefinitely. Paul O'Dwyer announced that Arthur Miller and I had been appointed to draft a resolution; I found Arthur Miller, who was no more able to think of a resolution than I. We told Paul as much, and he smiled and was unable to think of one either. I allowed a suspicion to enter my mind and grow to a certainty: Anyone with the range of Paul O'Dwyer's spirit has numberless souls, inimical to one another, in his care; he had to worry not only about our heads but also about the immortal souls of policemen, which had quite enough to answer for without having further objects of temptation thrown up to them. He wanted us to go home, and the natural successor to any resolution on anything is a motion now to adjourn. I agreed with him, but no inspiration came to our assistance, so we sang a while longer and then formed to march to the Hilton.

On the way I thought of the proper resolution—a poor thought, forgotten now—and ran forward, calling, "Paul O'Dwyer, Paul O'Dwyer." I found him dealing with a police inspector with that mystical mixture of kinship and authority possible only for one Irishman immediately identifiable to another Irishman as having, at an early point in life, on pure principle, refused the king's shilling. I knew at once that there was nothing I could contribute to this communion; turning away, I slipped and looked back, on righting myself, into the face of the enemy—a wide-eyed boy in the helmet liner of the National Guard. I said, very seriously, that I was sorry to be keeping you up so late, son, and Arthur Miller and I went in search of something to eat. Even the meanest holes were shut and we walked back past the Hilton. A young man was standing in the entrance; he looked much too respectable to be a delegate to a Junior Chamber of Commerce convention; a patch on his head had been shaved, and there was the cross of a bandage upon it.

"And just when do you think," Arthur Miller said, "the Conrad Hilton will be headquarters for a Democratic Convention again? The phone will ring; a voice will say that this is the Democratic National Committee and the manager"—he was starting to shake with laughter—"the manager will get his gas mask out of the drawer, cough, and say, Mr. Conrad is out of the country and Mr. Hilton won't be back for a month."

We parted, weeping with laughter. There was no way to the Sheraton-Chicago except walking; down Michigan Avenue, whose resident devil maintains his effect of crowds angrily roaring on both sides of you even at four in the morning, I felt again how I love this evil city, which has always given me more of life than anyone has a right to expect in any four-day segment. There was an envelope at the desk inscribed to Honorable James Murray Kempton. The letter inside said: "Hope you can join us for brunch in the Humphrey Hospitality Suite, Thursday 10 A.M. to 1 P.M., Tally-Ho Room, 9th Floor. We look forward to seeing you!" I would have to be downstairs in the morning to say good-bye to my friends on their way upstairs to the ninth floor.

[Thursday, the Day After]

AND NOW THE thing was finally done; no constituent could complain
if I played no part in choosing a vice president; my son and I had a day
to ourselves, beginning with a long slow breakfast, and then maybe the
Giants on television or the Art Institute possibly, and then an evening
watching television. We went to the Hilton on the chance of finding
Senator McCarthy. In the lobby we looked at the *Daily News:* David
Dellinger proposed that five hundred delegates march to the amphitheater this night, demanding admittance with countless protesters behind
them. I could conceive of no chapter in the annals of human freedom
quite so exotic as myself advancing behind banners, claiming my right
to penetrate an assemblage that I didn't want to attend and for which
I had my card of admission in my pocket.

Senator McCarthy was in the lobby; I asked if he might have time
for us; Norman Mailer was there too; wearily, McCarthy swept us all
up in his bag of social obligations and said, all right, come up to the
room in half an hour. And Norman said that he could use the interval;
he had a proposal to make to me. We all went to the Haymarket Room,
Mailer, my son, Robert Lowell, and I, and were served beer by a
waitress in thighs. Norman began his proposal by saying something
irresistibly brilliant about the condition of men.

He went on to say that we must answer Daley. We must make the
ante higher. "Why is it," he said to me, "that I have never hit you? It
is because you represent the face of decency." I thought, first, that he
might have chosen a better example, second, that such distinctions
among faces cannot have inhibited Norman at every moment in his
prior experience, and, last, that I must explain to my son that the
recognition that you are in the presence of a truly large personage is not
hampered but completed when you understand that you can laugh at
him a little. I said none of these things and went on listening. We must
raise the ante, Norman continued; we must make him hit the face of
decency. Since I happened to have been assigned the face of decency
in this discussion, my normal response would have been to decline the

nomination; but the cold madness of the delegate was encroaching again upon my interior, so I merely asked "How?" Norman answered something to the effect that he had told the protesters yesterday that they should not march unless at least two hundred delegates had the kidney to go with them. There would be a caucus of McCarthy delegates this afternoon—my guardian angel, having released me for rest and recreation, had until now protected me from knowing about any such thing and thus being torn between duty and pleasure—Norman's proposition was that I go with him to that caucus and introduce him and that he would ask for two hundred delegates—no less, and, if it turned up less, no march. I understood then that Norman was my better in everything that could be imagined, except that I was four days, which means light-years, older than he in those ballrooms where delegates meet. *When the Civil Rights Act of 1964 was being debated, Senator Everett McKinley Dirksen was set upon by a flock of clerics cawing that this was a moral issue. And Senator Dirksen freed himself and said, with the pride of Richelieu: "Gentlemen, I am not a moralist. I am a leg-is-la-tor," and escaped to work out the sinuosities of his scheme to pass the law.* I was not a wandering prophet; I was a delegate. "Norman," I said, "I am a delegate and I have learned things I did not know and will too soon forget. I know that when a delegate rises to say that he will go only when one hundred and ninety-nine other delegates go, he has not introduced a resolution; he knows, and they know, that he has found the exit." He might get 198 but, I was sure, he could be certain that neither he nor they would be embarrassed by the discovery of the 199th. "All I could do for you as a delegate would be to open by saying that I think that this is one thing that some of us ought to do, and that I have decided to do it even if no one else does. Then we should need another speaker and, if the thing builds, he can introduce you and we might get two hundred." I knew the other speaker almost without thinking; I had already recognized the Reverend Mr. Richard Neuhaus, a Lutheran pastor from Brooklyn and a delegate, as one of those persons into whose quiet mind the urge to bear public witness comes where only the temptation to sin comes to the rest of us.

Norman said that if I would go alone, I had more guts than he did. And I wondered again, as I often have, how insubstantialities like guts can worry men so much more intelligent than I. *I remember the war and its few patrols, and that acceptance of death that occasional soldiers know just once or twice and real soldiers know many times before it kills them. I remember coming out of the hills in that state of peace possible only to a man when he has known the enemy, and assured that I would never again fear gunfire. Then I was asleep in my tent, and some lonely Japanese Betty came over and began firing those silly white tracers and I, with nothing to fear, ran panting, almost gibbering, from tree to tree.* The one thing that guts is not is a quality that can be depended on. That is why it is useless continually to test it, because there is always a time when it fails almost anyone. Bravery is irrelevant; unless you have the dangerous good fortune of not knowing you are in danger, the trick is to anticipate; as often as not, you will act badly anytime you are surprised. Dignity, not courage, is all anyone can hope to keep; how odd that Mailer should so little understand his life as not to see that one of its more significant achievements has not come from its tests of his bravery but from its continual salvage of dignity intact. I spared him these pomposities and simply explained that my estimate of the terrain was much more complacent than his; we were in what my experience suggested was the postlude of riot, when the indistinguishable forces of order and disorder were exhausted and in need of some fraudulent rite of purification; my assumption was that to enter the delegates into the situation would provide the excuse for such a rite and that we should have a most comfortable evening. At the hotel later I found my notes on Norman's proposition; they read "1) common public decency ante higher 2) 200 delegates march amphitheater"; never had a lesson of the master been so basely transcribed or, I'm afraid, so summarily dismissed as of no use for its circumstances.

Going back down Madison Avenue, we came upon Tom Braden, once of the CIA and now one of Robert Kennedy's bequests as a California delegate, standing with his arms folded, looking, like Cortés, toward the Art Institute; how marvelous, I thought, even here, to maintain the posture of a man who, though fallen into California, would never let a stranger doubt that he had gone to Dartmouth and who was still, at the same time, a delightful fellow. He asked if I was going to the convention. I said I was commencing to think it might be more useful if delegates would do what they could to stand between the police and the protesters; and I was of a mind to go into the streets.

"Sounds right, put like that," Braden said.

At the caucus I performed lamentably, in part because I am a lamentable performer even when aroused, and in part, I am afraid, because something inside me wanted me to be worse than usual. For one thing, Paul O'Dwyer had to be on the other side, for reasons I knew to be the best ones. He was a candidate for the Senate; and, even though he would not endorse Mr. Humphrey, this meant that he had to be a Democrat through November. It was his job to stay in the party and do what he could. And that meant that he must go to that night's session; he could manifest his objections on the floor, but he was not entitled to demonstrate them in the street. Beyond that, he would not feel entitled, as I remained sure I was, just to sit passively in his hotel, withdrawal being against his nature.

We all met in that same ballroom where we had wrestled the regulars so long. The Reverend Mr. Neuhaus was where I had expected him to be, near the platform, ready to speak the tongues I had known his particular angel would inspire in him. We consorted together; and then since O'Dwyer's particular angel had other commitments than mine, I felt it best not to trust Him for any contract not stipulated in advance; Paul O'Dwyer might not notice Neuhaus and me beckoning for the floor, so I went to him and asked that our names be inscribed to speak.

When our time came, Paul O'Dwyer had explained why he thought we should all go to the floor. I said that I did not think I could, because it would only be to play jokes on poor Mr. Humphrey. But what I might be able to do was to honor the commitment of my constituents to peace and order, which meant standing between the two hostile camps. I should go and try to do that even if no other delegate did. Or, if I didn't say just those words, what I did say was as limp. I ended by saying that I understood and honored Paul's position, but—and I hesitated, struggling to find some substitute for an expression I had never thought to use and then giving up and saying it:

"I think the time is here, now, for every one of us to do his own thing."

No flames danced in the back of the room when I finished; I felt the comfort that attends respectable failure in something you did not want to do, but I also felt very tired. I should not wait for Mr. Neuhaus to speak; as for Mailer, I doubted he would ever get his chance; he could only be summoned on a rising note of passion, and who could raise a pitch from the flat I had set? I told Mr. Neuhaus that he could find me in Room 1917—you know, "October"—and went up to lie down and look at television, seeing for the first time Senator Abraham Ribicoff looking down upon Richard Daley, as some magnificent old Whig might have looked down at a king, and here was a man who I had thought never felt deeply about anything but traffic safety. This of all politicians to be Algernon Sydney at the scaffold? "Grant that I may Dye glorifying Thee for all thy Mercies; and that at the last Thou hast permitted me to be Singled out as a witness for Thy truth; and even by the Confession of my Opposers, for that OLD CAUSE in which I was from my youth engaged, and for which Thou hast Often and Wonderfully declared thy Self." Oh epiphany, epiphany, wherefore come thou never to me?

Neuhaus came in after a while—there was no need to ask how the meeting had gone, thank heaven—and for two hours I bored my son and annoyed Mr. Neuhaus with peevish impertinences about the inconvenience of our collaboration, and expressions of deep desire that we would have no flock except ourselves and that therefore I could make my excuses. I liked him immensely for abstaining from either quarreling or agreeing with me, and I am sure that his Christian struggled with the temptation to dislike me and lost. Then from downstairs Dixon Bain, a New Jersey delegate, called to say that our fellow marchers were waiting.

On the street outside there was a small company of delegates, which I did my best to reduce by demanding that everyone swear that he did not bear a fake credential, but only two confessed they did and dropped out; that was not enough; we should have to go. Dixon Bain had been told that Dick Gregory would lead a march to assert the right to demonstrate outside the Convention Hall; he was to start in twenty minutes; that was our place of duty then.

The name Gregory brought the day's first joy to my heart; he is a companion who delights me. But I knew that one of his jokes on US is to do everything five minutes early because WE think THEY are always late, and I told Neuhaus that my son and I would go ahead and try to hold Greg up until the delegate battalion could be assembled. So we almost ran to the Hilton, coming at last to a ragged band headed south. I cried, "Greg, Greg" and found the head of the column at last. He walked in deep converse with bearded pards. "Greg," I said. "Hi, baby," he answered distractedly. I introduced my son. Greg smiled at him. "Greg," I said, "just what do you want us delegates to do?" "Baby," he replied, "Later? Later? OK? I got *problems* to talk about." That was it. There were Greg's pards, in variants of the costume one of my sons had told me is called "Hollywood African," a few other blacks in front, and behind them strays of the grays of David Dellinger's mobilization, come to show themselves against the good advice of their leader. Television has made actors of all rebels; I had been conscripted into the theater of the streets: Its various troupes—the delegates, the blacks, the young grays—had nothing in common; they had, in fact, every reason for dispute; America is a two-party country in which two, three, or four different repertory companies perform their dramas at once on the same stage. We were lucky to have only three. I walked south with Dixon Bain in the column of actors from other productions. Tom Buckley from the *Times* noticed the black flag of anarchism bobbing ahead, and wondered if I was sure I wanted that in the line. I started to answer that a flag good enough for Prince Peter Kropotkin was certainly good enough to walk with me—why do I invariably choose heroes of high birth, if I'm a real Whig?—and then came the thought that this answer was not the point. Above all things, believe though I might in every subversive challenge it represented, this was *not* my march. It was the *right* to march, not the *idea* for which anyone might march, that was my mandate that night; and I had a duty to the

Twentieth Congressional District, in these hours just before it released me, not to assume any wider mandate from it. The point had to be that I would do the same thing for Lester Maddox.

We had arrived at Eighteenth and Michigan, where the guard and the police waited to say we could not go farther. The delegates had all found us and efficiently lined up behind Neuhaus and me, since, for reasons obscure but connected with the failure of its beginning, ours was known as the Neuhaus-Kempton group. Such then was my last caucus; and, when Gregory went forward to get himself arrested and the Reverend Mr. Neuhaus to treat with the police, not knowing the procedure for getting arrested in Chicago as well as Gregory, I found myself stranded as its leader. Gregory's blacks were juking in front of us; and Dellinger's strayed grays were no doubt preparing some manifestation behind us; and there fell upon me the sickening dread that at least two of our repertory companies were about to start their productions while ours, the amateur one, could not even think of its script.

I saw a tall young man in a *kente* and hair not so much natural as in the state of nature, and I felt achingly the need for an immediate bridge now to Jeune Afrique. I said "Excuse me" to him, and he came over, and I said that I knew a young reporter he would call a brother and that he had the closest to a natural hairdo a man could wear and still seem promising to *The New York Times*. The reporter's name was Earl Caldwell and I had seen him around a little while ago; could he be found? Earl Caldwell was delivered with courtesy and dispatch on that poor description to a stranger, and I asked him if he could keep within sight, consonant with his job as a journalist, because we might need an interpreter with the brothers. Earl consented; but I was starting to feel the need less: Man had begun to seem to me altogether wonderful if you and he can just stay offstage together.

And then a young man in shirtsleeves appeared with a bullhorn. "I am a delegate to this convention, and I will tell the delegates what we are going to do." I started yelling at him that he was not a delegate to this convention, that I seemed to be the leader of the delegates for this occasion, heaven help them without Neuhaus, and that I hadn't the remotest idea what we were going to do, and we failed to communicate at that squalid level for a while, and Jeune Afrique came over to restore our manners and I explained that we'd just have trouble if that kid raised his bullhorn and started off on a speech again, and I wondered if the brothers could just roust him, very delicately. Jeune Afrique did not need to do that; he simply mixed a contrivance of slight menace with the authority of being its object's elder in being oppressed, and the young man went peaceably back to a place among the delegates. Then Neuhaus returned at last, welcomed as no servant of the Lord often is, and said we should advance to confront the Guard. There was nothing to do but get arrested, which took an unconscionably long time, during which we sat down symbolically, and then got up, because Gregory's pards felt that it was about time to go into their performance and that we ought to stand and afford them free passage. I wanted to thank Jeune Afrique but he was chanting sightlessly, being needed no more for works and being freed for faith. A National Guard lieutenant colonel finally read his office over me, and I was moved, correctly but not cordially, into the wagon. Its bag was a mixed one of delegates and stray young people; riding over, the young called out "Free Vietnam" to the invisible streets outside. "Free assembly," I ridiculously croaked.

In my usual job, you come to think of policemen as very much the same; when you are under arrest, they turn out to have quite extraordinary range. I should say that I met three nice cops for every nasty one; what surprised me was how far our permissive society has gone even with cops: A pleasant one feels free to be unusually pleasant and a mean one feels free to be unusually mean, neither of which tones is exactly what the book must command for treatment of that offender against society who is also its ward.

"Give me everything you've got with a sharp point," the one who searched said. "One of you peace lovers put out an officer's eye with a pin once. Do you know that?" He found a token that somebody had slipped me a long day ago and that I had put in my pocket without even looking at. It turned out to have the likeness of Martin Luther King, Jr., on it; and he threw it to the floor. "Martin Luther Coon," he said, grinding it with his shoe; "you all come from the same bag." To my shame I did not make reply and only shuffled along, which is why it is so necessary never to be surprised. Yet, after this caricature, the trip to the Dark Tower, while tedious, had illogical moments of good manners. "What is a distinguished-looking man like you doing being arrested?" one of the booking detectives asked. I had no answer; the question, kindly meant, could only make me understand that I was getting old.

But, after a while, these desultory excursions into the study of policemen were driven away by the revelation of the other persons who had been arrested that night. The journey crept along in the company of The Professor of Physics at Stevens Institute and The Personnel Director of the Perth Amboy Hospital, The Telephone Company Lawyer, and then it would end in the waiting outside Riot Court, the Dark Tower itself, with the finding there of Harris Wofford, the President of A New York State University, of The Man from *The New York Times* and, unknown but commanding, a solitary figure, young but of a distinction that made me instantly conscious of the difference between the cut of his cloth and mine. I approached his presence and deferentially put the question. "My name is George Walton," he answered. "I was youth chairman of the Rockefeller campaign in Kentucky. I came here for the platform hearings. And . . ." I excused myself. No matter. The final crown of our company was The Rockefeller Man from Kentucky.

What could have brought them here in police custody on this night when Mayor Daley and I both listened to Vice President Humphrey intone a prayer of St. Francis, the mayor in his hall and I, in one of his detention rooms, listening to a radio, free of the Vice President, because free of any bitterness toward him.

I knew why I was here; I had taken a contract. But what brought them, these safe men who had never before been arrested and probably never would be arrested again? It must be this night of all nights; not just the night of the Defeat of the Antihero for the McCarthy delegates among them, or the Death of the Hero for old friends of Robert Kennedy among them, but the indefinite suspension of their assurance of the virtue and redemption of America. The means of grace and the hope of glory had been taken away, because, after all, America had been their real God. And this night, otherwise inconsequential in our dreadful recent history, was The Night They Knew It.

But I could almost feel each of them, in his private heart, tending all afternoon toward this least dignified of places as the only one where they could be sure of being alone with their dignity. For them to have been in public that night would have been to rail or make bad jokes there; they had gone to the patrol wagon for privacy.

We stood about and talked among ourselves as men unused to arrest probably do; Dellinger's stray young grays, who had been there before and would be again, slept on the floor. I felt quite tender about them, because I had noticed that although they sometimes carry signs bearing the device of some four-letter word or other when they are on-camera, they do not write dirty words on the walls of detention rooms. Do they, among other reasons, go to jail for privacy too?

There is very little to the rest. We went on talking; The Man from the *Times* came out from the Dark Tower and said this was a rough judge; he had been told to stop slouching. (I cherish The Man from the *Times*, but, in fairness to the judiciary, he does slouch.) My name was called; I entered the Dark Tower. And there, as usual with me, the first sight, instead of the Beast, was the warm bright greeting of William Fitts Ryan, my congressman; the convention was over and he had generously come down to be my lawyer. Bill Ryan unsheathed his congressional identification card, and gave rein to his imagination for hyperbolic explanations of the distinction of his client; the judge struggled to the summit of whatever foothills of grace are afforded by night courts, and I was set loose.

Back at the hotel I was surprised to find my son awake and waiting. I had said good-bye to him just before I followed the Reverend Mr. Neuhaus up to the police barrier, not even bothering to tell him to go home because I knew him to be so sensible. But he had stayed around, while I was safe with the peace officers, and a guardsman had hit him on the fingers with a gun butt. He seemed very happy with the evening; I prayed that he would be soon again his old sensible self. My son said that the *Tribune* had an editorial saying that we were all a bunch of Commies, leftists, and other agitators. Sounds like a fair description, I answered.

"You were right," he said, "and O'Dwyer and the people who went to the convention were wrong." I thanked him, and thought of a proper answer only later. It was, "No, Davy, the good thing is that, for once, nobody was wrong."

At the airport I looked at the Americans around me; had we really, all of us, the same faces of the lost, shuttling between the unknown city of Basic and the unknown city of Cursic, back and forth, back and forth? Suddenly I remembered that I had been supposed to see my candidate twenty hours ago and had forgotten even to telephone to apologize.

Saturday Evening Post, November 1968

Ronald Reagan: The Performer's Art

I

Question: Governor, last week at your press conference you indicated that there would be no cutbacks in the University appropriation. Then, shortly after that, you announced that there would be a cutback. Could you clarify your position on why there suddenly was a cutback?

Answer: Yes, I goofed. It's as simple as that.

Question: Why can't you figure out where the $40,000,000 came from (to pay off a deficit)? You paid the money, but you don't know where it came from?

Answer: That's right.

—GOVERNOR RONALD REAGAN, *press conference, January 17, 1968*

THAT IS THE relevant documentary history of the first year of the Ronald Reagan series.

Still it leaves out the music and poetry of Governor Reagan's administration. The most suggestive source for these intangibles are the television listings of those weekday morning shows where characters broken and exhausted by the struggle for prime time chew contentedly over the engagement and resolution of their happy problems in the grazing land of the residual—Dobie Gillis who takes up boxing, Gidget who keeps accidentally accepting dates for the same evening, Daddy who feels like a forgotten man on Henry's wedding day.

TV Guide's day begins on Channel 2 at 6:30, with the crises of Jackie Cooper's career as a city councilman. (Sample: "PEOPLE'S CHOICE.

'The Ink Blots.' Mandy's well-meaning father asks a visiting psychologist friend to determine whether Sock is the right man to marry his daughter. Cast: Jackie Cooper, Pat Breslin, Paul Maxey, etc.")

One of Ronald Reagan's recent days began with his prayer breakfast for the legislature. He must be there by 8 A.M. "The alarm clock rings at an unexpected hour . . . the agony of arising in a too-cold room."

He told his guests that there would be no differences between people if they would do just a little digging and finding out about one another.

"Not long ago my son came home from school and said that a bully was picking on him. I talked to him a long while. 'At the proper moment,' I told him, 'you hit back.' But then I found out why this boy was acting this way. He had had a deep personal tragedy in his life not very long ago. So there was a small boy in trouble, and another small boy's father very ashamed of what he had been saying to his son."

(PEOPLE'S CHOICE: Skipper has trouble with a bully at school. Ronnie tells him to hit back. But then Ronnie finds out why the other boy acts the way he does. Cast: Ronnie Reagan, Nancy Reagan, Ronald Reagan, Jr.)

Nancy Reagan thinks of her husband's elevation to governor of California as a victory over bigotry.

"It used to annoy me," she remembers, "when they said that Ronnie wasn't fit to be governor because he was an actor. Isn't that like saying a man shouldn't have an opportunity because he's colored or Jewish? Isn't that prejudice?"

Even so, the habits of the old occupation really *do* seem to regulate one's attitudes in the new one. Ronald Reagan's is best described as a situation government; it is impossible to find in it an event whose challenge and resolution could not be fitted into half-hour time segments. There are even signs of unconscious adherence to the rule that, while a television series can hardly avoid stealing someone else's episode, it can never repeat one of its own. Governor Reagan came to office pledged to maintain the death penalty; and Aaron Mitchell, the first of the sixty-odd condemned murderers eligible for execution at the time of Reagan's inauguration, went suitably to the gas chamber.

But the only two other prisoners whose execution dates have come up so far in his term have been reprieved, on technical grounds to be sure. Still, for all the distressing promises, the performance so far would appear to fit the formula: one series about a governor, one segment with an execution.

NATURALLY, A DOMESTIC situation produced the only battle the Reagans have so far fought through with any real determination and the only historic change they have brought to the government of California.

They live now in the largest house on a not very pretentious suburban block in Sacramento, having moved at Mrs. Reagan's insistence from the old Governor's Mansion, a ninety-year-old white Victorian Gothic treasure, long since condemned by the local fire department but until now so sacred in the state's political tradition that Governor Earl Warren endured it even though he had no fire escape for his daughters except a rope ladder.

Progress has left the Governor's Mansion stranded on a street of blighted car washes.

"My responsibility is to an eight-year-old child," Mrs. Reagan says. "You can't raise a child in the city."

"I told the legislators when we moved," she said, "that it should have been done years ago. More and more young people are coming into government and they can expect their governors to be younger men with younger families."

And Ronald Reagan is fifty-nine years old. But Mrs. Reagan is right; doesn't Robert Cummings still caper on weekday morning television ("Though he's still madly in love with Kay, Bob finds time to notice a curvaceous Hawaiian girl") twenty-eight years after he and Ronald Reagan were in *King's Row* together?

You leave their new house, with its shelves of the sort of books television producers use for backdrops and its dishes of soft chewy candy with pecan centers—the appointments rented, to be sure, but still an unobjectionably modulated setting for a play about the tenth most-admired man (Gallup Poll) married to the ninth best-dressed woman—and there behind you, made flesh, sits the world of television, with its fathers fixed forever in boyish middle age, with its little son, as Skipper Reagan has on occasion, livening up the dull stretches by shooting his water pistol at stuffy visitors, a world frozen in time, insulated from dust and rot, where no one is old and ugly unless he is redeemingly comic.

The program is curiously irrelevant to real life. Ronald Reagan developed his philosophy of government while attacking government as a wandering orator for General Electric. Now the condition of things he was elected to overthrow remains very much the same as it was when he came to office; the state government is larger indeed than when its excess of size and cost appalled him on the platform. This year Reagan will present the legislature with the largest budget in the state's history; California is still close to the first state in the nation in the dimension and quality of free service to its citizens.

Yet this failure both of public promise and sincere intention in no way affects either his popularity or his cheerfulness. It does not even intrude into his speeches; he still comments on the operations of his own government as an alienated outsider would. This year's season could just as well have been filmed two years ago.

You find the governor in his office dictating a letter:

"I agree with you that we all want peace in Vietnam," he intones, "but we have to know what we mean by peace."

"He always answers every letter," a press assistant says. "He signs every request for a photograph. He did it when he was an actor. It goes back that far; the actors knew how dependent they were on their fans."

THERE IS NO wound in the governor's smile when he is asked whether the first year's struggle with the beast has disappointed him.

"Oh, I've learned," he answers, "you can't just wave a wand. But I spent a lot of years on the mashed potato circuit. My job then was to rouse the people and to ring the alarm bell. But this is different: You have a chance to grope—uh, to grapple—with the thing yourself."

Ronald Reagan's election as governor was rather as though General Electric had decided that, having done so well as an orator, he deserved to be put in charge of production. The plant would remain pretty much the same. So would the speeches.

II

"He was always an oddball. He was a well-accepted actor at a time when Bette Davis, Errol Flynn, Humphrey Bogart and James Cagney were at Warner Brothers with him. They were all troublemakers. But Ronnie never fought Jack Warner. He was a professional; he never went on strike for himself. Jack Warner never thought about that at the time, because Warner hated all actors. But, when Ronnie decided to run for governor, Jack Warner remembered this about him. 'He's no politician,' he said, 'he's a great man.' "

—TAFT SCHREIBER, *once of MCA, now of Universal Pictures*

IT WOULD BE odd in any case except Ronald Reagan's for J. L. Warner now to have forgotten that they once quarreled quite bitterly indeed and over an issue most suggestive of the troublemaker's temperament—the governor's wardrobe in *Working Her Way Through College*.

"Things reached a peak," Ronald Reagan remembers, "about midnight one night when I received a telegram citing my contract and the studio's legal right with reference to wardrobe . . . I suddenly stepped into a phone booth and called Jack Warner in his office. He was understandably wary . . .

" 'Jack,' I said, 'when I got your wire last night, I felt pretty foolish. We've been together thirteen years and something is awfully wrong if we have to start sending telegrams to each other. I've done a lot of things for which I'm sorry, and I want you to know that there won't be any more.' "

He had neither the talent nor the passion to inflict himself upon our consciousness as a god from the Warner Brothers Studio of the thirties which is now a camp Pantheon. There could hardly be a Ronald Reagan Festival at the New Yorker Theater, except as some gesture of alienation on the day of his inauguration; there are no Ronald Reagan posters at the New Yorker Bookstore. For the governor had a guardian angel to instruct him that for a movie actor divinity is most often an achievement through private disaster; he never asked for more than an attendant role.

AND YET, IF he did not have the talent to leave us possessed by the myth of those scripts, he had the greater genius to be possessed by it himself. His lifestyle is the movie of the thirties; even now, at fifty-nine, he still plays out the confrontation and reconciliation of rebellious youth with wiser middle age, of Gipp with Rockne, of young Kildare with Dr. Gillespie. And so, alone among actors, he is cherished still by J. L. Warner because once, in a crisis, he made J. L. Warner feel himself Claude Rains.

A Republican who was elected to state office with Governor Reagan but who has seen him only occasionally since has to confess: "Even after a year up here, he is an enigma to me. But I do know this; he is a thoroughly nice man."

The whole life supports that estimate; Ronald Reagan convinces you in his autobiography[1] that he has always been decent, personally responsible, persevering but not voraciously ambitious. He is a man who will go bravely anywhere, just so long as someone else points out the way to go:

1. His first public triumph was when he was a freshman at Eureka College and made the speech which brought the student body out on strike against cuts in the budget for instruction. "*I'd been told* that I should sell the idea so that there'd be no doubt of the outcome . . . I discovered then that an audience has a feel to it and, in the parlance of the theater, that audience and I were together."

2. He was a scrub with a most dubious future in Eureka football

[1]Reagan, Ronald, with Richard G. Hubler, *Where's the Rest of Me?* (New York: Best Books, 1965).

scrimmages when Bud Cole, an injured professional, took an interest in him. "Bud made the decisions and I became a purely physical means to the ends he dictated . . . He would whisper: 'Knife in—they're going the other way.' Doing as he ordered, I was on the ball carrier three times in a row." He made the first team.

3. After college he went to the only family friend who was remotely successful and asked about his career. "What do you want to do?" the family friend asked. "All I could do was say 'I don't know.' " There followed "sleepless nights [when] I truly faced my future."

4. His night mind at last instructed him: "I wanted some form of show business." He became a radio sports announcer. "I was one of a profession just becoming popular," he says, in anticipatory revelation of what is still his function in politics, "—the visualizer for the armchair quarterback."

5. But he still wanted to be in the movies. One spring, in 1937, he was in Catalina with the Cubs and sought out Joy Hodges, whom he had known at his radio station in Des Moines and who had risen to sing at the Biltmore Bowl.

"Joy got right to the point. 'Take off your glasses,' she said. Her reaction was such that it implanted in me the desire to rid myself of glasses forevermore." She called her agent and he got the screen test.

That last is the seminal anecdote about Governor Reagan's extraordinary passivity.

The scene comes at once to mind from the old scripts: the exhausted employer, the office drab he has never noticed, the accident when she takes off her glasses, the dazzling revelation, "Why, Marilyn, you're beautiful."

HE HAS BEEN, at least up until now, one of those truly fortunate people whose good fairy governs any impulse to crowd their luck. He was always satisfied with the second part; his first wife, Jane Wyman, was a star of a magnitude brighter than his own modest glow; yet his friends remember, because it was so unusual for Hollywood, how contentedly he yielded her the center of the stage. He fought the studio for a role only once; it had long been the extreme ambition of his secret heart to play George Gipp, the Notre Dame tailback, in a movie about Knute Rockne; it was a part supporting Pat O'Brien, to be sure, but there was the eighty-yard run and the death scene, early in the picture of course, but assured of elevation in the recollection by O'Brien's climactic harangue about winning one for the Gipper.

Errol Flynn exercised the star's prerogative of insisting that the writers transfer to him such bright lines as had been allotted to the governor when they acted together; Lionel Barrymore ran his wheel-chair over the governor's toes; Wallace Beery almost knocked the governor down to get his own face in front of the governor's in close-ups. In all these wars, he bravely fought his betters for his rights; but he always knew that his rights were for no more than a decent corner and seldom the middle of that narrow frame.

He began to run down in the fifties, having grown older, on the calendar at least, and reached that delicate condition when the supporting juvenile must die or age into the character actor, with all that means in the coarsening of the skin, the rasping of the larynx, the running of the spittle. The ambiguities of his situation first suggested themselves to him in 1947, when he was only thirty-eight, and Warner's, trusting him as always, assigned him to shepherd Shirley Temple into maturity in *That Hagen Girl*.

"Came the moment on screen when I said to Shirley 'I love you' and the entire audience en masse cried, 'Oh no.' Maybe a late night TV sponsor can run a contest: 'Was I passionate or paternal to the present Mrs. Black?' "

But he fought against the transition to the ugly realities of middle age; there had been ingrained in the young Ronald Reagan that lesson of Eddie Foy's whose mark is still so heavy on the style of Governor Reagan: "Sing pretty, act pretty; pretty things they enjoy."

BUT, BY 1952, he was forty-three and time had quite withered him as vessel for the illusion of ardent youth; he was in the clutch of the back-income-tax collector, that monster of career twilights, and he was reduced to introducing acts at Las Vegas.

Then he was pulled back from that abyss by the Music Corporation of America.

"That was the greatness of MCA; we never waited for the worst to happen to a client," Taft Schreiber says. "We diversified into radio; we went into television in 1949. In 1951, Ronnie was still well thought of and still making money and television still wanted him. GE offered us this deal for a weekly show and I told Ronnie he should take it."

There was very little argument. "He knew he'd kind of had it in the movies. The deal was not too much work and he'd be starring again. And he rather enjoyed the idea that GE wanted him to make four weeks of personal appearances a year."

The four weeks soon thickened out to eight. It was Ronald Reagan's conscientious professional habit to give the sponsor a little better than he expected; GE had asked for little more than his smile and a few anecdotes about Hollywood; Ronald Reagan worked out a long sermon on our moral decay and our surrender to government to go with the smile and the anecdotes.

He had moved by now across fifteen years through a succession of private political roles—from One-World liberal, to anti-Stalin liberal, to anti-Communist liberal, to anti-liberal anti-Communist, and at last to anti-liberal, anti-welfare-statist.

He had always been insistent about any article of faith so long as he held it, and, by 1959, his integrity had become something of a trial to General Electric which, while generally as dissatisfied with other people's morals and dependence on the state as respectable Americans can be trusted to be, happened to be dependent on government orders for much of its profit.

One ornament of The Speech was a denunciation of the Tennessee Valley Authority, a GE customer. When TVA protested, GE wondered whether Reagan could find another example of government waste, extravagance, and tyranny.

Ronald Reagan refused. "I'm gonna say what I'm gonna say," he told Schreiber. He called General Electric with the same brave defiance, and General Electric sadly answered that, if he felt that way, it wouldn't censor him.

Ronald Reagan hung up. "Golly," he told Schreiber, "what a great company to work for. It's not right for me to make them unhappy. After all, the TVA isn't the only government agency. I can talk about some others."

And so he excised from The Speech all references to the Tennessee Valley Authority as cause for alarm and returned them only in 1964 when he delivered it in its virgin state on television with the Goldwater campaign as his sponsor.

This is a life of successive confrontation of his integrity with the demands of authority and then, once his integrity has been preserved in struggle, the sincere recognition of the higher wisdom of authority. Ronald Reagan has fought very hard to attain the position which is now his: He is the company man who has kept his honor.

III

"Hollywood has a way of talking to itself and believing everything it says."
—RONALD REAGAN, *Where's the Rest of Me?*

LAST SPRING, FOR a very little while, Ronald Reagan undertook to do what politician-governors do and set out to cultivate his legislature.

"Dinner was elegant with candlelight and California wine," Lee Edwards reports.[2] "Cocktails were served by Orientals in native costume. Conversation was kept flowing by the always gracious Mrs. Reagan. The guests were enchanted. Upon the completion of the dinner the evening took a typically Reagan turn. The governor would rise and say, 'Gentlemen, let's go downstairs.' There the men were confronted by a gigantic electric train set covering nearly one-half of a large recreation room, an upright piano and a pool table. Taking off his tux, the governor would run the trains while a senator would strike up a tune . . ."

[2]Edwards, Lee, *Reagan: A Political Biography* (San Diego: Viewpoint Books, 1967).

These feasts of innocent merriment belong to the governor's past now; he is, granted the large consolation of his family, almost as isolated in Sacramento as he was a few weeks after his inaugural when former Governor Brown inquired about the problems of state and Ronald Reagan answered, "What do *you* do in this town at night?"

Mrs. Reagan does not seem to remember this transient courtship with much pleasure; she does not enjoy politicians. ("I do not think of Ronnie as a politician.")

"I like sincere people in government," she says severely, "but people who think only of elections—I haven't much regard for them."

Legislators representative of that vast majority of their kind which the Citizeness dismisses as thinking only of elections recall this interlude of cultivation with proper pleasure but some puzzlement about its relevance.

"His whole social conversation excludes politics," Assemblyman Charles Warren, a Democrat, has decided. "The evening I went there, he had just cut medical services. All he talked about was Hollywood. 'When you make an entrance,' he said, 'a doorway makes a nice frame.' I don't remember anything else."

HIS FRIENDS FROM Hollywood remember a Ronald Reagan who talked about nothing except politics. Now that he is a governor, he talks more and more about Hollywood. He is that pleasant, distinguished visitor who is doing something else.

It is a device which, innocent though it may be in its origin, has for him a powerfully useful effect; when it is your style to be against government, nothing can succeed for you like failure to govern.

A month after his inauguration, he submitted a $4.6 billion budget to the legislature, a cut, he estimated, of $250 million in the annual expenditures of his Democratic predecessors. In March, he raised the figure to $5.06 billion, $184 million higher than any previous budget and increased taxes nearly a billion dollars.

"I will tell you now," he told the voters in July, "—this tax bill, like the budget, does not represent my philosophy."

The reward of this manful disassociation from his own actions as governor was an 8 percent increase in his popularity in the polls; he closed the month with a 74 percent performance-approved rating.

And so, the governor always smiles when he speaks of the "frustrating impatience" of his job.

"You can't predict the budget," he says, "and that gets you pretty impatient."

He will still certify his $23 million a year in economies, but adding up all the little occasions of string saving exhausts him very quickly and he finally says: "We'll never know how much we've saved. It's an atmosphere. Do you know we've been able to triple our awards to the Civil Service for suggestions about economy? That's what can happen when people know there's somebody who wants to listen."

All the same, he accepts the condition that his budget will go up 8 percent every year because of California's growth rate and President Johnson's "policy of planned inflation."

"I don't have much respect for those legislators who won't let my husband do the things he said he would," Mrs. Reagan says. "Last year they wouldn't let his bill against pornography out of committee. I can't understand people who won't vote against pornography."

But her husband is markedly more casual than she about progress in his special trinity of priority concerns for California—"crime, pornography, and traffic safety."

"In Paris," he smiles, "they're selling California postcards. We've got to do something about this." Still, he had no antipornography bill ready for this session and his pressure for the last one seems to have been distinctly languid. California still has the highest crime rate in the country; yet last year, the governor vetoed expansion of the Highway Patrol, which happens to be within his control; his most substantial action in the field of traffic safety was to veto a bill to control the drunken driver.

THE GOVERNOR'S IS a politics of myth, which so transcends reality, that when quite real persons are suddenly cast into his epics, they are chagrined to discover themselves rendered more mythic than they wish.

The recurrent example is H. C. McClellan, former president of the National Association of Manufacturers, who has consumed himself in the pursuit of jobs for poor Negroes ever since the 1965 Los Angeles riots.

The governor often talks about the poor; as occasion for homily, they rank indeed slightly behind crime and pornography and well ahead of traffic safety. We have, he pointed out last February, 320,000 churches in America:

> Do you realize that if you prorated the actual hard core unemploy-ment in this country, it comes out to a little less than three per church? . . . [Just stop to] think of that many people saying: Here are three people we should help—three families we should get on their feet—you begin to see the great power the people have.
>
> Every problem that besets us, from drop-outs to disease, from job training to student loans, is being solved someplace in this country by someone who did not wait for government.

There always follows the revelatory anecdote about H. C. (Chad, of course) McClellan. After Watts, all alone, the governor recalls, Chad McClellan moved to the breach and persuaded industry to hire 17,049 Negroes. Now more than half of Watts's unemployed Negroes have been put to work without expenditure of one dollar of government subsidy. And now Chad McClellan is doing the same thing for Califor-nia at no drain on tax revenues.

But then a reporter calls upon H. C. McClellan in his Los Angeles office, clutching the telephone, bullying one of his friends into hiring a Negro. McClellan is seventy years old and there has fallen upon him the divine madness of possession. Things are almost as bad in Watts as they ever were, he says, although there are rewards: The other day a Negro came up to him after a meeting and said, "Mr. McClellan, I don't know much else after I've heard you, but now I know you're not a fink."

He wishes the governor would stop "playing that numbers game"; he himself learned long ago that numbers mean nothing.

Governor Reagan came in to see me when he was running; we had it out here hammer-and-tongs. His reluctance to understand the need for the national government is understandable. But I thought I'd convinced him that this isn't just a Republican problem; I think he's reconciled to the federal government. Federal training programs? Hell, our trouble is we don't get enough of them. If we could double the production of the Manpower Defense Training Act skill centers, we could still get every one of them hired. Sure, I give the federal people hell frequently. But I work hand in glove with them, because I know I have to.

Even so, the governor moves through his ceremonies and composes his little stories with instinctive abstention from reference to real toads in real gardens.

It follows quite naturally from his refusal to be anything so low as a politician that he would not ascend to anything so useful as being a political manager; he seems indeed to regard it as rather a refreshment of his image that he must live with a Democratic legislature.

He campaigns, of course, for a Republican legislature, because that promise offers an excuse for those exercises in self-fulfillment he calls "fund-raisers." Last fall, he was imperiled by success; a Republican won a special election to the Senate from San Francisco; this victory meant that, if party discipline was maintained, twenty Republicans would be on hand to offset twenty Democrats and that a Republican lieutenant-governor could cast the decisive vote giving the governor's party control of the upper House for the first time in his tenure.

But, in real life, a Republican legislator persuades us when he doubts that there are three real Reagan men in either chamber. And so, when the legislature convened, eight Republican senators, including the latest anointed, voted to elect Hayden Burns, the designate-Democrat as leader of the Senate, Governor Reagan's victory was thus confined to his Neilsen rating, where he is, after all, happiest. It was a mark both of his good nature and indifference that eight Republicans could stray and know that he would not punish them; when a governor does not accept government, he can hardly, after all, conceive reprisal by government.

And so, affairs remain under the control of Jesse Unruh, Democratic Speaker of the Assembly. We unengagedly examine one of those screenplays where Unruh steals any scene he wants, being Wallace Beery, and the governor lets him, being at last the certified star, and assured that no excess will give Unruh possession of any scene. Occasionally the governor rouses himself to the measured response, or one of those cinematic confrontations where the man in the white hat crumples the man with the black hat with a balsa chair.

Otherwise, when Unruh goes too far, the governor just exercises the staying hand of his veto power. He vetoed one bill which would have increased the budget for crippled children—a disability, he explained, must detachedly be judged as to whether it is a disability which deserves to be corrected at the expense of the state—and he vetoed another bill to control parents who, whenever their hatred of the boss overwhelms them, take sanctuary in the sublimation of beating their children.

All of which makes the governor sound terribly cold; and yet his problem is simply that his imagination is incapable of compassion in the general. Show Ronald Reagan a crippled or beaten and broken child and he would first weep and then loot the treasury to make it right. The general is beyond his scope; only the particular can fit into one script and half an hour.

IV

"FDR was elected President and [my father] went to work for the government. [His] job was handing out the foodstuffs the government bought and shipped in . . . Every week the line would form—not bums or strangers but friends, fathers of kids I'd gone to school with. Most of them were first names to [my father] and he was Jack to them."

—RONALD REAGAN, *Where's the Rest of Me?*

Question: Assemblyman Willie Brown added a little bit to that charge about the Negroes that you met last week. He said all but one of them were Republicans and that they also had some connection with the 1966 campaign.

Answer: How else could I get acquainted with them?

—GOVERNOR REAGAN, *press conference, July 12, 1967*

IN THIRTY-FOUR YEARS, Ronald Reagan has traveled from a time when almost everyone he knew was dead broke to a time when he knows almost nobody who is poor.

And he is tuned to the dominant majority of his voters as no viable politician except George Wallace is, because they have that same history, which is not their state's history, because, in so many cases besides his own, California was not their first state.

It is hard, at least in Southern California, not to think yourself in the only foreign country on earth which consists entirely of its American colony. Ronald Reagan's own rural Middle West seems to have sent most of its student cheerleaders to Los Angeles as it sent so many of its student editors to New York; and these expatriates dominate the tone of the Reagan country.

They are the counterrevolutionary sons of the Roosevelt revolution and their governor may be right when he says, in natural echo of Pat O'Brien as Knute Rockne, that "they can start a prairie fire that will sweep the nation." The Roosevelt revolution began the process which elevated America to its present eminence as the greatest instrument for the care and feeding of incompetent white people in the whole story of man.

RONALD REAGAN EMBODIES that generation which was familiar with penury and privation when its members were children and has known very little except comfort and abundance when its members were adults. And suburban Southern California, as the most comfortable place in America to live, would have to be one of the farthest removed from the experience of crisis and the sense of adventure.

"Of course, it's unfair to complain that Ronnie doesn't work hard enough as governor," a Sacramento Republican says. "What has been his experience with work for the last ten years? He would drive up from his ranch on the freeway once a week and work about four hours."

THEN THERE IS the sort of work Southern Californians do. "There's nothing, by God, but real estate offices and hot dog stands," Ronald Reagan's father complained when he came there to die in the thirties. It is not, in general, a place where jobs present those real problems associated with tangible production. Naturally then, its governor has so little functional sense about affairs that he continues hopelessly to confuse serious vocations with quite trivial ones; to describe Gordon Smith, his state finance director, as a former management consultant when what Smith did in real life was to make sales presentations for a firm of management consultants.

What the governor knows about the city is not very far from the only apparent scar on what is an otherwise unspotted memory of childhood. His father, in the course of a generally luckless career, set the family briefly down in the south side of Chicago. He and his brother were alone in the apartment; "we got scared, with twilight coming on and went to scour the city for our parents." When they were found, his mother "had almost lost her mind." They moved to Galesburg, Illinois, shortly after this experience, and he never lived in a city as huge, black, and anonymous as Chicago again.

His mind was formed in a community of ten thousand persons and fixed afterward by those Warner Brothers movies about the American small town. He has all the kindness of that rural Midwest which can reach out so generously to anyone in need it knows; but his mind cannot deal with great numbers of strangers; and he has no capacity to imagine human suffering in the abstract.

He speaks, because they are his friends, for those people to whom the tax collector is the nearest equivalent of the menace the landlord is to the welfare mother. He is, of all politicians, the least inclined to grasp for new friends or unfamiliar adventures.

You would think, for example, that when he became governor of California his mind would have been consumed by the challenge and burdens of this journey into the unknown. Instead, Mrs. Reagan remembers him only as lonely, like any good family man called away from home.

"It was so dark in that mansion, so grim in that office," Mrs. Reagan says. "To have to go from that mansion to that office. I began to make over his office because I was determined to give him one pleasant little room."

Change disturbs the governor that much, which is why he is so well suited for the moment in our politics when more and more voters want nothing else but to keep what they have.

"I HAVE CONSIDERED myself a rabid union man ever since" he joined the Screen Actors Guild, he said in 1964, when he was denouncing every other consequence of the New Deal. His union even remembers him as probably the best of its presidents; it brought him back to leadership in 1959, because, one of them says, its executives knew no other figure who could both lead the strike and convince the membership to accept a settlement. But, then, if there is one vestige of the New Deal to which the governor would cling while discarding all others, it would be the labor union, the instrument of the workingman to protect what he has against outsiders; the stagehands' union and Orange County, California, are both forms of the closed shop.

He speaks then to audiences essentially incurious because their main demand is not to be disturbed; and that may be why, if Richard Nixon was the first politician to make proper use of the illustrative anecdote and President Kennedy the first to make proper use of the illuminating statistic, Governor Reagan is the first to be able to take these two dubious enough devices and transmute them, unchallenged, into material unbelievable on its face:

From the New Frontier of 1960 we have progressed to a "Great Society." . . . The payroll has increased 7½ times and total government spending has gone up 8½ times.

The governor has intoned these figures at least seven times in public places since his inauguration, and not once does anyone seem to have pointed out to him that President Eisenhower's 1960 budget was $80 billion and President Johnson's 1968 one is $186 billion. That is quite depressing enough, but it is not an 850 percent increase; it comes out, in fact, if you adjust for the cost of the Vietnam War, closer to 85 percent.

"You realize that today the federal agencies receive five reports a year for every man, woman, and baby in the United States."

That would be 1 billion separate reports a year, all to be stored in Washington, at a rate of 5 million a day.

Then there is the illustrative anecdote:

> I don't have to go too far to tell of an actual case within the last several months of a man who refused employment. He was on welfare with his family and he was reinstated on welfare because it was ruled that his extreme laziness was an incurable ailment and, therefore, he was entitled to welfare.

It is possible to retain an open mind as to whether a real prime minister ever told Mr. Nixon what Mr. Nixon says he told him, but there are some anecdotes against which the reason closes. The softest welfare department in the country wouldn't go on record with that ruling.

The governor can move serenely through this litany of the ridiculous because his audiences are not people who question or challenge. Just once, in the collected utterances of his first year, is there reference to the condition that California's unemployment rate is 28 percent higher than the national average.

For all human troubles, the tone is otherwise the curious indifference of his answer last November when he was asked why he had cut back the crippled children's program:

> I have a question whether there has been a cutback. It would simply be where do you draw the line at what is a disability on the part of a child? But, *as the state continues to grow*, you may find that lines are drawn. What lack of ability, what physical defect do you constitute as a disability that requires special attention or care?

And yet he is a kind man; the coldness comes simply from lack of imagination. If he were not kind, he could not have held California as he has. What was plainly wanted, and what still contents is the man who soothes rather than the man who arouses. For touching a people who want to forget ugly problems, no politician equals the one who has already forgotten them himself.

The governor who addressed his legislature when it began its session last month showed his boredom with matters of state both in his tone and in the revelation that he had come to his second year with no legislative proposals ready for submission.

He did make one essay at the posture of dedication: He reminded the legislature that a poet had once wished for California "men with new eras in their brains."

"Let that be us as we go about the people's business. Let that be us as we build tomorrow."

After this climax, the governor finished:

"While there is still time, let me wish you a HAPPY NEW YEAR. As a matter of fact, I might even go farther and ask you for the same thing myself."

The film editors who would show the governor to his people that night were thus left with alternate endings—either the ritual peroration which sought to inspire or the feeble little joke which sought to disarm. Without exception, that night's films excised the governor's exhortation to build tomorrow and kept in his expression of hope not to be bothered this year. The governor and the majority of Californians he represents would probably make the same choice between the two aspirations.

New York Post, January and February 1968

[Postscriptum]

IF SUPERIOR BRILLIANCE of technique were all that mattered in a political campaign, we might very well have a roster of First Ladies rather different from the one that graces page 304 of the World Almanac. But even so, just as art, the fourth rerun of Governor Reagan's debut as a presidential candidate shone with a brilliance that ought to be taught in the textbooks.

The geographical setting was superbly selected. The governor's choice of New York as the stage for his proclamation was one of those bold and resolute forays into presumably hostile country that are designed to crush one's enemies before they can group.

Even as the day broke for Reagan's announcement there were reports in respected quarters of a tide sweeping the Republicans of New York, New Jersey, and Connecticut his way. The waters did not rise quite as high as promised at the Hilton last night.

Few of the movers and shakers in evidence sit on any throne loftier than a seat in the state legislature. Still, as Senator Kennedy has said, in politics what is perceived counts more than what is real; and a daisy might as well be a redwood if it is blooming in a desert.

The selection of New York was a dazzling concept; and the set was worthy of it. The basic premise of Governor Reagan's producers is that, while many Americans of his generation aren't sure that Roosevelt did everything right in the thirties, they are positive that Warner Brothers did.

The lights in the ballroom were out; the stage was dark and then a spotlight fell on the curtain and Governor Reagan slipped into it, endlessly unassuming but permanently true-blue.

There was no way for any of us to avoid feeling the way Priscilla Lane was supposed to when she sat on her porch beside the only streetlight in the Warner Brothers notion of a midwestern town and Ronald Reagan suddenly walked through its beams toward her and the last, painful fugitive memory of John Garfield fled and she could only wonder how she had been so blind all those years since high school.

The speech was reasonably well-crafted but it had the woodenness we have come to associate with its genre; and it could be noticed how well Reagan has kept the instinct for tone that no manager can impart. As he moved along, he improvised subtle changes from the rhetorical to the conversational, altering "nation" to "country," turning "the American people" into "us," saying "we've" instead of "we have." The Brothers Warner taught him and he has never forgotten the power of the homely style.

He does not have to sound like a hard conservative; that painful necessity presses only upon moderates like George Bush and Howard Baker. He even used the noun of assembly "oil company profits" and that subversive expression "unfairly exploited" in the same paragraph, although not too dangerously close together. Still, as time goes on, it becomes plainer that the oil companies, having too soon given too much to John Connally, will have to endure unaccustomed disrespect from all the other candidates until fall.

He rushed through his words with unusual speed, but that pace may have been designed to produce the effect of the breathless energy of youth. He does look older, but that shadow would lie much less heavy upon him if he did not work so hard to look young. Nothing ages a man like persistence in dressing the way Russ Hodges used to when he was broadcasting Giant games. His hair, which used to flourish various *bizarreries* of color, has now settled into a glossy black, which is still unsatisfactory.

Not cosmetology but rigorous abstention from it can, however, easily free him from this time warp: a touch of gray at the temples in New Hampshire, a progressive whitening in Florida, and then the glory of his natural mane in Illinois; a vest, narrower lapels, darker suits, small-figured ties, perhaps a gray wool muffler, and he will be seen for what he is, seasoned in years but young in heart.

Still, even with that look of someone afraid he has grown too old for his part, his appearance seems by no means too much less fit than it used to and his performance not a whit less masterly.

New York Post, November 14, 1979

Born-Again Republicans

THOSE OF US lucky enough to be detached from the sufferings of the Republicans were drawn to the Kansas City convention to an ignoble extent by the promise of watching them let one another's blood. We were cheated, as those all too human parts that are instinct with the thirst for gore deserve to be cheated, and we knew we were almost at the first sight of this lowing herd, which anticipation had confused with a bedlam of bulls. For the moment the Republicans have no blood to let; they are drained by the prolonged biting of flies.

They have not been so much gored as galled. They are resentful, of course—and who in their income bracket has a larger claim?—but they have lost count of their resentments. The endurance of their factions is no more than one of those habits that outlive passion. They cannot hate each other as they sometimes used to, being bound in the fraternity of a shared victimhood. Their bitterness is diffused, unfocused, and of that order that brought Vergil to speak of "the tears of things"; but these are not the *lacrimae* but the *acrimoniae rerum*. If they could give a face to their rancor, it would probably belong to the uneasy ghost at San Clemente, and yet a part of them is tied even to him by the bond of a shared misfortune. Of all the afflictions that have deadened them, the heaviest is the possession of this martyr who is also their cross. He is everywhere and nowhere, the more noticeable in a convention hall barren of any graven image, even Abraham Lincoln's let alone Mr. Ford's. It is as though we have been confronted by a universal will to believe that the Republican party was founded in Ripon, Wisconsin, sometime in August 1974 and dedicated to the liberation of Washington from generations of misrule by the Democrats. The Republican distaste for government has almost forced them into a compact to forget that, come January, they will have been at the head of government for sixteen of the past twenty-four years. We cannot even be sure that they will not thereafter be cursed by title to the estate they so dislike. They have become the inert party, and the size of the inert vote is by now incalculable, since we have no way yet to measure how far their numbness extends to the rest of us.

[Republican Semiotics]

MEANWHILE, IF ONE emotion controlled their rounds, it was their ill-concealed mutual goodwill. Our habit of thinking of the Republican party as an arena of quarrel between its conservatives and its moderates went its way even on this scene where the only contention was be-tween two factions of its right wing, one putatively if dubiously pur-poseful, the other plainly without need of purpose. It would be an altogether easier case if the thing restored itself to the brutal simplici-ties that governed it before Mr. Nixon, and provided us some banner of the truly committed like the California delegation that former Sena-tor William Knowland led into the lists for Barry Goldwater in 1964. Knowland was a tower of certainty then, remembered as a somewhat elephantinely graceful man once, but now half-seas-over from the grievance of the lost cause of himself, his every hair standing up from the very electricity of his vehemence, and his troops howling at his back, every man in his orange jumpsuit as though made ready for whatever befell from the creeps, the Commies, and the epicene snobs, and dressed so as to make each good American identifiable to every other in the melee. But here there was no symbol to suggest the fanatic heart except the red celluloid cowboy hats of the unanimous Reagan delegation from Texas. Only an aisle separated them from the New York delegation and Richard Rosenbaum, that state's Republican chairman and Vice President Rockefeller's whipper-in charged with holding its pack to Mr. Ford. That cannot have been a cause commanding the utmost from Rosenbaum's spiritual fervor, since his own great principal had been treated with extreme shabbiness by the President. Yet here was one of those men who, if he cannot love those he serves, all the same exults in the crudities and cruelties of the service. Rosenbaum strode his beat like some rogue cop, bullying the poor huddle of Reaganites in his captivity, his rasping voice and hairless head the incarnation of the pitiless and terrible authority that cares not for whose sake it asserts so long as it can assert itself. There was a time whose passing it would be ridiculous to mourn when Texans of rightward cast knew how to hate, and the sight of Rosenbaum in the bloom of his frenzy would have excited extremes of nativist bigotry toward any such offering from what Governor Carter has called the heritage and Mr. Ford the treasury of our ethnicity. But, as things were now, when Rosenbaum's polished skull rose and shone with a special arrogance, the most aroused of Texans could summon up no cry of protest beyond an almost complicit "Sit down, skinhead." On the convention's final night, Rosenbaum was carrying a Texas hat, the parting gift, no doubt, of these new friends, his enemies. There are no second acts for the politics of the *enragé* in American life.

NATURALLY, THEN, THE quarrel over the soul of this party we had come to think of as endemically diseased by the bad blood of its amateurs was a contest between mercenaries, exhausted in the case of Mr. Ford's subalterns and quick with the rakish energies of youth only in that of John Sears, Governor Reagan's master of the horse. Mr. Ford is, one supposes, the Eternal Husband, and the array of his campaign servitors ran to old stagers who had collapsed into his arms, their great loves forever lost to them. There was Harry Dent of South Carolina, who had first come to notice as a junior flugelman for the Dixiecrats in 1948; there was William Timmons, last seen as chief whip of Mr.

Nixon's resistance to impeachment by the House of Representatives, a masterpiece of tactics that worked its way down from a garrison of two-hundred-odd loyalists to a cadre of twenty-five; there was Clifton White, who had been Goldwater's chief master of ceremonies and of delegates; there was Senator John Tower, who had been his convention floor manager; there was Dean Burch, who had directed his campaign; and there was Goldwater himself, who had never been much of a Goldwaterite and had a while ago muddled his convictions into a general fraternal benevolence. Their days are in the yellow leaf, and their history even when they were in the green is so dismal a logbook of pilings up on rocks as to exclude them by definition from any suspicion of bare competence; but they brought the ship home this time and were universally hailed for the dexterity of their address in clutching a desperate victory from what ought not ever to have been a battle. The affairs of the Republicans belong by now more to paleontology than to any politics familiar to us; we do not lard the Cretaceous period with compliments for having outworn the Jurassic. But if for Acton there was no worse heresy than that the office sanctifies the holder of it, there is for journalism no credo more sacred than that victory, however seedy, certifies the brilliance of the victor.

In the fortunate defection of their tribal chiefs, the Goldwaterites had turned to John Sears, a *condottiere* who was a stranger even to Governor Reagan. As the faction appointed to represent moderation was staffed and led by these depleted veterans of a Republican campaign whose defeat is generally blamed upon its extremism, the faction deemed extremist was directed by the former chairman of Students for Kennedy at Notre Dame University. John Sears had gone on to further his political apprenticeship as a junior in the law firm that somehow sits in the memory as Nixon, Mudge, Grudge, Nasty, Brutish, and Short. Mr. Nixon may well have had John Sears in mind as exemplary pupil when he used to say in those days, "I tell the young men around me that politics is nothing unless it is also poetry." His addiction to flourishes of nonsense like that is one of several encouragements to forgetting that Mr. Nixon had a very long head for the business of any politician except himself and could therefore have been that best of instructors, the one at once informed enough to teach the acquired wisdom of his discipline and deformed enough to be a useful warning against its follies. This least lyrical and most prosy of artisans may even have been on to something in his fantasy of a politics that is nothing unless it is also poetry. Politics does occasionally attain poetic occasions; but they run to just the ones that persons most serious about success ought most earnestly to avoid, being limited as they are to what Apollinaire had in mind when he wrote that there is a poem in the bird that has but one wing.

Governor Reagan was just that species of bird. It is hard otherwise to see what could have brought John Sears to him. There had, to be sure, subsequently grown between them a bond as unmistakable and as mysterious as the one that might, in the best of cases, tie trainer to horse to trainer. It was nonetheless an incongruity to find the most unremittingly incantatory ideologue in our politics giving all his trust to a campaign manager who never ceased to insist that this was not an ideological year. There was in the sight of Sears at work all the puzzlement and the final admiration that would attend any agnostic masterfully captaining some army of the faithful, now and again lighting up the solemnities of its march with his drolleries, and making it altogether clear that the continually refreshed impulse of his employment had been his delight in the game as game.

IT MUST BE said for Governor Reagan that he was a horse worthy of such a trainer. He deserves, when you consider the weight assigned, to be counted as one of the great candidates in our memory, perhaps the greatest who never got his chance. As it was, he finished the primaries with more votes from Republicans than a President who, however dim otherwise, was their own and who had the support of all such paladins, however reduced in fortune, as are left for them to revere. Reagan rode over Goldwater in Arizona, in Texas reduced John Connally to an unwonted silence, and, if Sears had not, in this one instance, underestimated his proportions, might conceivably have added to the load of Rockefeller's embarrassments if he had chosen to challenge in New York.

His gifts were the actor's, some native and others, no less formidable, acquired in the craft. It was not merely that no one who had ever taken the field against him could be Reagan's equal at telling a story, providing, as Shaw said of Shakespeare, that someone else had told it to him first, or that he could suggest that fluoridation induces hair on the palms of the hands and maintain a tone pregnant with common sense. That his talents as an actor had always been of the respectable rather than the transforming sort added significantly to his dimensions as a candidate. Modest talents learn to be modest, since their survival depends upon the subordination of their temperament. Ronald Reagan, when young, had grown used to doing what his director, his producer, and, beyond all others, his agent told him was best for him. If he had not, he would have been forgotten long since. In the forties he lost his bloom just at the awful moment when Hollywood was losing its. Taft Schreiber of the Music Corporation of America was his agent then, and nearly twenty-five years later he could still speak with reverence of the noble fashion with which Reagan pulled down vanity.

"Bigger performers than he were in the same trouble he was," Schreiber remembered. "All they did was complain that we didn't get them parts. They couldn't understand that movies had stopped being made in those days. But Ron would do anything. I think he would have put on a clown suit and helped open a shopping center if we'd suggested it. We finally got him work speaking at General Electric sales meetings. He had only started when we got a letter from GE saying that one of the dealers had complained about some wisecrack Ron had made. I thought that was pretty insulting for a performer of his stature; but I thought I ought to show him the letter. And do you know that Ron picked up the phone and called GE and told them that he was glad they had told this to him. He said that this was a new job, and he knew he would make mistakes, and he was working for GE now, and that he'd be helped and not hurt by being told what it wanted."

He was not sunk but had only dived and would yet get up again. This habit of being pliable won Reagan a campaign that ought to be remembered as one of the epics of our politics. For what are epics about, after all, except how this man or that one played out a bad hand? He had begun in the East, mild as milk, and failed, although narrowly;

after Illinois, all seemed up with him. He fell boldly back upon those tested untruths that bad memory transforms into verities—the enemy with his talons at our jugular, the Panama Canal as holy ground—and he went through the West like a devouring flame. He was once again in being as a candidate; a lesser man with a lesser agent would have been intoxicated by principles not only cherished for themselves but so lately proven in the service of his recovery, and would have gone on trusting them and would have expired with increasingly hoarse and decreasingly attended preachments against the Mongol horde. But it was the peculiar element of Reagan's genius that he would yield any trust in his own convictions to his higher trust in his agent. Sears had divined that what had brought them to Mr. Ford's very gate was not enough to carry them through and that no hope remained unless the troops of the committed could be reinforced from the dwelling places of the calculating. He set to scouring the countryside, returned with Senator Richard Schweiker of Pennsylvania, and introduced this most bizarre trophy to Reagan as his vice president–designate. It was a piece of superb impudence; the smell of heresy to stern Republican principles that the orthodox had so long sniffed in their Eastern dioceses was a stench of sulphur on Schweiker. While Rockefeller groaned for pardon of his seldom ardent and long ago renounced traffickings with the liberals, Schweiker was writhing unashamedly at their orgies. His votes in the Senate could be seen to deviate from the desires of George Meany only when they had given precedence to some contrary wish of the Americans for Democratic Action. There is no telling how far Sears had worked his way through the muster roll of the enemy's camp before having resort to any prospect as seemingly unpromising as Schweiker; he might well have turned to him early on the sound premise that the likeliest deserter is the trooper with some prior experience of absences without leave. Schweiker defected with an alacrity hardly more decent than his voting record and seems already to have been the chosen vessel when he was borne to Reagan for inspection. Their first meeting is said to have consumed five hours and distilled a broad agreement that hearths ought to be warm and homes proof against termites. Schweiker is a fair-seeming fellow with one of those orator-on-the-windy-hilltop faces that would have impressed Vachel Lindsay for at least a minute and a half; but, all the same, Reagan's occasional lapses in identifying this brand that had leaped to him from the burning suggested a probe of the smallest degree of intimacy. But then to work overmuch to contrive the pretense that such an alliance could have the remotest connection with the logic of the convictions of either of these comrades-in-arms would have spoiled the symmetry of a gesture whose entire point was to give proof of Reagan's readiness to cast off his principles at need. His progress had been halted at its final barrier by the fears of the prudent that he was overprincipled, the terror of another Goldwater campaign having driven even Goldwater to Mr. Ford's standard.

[A Change in Doctrine]

AND SO REAGAN raised himself for one final demonstration that he was capable of as many roles as there are sins to commit. As he had begun sectarian, he ended ecumenical. When the faithful gathered to welcome him to Kansas City and the final conflict, they found him preaching the same heresies that he and they had stood together so long to extirpate.

"I got in this," he said, "to win an election." For all too long, the Northeastern Republicans had felt abused and scorned and traduced. "It was time to reach our hands across the border," and that was what he alone had been bold enough to do. And there in the sun, with the balloons bobbing on the hills around the Alameda-Plaza Hotel, the young mothers held up their children to see Schweiker, who, had they known of his existence a month ago, could only have imagined him as a sight fit to turn any innocent gazer to stone. Their devotion to Reagan had begun with their antipathy to all the Schweikers of this earth; and now they listened to a lament over the wounds of the Eastern Republicans that they themselves had gloried in inflicting, and they accepted with cheerful complacency the honors due them as the saviors of their own victims. When Mr. Nixon reached out his hand to Mao Tse-tung, he knew his audience. It is foolish to think of the Republican party as an institution that will not endure to Judgment; it is protected by its own imperviousness to every irony.

The stroke was no less masterful for having made no difference. Schweiker brought no delegates with him, and Reagan lost none that he already possessed, except a few from Mississippi who would have found some other excuse to desert him soon enough. There arrives a time in these affairs when the lines are drawn beyond assail by so weak a force as reason. The generic Reaganite, being principled, could no more be disillusioned at seeing his principles mocked by their appointed champion than the generic Fordite, being realistic, could be seduced by any appeal, however shrewd, to his bent for the practical.

But John Sears cannot have expected much from any device of his by then. He could do no more than come up with the best that was left. His campaign had been notable for the acuity of its anticipation of the moment when the vein it was mining would be tapped out. There now remained to him nothing except to display Reagan to the professionals as a candidate even more anxious to win than they, even quicker to sacrifice fantasies of honor, and in every way more venturesome and readier to dare all. But to appreciate the promise of qualities of that distinguished order required imagination at its keenest pitch; Sears must have known that his case was terminally desperate when he understood that it had no hopes of salvage unless it could arouse the imagination of a party rendered by dreadful circumstance incapable of imagining anything except some fresh horror.

STILL AND ALL, when the convention entered upon its formalities, there were eighty or so delegates still confessing themselves unable to choose between the two candidates. Their mystery was the only prop to the fiction that the game was not up. It was widely thought that, having led obscure lives, they were only indulging the itch to stay conspicuous as long as they could. And yet the attention paid them seemed more an embarrassment than a gratification, for they were Republicans and, as members of the party of order, unable to go their way unconscious of the sin of having lapsed into being an occasion for uncertainty. They ran to a marked degree to persons whose hope for rescue abided now in the intervention of some supernatural agent: There passed in view the congressman from Denver who called a press conference to announce that that afternoon he was going on his knees to pray the Almighty's counsel, the lady from Mississippi who said she was waiting for a vision, and the spiritualist from Virginia who felt that she could at last relax because she had ordered up a dream for that very evening; by then it had come to seem that victory might well belong to the faction with the wit to fix the horoscope in Wednesday afternoon's *Kansas City Star*. Most of these devotees of various competitive powers and principalities of the air ended up in Mr. Ford's custody; but then, if one is a Republican and summons the Angel of God, He can, I suppose, be trusted to arrive terrible in His majesty and deliver the injunction "Always keep a-hold of Nurse/For fear of finding something worse."

By now John Sears was left with only two instruments that might provide for him some plausible diversion from the counterrevolutionary bias that seems to be common to all messages from the Other Shore.

One was a proposal that the convention revise its rules to require any candidate for president to designate his choice for vice president the morning before the night he submits himself to the mercy of the delegates. That had been Sears's idea. The other was an amendment to the platform which, under the guise of a pledge to "morality in foreign policy" was a litany of the perfidies of a secretary of state who had been named as the most admired American the last time the Gallup firm dared to test the proposition that there might be one, and who was here rent limb from limb by the exaltation of Alexander Solzhenitsyn, whom he had snubbed, and the denunciation of the Helsinki agreement, which he had sponsored. That had been the concoction of the more ferocious tribes around Reagan's campfires. Sears seems to have regarded it as of little purpose except for sport; and, when he was asked why the amendment did not content itself with a simple "Bring me the head of Henry Kissinger," his interior laughter seemed almost loud enough to be heard; he rolled his tongue about his cheek and made a protracted show of studying the document at hand and emerging to report that nowhere upon the page had he been able to find the name of Secretary Kissinger.

He clearly regarded all such wrestlings with the cosmos as irrelevant in a politics whose ultimate struggles are not over ideas but property, and are decided on matters of procedure rather than ideology. To force Mr. Ford to name his vice president and create one future ingrate and a dozen enemies would be to weaken Mr. Ford, while to have his own party abuse his foreign policy would do no more than insult a dignity that had long ago surrendered itself in supplications to ladies from Mississippi who, while they were waiting for their vision, would as lief pass the time with the President of the United States as with any other mortal.

THE CHALLENGE TO reform the vice-presidential selection process had more definitive promise as a weapon and even some modest merit as a proposition. Here, after all, was a party that had seen both its vice presidents of the past twenty-four years end up as putative co-conspirators on felony indictment sheets. Even though a candidate for president could hardly be more perceptive in his blunderings toward the choice of a running mate while distracted by the imminence of the convention than while exhausted after it, he could certainly not be less so; and, given the record, even the most languid wave in the direction of reform might be taken as a minimally decent show of conscience.

Mr. Ford's majority on the rules committee had rejected Sears's proposal even so; it would come to the convention floor only as a minority report on the second night of the convention. Sears met the journalists at noon of the evening of this last go at the tables with his gaiety undiminished. It would, he promised them, be one of the most exciting nights in history. He must have known that it was all up with him; it had been twenty-four hours since he had been able to take note of the emergence of a closet Reaganite; he had instead taken to speaking of forty or fifty delegates that were his and that no one had counted as his because they preferred to reveal themselves on the floor. He moved through these fancies with an air of such careless assurance—as of one so rich that he no longer bothers to count his fortune—that the bare rumor of him must have sent Mr. Ford's captains to a frantic recanvass of figures whose accuracy he perfectly appreciated but whose dubiety he managed alarmingly to suggest on no evidence except his manner.

He was asked about Mississippi, whose thirty delegates had made their entrance marked as movers and shakers and had met that challenge by collapsing into a midden of intermingled and shuddering flesh from which no signal came more coherent than now a moan and then a lamentation. Sears affected to have stopped thinking about Mississippi except with the sympathy for the unfortunate that noblesse obliges:

"That delegation is full of gentlemen I have known for many years. In all this excitement, if one more question is asked of them, these people will drop dead of fatigue."

His impulse to mischief had carried him one half-step too far; a campaign manager, no matter how ample his graces, cannot say that it would be indelicate of him to intrude upon the prayer and fasting of the troubled without suggesting that he knows by now that it would be an intrusion without hope. By now, some sense of injury was arising among the journalists. A serious man does not like to think of his business as trivial; and how to go on affirming the importance of this tapestry when the faces of the defeated showed themselves so all else but suffering?

"How about some *real* figures," one of us growled.

"There will be real figures tonight," John Sears answered, and with more bitterness seated in their ranks than they had before known with this droll companion, the journalists trailed away. And yet he had only said, gentlemen, the dice will be on the table this evening, and, although I concede that thirteen is not the easiest of all points to make, we propose to have our throw. It was difficult not to feel a little ashamed of us; but it is not easy to be better than one's circumstances; and given the debasement of the playing level of politics—even hockey is no more inept—it was inevitable that some practitioner with a feel for the art would appear by chance and there would come a moment in the course of one of his disquisitions when we would know how things might have gone if Mozart had submitted himself to the inquiries of a convention of country and western music editors in Nashville, Tennessee.

That afternoon, there was manifested in the pressroom the agenda for the night's great debate. The climactic confrontation over the soul of the Republican party was identified as one of "two and only two amendments" to the platform, "which are in order: Two. Insert morality in foreign-affairs language. Ten minutes pro and con."

Giants would stalk among us. The question: "Resolved, that our Secretary of State is the scourge of our friends and the solace of our enemies" would be put by "R. Obenshein, Virginia; J. Baxter, Delaware; L. Leonard, West Virginia; Congressman P. Crane, Illinois." The reply in the Crown's name would be given by "Sen. R. Hruska, Nebraska."

But long before then the proposed rule to force Mr. Ford to confess whatever shabby disposition he proposed to make of the vice presidency of the United States would run its hurdles and the matter of the property would have been for all realistic purposes settled.

The proponents of the change had no argument to offer except that the delegates had a right to know, an ideal that, however handsome in other quarters, cut the meanest of figures on a floor crowded with so many persons who had been granted all too much of their right to know in recent years and found it invariably accompanied by the nastiest of shocks. Its opponents barely argued at all and would have been unheard if they had; the delegates had ceased all attention to the podium, having been distracted by Vice President Rockefeller, by now consumed by his role as aging pantaloon fallen from notice and remembering that his most infrequent moments of grandeur at Republican conventions had been confined to those occasions when he was able to shine forth as their victim, and bent upon restoring his importance by rousing the beast that slumbered around him. A North Carolina delegate teased him with a Reagan sign, and gratefully the Vice President snatched and made away with it. A Utah delegate retaliated by ripping Richard Rosenbaum's telephone from its moorings. While these buffooneries rolled forward, Sherry Shealy Martschink, South Carolina's rules committeewoman, did her plaintive best to set forth her objections to any change in the sacred rite of vice-presidential selection.

"Take Checkers," she began. There was no noticeable flinching; all the week's elaborate precautions against disturbing the peace of this house of the hangman with infelicities about ropes had been superfluous after all. "Take checkers," Mrs. Martschink proceeded. "In checkers, we decide on the rules before we start the game. I am in favor of change, in 1980—not in the middle of the game." The major debate of the convention of the great party that has ruled the air above and the earth below us through two-thirds of the lifetime of any American twenty-four years of age had taken full flight from reason and reality.

No one thought to make the point that the game had not started, and the writing of the rules before it did was the exact subject on the agenda. And no one pointed to the Vice President waving about his martyred telephone on the floor and doing his best to add to the crimes that stain the memory of recent American vice presidents the especially baroque one of inciting to riot. The case for sober consideration of improvements in the standards of vice-presidential selection could rest on the solitary exhibit of that office's incumbent ornament at his revels. But then, what matters the argument if the vote be lost, as lost it was? Mr. Ford had at least fifty votes more than he needed for nomination; there was nothing left but sullen resignation. What with the snufflings over the investiture of Representative John Rhodes as permanent chairman, the platform could not be served up until midnight and it was one-thirty in the morning before the proposal "Insert morality in foreign-affairs language" could claim the floor. By then, Mr. Ford's managers would have seen Henry Kissinger hanging from the highest beam before flogging these drooping spirits through yet another roll call, from whose torments they could wake only to howl for vengeance; it was quickly announced that Mr. Ford had accepted the amendment, and it took its place in the Republican platform of 1976, which gained from it, in fact, an improved artistic unity, because there had been needed only this warning against spiritual wickedness in high places to make complete the impression it conveyed that, for the past eight years, the country had been governed by a myriad of faceless scoundrels whose infamies oppressed every decent Republican nostril. The dismembered limbs of the secretary of state were left to reappear miraculously sewn together and sitting in the seats reserved for important guests two nights later when Mr. Ford was safely home.

[The Suppliant Candidate]

THE SPEECH MR. FORD made in accepting his prize was generally accounted a rouser. I suppose it may be thought such if we compare it only with his others; he remains a long way from ceasing to remind us of Kafka's image of the candidate about whom it was no longer possible to tell whether he was outlining his program or crying for help. When he had finished, he made an imploring gesture to the Reagans to join him on the platform, and they made their way there so graciously that the desperation of the President's entreaty seemed entirely unnecessary. But then, having been reduced to beggary in the extremity of his ordeal, he may have become a beggar by habit; and we may never see him again except pleading, when he need only invite. He fills the mind with the sense of how ordinary he is and how vulnerable, with his wife and children to worry about, and so little capital that he even pays almost his fair share of his taxes, and us not all that certain that he is even employable. He impels you to think of the vote, so otherwise unserviceable, as at least of some use as a handout. We may have been brought, by the distortions worked by the urge to be great upon the characters of so many who came before him, to an exhaustion where we can hardly conceive of believing again in a President we dare think of ourselves as needing; if Mr. Ford survives, it will be because he is so patently a President who needs us.

Mr. Ford wondered in his abject way whether Governor Reagan

might have something to say. The governor talked about how honored he and Mrs. Reagan were by the President's generosity and kindness in bringing them here this last time; he had given them a memory that would live in their hearts forever. And then he took wing. He remembered that he had been asked to compose a letter that would be encased in a time capsule to be opened in Los Angeles a hundred years from now.

"We live in a world," it had occurred to him, "in which the great powers have poised and aimed at each other horrible missiles of destruction. . . . And suddenly it dawned on me, those who would read this letter 100 years from now will know if those missiles had been fired. They will know whether we met our challenge."

And there could suddenly be felt the assault of the awe of the thought that, meaning no offense to the speaker, only the votes of 117 inert and unknown strangers had saved us from being fooled once more. The Republicans had begun to weep, the Reaganites mostly, of course, weeping not for the loss of a nomination but for the loss of their chance to be fooled again, for the departure of the last object of unreasonable faith they could expect ever to know. After us, the worthy clod. Even John Sears was seen to weep. He will be old and gray and remember a dozen other candidates, some of them successful, but none like this one. He had gone through his one grand passion; he would never again travel with that high heart on the quest for the Absolute. You felt his bereavement like an ache; for here had passed an artist who would never come this way in this form again. There was, however, a considerable measure of relief to go with the regret; the Quest for the Absolute is a damnable piece of mischief.

Harper's, November 1976

The Making of the Pope

The Cardinals made their way into St. Peter's for the last mass before their withdrawal into conclave through the entranceway beneath the tomb of Alexander VII, where the bare-boned black arm of Death holds up its swirling blanket of the rosiest, cheeriest jasper. They walked, savoring the presence of gossip, through an aisle of the gossipy—Cardinal Pignadoli of the Secretariat for Non-Christians in smiling communion with himself, Cardinal Benelli of Florence in the smiling community with all the world that defines the man who has arrayed his forces and knows that very shortly he will be, if not king of Rome, the mayor of its palace. Cardinal Gouyon of Rennes, as tall as but by no means so solemn as the husband in a Feydeau farce, kept stopping, plunging to the barriers to shake hands with believer and doubter with absolute impartiality, at once a bottomless fount and a universal object of merriment. Charm is a cardinal virtue.

They went sauntering without gravity across the largest indoor piazza under the eye of God, past the great altar where Bernini indulged his pranks high above with the little angels that seem almost to play toss with the papal tiara. No one, of course, paid the slightest attention to the patriarch of Venice.

The bronze statue of Saint Peter seems to have been appointed as a sort of caution light for solemnity. As the cardinals came to it, every now and then one of them would halt there and kneel for a moment's prayer. They were by all odds praying to Jupiter, whose fourth century

B.C. statue in the Capitoline is this one's very likeness and a compelling argument against the Christian origin of either. You think of Saint Peter as looking altogether more like Cardinal Wyszyński of Warsaw, that least inauthentic of modern heroes, with the step of an old lion and the look of a by no means welcoming innkeeper. No matter: St. Peter's is a mountain over the graveyards of its enemies.

Michelangelo for terror, Bernini for caprice, Raphael for refined reason, Caravaggio for divinely coarse reality, the pagan statues chained to their altars for trophies of victory, the martyrs in their catacombs for memories of defeat—vanity, humility, awe, condescension, simplicity, guile, gaiety, and melancholy, all of it, the whole uncountable mix of incompatibles that makes up the single impenetrable mystery of this church. And below, at its feet, the Romans, who have faith in nothing, except of course, this evening's miracle.

Rome is where the gypsies steal your wallet and the church robs you of every faith in the laws of probability. Only eleven of these 111 cardinals had ever been in a conclave until now. They ran a range whose distance may have extended even beyond the one side of Cardinal Silva of Santiago, who has gotten himself called "an ally of Communist subversion" by the lay votaries of the Pinochet government, and the other side of Cardinal-Deacon Felici of Rome, who is supposed to have pronounced on the reforms projected by the Second Vatican Council with the judgment that Pope John XXIII had simply gone mad.

Beyond their disparities, these cardinals were so tenuously acquainted with one another that the holy office thought to forestall any possible embarrassment at mistaking a face or a name by giving each one a booklet with a photograph and a biography of all his brothers in Christ. There was no evidence of the mutual spite so often unconcealed in the days following the death of Pope Pius XII, twenty years ago, but then everyone knew pretty much everyone else. Nothing advances amiability like unfamiliarity.

Even so, for all their social harmony, the cardinals seemed much too divided in principle to arrive at an easy agreement. Naturally, then, they needed only nine hours to elect as their pope Cardinal Luciani, the patriarch of Venice. It had taken six ballots to elect Cardinal Montini, who everyone knew would be pope. And now it has taken only three ballots to elect Cardinal Luciani, who had been imagined as pope by almost no one.

The result has so confounded the speculative and abashed the informed as to have produced the miracle of a Rome without gossip. The Italian press normally treats the Vatican's affairs with altogether less reverence than our own extends to the White House, and the pleasure it habitually takes in intimations of intrigue once stung Cardinal Felici into describing the journalists attendant upon the Second Vatican Council as "parasites and fungus growths . . . promoting confusion, insubordination, and error." But now all the journalists have been struck dumb and gone to their knees before this prodigy. Even *La Stampa* of Turin, for which only Fiat is holy, has in its stupefaction made *L'Osservatore Romano* sound like the *Protestant Herald*.

Still there are explanations—governed, of course, by the device the church holds up to all who dare pretend to understand her: "You think, and therefore I am not what you think."

Whatever the workings of the Holy Spirit, the operations of the memory of Pope John XXIII are unmistakable: Angelo Roncalli, patriarch of Venice, brothers who were socialists; Albino Luciani, patriarch of Venice, father who was a socialist. Both easy smilers, both kept a pleasant acquaintanceship with other primates whose Romanism was so much less orthodox than their own as to smell like heresy to the traditionalists. The parallels are obvious, but so are the differences. For all his air of the country priest, Roncalli was an intricately sophisticated papal diplomat who had charmed Paris not just with his good humor but with his wit. Question: "Monsignor, do you *really* believe in the miracle at Lourdes?" Answer: "I am sorry, but I never discuss religion at cocktail parties."

There was just the trace of the serpent in Roncalli's smile. The scanty published conjectures that Cardinal Luciani might emerge as the elected were all too often accompanied by adjectives like "gray" and "colorless." When you have seen one humble origin, you have by no means seen them all. Roncalli was from a farm near Bergamo, and Luciani is from a town in the Veneto. The inhabitants of Italian towns tend to separate into the gullers and the gulled, and there are certain suspicions of the gulled in the radiant innocence of the smile of Pope Giovanni Paolo I. If he is Roncalli, it is not without point that Roncalli was twenty hectic years ago, and to be Roncalli now is almost to promise the restoration of the papacy as it was. He was the candidate of the right—for Cardinal Felici, one more chance with a Roncalli who this time might not go crazy—and acceptable to the left for its sentimental recollections of a Roncalli it had cherished. But then the church's rule of never being what it seems is so rigid that victories for the right quite often turn out to be disasters for the right, as the left's anointment of Pius XII turned out to be a disaster for the left.

If those cardinals with ecclesiastical duties outside of Rome had a single sentiment in common, it was their desire that the hand of the Vatican be light upon them. There begin to be signs, uncertain as always, of a certain rhythm of alternating pastoral popes with political popes: Pius XII, political; John XXIII, pastoral; Paul VI, political. Now John Paul I, presumably pastoral. Political popes tend to tighten the government of the church and pastoral ones to loosen it.

Pope John's memory is a particularly blessed one in the Sacred College because he left the cardinals alone and was no less pleased to see the archbishop of Naples holding aloft the liquefied blood of San Gennario in the unpromising expectation of saving the souls of Neapolitans than he was to hear that the bishop of Recife was fomenting unrest among the poor. He combined a French affection for the priest who was interestingly venturesome and an Italian affection for the priest who was properly superstitious.

POLITICAL PAPACIES GENERALLY come to an end with the Vatican cadre more intrusive and interfering than the bishops enjoy having it be. Even though Pope Paul is tenderly remembered, for his sorrows and for his generosity with the hats, the curia that enforced his decrees when they were rigorous and occasionally overlooked them when they were too gentle for its taste is by no means the object of the church's otherwise universal love. It cannot be an accident that all the candidates thought most likely were curialists and that all were so swiftly discarded for a patriarch whose experience was entirely pastoral.

All the same, the ascension of John Paul I is a triumph of that Italian subtlety of which he himself appears so remarkably innocent. The Italians were enormously outnumbered in this conclave, and it had seemed reasonable to suppose that, if the bishop of Rome would probably be an Italian this time round, he could hardly be on the next. The longer the conclave, the more likely a foreign choice would be.

The Italians addressed this problem with the suppleness born in their natures and developed by their experience. Their motives were in few ways selfish and in none ignoble. They were simply acting on their belief that Rome is the teacher and the provinces are her pupils. To consider, or more precisely to guess at, their performance is to understand that Machiavelli was put on the index not only because *The Prince* is evil but also because its prescriptions are clumsy and crude.

Every day for two weeks before their conclave, the cardinals met in congregation to discuss the general state of the church. Cardinal Felici, who is at the same time a great classicist and a student of Freud, a genial spirit and an autocrat, suspended his vanity as a Latinist and made the welcoming address in Italian, thereby establishing it as the language of the congregations. All the cardinals had studied in Rome and earned themselves a working knowledge of Italian. But they had grown so used to employing it with docility and diffidence toward those older and wiser than they that, as it turned out, the Italians, with less than a quarter of the representation, delivered more than two thirds of the utterances. The conclave was, of course, a forbidden subject, but the very tone of the congregations had to be a most forceful reminder that Rome is the mother of churches and Italians first among her servants.

What Felici had commenced with style, Cardinal Benelli completed with cunning. At fifty-seven, he was too young to conquer the college's ingrained distrust of twenty-year papacies, and since he had been Pope Paul's chief executive assistant he was additionally burdened with the rancors that function inevitably attracts to its holder. His pre-conclave role was an infinite run on all the changes of the obscure and the ostentatious. He at once let it be known that he had an active strategy and managed to hide it in realms beyond comprehension. Now he seemed to be promoting Cardinal Felici, then Cardinal Baggio, and from time to time Cardinal Luciani. Luciani's views were old-fashioned enough to content many traditionalists; he was far enough from the curia to satisfy several moderates; and he was open enough to discussion to be more than attractive to a few progressives. That combination of agreeable qualities promised the collection of some votes in his name—perhaps as many as twenty—from all around the board. But no one outside the walls could conceive of his candidacy as having any use except as a bank for holding votes in reserve. He hardly seemed enough of a presence to fit whatever grand design Benelli might have.

In Rome the cardinals are conditioned to do as the Romans do, and the Romans, a people made savage by necessity, are fond of saints so long as they are mild-mannered and forgiving by nature. The day before the conclave, Benelli publicly pointed to the church's duty to extend more power and authority to the diocesan bishops. He could not have emitted a shrewder campaign promise, and by nightfall he had become the maker of a pope and perhaps in due course would become a pope himself. There seems little doubt that he will be Richelieu to Pope John Paul's Louis XIII.

Not the smallest stake in Benelli's search for an acceptable Italian candidate may have been his concern for the weakening of the church's role in the politics of Italy. Curiously, although the church's world dominion has not in centuries seemed broader and more vigorous than now, she is stronger in Latin America, where until now she had always been weak, and weaker in Italy, where she has always been strong. In the past two years, the Italian parliament has enacted an abortion law and Italian voters have returned a thundering no on a church-sponsored resolution to repeal the divorce code. Catholics who otherwise think themselves comfortable in a state of grace serenely vote the Communist ticket, and the Christian Democrats, the official Catholic party, have been reduced to trafficking with the Communists in their anxiety to save the property they have increasingly abused. There has always been the suspicion, even outside the Vatican, that, if church and state were ever separated, the state would collapse. But separating they seem to be by the will of a populace that more and more prefers its convenience to its salvation.

Benelli actively pushed the divorce referendum, which the new pope is said to have thought a risk the church would be wise not to take. Benelli is reputed to be the chief inspiration for the Italian Right to Life Movement, and he insists that Catholics have a duty to vote for a Catholic political party. These are all articles of faith that have been held equally, if less aggressively, by Cardinal Luciani, and Benelli may well have judged that, if Italians could no longer be usefully exhorted, they could well be beguiled for their own good by a pope as persevering in his affability as in his adherence to tradition.

Certainly Rome—even evil old Rome—has never seemed more depleted of faith, whether sacred or secular. Romans are not gloomy of course; as Stendhal said, to be gloomy one must have hope. The Communist party is ashamed of its past and weary of its present. When Ignazio Silone, its grandest apostate, died two weeks ago, the Communist press was plunged into mourning for this "socialist without a party and Christian without a church" who was expelled as a Trotskyist fifty years ago. So much for the religion of the twentieth century. It has no one to canonize except its heretics.

And, as to the faith of the seventeenth and every century before it, St. Peter's was hardly half full for the mass for the election of the pope, even though, just as sound and spectacle, it had to be altogether superior to the nudes at Piper's Theatre Restaurant. Very few of those present were young—and most of those were plainly tourists. There were far more nuns than priests in attendance, and far more women than men. A rebel priest in Florence wrote twenty years ago that, in Italy, religion was becoming the stuff of women, and that seems more and more the case now. They are, of course, women in the awful torment of being condemned to serve and never to command, women who seem desperate for a miracle. Where the faith keeps its amateur passion, it is almost hysterical. And where it is professional, at least at the journeyman level, it seems bored, which is, if anything, considerably worse.

During the cardinal's mass, a priest walked the aisles by the high altar handing out the platens and repeating in a tone mechanical and distinctly put-upon, "Body of Christ, body of Christ, body of Christ," while the women clutched at him in the extremity of their prayer for some hope somewhere, until you almost wanted to grab and shake him with all the consequential perils of hellfire and fairly scream at him to remember that what he had in his charge was, after all, a flame.

The election of the new pope seemed to draw a marked lack of attention in Rome until it produced the delight of a surprise. But then, this was August, when you can ask of her no more than the somber pleasures of a melancholy heart. Rome is never crueler than in August, when its luckier citizens always flee, leaving only unfortunate savages behind them. The prices made it certain that it wasn't the Borgias who drove Martin Luther to heresy but the Roman hotel keepers in a jubilee year. Thievery was a plague: My pocket was picked in St. Mary of the Angels and Martyrs. I reported it to the police, who laughed with that affinity between cops and bandits that can be found only in Balzac and the Roman *questura*. Then I trailed to the American Embassy to find my identity, feeling that no one could be so wanting in vigilance as I, and there I found the largest group of pilgrims the town had drawn to its sacred ceremonies, Americans seeking a replacement for passports stolen on the street. There are only two basic consumer rules for Rome in August: When you look upward at a cupola, always put your hand on your wallet, and, unless you are very rich indeed, never sit down at a trattoria that has a splendid view.

St. Peter's Square was all but empty for the conclave's first day, since everyone sensible knew that it could produce nothing. The black smoke came up at noon to be lustily cheered by the cabdrivers who thought it assured them another day's business. By then the sun had stopped in the sky, as though Joshua had chosen this high moment to make a fool of Galileo and ratify the judgment of the Inquisition. August is vicious to Bernini's Colonnade, bleaching and desiccating and blotching it. The most stupendous work of man I have ever known had been transformed into a waste habitable only by the camels of the desert.

As the day continued its torments, the little clusters of the curious began to collapse into what patches of shade the sun permitted the columns to provide. They seemed not so much curious any longer as drained of the will to move anywhere. By 5:30 P.M. someone kindlier among the gods relented. There was almost a breeze. The light that had been so brutal on the façade of the cathedral grew suddenly soft and darkening and lovely as ever, and an hour or so later a cloud of white smoke began floating from the chimney over the Sistine Chapel.

On the balconies outside the papal apartments, attendants could be seen running. The signal appeared plainly white. But then in a few moments it darkened or at least began to muddy a little, and confusion rose to assert the rule that, with the church, you can never be less sure than when you find yourself most certain. For this conclave, the Vatican had bought chemicals guaranteed to produce unmistakably black or unmistakably white smoke, and yet the thing was unclear still. The church has never been on safer ground than in its distrust of everything modern.

The feeders of the fire went on and on in the search for clarity, and, over the next half hour, there were five emanations of acceptably white smoke. The square had begun to fill. After fifty minutes, the longest wait between the signal and the proclamation in this century, the glass doors of the central loggia opened, and, with great deliberation, the purple papal tapestry was spread over the balcony, and there appeared Cardinal-Deacon Felici to pronounce the old words with the Ciceronian perfection he must always have found wanting in every messenger before him:

"Annuncio vobis gaudium magnum. Habemus papam . . ."

He paused. The church in her supreme moment could not forbear to tease.

He rolled on: "Eminentissimum ac reverendissimum dominum ecclesiae sanctae cardinalem . . ." He paused again. "Albinum."

A thousand heads laboriously prepared for a Sergium, a Sebastium, or any one of four Johannim began scuffling vainly for an Albinum. And Cardinal Felici waited for the shout to die, and then finished: "Lucius."

After that, every window on the loggia was thrown open, and the cardinals looked sociably out of them, now and then waving to the crowd. And then Pope John Paul appeared. At that distance he looked surprisingly the way Pope John had, small, smiling, and wonderfully uninhibited with his hands.

He read the blessing to the city and the world in a voice rather high and tremulous for an aria in an opera that had as much of the *jocoso* as the *serioso* in it. The Swiss Guards entered the plaza and performed their drill march in his honor.

"Look at that scene," I said pompously to my neighbor. "Michelangelo saw it. Stendhal saw it. Henry James saw it." That happened, of course, to be even less true than most assertions about the church: Michelangelo was dead long before St. Peter's had its façade. Stendhal, if he saw the scene at all—and he was a most adroit fabulist—would have seen it at the Quirinale. And as to James, I forget, but he would have needed to have been in Rome in 1878 or 1903, and he does not impress me as having often enough been that lucky. One of the somber joys of the melancholy heart is that one is sometimes more fortunate than one's betters.

And why do you suppose that seventy-five cardinals, in so many profound ways so different from one another in temperament and visions, could come so quickly to agreement in this case? Naturally, of course, in this church of contradictions, divine and profane, so that they would thereafter be free to disagree with one another about everything else.

New York, September 11, 1978

As the World Turns

COMMUNISM HAS BEEN driven to yield over its Eastern European garrisons to an unknowable future not by force of arms but by the collapse of its will for further struggle under the weight of all the history that had piled up before it seized what it had felt assured would be its time. If there is such a thing as an inevitability in history, it is that those who think they can ordain what will henceforth be always end up finding themselves overcome by what has ever been.

Fewer great historical events are brought about by the power of the new than by the enduring strength of the old. It is altogether more serviceable for us to search for the destiny of nations in the permanence of their culture than in the transience of their political systems. That is why the novelist can always teach us more than the political scientist, because the realm called fiction is ruled by what is real, and the territory called fact has to make do with the dubieties of the fancied.

The most enlightening guide I have found to Central America is not the product of a social scientist's research but *Nostromo*, the novel Joseph Conrad published in 1904 when his direct experience with the neighborhood was nearly thirty years past and had never extended beyond a tarrying or so in ports when he had sailed as a schooner deck officer in the Gulf of Mexico.

Yet, here as nowhere in the reports of embassies and the monographs of researchers, is the El Salvador of last week where, in Conrad's words, "the cruelty of things stood unveiled in the levity and sufferings of that incorrigible people."

There are the poor of the barrios walking stoically about their errands with grenades crumping and machine guns chattering in the near distance, awesomely brave and pitifully passive and unchanged from the citizens of Conrad's Sulaco who were "surprised but not indignant" when the cavalry of the revolution suddenly lowered lances and cleared them from the streets, because "no Costaguanero had ever learned to question the eccentricities of a military force."

There is the president of Salvador who has just the look of the "more pathetic than promising" of Conrad's freshly installed soon to be unseated chief of state. There is the Western diplomat who observes that, "There is no center in El Salvador" and who but echoes the judgment of Conrad's Englishman that "The fault of this country is the want of measure in political life." Conrad's disenchanted liberal remembers Bolivar's bitter summation that "[South and Central] America is ungovernable. Those who worked for her independence have ploughed the sea."

Conrad's Spanish elite hate their Catholic vicar general whom they suspect, with reason, of rousing the Indian peasantry for land reform and of sympathizing with the bandits who control the countryside.

"If it had not been for the lawless tyranny of your government," the wife of the administrator of Sulaco's silver mine says to its superintendent, "many an outlaw would be living peaceable and happy by the honest work of his hands."

"No wonder there are bandits in the camps," he answers, "when there are none but thieves and swindlers and sanguinary [posturers] to rule us."

The cruelty and indifference of misgovernment explain the bandits of Conrad's Costaguana, and perhaps the same things explain the FMLN in El Salvador's hills today. We must look to the novelist if we hope to understand. His is the matter of fact. Social science and intelligence reports are the mere poor stuff of an unadorned imagination.

New York Newsday, December 10, 1989

The Gift of Thought

NINETEEN-NINETY SEEMS to be progressing in a fashion all else but kind to the prophets we had trusted to relieve us of the inconvenience of having to think for ourselves. First, the Communists cut out and leave Karl Marx to shift for himself in Central Europe. And now the psychoanalysts are having at Sigmund Freud, whose reports on the cases he treated, one of them has told *The New York Times*, "just don't stand up in light of historical fact."

The only surprise in this judgment is that it could still be offered as a surprise. Marx happened to have been remarkably scrupulous in his treatment of facts, if not people, but rigging the data was almost an obsession with Freud. No reader as brilliant as he could have been as wrongheaded except as a matter of deliberate policy.

The Oedipus complex may or may not be a problem for some sons. But it certainly wasn't for Oedipus. First Laius, his father, pierces his ankles and leaves him naked in the chill of the mountains. Somehow Oedipus grows up and sets forth on the road to Thebes. Laius is out for a drive, spots Oedipus from afar, and turns his chariot wheels in haste to attack him. Oedipus kills him. That homicide is a response entirely justifiable in a victim of the Laius complex.

Electra was no less immune to the Electra complex. She could not even have known her father, who had been at the Trojan War all her life. Her hang-up was with her mother, Clytemnestra, whose affair with Aegisthus too much distracted her from paying the attention that is a daughter's due. So Electra arranged the murder of both, which was, of course, an excessive reaction; but then, what's a girl to do when the Clytemnestra complex is tearing her soul?

Freud's particular gift to his devotees was to spare them the trouble of reading Sophocles or anybody else, which is why we so seldom encounter a psychiatrist without sustaining a powerful impression that, however bad our own education in the humanities may be, his is worse. Yet Marx and Freud were both so well up on the humanities as to find there the inspiration for the marvelous poetic metaphors that the Marxists and the Freudians have since mistaken for the materials of scientific system.

Leonardo da Vinci, whose common sense was of an order curiously mediocre for a genius, once observed that it is a poor disciple who is not better than his master. But most experiences of life and history ought by now to have taught us instead that it was a poor master who was not better than his disciples.

What we so long referred to as Marxism-Leninism was only Leninist Marxism. Lenin read Marx not to enlighten himself but to quarrel with others. You cannot find a citation from Marx in *State and Revolution* that has not been purposefully employed to encourage the suspension of the critical intelligence. Lenin was not an empirical observer but a hagiographer; the church would have become a fossil centuries ago if its theologians had frozen their doctrine as solidly as he did his.

Freud and Marx are always fun to read and the Freudians and the Marxists most often aren't. And so the Leninists dried up all the juices of Marx and themselves with it, and it has taken just one rising of the wind to blow them away and leave behind uncountable disciples stuck with thinking for themselves.

When Justice Oliver Wendell Holmes was along in his eighties, one of his acolytes found him reading Plato and wondered why. "To improve my mind," Holmes replied. Too many of us have been too beguiled by those terrible simplifiers, the systematizers, to keep up the practice and, now that their spell seems broken, the prospect of being forced to work at it again is most exhilarating.

New York Newsday, March 8, 1990

Index

Murray Kempton was born in 1917 and has been a columnist for the *New York Post* and an editor of *The New Republic;* he is now a regular columnist and contributor to *New York Newsday* and *The New York Review of Books.* He is the author of three previous books: *Part of Our Time: Some Ruins and Monuments of the Thirties, America Comes of Middle Age: Columns, 1950–1962,* and *The Briar Patch: The People of the State of New York vs. Lumumba Shakur, et al.,* for which he received the National Book Award in 1973. In 1985, Kempton was the recipient of the Pulitzer Prize for commentary. He is also the recipient of two George Polk awards, and one-sixth of a Grammy for his contribution to the liner notes of a multi-disk Frank Sinatra album. He lives in Manhattan.